A World More Concrete

HISTORICAL STUDIES OF URBAN AMERICA
Edited by Timothy J. Gilfoyle, James R. Grossman, and Becky M. Nicolaides

Also in the series:

Additional series titles follow index

A World More Concrete

Real Estate and the Remaking
of Jim Crow South Florida

N. D. B. Connolly

The University of Chicago Press
Chicago and London

N. D. B. Connolly is assistant professor of history at Johns Hopkins University.

The University of Chicago Press, Chicago 60637
The University of Chicago Press, Ltd., London
© 2014 by The University of Chicago
All rights reserved. Published 2014.
Printed in the United States of America

23 22 21 20 19 18 17 16 15 14 1 2 3 4 5

ISBN-13: 978-0-226-11514-6 (cloth)
ISBN-13: 978-0-226-13525-0 (e-book)
DOI: 10.7208/chicago/ 9780226135250.001.0001

OUP Material: p. 149 extract (531w) from "Games of Chance: Jim Crow's
Entrepreneurs Bet on 'Negro' Law and Order," from *What's Good for Business*,
edited by Kim Phillips-Fein and Julian E. Zelizer (2012).
Free permission. Author's own material. By permission of Oxford University
Press, USA.

Library of Congress Cataloging-in-Publication Data

Connolly, N. D. B., author.
  A world more concrete : real estate and the remaking of Jim Crow South
Florida / N.D.B. Connolly.
      pages ; cm. — (Historical studies of urban America)
    ISBN 978-0-226-11514-6 (cloth : alk. paper) — ISBN 978-0-226-13525-0
(e-book) 1. Real property—History—Political aspects—Florida—Miami.
2. Rental housing—History—Political aspects—Florida. 3. African
Americans—Housing—Florida—Miami—History. 4. African American
neighborhoods—Florida—Miami—History. 5. Urban renewal—Florida—
Miami—History—20th century. 6. Racism—Florida—Miami—History.
I. Title. II. Series: Historical studies of urban America.
  HD268.M45C66 2014
  363.5'99960730759381—dc23

                                                              2013040478

⊗ This paper meets the requirements of ANSI/NISO Z39.48-1992
(Permanence of Paper).

For Shani, naturally
And for my mother, Diane Connolly-Graham

CONTENTS

ACKNOWLEDGMENTS

Thank you, Jesus!

I've accumulated a dizzying number of personal and professional debts over the life of this project. Only through the generosity of many wonderful people does this book exist at all.

My most heartfelt gratitude, first, to Ashraf H. A. Rushdy, who read far more (far more closely) than he had to, and who continues to inspire me with his discipline, insight, friendship, and genuine sense of perspective. Thank you for your mind. And thank you for helping me appreciate the relative value of ideas and relationships.

I'd also like to thank Thomas C. Holt, Nell Irvin Painter, Barbara Jean Fields, and the late Michel-Rolph Trouillot. I've never actually met any of you. Nevertheless, your intellectual courage and the naked brilliance of your work kept me both heartened and humbled as I wrestled with institutional power and our country's troublesome racial past.

My sincere thanks to Robert Devens and Tim Mennel, from the University of Chicago Press, as well as to Becky Nicolaides, who first solicited this project. Thanks, too, to Jim Grossman, whose professionalism and insight made this a better book, and whose passing words of encouragement, some fifteen years ago, kept me on the path to being a historian. I owe a tremendous debt of gratitude to my friend, collaborator, and manuscript reader, David Freund. Most first-time authors never enjoy as much thorough, thoughtful, and encouraging feedback as that which David provided—unless, of course, they, too, had David read their work.

As a member of the Department of History and the Center for Africana Studies (CAS) at Johns Hopkins University, I've had the benefit of growing among an exceptional collection of warm and unfailingly sharp scholars. In Africana Studies, I wish to thank Michael Hanchard, Hollis Robbins, Pier

Larson, Floyd Hayes, Siba Grovogui, Jane Guyer, Lester Spence, Claude Poux, Kelly Josephs, Moira Hinderer, Asantewa Boakyewa, Sara Berry, Jared Hickman, James Calvin, Adrienne Breckenridge, and, of course, Franklin Knight and Ben Vinson III, who directed CAS with such a high sense of duty. I thank each of you, my CAS colleagues, for your often-thankless dedication to advancing the study of Africa and its diaspora.

There is, perhaps, no better place than the Hopkins History Department's Monday Seminar in which to appreciate the importance of a well-formulated question. Yet, I most value the camaraderie and holistic schooling about the profession I have received as a member of "Hopkins History" over the last six years. My most profound gratitude to Michael Johnson, John Marshall, Angus Burgin, Judy Walkowitz, Toby Ditz, Lou Galambos, Richard Kagan, Michael Kwass, Marina Rustow, Jeff Brooks, Ron Walters, Peter Jelavich, Bill Rowe, Franklin Knight, Ben Vinson III, and Phil Morgan. In all matters dealing with public schools, children's literature, Washington, DC, and how to write about human loss, I enjoyed the finest friend in Tobie Meyer-Fong. Thanks, especially, to Gaby Spiegel for opening her home to my family when I first arrived in Baltimore, and for so much more since. My indebtedness to Melanie Shell-Weiss runs deeper, farther, and wider than just the history of Miami. In terms of archival rigor and honoring the personhood of your subjects, you, Melanie, continue to cut a path for me to follow. To Sara Berry and Mary Ryan, with whom I had the pleasure of team-teaching and sharing chapters, I convey a most special thanks as well. Your respective skill and attentiveness as writers, scholars, and teachers improved this book to no small degree. Deepest thanks to Michael Hanchard, Todd Shepard, Gabe Paquette, Ken Moss, and Pier Larson for helping me weather the unique hazards of being both racially literate and a dad to small children while on the meager end of the tenure track.

Elsewhere at Hopkins, I benefited from the insight, collegiality, and support of Eric Sundquist, Erica Schoenberger, Katherine Newman, Adam Sheingate, Steven Teles, and Erin Chung. Tara Bynum deserves special thanks as a meticulous reader of chapters, a lover of Baltimore, and a packer of boxes. I thank Ann Eakin Moss for the many warm and edifying conversations around her dinner table. I hope to one day wear my learning as gracefully as you do. Carla Hopkins and Joe Colon introduced me to Ghana, and to a side of Johns Hopkins, in its humor and selflessness, that I so needed to find. Thanks to Stephanie Farquhar and Josh Garoon for helping me appreciate Baltimore politics and the depth of urban redevelopment issues in the present day. And perhaps no single person in recent years has improved my pedagogy and writing about the American past more than Sarah Manekin.

Thank you for being such a dear friend, master teacher, and superb historian. Very important thanks must go to the late Harry Marks, whose e-mails I still consult, years after the fact, and to the late and incomparable John Russell-Wood. Not a day goes by that I do not miss your clarity, thoughtfulness, and humor. Ever my office mate, John, ever my friend.

In the wider profession, I've had the benefit of amazing (and amazingly generous) scholars who have made my early years as a working historian more rewarding than I could have ever imagined. Full and hearty thanks go to Brett Gadsden, who read and reread much of this book, in some form or another, and with whom I hope to argue and laugh for years to come. Thanks, too, to Robert Blunt, Millery Polyné, Davarian Baldwin, Andrew Kahrl, Rabia Belt, Tom Guglielmo, and Donna Murch for their unflinching support and equally unflinching critique over the many iterations of this project. This book would be greatly diminished without insights and encouragement from Sarah Thankachan, Zita Nunes, Marcus Allen, Reanna Ursin, James Dator, Leandro Benmergui, and Paula Halperin. For their empathy and earnest engagement, I also wish to thank Claire Pettengill, Leah Gordon, Dan D'Oca, Angela Dillard, Rhonda Williams, Heather Ann Thompson, Yenisey Rodriguez, Lara Stein-Pardo, John Stuart, Kelly Quinn, Chantalle Verna, Angela Parker, Alex Cornelius, Chanelle Rose, Michele Mitchell, Martha Hodes, Jennifer Morgan, and Elsa Barkley Brown. Roger Biles and Mark Rose gave this project an attention I can never fully repay. Raymond Mohl not only laid the historiographical foundation for my and every other recent book on Miami's urban history. He also took the time to improve this book as he fought through his own grave health issues. For both efforts I will be forever in your debt, Ray.

I'm also thankful for Robert Henderson, Michael Katz, Andrew Weise, Laura McEnaney, Kevin Mumford, Luther Adams, Nicolas Kenny, Megan Francis, Angel David Nieves, Jennifer Hock, Christopher Klemek, Christopher Wells, Allison Isenberg, and Victoria Wolcott. Each of you helped affirm or revise my thinking in ways that made this a smarter book. I must also thank Andrew Needham, Nancy Kwak, Volker Janssen, Daniel Martinez HoSang, Carl Abbott, Darren Grem, Sylvia Manzano, Elizabeth Shermer, Shana Bernstein, Jeff Gonda, Julia Guaneri, Jonathan Holloway, Françoise Hamlin, and Michael Carriere for providing excellent advice during this project's early second life as a book manuscript. Of late, Colin Gordon, Todd Michney, Andrew Diamond, Rachel Guberman, Adam Ewing, and especially Nicholas Brady have helped this book feel even more at home in the world.

Much credit goes to Bob Lockhart and Susan Ferber, at the University of Pennsylvania and Oxford University Presses, respectively, for their fine editorial work on ideas that eventually wound up in this University of Chicago monograph. I owe additional editorial debts to Michelle Nickerson, Darren Dochuk, Phil Ethington, Janice L. Reiff, Robin Bachin, Julian Zelizer, and Kim Phillips-Fein. Thanks to Brian Balogh, Guian McKee, Julian Zelizer, Louis Hyman, Donna Murch, Harvey Graff, and Bruce Schulman for offering excellent venues and avenues for improving my work. And an extra special thanks to Kevin Kruse, Tom Sugrue, and Joe Crespino for their levity, scholarship, and general excellence in supporting junior scholars like me.

Since graduating from the University of Michigan in 2008, I've grown even more to appreciate my onetime mentors as valued colleagues and fellow travelers. Thanks to Matthew Countryman and Jesse Hoffnung-Garskof, whose questions continue to inform my thinking. My deepest gratitude to Gina Morantz-Sanchez and Geoff Eley for their remarkable care and attentiveness over the years. Rebecca Scott and Julius Scott still model what can only be called love for this work we call history. And Matthew Lassiter continues to hold a singular importance in my intellectual growth. Thank you, Matt, for holding on to your healthy contempt for Americans' intellectual hardwiring, and thanks, more, for setting a high bar for how to support and elevate one's students. I still aspire on both counts.

The University of Michigan's Institute for the Humanities deserves special mention for electing to grant me its Emerging Scholars Prize in 2009. Its substantial support, and the timely support of Marsha Holmes while I was still a graduate student, helped this project tremendously. And I would be remiss if I did not thank the several classes of dedicated doctoral students who have kept the torch of Michigan's Black Humanities Collective (BHC) burning since its founding in 2004. Presenting my work to the BHC nearly a decade after we convened our inaugural group represents the highlight of my career to date.

As for my own students, I thank all of them for their patience as I stole away to finish chapters and footnotes. To Amira Rose Davis, Mo Speller, Jessica Levy, and Adam Thomas, I say thank you for probing historical questions that, in our shared search for answers, made my own work better. I say that and more to Paige Glotzer, one of a handful of people who read my whole manuscript and never sought a scrap of compensation for the pleasure.

As with most historical works, any durable contribution I hope for this book to make owes its existence to an archivist. I wish to thank, above all, the archivists at the Black Archives History and Research Foundation of South Florida—Dorothy Jenkins Fields and Timothy A. Barber. I also wish to thank Stephanie Wanza, whose work at the Black Archives helped launch this project many moons ago. Joanne Hyppolite and Dawn Hugh at the Historical Museum of Southern Florida deserve special mention for their research and image support over the years. I also thank all those who have labored to archive Miami's past in their own homes, schools, and nonprofit organizations, including Enid Pinkney of the Dade Heritage Trust and the Hampton House Trust, Greg Bush of the University of Miami, and Dinizulu "Gene" Tinnie of the Virginia Key Beach Park Trust (and several other organizations). I also thank Donnalyn Anthony, Thelma Gibson, Eugenia B. Thomas, Georgia Ayers, Leonard Barfield, and Margie and George Harth.

In no uncertain terms, my family is my history. My mother deserves all the credit for me daring to ask questions and daring to become a writer. (I still hope, even now, that you won't find any typos.) Thanks to the entire Connolly and Mott families. Thanks especially to my godmother and aunt, Danielle; my aunt Tamé; my brothers, Josh and RJ; and my sister, Janelle. The late Rodney Graham and Cherrie Connolly, my grandmother, are always with me. Much love goes to the Means and Beauttah families, who made the Connolly-Motts more than friends. The Beardsleys—and my dear compadre, Steve, in particular—remain ever in my heart. Robert Blunt deserves another mention for his unshakable friendship over the years. And to my most stalwart and longtime friends, Louis Jacques, Ikello Brown, and Matt Puglisi, you know what it is.

My children are mighty and awesome at all times, and they demand nothing less from me. To London, Clarke, and my infant son, Elijah, Daddy thanks you for reminding me what's at stake in the history of American inequality, and for helping me, at the very same time, not take myself too seriously.

Shani, I hesitate to call this book my love letter to you because it is too imperfect. Please accept it, though, as my attempt to honor the many perfect hours, months, and years you gave to this absurd little project. You weathered my absence and my distracted presence, and you lived every soaring breakthrough and excruciating revision right alongside me. I'll never know just how often you had to shoo London and Clarke away from my office door, or how many ways you assured them that I *really* did want to play. What I *do* know is that your love made this book. It also makes me fearless every single day.

N. D. B. Connolly
Baltimore, Maryland

America's Playground

Figure 0.1. "One of America's First Underexpressway Parks," 1969. (Courtesy of the Black Archives History and Research Foundation of South Florida Inc.)

It seemed like a good idea at the time. During the afternoon of 30 July 1969, more than a thousand men, women, and children gathered beneath Interstate 95, in the heart of Miami's Central Negro District. The occasion was a ribbon-cutting ceremony for "one of America's first underexpressway parks." Over the previous year, city officials and corporate and individual donors cobbled together thirty thousand dollars to erect jungle gyms, swings, and other amusements on nearly five acres of what city planners had already deemed "dead land." Playground equipment replaced hundreds of houses and apartments that state road builders bulldozed, just a few years earlier, to make room for I-95.[1]

The park was the brainchild of the city's first black city commissioner, M. Athalie Range. The owner of three funeral homes and several rental properties, Range had become the most recent entrepreneur to assume prominence as the nominal leader of Miami's "Negro community." A widow with children, she was also, notably, the first woman to do so. The city's underexpressway park would bear Range's name and enjoy endorsements from an influential, interracial coalition that included the city's mayor, several white city commissioners, and past and present heads of the local chapter of the National Association for the Advancement of Colored People (NAACP). The City of Miami's Tourism Bureau took scores of photographs at the opening ceremony and later publicized the event in national news outlets.[2]

Shadowed beneath a bustling freeway, Mayor Stephen Clark spoke to the residents of South Florida's poorest neighborhood with what was likely unintended irony. "Miami does not shove socio-economic problems under the rug," the mayor assured, "but in the spirit of enterprise, copes with them."[3] Celebrants at the park's opening paid little attention to the new and already wilting grass, which lay, in some places, right up against the legs of playground equipment. Somehow, dry sod, hastily planted, was supposed to grow in weak soil and scant sunlight. No one would say that a similar expectation had been placed on Miami's poorer black children, even if the comparison seemed apt in the midst of underfunded schools, substandard housing, and minimal access to decent city services. Nor would anyone comment on the potential symbolism of a park that effectively rendered these kids invisible to travelers whisking above between the region's airports, beaches, and suburbs. Below that freeway, in one of the most spectacular year-round climates in America, the embodied future of black Miami looked up at a concrete sky.

The city's black newspaper of record, the *Miami Times*, affirmed the general tenor of the occasion. It avoided reminding its readers about the twelve thousand people displaced to make room for Interstate 95. Over the previous decade, the freeway, as an instrument of slum clearance and regional prosperity, had been a project that Miami's preeminent Negro weekly repeatedly championed. Now, the hum of half a million cars and trucks passing overhead provided an audible reminder of Greater Miami's innovative leadership and economic progress, not of the park's compromised air quality. "This startling new concept in play areas," the *Times'* editorial page professed, "is expected

Great Idea, Commissioner Range

Figure 0.2. *Miami Times*, 31 July 1969. (Courtesy of the *Miami Times*.)

to sweep across the nation." "We are proud that it was started in Miami," the paper continued, "and more so that the idea came from one of us."[4]

This book does not principally concern a single park opening or the disruptive force of an interstate highway. It attends to the political and commercial transactions that inspired these *kinds* of events, and it endeavors to render a world in which "colored only" beaches, mass displacements of working families, and even playgrounds under highways seemed, at one point or another, like good ideas.[5] *A World More Concrete* argues that Americans, immigrants, and even indigenous people made tremendous investments in racial apartheid, largely in an effort to govern growing cities and to unleash the value of land as real estate. Even today, land and its uses serve as expressions of acceptable governance. And between the 1890s and the 1960s, people built a sturdy and supple infrastructure for white supremacy that remains very much in place.

Contests over land allowed certain aspects of Jim Crow's culture to become America's culture—politically, economically, and at the level of the built environment. Acceptable governance in Jim Crow America required minimizing the discomforts of white Americans, protecting the political power of property owners, and ensuring that poor people continued to generate other people's wealth. Good governing also meant making "colored people" the principal bearers of difficult or unpopular policy choices. It means all these things still.[6] Over the course of the early and mid-twentieth century, investment in racial segregation became so great and multifaceted—enabled by every level of government and people of every color, every class—that even when challenged by something as forceful and many-headed as the black freedom struggle, it could not be undone. Indeed, the very means and methods of race reform often helped make both the natural world and the social world of Jim Crow a world more concrete.

As a *system*—or a set of historical relationships—white supremacy was and is far more than the overtly and occasionally racist act. It includes laws and the setting of commercial and institutional priorities. White supremacy also includes the everyday deals that political operators and common people strike in observance of white privilege or, more accurately, white power.[7] Even by the time of Athalie Range's park opening in 1969, racism in the United States hardly looked like the morality tales that many Americans still consign to the distant past. Ku Klux Klan cross burnings, "colored only" water fountains, or even the pronouncements of frothing segregationists were already relics of what seemed like another country.[8] America suffered, instead, under the kind of racial violence that I-95 wrought and that Miami's underexpressway park echoed. Since the late nineteenth century, in fact, slum tenements, the devaluation of black suburbs, and forced land expropriation gave a brick-and-mortar quality to the hardships of those once known as "colored." And in its overt and more infrastructural forms, white supremacy realized and maintained its power over several decades through its ability to preserve order and to narrow the range of acceptable political expression.[9]

White supremacy required political, cultural, and business transactions, especially as it related to the meaning and value of real estate in twentieth-century America. The culture driving growth politics in segregated US cities and suburbs, for nearly a century, could not have worked through a simple imposition of so-called white people pressing down on colored people. It required repeated buy-in from people across the class and color spectrums, trade-off after trade-off, year upon year. Driven by individual self-interest and, often, communal ideals about race, people of every complexion made Jim Crow work. And they did so by pursuing frail promises about the benefits of property ownership, the acceptability of state violence, and the potentially reparative power of urban redevelopment. Through projects as everyday as paved streets in the city or new houses in the suburbs, even Jim Crow's most beleaguered and maligned people placed their hopes in one day morally perfecting American capitalism.

The unexceptional and mundane qualities of racial governance and the built environment remained evident even in a region many consider one of the United States' most unique and spectacular: Greater Miami. Since Miami's founding in the 1890s, investors and boosters have conferred on the region resplendent titles such as the Gateway to the Americas, the Magic City, or America's Playground.[10] Through such monikers, hoteliers and suburban real estate developers, alongside countless other investors and publicists, hoped to describe and enact Miami's beckoning call on migrants from the icy north and the foreign nations to the south. America's Playground was where one made fast fortunes or perhaps chanced upon a forbidden tryst in the tropics. Miami's nicknames, in proclaiming the city's luxury and otherworldliness, passed by word of mouth and on the travel pages of the nation's most prominent newspapers. South Florida's exotic labels also served to conceal the brutality and racism so often required to create and preserve one of the nation's most celebrated tourist destinations.[11]

Indeed, southern Florida's unlikely development from a turn-of-the-century "frontier" to something far more fanciful seemed to give the entire region an almost mystical quality. "The Magic City" became Miami's most permanent label, and, as one 1968 *New York Times* article explained, the Magic City's sister city, Miami Beach, "worships two gods—the sun and the fast buck—and there's every evidence that its prayers are usually answered."[12] Local entrepreneurs and politicians seldom left growth to prayer or incantations, of course. They managed it, for decades, within an apartheid system reliant on layer upon layer of violence. White vigilantes, excessive law enforcement, and serial acts of forced land expropriation were just a few of the instruments that scrawled Jim Crow's rules onto the Florida Peninsula. Over time, the violence needed to maintain the color line went through its own evolution, as lynch law from the 1910s and 1920s gave way to more benign tools of segregation, including racist zoning practices and promiscuous use of eminent domain.[13]

Eminent domain, the taking of private property for public use, became one of most particular and dramatic ways to help check encroachments of one racial group upon another. It served, in fact, as part of Jim Crow's broader regulation of people and profit within America's Keynesian economy.[14] When the buying and selling of real estate threatened to transgress the color line, or tales of rancid slum housing threatened to overtake the Magic City's more favorable publicity, Miami's local politicos looked to land taking as a market "corrective." Eminent domain helped protect white homeowners, contain black renters, and keep the racial peace. And true to the equations studiously formulated by economists and financiers, careful—albeit racist—land regulation facilitated remarkable economic growth. Greater Miami's "whites only" beaches, hotels, apartments, and suburbs churned out millions of dollars on one side of the color line, while landlords and property managers in the region's hulking, cramped slums harvested millions in rent money on the other.

Despite its glittering reputation and its tremendous cultural and linguistic diversity, Greater Miami was nothing special. It remained as economically dependent on a white-over-black system as more industrialized US cities, such as Birmingham, Alabama, or Chicago, Illinois. It also enjoyed violence as grisly as any found in the Mississippi Delta or rural Texas, especially in its early years.[15] If anything makes Jim Crow Miami unique, it's perhaps the city's ability to help present-day observers appreciate apartheid there for what it was everywhere—namely, a variation on colonialism.[16]

As a city founded with *northern* money, in a *southern* state, off the *Caribbean* Sea, Greater Miami belonged to a nation and region where white elites often governed with and through their colored counterparts, cultivating a kind of indirect rule.[17] Greater Miami, like the wider Americas, was also a place where colored people of means aspired to appropriate state violence in an effort to assert control over "their own" communities.[18] Perhaps, though, Greater Miami's colonial qualities remained most evident through the ways in which state actors racially allocated land and in so doing made nonwhite people generators of fantastic wealth, often for those who seemed to live a world away.[19] Rather than disconnect Greater Miami or, for that matter, the United States from their regional or political sisters, Jim Crow in South Florida binds the history of the US metropolis to the history of resource extraction in the formally colonized and postcolonized world. Similar to conditions in Havana or New Orleans—Caracas or Colón—apartheid in Miami, and its accompanying violence, made money. Jim Crow's money, in turn, shaped the development of American politics.

As with the segregation of jobs or schools, real estate and its racial uses captured apartheid's economic utility.[20] Racially dividing real estate generated wealth because it limited the mobility of consumers, thereby confining demand, manufacturing scarcity, and driving up prices on both sides of the color line. And real estate itself—defined as land turned into property for the sake of further capital investment—served as one of the chief vehicles for the development and continuance of antiblack racism. As scholars have explained (largely unheeded) for several generations now, techniques for setting property values, the confinement of black people to rental housing, and white flight in the wake of increased black property ownership had profound social and political consequences.[21] All, for instance, contributed to white Americans' evolving ideas about the appropriate reach of government in observance of an apparent "free market."[22] And all have affirmed negative associations between black people and poverty, black people and crime, and black people and sexual immorality.[23] Those perceived associations are part of what make all-white communities more appealing and thus, to this day, generally more expensive.[24] They also make black people, relative to whites, appear generally less deserving of state assistance and protection. Racial logic, in other words, did double duty through real estate. It helped create niche markets by way of segregation, and, in the midst of seemingly objective models of real estate economics, it offered a handy explanation—supposed black inferiority—for why capitalism never quite worked the same way for everybody.[25]

Make no mistake, real estate, from the perspective of nonwhite property owners, proved critical to the cause of racial justice because ownership of real estate served, in itself, as a symbol of racial equality and a means for community uplift. Despite real estate's more noble associations, however, the cultural and social mores tied to real estate, as capital, encouraged even nonwhites and working-class people to believe that black people, and especially black *poor* people, had an adverse effect on the property aspirations of others.[26] Real estate was not a blank slate onto which people simply scratched their own meaning. It was, by the mid-twentieth century, certainly, the latest form of landed investment in a country built through slavery, racial exclusion, and repeated acts of race-based land expropriation. Through the burden of history, real estate carried an inherent racial politics—a white supremacist politics—that made white Americans, immigrants, Native Americans, and even black Americans themselves understand black people—and, again, the black poor, especially—as potential threats to property values.[27] At times, even self-identified activists and reformers failed to understand the difference between the black poor and the environment built to profit from them. Thus, under Jim Crow's folk wisdom, "niggers" seemed to be natural impediments to the making of moral communities. These ideas did not begin in the twentieth century. But, through generations of "sensible" race reform over the course of the last century, Americans fashioned these ideas into sturdy common sense.

Landlords

In illustrating the relationship between racism, real estate, and governance, this book offers an unprecedented look at the complexities of rental property in Jim Crow America. Landlords shaped US politics profoundly because of their ability to inspire dramatic government land projects and to capture and impair the New Deal and post–World War II regulatory state.[28] Between the 1940s and 1970s, local and federal agents destroyed some sixteen hundred black neighborhoods through various slum clearance, urban renewal, and interstate highway projects. The resulting disruption and pain many of these projects wrought was not, as some have argued, the result of some political accident or bureaucratic misstep on the part of otherwise earnest housing reformers.[29] Displacements were intentional. They represented, for growth-minded elites, successful attempts to contain black people and to subsidize regional economies with millions in federal spending. More than that, though, many of the most injurious and dramatic urban land projects of the postwar period enjoyed wide support and crucial black political cover because urban progressives and moderate reformers explicitly framed land expropriation as an effective weapon against abusive and intransigent landlords. To various degrees, black and white housing activists, urban mayors, and even more moderate southern governors lauded bulldozers and land condemnation as instruments of civil rights reform. Through demolition, advocates of fair housing who hated "the Negro's" wretched living conditions found common cause with proponents of regional growth who simply wanted to repurpose the land rental owners held. Landlords offered a common enemy for Jim Crow's liberals. Yet, they were enemies not easily bested.

Rental property owners dominated debates around property rights and urban redevelopment in much of the country with the aid of ironclad constitutional protections of private property and the selective enforcement of real estate regulations at the local and state level. Especially in the American South and West, landlords repelled federal slum clearance provisions for nearly a decade longer than their counterparts in the urban North. During the 1950s, in particular, landlords kept many redevelopment efforts at bay by keeping state eminent domain laws weak and by carefully utilizing government mortgage subsidies from the Federal Housing Administration. Freeways and urban renewal programs (and their accompanying millions of dollars in federal spending) helped dissolve the last of Jim Crow's wood and tarpaper shacks by the early 1960s. Yet, largely because of landlord power, redevelopment only brought about the proliferation of concrete tenements and the less overt and sturdier color lines that continue to define post–Jim Crow America.[30] The remarkable regional, and indeed national, scale of landlord power must be understood as critical to the course of metropolitan growth and political development in the United States. That requires looking where landlord power originated and where it remained most acutely felt—during the Jim Crow era, at street level, and in everyday contests over segregation and property rights.

Truly, with all we know about white suburbanites, corporate interests, and southern politicians in Jim Crow America, we still know precious little about the white people who fought for the ghetto's endurance, those who profited from its strengthening, and those who steered city governments in the interest of protecting landlords' property rights. Moreover, with all that's been written on black life in America, the men and women who actually owned and managed black rental communities remain largely faceless historical agents, to say nothing of the role these mostly white entrepreneurs played in the daily cultural and political lives of their mostly black tenants.[31]

White real estate interests play a particularly important role in the chapters that follow because of (1) their ability to take advantage of the legal protections afforded them as *white* property owners and (2) their willingness to use that power, often in surprising ways, to protect the interests of *black* property owners. It may astonish some readers to learn, in fact, that Jim Crow provided little impediment for black and white rental property owners and real estate developers to understand themselves as a class. This remained true even when, as was often the case, white landlords deployed "states' rights" arguments to win over segregationist white voters for their various causes. If anything, the dual traditions of Negro self-help and white paternalism on display in southern cities encouraged interracial collaboration—dare one say, class formation—among the region's landlords. White and black landlords loaned each other money and jointly invested in any number of real estate projects during Miami's early development in the 1910s and 1920s. They also shared views of colored tenants as lazy, dirty, impressionable, and in need of landlord benevolence and philanthropy, which, at times, they also organized jointly. Through a combination of tenant paternalism and savvy property management subcontractors, black and white landlords compromised tenants' electoral voice. They routinely exploited tenants to the point of destitution. And they thwarted housing reformers looking to alleviate the privation of Negro tenements.

Black and white landlords worked different sides of the political equation that bound real estate to structural racism and white supremacy to political power. As leaders of a perceived "Negro community," many black rental owners would insulate landlords, in general, from the possibility of black tenant organizing. And white landlords, through lobbying groups and personal connections to well-placed elected officials, would ensure that the legal and policy regimes of all-white governing bodies protected rental interests. Separate yet one, like the fingers of the hand, property owners' collaboration worked less as some kind of conspiracy than as a simple cohort of entrepreneurs protecting shared interests from contrasting social positions. In tandem, if not always in direct consultation, black and white landlords helped ensure white supremacy's profitability.

Often, the principal political fault lines in Jim Crow America were not between blacks and whites, but between those advocating for a strict defense of property rights and those favoring a vision of liberalism dependent on land expropriation. In fact, through what may have been their most important and least understood joint action, black and white landlords regularly used their political influence and legal resources to keep large-scale land use projects from claiming black homes. Many times, the only people fighting most immediately—most intimately—alongside black property owners, even in emergent black suburbs, were well-connected white rental landlords. In Richmond, Virginia; Birmingham, Alabama; and elsewhere, black property owners and white landlords with vested interests in Negro rentals teamed up again and again to oppose slum clearance projects of the 1930s and 1940s, highway development and the forced expansion of "whites only" suburbs in the 1950s, and public housing and urban renewal in the 1950s and 1960s.[32] Quite ironically, white supremacy—in this instance, the legal defense of exploiting black tenants—could actually offer black property owners a modicum of defense against state officials looking to carry out their own racially inflected urban redevelopment projects. Through protecting their own property interests, landlords affirmed a notion of black property rights that, unlike many of its contemporary liberal alternatives, did not depend on the possibility of mandated integration or the even more remote prospect of changing white people's hearts and minds. Landlords reinforced, instead, what had become yet another piece of folk wisdom during African Americans' long history of enduring disenfranchisement and serial land divestment—actual ownership meant more than promises of citizenship.

The point is neither to lionize black property ownership nor to absolve racist economic exploitation. Rather, the point is to unpack the shared assumptions that real estate and white supremacy nurtured in their subjects, regardless of skin color and regardless of class status, and to demonstrate how those assumptions bore drastically different consequences because of skin color and because of class status.[33] A vision of freedom made from property and growth—a vision that remains today America's centrist understanding of civil rights—began as a pragmatic feature of segregationist statecraft.[34] And Americans' very understanding of freedom *as* real estate remained and remains steeped in many of Jim Crow's political practices and regrettable racial assumptions.

From Property to Protest

Much has rightly been made of the labor/leftist origins of direct action campaigns in literature on the black freedom struggle.[35] Yet, we have also known for some time that black business and property interests often provided the organizational resources and personal connections that proved critical to race reform.[36] Real estate mattered to the life and death of black political movements because it was property owners who mostly set the agendas for formal civil rights protest. As the holders of church land, homes, and storefronts, black property owners often determined the time and the place that everyday agency would become public activism.[37] Just as critically, black property owners, following acts of public protest, handled the negotiations with white elites that ultimately arrived at "pragmatic" solutions.[38] Black property owners were responsible for preserving an abiding conservatism that existed within civil rights organizations.[39] At the very same time, though, it was also largely property owners and aspiring property owners who, through the discourse of property *rights*, expressed how economic and political justice worked together. They articulated a "freedom dream"—ownership—that many still associate with the most ambitious forms of civil rights struggle.[40]

Property and real estate, in other words, occupied a privileged position within black politics. Owning rental real estate and owning one's own home promised black people a measure of individual freedom from the coercive power of wage labor, landlords, and the state. Voting rights and civil rights remained bound to black property rights. Often, the acquisition of real estate represented the cardinal goal, the protection of property the chief purpose, and the assets from property the principal economic means of sustained black agency and activism. And, just as property ownership complicates what we know about white Americans in a Jim Crow system, the centrality of real estate for so-called colored people created profound, long-term contradictions within black communities.

Around roughly the same time she launched her underexpressway park, Athalie Range owned several houses in Greater Miami's Liberty City and Brownsville neighborhoods, including a house at 1184 NW Sixty-Second Street. In keeping with Range's other income properties, the house at Sixty-Second Street suffered from several violations of the minimum housing code, including sizable holes in the floor and walls. The house was in such bad shape that, according to the tenant, Rose Lee Wyatt, Mrs. Range threatened simply to tear down the house if Rose Lee, also a black woman, did not dip into her own pocket for the repairs. For about two hundred dollars, Mrs. Wyatt recounted, "I had to buy a couple doors and fix a couple windows. She still not refusing to take my rent, though." Others among Range's tenants told similar stories: substandard units in need of massive repairs that tenants would have to pay for and carry out themselves.[41]

Speaking to investigative reporters in the mid-1970s, Wyatt described suffering repeated coercion, with little recourse, at the hands of her landlord. For even as Athalie Range stood scarcely five feet tall, she was nothing less than a civil rights giant in South Florida.[42] From the 1950s until she passed away in 2006 at the age of ninety-one, Range built an impressive record of legislative successes as a city commissioner and political advocate. She also enjoyed an unequaled status as black Miami's matriarch. She was widely known, until her final days, in fact, as "Ma Range."[43] Much of her renown during her younger years came, somewhat ironically, when she took on absentee landlords from her seat on the Miami City Commission.[44] Range also fought for school integration when it was highly unpopular and potentially dangerous to do so. She was the first black Miamian to be appointed by a sitting US president (Jimmy Carter placed Range on the governing board of AMTRAK), and she won countless commendations for her fights to open parkland, improve trash collection, and tighten gun control. Range spent her final years protecting beachfront land from real estate developers for the purposes of a one-of-a-kind museum commemorating Miami's only Jim Crow era "Colored Beach."[45] Her success, for years, was black Miami's success. And her skill as an entrepreneur and investor played no small part in her lifelong activism. Yet, despite all this, from the perspective of Rose Lee Wyatt, Athalie Range was a slumlord.

Among the most elite of America's black middle class, Range was not so much the exception as the rule. Miami's most powerful black newspaper editors, physicians, judges, attorneys, and ministers were leaders all and, with scant exception, landlords all. The same was true of nationally iconic activists like W. E. B. Du Bois and Mary McLeod Bethune, as well as more local heroes like Chicago's Carl Hansberry and black US representative Oscar De Priest, Mississippi's T. R. M. Howard, or the prominent Spaulding family of Durham, North Carolina.[46] Black property owners, as in Du Bois's case, used sparsely maintained rental units to provide themselves with some form of personal economic security.[47] Others, such as Bethune or the Spauldings, spent money generated from apartments to build "colored only" schools, libraries, and a score of other segregated institutions.[48] With whites largely in control of federal, state, and local government, black landlords and their white allies routinely subsidized community building and racial uplift with rent monies gained from those in most apparent need of uplifting. In short, much of Afro-America, like the rest of America, ran on rents.

Because one could never fully separate Jim Crow's Negro neighborhoods from the political and social sensibilities of the wider, capitalist world, the desire to "have something" always ran far and deep for black people. Real estate and the pursuit of property influenced the political behavior of everyday folk who may not have been in charge of churches, businesses, or civil rights organizations, but who nonetheless sought income properties, suburban homes, and other means and symbols of independence. In this way, working people, too, served as the hopeful architects and advocates of making liberalism more responsive and capitalism more humane. In contrast to whites with similar aspirations, however, black property owners suffered greater difficulties securing loans, paying property taxes, and making repairs on their homes and apartments, even after their occasional collaboration with white rental interests.[49] Such structural hardships greased the wheels of black-on-black predation. They also inspired practices through which black suburbanites fought, unsuccessfully, to repel their poorer, colored counterparts.[50] Extracting capital from colored renters or moving to "the 'burbs," though, was not about Negro property owners thinking or behaving "white," a stubbornly resilient interpretation of such practices.[51] It was about becoming a richer and better "black" for oneself, and, if pushed on the matter, for "the race."[52]

Athalie Range promised at least two more underexpressway parks at her 1969 opening ceremony. One would serve black senior citizens and the other would be "for the teenaged, the ones who are causing our problems." Her voice carrying over seesaws and hobbyhorses, Commissioner Range reminded the crowd, "These are still explosive times." Her remarks marked the park's opening with an unfortunate anniversary in Miami's more recent history.[53]

Just a year earlier, almost to the day, Greater Miami suffered its most disastrous national news event. The onetime suburbs of Liberty City and Brownsville burst with what observers were calling South Florida's first "race riot." During the late 1940s and 1950s, Liberty City and Brownsville attracted upwardly mobile West Indians, Spanish-speaking Caribbean folk, and American blacks, all known, in those years, as "colored people." They came by the thousands in search of parks, swimming pools, homeownership, and freedom from downtown slums. By the early 1960s, however, the promise of suburbia seemed unmade. White rental speculators and a wave of rezoning initiatives had turned much of Brownsville, and especially Liberty City, into a suburban ghetto. By the summer of 1968, privately owned

Figure 0.3. Hard Power. The Liberty City riot, 1968. (Courtesy of Corbis.)

tenements and other relocation housing had left residents of these communities in the same predicament as the people living "over town."

To live in Miami's black suburbs meant to be trapped in a web of stop-and-frisk policing, insufficient city services, unemployment, price gouging, and worsening rental conditions. Perhaps unexpectedly, there was also a noticeable increase in cars driving through the neighborhood with "[George] Wallace for President" bumper stickers.[54] Alabama's archsegregationist governor—who famously declared in 1963, "Segregation now, segregation tomorrow, segregation forever"—had little chance of becoming president in 1968. Nevertheless, that year's Republican National Convention, going on just seven miles away in Miami Beach, created a spiked political atmosphere that fed black Miamians' simmering frustration with a white supremacy that seemed everywhere and, increasingly, nowhere in particular. Over two blistering days in August, a mix of suburban ranch homes and low-rise housing projects served as the backdrop for clashes between neighborhood youth and police. Black Miami inaugurated America's Sunbelt era wreathed by a police blockade and beset by burning storefronts, hundreds of arrests, dozens injured, and three people killed.

In light of the unrest, Miami's underexpressway park stood as far more than a park. It was politics. It was governing. It was capitalism. To our present-day eyes, opening a playground under an expressway in sunny South Florida

Figure 0.4. Soft Power. Miami's mayor, Stephen P. Clark, and City Commissioner M. Athalie Range. (Courtesy of the Black Archives History and Research Foundation of South Florida Inc.)

might seem absurd or, perhaps, as regrettable as Klan marches or other relics of a racism long dead. It was certainly true that, at points during the opening ceremony, black poor people seemed fit mostly to stand and watch as their wealthier race-mates moved back and forth, up and down, crafting with white elites a seemingly more acceptable segregation.

Yet the park's opening and events like it were, at one point, appropriate demonstrations of neighborhood pride and effective, sensible politics in local America. Built for better or for worse, Athalie Range Park served to symbolize the Negro's new political power, for some even "Black Power." In its contradictions, it may well have been a more fitting example of "America's Playground" than even Miami itself.

To appreciate Athalie Range Park as part of a broader governing template for managing the social pressures of poverty, one must understand that the racial theatrics on display under I-95 were not really prompted by riots or even the arrival of new black politicians. They followed Jim Crow's political script, with the better-off speaking for the worse-off. They were part of timeworn practices intended to preserve how money moved, what land was worth, and how power worked. What follows, therefore, does not chronicle the bigoted folkways and state provisions that evaporated under the heat of civil rights activism and heroic acts of self-sacrifice. It explores the more durable world that held and hardened under the very feet of protest marchers and rioters as Jim Crow died and segregation remained.[55]

PART ONE

Foundation

Figure 0.5. Seminoles performing at Miami Beach, 1922. Growing Greater Miami's economy during the Progressive Era relied on selling Florida real estate as part of an untamed frontier and on allowing white tourists to enjoy watching colored people engaged in elaborate displays of primitivism and subservience. Here, in this photo dated 4 March 1922, onlookers enjoy alligator wrestling and a Seminole poling a dugout canoe in a Miami Beach swimming pool. (Courtesy of the Charles W. Tebeau Library, Historical Museum of Southern Florida.)

CHAPTER ONE

The Magic City

In 1845, Florida gained the fifty thousand white people required by federal law to achieve statehood. That year, Miami was what it would be for at least another half century, a remote and desolate outback. Until the 1890s, the region's population, which cropped up around Fort Dallas, an old outpost from the Seminole Wars, consisted of a handful of homesteading white families; the families of freed slaves; fewer than five hundred Seminoles; and a few dozen, mostly black, Bahamians.[1] With no bank, and therefore little access to credit, these early residents held their economy together through cash transactions. Most of the hard currency circulating through the local economy came by way of Seminoles who traded bird plumes, alligator hides, and animal furs of high demand within a growing international fashion industry.[2] Through at least the late 1880s, Miami's denizens were connected to one another and parts north by sailboat and canoe travel and by the on-foot trekking of those later known as "barefoot mailmen." In the absence of roads and freshwater for horses, contracted mail carriers covered in three days the sixty-plus miles of coast between Palm Beach and Coconut Grove. Southern Florida's Seminoles, black people, and white settlers fought each other and among themselves for any number of reasons. The relatively small population and the harshness of daily life, however, left very little use for what one would recognize as Jim Crow segregation.

Whatever yeoman way of life existed during Miami's homesteading years began receding with the arrival of big money from the North in the 1890s. Julia Tuttle, Miami's first booster, was also a widowed entrepreneur from Cleveland, Ohio. Touting the region's lack of frost during the winter months, she enticed several northern investors, most notably Henry Flagler of Standard Oil, to take an interest in southern Florida. "As if by magic," early residents liked to brag, Miami turned from a wilderness to a fully de-

veloped city. Tuttle offered massive land grants and Flagler, through his railroad, transported people into southern Florida by the hundreds.

Publicists and businesspeople agreed to call Miami the Magic City as a
way of capturing the almost supernatural speed with which early developers
built a city out of what seemed like thin air.[3] Work crews first hacked through
Dade County's bush to lay track for Flagler's Florida East Coast (FEC) Railway in early 1896. They pressed through water moccasins, a near constant
fog of mosquitoes, and dense mangrove forests. In less than six months,
Miami had the semblance of a city grid, a newspaper, a bank, and several
stores and churches. It also had about 500 voting-age residents—whites and
Negroes—which was 200 more than the number necessary under Florida
law to incorporate Miami as a city. Incorporation granted Miami's first generation of civic leaders the power to collect taxes and start lobbying state
and local governments for assistance in infrastructural development.[4] As
historians in South Florida are still quick to point out, 162 of the nearly 400
voters who incorporated Miami were colored men.[5]

Contrary to common depictions of electoral politics in the turn-of-the-
century South, Miami's white civic leaders would not summarily disenfran-
chise black voters after the city's 1896 incorporation. Rather, white politicos
would strategically deploy the Negro vote to accommodate one investor or
another's development vision. As laborers and swing voters, in fact, Negroes
were integral to Miami's early "magic." John Sewell, who would become the
city's third mayor, proved particularly adept at tipping close elections with
what he liked to call his "black artillery." "I had about one hundred of my
negroes registered and qualified to vote, and held them in reserve for emer-
gencies."[6] Sewell kept his colored voters up to date on their poll taxes. One
can also presume that, given the frequency of special "freeholder" elections
for early land development projects, Sewell also ensured these men met the
state's property requirements.

Sewell first began building his "black artillery" as a foreman on Flagler's
FEC Railway and, later, during the construction of the Royal Palm Hotel.
Built in 1897 as Miami's first tourist destination, the Royal Palm sat on the
banks of the Miami River and boasted four hundred rooms, six levels, and a
six-hundred-foot veranda. A structure of that size looked like a palace standing alone amid surrounding swamp and wildlife. Building the hotel also
required unearthing the burial mound of marsh-dwelling native peoples
known as the Tequesta, a group who predated even the Seminoles by at least
one hundred years. At the site, Sewell gave away as souvenirs some of the
sixty or so Tequesta skulls his workers found while digging the hotel's foundation.[7] He ordered the rest of the bones removed to an unmarked grave. "I

took about four of my most trusted negroes," Sewell later wrote, "and hauled all those skeletons out by where there was a big hole in the ground, about twelve feet deep, and dumped the bones in it." On top of displaced Indian remains, Sewell built and sold what he called "a fine residence," adding, "The things that the owners don't know will never hurt them."[8]

Errand into the Wilderness

Indian bones glibly discarded captures the kind of disregard South Florida's early real estate men brought to the region, especially as it concerned the natural environment. Fancying themselves as the next generation of Henry Flaglers, a second wave of millionaire developers, again mostly from northern states, came to Miami just after 1900. Like the robber barons they emulated, these men paid very little mind to the ecological and social impact of their land reclamation efforts. The eccentric industrialist from Maine, James Deering; Missouri's Locke Highleyman; Carl Fisher, an auto-body magnate from Indiana; and the aged New Jersey–born farmer John Collins were but a few of those who paid millions of dollars and secured millions more in government funds to build docks and bridges, to expand the railroad, to dynamite narrow streams, and to continue the slow, steady drainage of the Everglades with over 125 miles of new canals.[9]

Since at least 1906, drainage projects, in particular, began cutting off Seminoles from their seasonal marsh settlements and hunting grounds farther inland. Several native families, in response, elected to move closer to Miami's slowly urbanizing sections. Seminoles traveled daily down the Miami River to work in small shops or sell animal pelts and Indian crafts to merchants and other recent arrivals. Where the Miami River met NW First Street, one could find more than a dozen dugout canoes parked on the river's landings on any given day. Newly arrived whites often marveled at the sight of "real Indian" families in town on everyday business. Admitted one resident who spent his youth in Miami during the 1910s, "I liked to watch an Indian family walk down the street, always single file, with the father in front, followed by the boys . . . then the mother, and after the mother, the girls."[10]

By this point in Miami's development, Seminoles were hardly the warring nation so many whites associated with Florida's frontier history. Their numbers had dropped to as few as 160 people in the 1860s, and they seemed, in the words of one official, "doomed ultimately to extinction."[11] Natural population increases had caused their numbers to approach 400 by 1910. Yet this growth brought with it spikes in rates of malaria and infant mortality. Public health crises ran headlong into dramatic reductions in the desirability of furs and alligator skins by 1915, driving Miami's native communities further into poverty. Seminoles who saw little future success or stability as the 1900s wore on joined earlier migrants, and fled for reservations in Oklahoma. Others moved to Seminole settlements near Lake Okeechobee farther upstate. Others still, at the behest of John Sewell's younger brother, Everest, would eventually find work as caddies on golf courses and, later, as "tribal" performers in silent films, promotional events, and at alligator-wrestling spectaculars. Though their thoughts on the matter remain largely unknown, Miami's indigenous people, by their very presence, contributed to southern Florida's frontier feel and the money one could make from it.

Considered to be, in the words of one paper, "peculiar recluses," Seminoles also generally avoided sending their children to formal schools, and this further marginalized them from the rapid growth transforming the region. As reported by Indian Affairs agents, white people's continually broken promises inspired the notion that white education taught a person to lie. Only careful negotiation among Seminole leaders, government officials, and local white educators finally got a single Indian boy, Hath-wa-ha-chee, into a white primary school in neighboring Broward County in 1914. Called Tony Tommie to ease white discomfort with pronouncing his name, Hath-wa-ha-chee was fourteen years old at the time he started first grade, and his initial difficulties in accessing "whites only" education prompted some to recommend that he attend a school for colored children. "I opposed this," said Lucien Spencer, Florida's federally appointed commissioner of Indian Affairs. "I know the Indians draw the color line even closer than we whites do." "Persons of negro blood among the Indians," Spencer continued, "have no tribal rights whatever, and to try and place a Seminole on a plane with negroes would destroy the work [of educating Indian children] completely."[12] During the 1910s, young Tony Tommie and other Seminoles remained largely relegated to being set pieces in parades and on golf courses.

Just as the presence of native peoples proved integral to Miami's early years, the interdependency of black and white residential life and labor was equally evident from the very beginning of the city's development. Wealthy white Miamians drew aesthetic inspiration from Mediterranean villas and British manors, and they built dozens of opulent winter homes, lavish waterfront estates, and hotels in full view of Miami's impressive bayfront. Raising luxury from Florida bushlands brought West Indian and American Negro workers shoulder to shoulder with Scotsmen, Englishmen, Italians, and other Europeans.[13] Two early Miami developers—the Canadian concert pianist Franklin Bush and Walter de Garmo, an Illinois-born architect—sold homes and lots in what would become Miami's Coconut Grove and Coral Gables

neighborhoods. Though concerned principally with catering to a white clientele, Bush and de Garmo made renting to colored people an ancillary benefit
of becoming a homeowner or developer in Miami. With every eight to ten
lots they sold in Coral Gables, they threw in a free "colored" acre in Coconut
Grove, the size of which accommodated nearly a dozen black rental houses.[14]

Black housing was mostly workers' housing, and, in Miami, black work
conditions, because of white racism, mirrored national trends. Almost as a
rule, affluent white homes brought in black women as domestics. Hotels
and white homeowners ran "colored preferred" want ads daily, with most
expressly looking for an "American colored girl" or a "competent colored
woman" for one kind of domestic task or another.[15] The preponderance
of wealthier white women among Miami's early investor families ensured
that most domestic work in the city was going to be done by black Caribbean women. Turn-of-the-century Miami also sat at the dawn of a thirty-year
blackening of domestic labor around the country. Roughly between 1900
and 1930, the number of white women engaged in domestic employment
declined by 40 percent. Most gained access to new clerical professions. Black
women largely took on white women's old menial labor, as evidenced by
the 40 percent *increase* in the number of black women working as domestics
and laundresses over those same years.[16]

Racism on the job and between jobs determined the nature of black
men's work as well. Beginning in the 1910s and continuing well into the
1940s, white union members enforced "whites only" membership rules
within the sectors of carpentry and entertainment. These helped exclude
colored people from Miami's most well paying jobs. Miami's Central Labor
Union, an umbrella organization representing workers throughout South
Florida's early tourist economy, argued in 1915, "Organized labor must
maintain the barrier between white and black in Miami."[17]

White union members and employers generally made poor-paying and
degradingly servile jobs the kind of employment most available to black
Miamians. The real estate developer Carl Fisher bragged of employing "the
most wonderful Bahama negroes you ever saw." They steered gondolas at
Fisher's Nautilus Hotel on Miami Beach, and, as Fisher explained to a fellow white entrepreneur, "They are all going to be stripped to the waist and
wear big brass rings. And possibly necklaces of live crabs or crawfish."[18]
Whites also preferred colored men for driving "Afromobiles" across the verdant grounds of the Royal Palm and other new hotels. An Afromobile was a
wicker chair mounted on a three-wheeled cycle frame and usually propelled
by a colored servant pedaling from the rear. "The negro chair chauffeurs," by
one account, "drive the chair along by vigorous pedaling."[19]

Afromobiles, thought of as a "chariot of wealth and beauty," were a favorite attraction for whites vacationing at coastal destinations throughout the seaside Deep South, and as far north as Atlantic City.[20] For working-class white travelers, in particular, being transported by Afromobile did much to help otherwise downtrodden white workers leisure, albeit temporarily, like wealthy capitalists. In South Florida, Afromobile conductors were supposed to provide vacationing whites with descriptions of Florida's exotic flora and fauna; they also contributed to the generally healthy atmosphere promised in Miami advertising. The "gentle side to side motion [of an Afromobile] . . . acts as a mild massage to the occupant. Two hours of such exercise is considered to be about enough."[21]

Apart from being "exercise" for its white occupants, a ride in an Afromobile was part of the wider colonial experience of apartheid in southern Florida. It performed the same racial work as a Seminole carrying one's golf bag on the links, and it was synonymous with the toothy greeting one got from a Bahamian maid or bellhop flaunting a freshly starched uniform and a patois brogue.[22] In South Florida, as elsewhere in the Americas, whites attended live minstrel shows or forced black waiters to race with full trays of glassware across the sands of Miami Beach.[23] At practically every site of white leisure, nonwhite servitude proved integral to the everyday theatrics and comforts of seaside recreation.

American, Caribbean

After a decade of construction activity, South Florida's marsh- and grasslands began to favor any other sleepy seaside town in Louisiana or South Carolina. Most of Miami's buildings were wood-frame construction or, in the general absence of brick, built from native rock, such as coral and limestone. Bahamian masons proved especially adept at fashioning these fossils of sea life into sturdy dwellings, mostly for white buyers. The childhood home of the eventual real estate developer George Merrick, for instance, was a coral rock house with a red gabled roof made from local pine trees. Merrick's father, Solomon, had bought acres of land from Bush and de Garmo, and he used lands surrounding the family home to establish real estate holdings for agricultural production and rental shacks.[24] Through young George's efforts several years later, the family home Solomon built in 1906, named "Coral Gables," would become the namesake for one of Miami's most exclusive communities.[25] But it would be the West Indian and American colored folk—those propping up Merrick family fortunes—who were most responsible for setting Miami's early coastal ambience. Mostly black work crews planted thousands of imported palm trees (which were not native to Florida). They also paved many of the city's otherwise dirt streets with crumpled white limestone. Summer sun shot between Miami's palms and onto streets the color of baby power. The glare was so bad, as one resident remembered, "it almost knocked your eyes out."[26]

During the early 1900s, black Bahamians and colored Americans made up 40 percent of Miami's total population, and 75 percent of colored people in Miami were born somewhere in the islands.[27] By 1920, after twenty years of population growth, over half of Miami's black population could still claim Caribbean birth or parentage. Among cities in the United States, only New York boasted more West Indian migrants than Miami.[28] As one Miamian described as recently as the late 1990s, "Black Miamians are Caribbean peoples in the first place . . . not the second place."[29] Miami, like New Orleans or many other Caribbean cities, served as an important crossroads for a region in perpetual motion. Jamaicans and American blacks traveled to dig the Panama Canal. Haitians migrated to cut cane on Cuban sugar plantations. Cubans landed in Tampa to roll cigars. And from the 1830s to World War I, East and South Asians reached every British possession between British Guiana and Jamaica. Oftentimes herded into dilapidated shacks in "black quarters" or "coolie" work camps throughout the circum-Caribbean, each group of workers tried to carve a sliver of livelihood from their colonial predicament.[30]

Between the 1880s and the 1940s, Miami's chief source of black in-migration was from the Bahamas. For many Bahamian migrants, the still-developing labor arrangements in early Miami seemed preferable to the ways in which white islanders and immigrant landowners exploited black workers under British colonialism. Few migrants arrived with the notion that Miami was some kind of racial utopia. A variety of economic factors, however, made the Magic City a preferred destination for Bahamians. For one, unskilled construction work and agricultural labor in Miami fetched wages, on average, three times higher than what black workers were paid in the islands.[31] The Bahamas also lost a major source of employment when US subsidies of American pineapple interests in Hawaii, Cuba, and the Philippines put Bahamian competitors out of business. This shift was then followed by the onset of a Greek monopoly in Bahamian sponge aquaculture by the start of World War I, further weakening black employment options. Finally, British property law made acquiring land exceedingly difficult for Bahamian blacks. Not only did planters hoard land or help price the land out of black people's reach; any land that fell into default was usually sold, with the help of British Crown officials, to foreign whites, many of whom were Americans, looking to establish large plantations.[32]

Such conditions made Miami a natural draw for poor Bahamians.[33] Between 1911 and 1921, migrants fled the Bahamas in such great numbers that overall population of the islands declined by 5.5 percent.[34] For only one British pound—the equivalent of five US dollars—black British subjects boarded mail-carrying boats in Nassau and landed in droves at Miami. Remittances back to the Bahamas became the chief source of income in the rural, depressed communities many of these men and women left behind.[35]

As one might imagine, the inequities of racism in Miami did not go unremarked by West Indians. "Having passed the immigration and customs examiners," recalled one migrant from the Bahamas, "I took a carriage for what the driver called 'Nigger Town.' It was the first time I had heard that opprobrious epithet employed, and then, by a colored man himself. I was vividly irked no little." The man likely passed the graying, eggshell facades of Miami's downtown hotels and the meager wood dwellings of poor whites that ran right up to the railroad tracks. Then, crossing the tracks and "arriving in Colored Town, I alighted from the carriage in front of an unpainted, poorly ventilated rooming house where I paid $2.00 for a week's lodging." "Already," he continued, "I was rapidly becoming disillusioned. . . . Colored Miami was certainly not the Miami of which I had heard so much. It was the filthy backyard of the Magic City."[36]

Colored Town stood as an invention of Henry Flagler. Initially, white and colored workers lived together on the grounds of Flagler's Royal Palm Hotel during its construction. But once workers completed the project, Flagler bought a separate tract of land on which his colored workers could build their own homes. Black workers bought 50-by-150-foot lots of uncleared land from Flagler at a cost of fifty dollars each. Flagler also donated a plot of land to every religious denomination represented among Miami's colored people. Cobbled together, these lots would make up Colored Town, with Flagler's railroad tracks, on the eastern edge of the black district, serving as the first and longest-lasting boundary between colored and white Miami. After working on the white side of the color line all day, black workers would carry discarded planks of wood and sheets of tin back to Colored Town. There, they worked by torchlight and lanterns to build their own homes and those of their neighbors.[37]

Upbuilding the Race

Miami's early black arrivals took full advantage of the opportunity to accumulate as many lots as possible, and they labored with great haste to build the homes that would provide many colored people with their first semblance of economic security. One of the laborers to take advantage of Flagler's land sales was Dana A. Dorsey. Born in 1868, Dorsey had been a carpenter working in John Sewell's "black artillery" at Flagler's Royal Palm Hotel. In 1900, Dorsey moved into a rented room in Coconut Grove and tried his hand at farming. A black sharecropper's son from Quitman County, Georgia, Dorsey had only a fourth-grade education. He nevertheless used his workman's income to buy several lots in Colored Town and a few in Coconut Grove. Dorsey then built a house for himself, before quickly fashioning dozens of small rental homes from scrap lumber and other cheaply bought materials.[38] Before his death in 1940, Dana Dorsey eventually built a million-dollar real estate fortune that included oil fields near Tallahassee and in Louisiana, land in Cuba and the Bahamas, and properties up and down the Florida Peninsula. The self-described "realtor and capitalist" was also primary stockholder of Pewaubic Mine Company, a copper mine in Gilpin County, Colorado.[39]

At his rental properties in Colored Town, Dorsey, for years, made a point of collecting his rents personally. After church on Sundays, he would spend all day traveling from one property to another to inspect his units and receive his weekly dividend. Roberta Thompson, a Colored Town native, lived across the street from a Dorsey-owned property. She described how tenants busied themselves on Saturday to prepare for their landlord's Sunday visit. "On Saturdays most of the people had their children get a broom and sweep in front of the house or . . . the yards." Thompson noted that, despite high renter turnover from one season to the next, the property "was kept clean . . . and . . . nice and quiet."[40]

In addition to his many real estate investments, Dorsey had dreams of opening a Negro beach for Colored Town residents on the South Florida coast.[41] In 1918, he bought twenty-one acres on one of Miami's nearby islands in hopes of constructing seaside luxury estates and resorts exclusively for colored people.[42] Less than two years after the purchase, though, tax troubles, possibly orchestrated by white competitors, forced Dorsey to sell his holdings to a white entrepreneur, Carl Fisher. Fisher Island remains today one of Miami's most exclusive seaside enclaves. Following Dorsey's loss, it would take another thirty years for blacks in Miami to access swimming and other leisure on the Atlantic Ocean.[43]

Florence Gaskins, a contemporary of Dorsey's, worked as a colored washerwoman, laundering clothes and linens for laborers and guests at the Royal Palm. She was recently widowed and in her midthirties when she arrived in Miami from Jacksonville in 1896. Gaskins saved her earnings as a laundress for several years, and eventually acquired considerable rental and commercial real estate in Colored Town.[44] As she grew in relative wealth and influence, Gaskins opened an employment agency for black domestics and established a colored auxiliary of the Red Cross. This provided a platform from which she, Dorsey, and many others battled child mortality and other public health crises associated with Miami's black poor. Gaskins became an especially important organizer of black women's activism through her ability to direct women's political energy in the service of community-wide efforts. She coordinated women's participation in civic events, and, in 1923, she and several women opened a branch of the Young Women's Christian Association in Gaskins's Colored Town home.[45] Like most of her black and white counterparts, Florence Gaskins also believed Miami's broader economic growth could improve living conditions for everyone. She repeatedly donated to deepwater dredging efforts and other initiatives aimed at improving Miami's infrastructure. Her generosity to these initiatives routinely exceeded that of Dana Dorsey and other notable colored men, in fact.[46]

During Miami's frontier era, Dorsey and Gaskins were but two among a growing number of black property owners who helped affirm and advance beliefs about the social benefits of enterprise and ownership. Heartened by the example of Booker T. Washington, black Miamians belonged to a national wave of colored community builders who would name clinics and schools after the man widely known as "the Wizard of Tuskegee." Well into the 1950s, residents of Colored Town would at times refer to their community as Washington Heights. It would be a mistake, though, to assume that black Miamians' pursuits of ownership were derivative of some distant or, by 1915, deceased Great Man. Washington was an echo, not the architect, of what the historian Juliet Walker called the "Golden Age of Black Business."[47] Faced with the broad erasure of electoral power, American Negroes and black immigrants in the United States used business and property ownership to dull the sting of local discrimination, international economic pressures, and racist federal and state law. It should be said, too, that whites also used colored people's strategic emphasis on business to develop the colonial relationships—the political culture of Jim Crow—that made black entrepreneurs part of a more general effort to maintain the link between governance, racial power, and property after slavery.[48]

Property and Citizenship

For black people in the wider, postslavery Americas, any hope of making citizenship more than a promise remained intimately bound to beliefs in and narratives about private property.[49] This remained especially true under US law at the end of the nineteenth century, where black people's civil rights and voting rights stood on shifting sand. The Fourteenth Amendment (1868), for one, offered little protection of black people's civil rights because its crafters in Congress emphasized prohibiting discrimination against the so-called slave race *as a group*. Over the next century, white politicians and jurists used that *group* standard to undercut complaints from *individual* black people about civil rights violations in voting, education, public transportation, and any number of areas.[50] By contrast, when it came to black people's legal claims on property, courts and other adjudicating bodies generally proved more responsive, for there it was often the integrity of capitalism, not white power, that was at issue. As the historian Dylan Penningroth points out, the presence of Union troops and military courts immediately after the Civil War created a space wherein black people could protect property, even when they acquired that property as slaves. Amid even the racial hostility of the post-Emancipation South, Penningroth notes, it was not unheard of for former masters to testify in defense of their former bondsmen's property rights. Such moments became constitutive of the South's broader conversion from relations of bondage to those of contract.[51]

Property rights, through the courts, remained coupled to white supremacy, however, as rights in property provided Jim Crow with its legal and extralegal bedrock. In its first official interpretation of the Fourteenth Amendment—the *Slaughterhouse* cases of 1873—the US Supreme Court deemed that there were only two kinds of rights: property rights and political rights. Property rights were protected by the US Constitution; political rights fell under the aegis of the states. By the late 1870s especially, the defense of black rights remained dubious at best under state laws.[52] Then, in 1883, legal arguments in explicit defense of white property rights moved the Supreme Court, in the *Civil Rights Cases*, to declare that the federal government had no right to impede white business owners who exercised their property rights by excluding black patrons.[53] In the wake of this ruling, white lawmakers in Florida and in state legislatures across the South passed a whirlwind of provisions exacerbating black disenfranchisement, peonage, school segregation, and, after *Plessy v. Ferguson* (1896), "separate but equal" public accommodations.[54] In a particularly active decade of black disenfranchisement in Louisiana—1894 to 1904—whites reduced the number of black registered voters from 130,000 to 1,300, a decrease of 99 percent. Meanwhile, beneath the lofty legal arguments about property rights, black people, on the ground, suffered violent divestments of thousands of acres of land at the hands of white southerners through a practice called "whitecapping."[55] Land confiscation at the turn of the century served as an extension of lynching, sexual assaults, and other forms of white terrorism meant to devalue the property and property rights of colored people. Many recognized that, in the South, *all* white people were, in effect, the state. And one observer went so far as to describe lynching as "eminent domain, not only in the estate, but in the living body of [the] citizen."[56]

Given the legal openings fought for and foreclosed in the late nineteenth and early twentieth centuries, black people developed very tangible—and, in some cases, corporeal—understandings of property rights. Many learned, in fact, to pair property rights with gun rights, since these served as the principal constitutional and personal guarantors of Negroes' "civil rights." All accounts of racial incidents in turn-of-the-century Miami point to extensive gun ownership among immigrant and American-born blacks. One report placed the rate of gun ownership among Miami's colored folk as high as 90 percent.[57] But survival required more than simply adopting a commitment to self-defense. It required political struggle over the long term. Many black people who fought for landed self-determination in the nineteenth century lived to carry the political and legal fight into the twentieth. Referring to the seemingly new militancy of the 1920s, the historian Paul Ortiz explains, "The New Negro had gray hair."[58] Many black people spoke out and testified to the brutalities of white racism publicly and in print.[59] Yet, many more, simply and quietly, remained armed, resolute, and committed to a vision of progress through property.

Negotiating Jim Crow

To expand community-building and ownership possibilities for colored people in Miami, older black businesspeople like Dana Dorsey strategized behind closed doors with an incoming class of young Negro professionals. One of those new arrivals was the physician William B. Sawyer. A migrant to Miami in 1908, Sawyer put himself through Atlanta University by cooking and tending a furnace for W. E. B. Du Bois. He went on to complete his medical training at Meharry medical school in Nashville, Tennessee, before eventually becoming a wealthy landlord, a hotel owner, and a crusader against tuberculosis in South Florida. In his more quiet moments, Sawyer enjoyed passing the time playing checkers with other men on the front porch of his doctor's office in Colored Town. Between jumps, according to observers many years later, Sawyer would encourage his friends and neighbors to pool their money, buy land, and "become taxpayers."[60] Sawyer likely explained how owning property allowed colored people to vote in "freeholder" elections. The names of new black deed holders were also printed in the newspaper every year, serving as a public recognition of "the Negro's" economic discipline.

Shortly after his arrival in Miami, Sawyer joined Dorsey; Miami's first black attorney, R. E. S. Toomey; and a handful of other black property owners and entrepreneurs who, in 1900, established the Colored Board of Trade. Made up entirely of men, many of whom, like Toomey, were veterans of US wars, the board committed itself to growing black American business in an otherwise Caribbean city. At the time of the group's founding, there were barely two hundred American-born blacks in all of Miami, and only a dozen or so of those were members of the board. The group nevertheless claimed to represent "the interests and residents of our section of the city," regardless of the fact that black Miami, at this time, was mostly West Indian laborers.[61] "Race," writes Earl Lewis, "was a powerful connector, but it was never as adhesive as whites made out and as blacks allowed them to believe."[62] It was in the board's interest, as Americans, to claim to speak for the entire black collective, even though contests between West Indians and American blacks remained a regular feature of Miami's early years. For the Colored Board of Trade's part, its members focused primarily on persuading the five white bank presidents who made up Miami's early city councils.[63] "Patriotically concerned for the best interests of the community," the board saw its role as working with white businesspeople to help preserve "our common citizenship and eliminate some of the causes for inter-racial discord, conflict and strife."[64]

The group attempted, principally, to win community improvements for Miami's black population. But its demands were usually thwarted by white city officials, union leaders, or homeowners who desired to keep Negroes confined to the worst jobs and housing. The board pushed for parks, a hospital, and paved streets in Colored Town. In almost every instance, whites cried they had not the money or, in some cases, the votes to make separate equal.[65] After a series of violent disputes between black and white chauffeurs and taxi drivers between 1915 and 1919, for instance, "compromise" yielded a monopoly for whites on all fares earned outside of Colored Town. Black drivers were entitled only to those fares generated in black neighborhoods.[66] Colored drivers, in short, remained confined to the city's unpaved streets. City officials had laid over fifty miles of paving in Miami by 1920, and not a mile of the new surfaces, in spite of pleadings from the Colored Board of Trade, covered the streets of Colored Town.[67]

The physical condition of South Florida's black communities, and the continued growth of the population therein, affirmed white assumptions about the link between Negroes, disease, and Miami's young, haphazard cityscape. "Miami is being badly injured and badly disfigured by the growth of . . . Negro sections," remarked the *Miami Herald* in 1911. The paper characterized "the advance of the Negro population" as "a plague [that] carries destruction with it to all surrounding property." Evoking, at once, images of both germs and dusky savages, the *Herald* reminded its readers, "White people do not care to live in the vicinity of colonies of negroes housed in buildings little better than cabins."[68] Colored Town's streets and alleyways seemed especially hazardous because they supposedly enabled "high incidence" of "misconduct between white men and negro women."[69] Reporters and city officials cited evidence of sexually transmitted diseases among black women, in particular, as proof of black people's being a "degraded race." William Sawyer and other physicians from Colored Town, however, pointed to those same numbers as indicators of the predations of roving white men and landlords.[70]

Colored maids, nannies, and laundresses, by white people's general estimation, were especially insidious carriers of tuberculosis and other contagion.[71] "It is common knowledge that very many persons of the colored race are infected with a horrible communicable disease," explained editorialists at the *Herald*. "No mother who lets her baby out of her sight in the care of an irresponsible colored girl can know for a certainty that the child is safe." Whites were especially concerned about black nannies running their daily errands among the "unhealthful" inhabitants of Colored Town, a place "where the infants are fondled and handled by various strange persons." In response to white demands, Miami police, in the summer of 1915, threatened to arrest any black women found in Colored Town with white children.[72]

The discourse of disease and cleanliness offered more than simple metaphor; since the 1880s at least, it provided rationales for segregationist governance within cities faced with migrating "pestilence" from China, Southern and Eastern Europe, the Caribbean, and the South's Black Belt. Whites would advocate for Jim Crow, as a prophylactic, in nearly every major and minor city between San Francisco and Baltimore. It became widely held that one could, in the historian Nayan Shah's words, "divide the contaminated from the uncontaminated along racial lines."[73] Within emergent Progressive Era discourses about public health, the racial associations between the city and the body politic ensured that city planners and health administrators around the country would make "lung blocks"—quarantined areas for those suffering from tuberculosis—synonymous with Chinatowns and "negro sections."[74]

Citing incidences of leprosy in India, South Africa, and the United States, the *Miami Herald* argued that, to stave off public health crises, "segregation is necessary."[75] Black Americans, too, made the argument for segregation within colored communities, citing threats of syphilis, tuberculosis, and the most feared infections and immoralities of the day. With the help of several white allies, members of the Colored Board of Trade successfully established vice and prostitution "zones" outside of Colored Town. As *Miami Herald* reporters explained, "If by moving the people complained of we can assist the colored man and his family to become more reliable, moral, and enterprising citizens, we are not only aiding the race, but are making white people safer."[76]

Property, Whites

In 1915, Miami experienced its first of many struggles between white landlords and white homeowners over where best to house black people. White landlords, seeking to expand their interest in the Negro rental market, started building homes for colored people ever closer to Avenue J, or what in a few years' time would be known as NW Fifth Avenue, the western boundary of Colored Town. These developments approached a mixed-income white neighborhood called Highland Park. The *Miami Herald* warned, "These [Colored Town] houses are said to be rapidly increasing in number and spreading over a wide territory in such a manner as to bring about friction between the races sooner or later."[77] At 1:00 one August morning, a dozen armed white men with masks and torches visited each of the forty black families that lived in the disputed section—between Sixth and Fourth Streets, and Avenues I and J. The men distributed handwritten notes reading, "No nigger can live in this house. Move out by Monday night or we will blow you up. Signed 200 white men."[78]

The *Miami Metropolis*, a local paper more moderate than the *Herald*, condemned the threats as "Ku-Klux-Klan methods," but many of the whites in neighboring Highland Park took exception to such characterizations.[79] Writing as a homeowners association, white residents granted, in a letter in the *Herald*, that they threatened to lynch whole families, and that they terrorized black Miamians under cover of darkness. But the act of driving blacks away, they argued, was an act of self-help, worthy, indeed, of the country's Founding Fathers.[80] "If you saw the value of your hard earned home being ruined by constant negro aggressions, saw your family debased by being compelled to live among negroes, and all proposed legal remedies snatched from your grasp, wouldn't you be enough of [a] man, husband and father, to invoke that self-help which has so honorably characterized and succored us Americans since our earliest colonial days?"[81]

Informed by a several generations of law and custom, white homeowners understood the violent management of Negroes as being integral to their vision of democracy. As with perceived threats of syphilitic colored prostitutes, fears of Negro neighbors drove white political participation and small-town civic engagement. Around the country, in fact, white Americans joined homeowners associations to play a role in the day-to-day monitoring of trash collection, road improvement, and the policing of potential "nuisances," like neighbors who might want to own livestock or sell to Negroes. One such association in Baltimore advised the following in a provision immediately following the banning of livestock: "At no time, shall the land included in said tract or any part thereof . . . be occupied by any negro person or person of negro extraction."[82] Newly opened suburbs made sure to notify potential buyers that they enforced (and expected their neighbors to enforce) all the necessary restrictions, including "building, liquor, negro, and sanitary restrictions."[83] Vigilant homeowners associations guarded every neighborhood that encircled Colored Town. The North Miami Improvement Association, the Highland Park Improvement Association, the Southside Civic Improvement Association, the Riverside Improvement Association, the Buena Vista Improvement Association: all claimed to be driven by the higher ideals of morality and red-blooded Americanism.

In the opinion of South Florida's white homeowners, white landlords were leading "the Negro" astray, contaminating the colored man's mind that something was possibly *wrong* with segregation. "Miami's negroes," contended Earl Padgett of the Highland Park Improvement Association, "are well disposed, when not misled or incited by scheming whites who exploit the colored man, and persistently vex and complicate our negro problem for their own private gain."[84] On the question of Jim Crow itself, "There ought not to be any sense of degradation in the matter of segregation": so argued the *Miami Herald* editorial page in 1916, echoing the *Plessy* decision. "And where [segregation] is attempted," the city's flagship paper continued, "there is no desire to inflict on anyone the imputation of inferiority." There were, rather, "facts . . . to be recognized," including the apparent fact that "the two races do not get along as happily close together as where they are separated," and the equally self-evident proposition that "each race can work out its own destiny much better [when] the question of mixing does not . . . cause friction."[85]

Members of the Colored Board of Trade, perhaps used to speaking for others, did not appreciate Miami's white homeowners speaking for them. Appearing, as they often did, "as taxpayers and citizens" in the pages of the *Miami Herald*, board members demanded to play a role in what was becoming a robust public debate about establishing a new and legal residential color line.[86] Like white owners of black rental property, many black landlords saw little to be gained by surrendering their real estate for the purpose of creating a racial buffer zone or some other instrument of formal Jim Crow. Dana Dorsey actually threatened to fight the segregation measure in the courts, alongside white landlords, arguing that residential segregation was unnecessary and that it threatened to take people's property unjustly.[87] As a group, the board argued, in particular, that "the enactment of a segregation ordinance by the [city] council would be ill-advised [because] segregation, by legal enactment is indefensible both in laws and morals."[88]

Not all black businesspeople endorsed allying with white landlords. For if it was, indeed, possible to have segregation without discrimination, then any segregation should follow the principles of "mutual segregation."[89] "We insist," the Colored Board of Trade wrote in the pages of the *Herald*, "upon a segregation that really does segregate, absolute and inviolate. . . . If we are to be shut in, simple justice demands that the white people be shut out."[90] The primary problem, as some of Miami's black entrepreneurs understood it, was the crippling potential of "invading" white capital squeezing out black money. "In times past, we left our former places of business and located in the section marked off for colored people; since that time we have not transgressed the line. . . . Can the same be said of the white citizens of Miami?"[91]

Experience in the Magic City's early development and in the rural South taught many black businesspeople to fear the inherent dangers of white investment capital. Many members of the Colored Board of Trade, after all, came from southern sharecropping families. They were not strangers to the pricing schemes, intimidation, and cycles of indebtedness that white landowners and merchants employed to sap black people's labor power and buying power. White landowners could take a black tenant's entire investment through a well-timed eviction. And, as many suspected happened to Dana Dorsey's own beachfront property, whites of means and motivation could organize to take black property through any number of dubious strategies.

White-on-black profiteering was a national and growing problem. Particularly with the onset of World War I, the promise of industrial employment and the continuance of white-on-black violence in the rural South propelled black people's migrations into northern, southern, and even a few western cities. Recognizing a new consumer base, white entrepreneurs around the country began opening dry goods shops in burgeoning black communities while also increasing their investment in colored rental housing. At the same time, Negro businesspeople, through various forms of racial exclusion, remained blocked from accessing customers beyond designated colored enclaves. As one response, Negro insurance companies like Atlanta Life and

North Carolina Mutual issued mortgages, in the words of Mutual's chief executive, to "keep white people out of our Negro section."[92] In New York City, black journalists and economists in Harlem complained about America's emergent Negro Mecca being "bled white" by white-owned businesses.[93]

Then, of course, there were the international dimensions of white profiteering, through which big planters and powerful white property owners continued to exercise great influence over national and local governments throughout the hemisphere. If nothing else, Miami's black Caribbean migrants, especially Bahamians, knew these forms of white supremacy all too well. At the beginning of what would become the age of US multinational corporations, American capitalists could count on what President Theodore Roosevelt called "international police power" to further their economic influence over Caribbean governments, often through actual or threatened military action. Starting with the taking of Guantánamo Bay under the Platt Amendment of 1898 and the US expropriation of the Panama Canal in 1903, American officials took over the customs services of the Dominican Republic (1905) and Nicaragua (1911), followed by protracted military occupations in those two countries as well as in Haiti (1915–34), and smaller operations in northern Mexico (1916), Mexico's port city of Vera Cruz (1914), and the Danish Virgin Islands (1916).[94] Across the Americas, white capital was as peripatetic as black labor.

Perhaps unsurprisingly, however, Miami's black businesspeople, appreciating certain aspects of capital's fluidity, had developed their own means of profiting across the color line. Several members of Miami's Colored Board of Trade owned stock in white businesses. Miami's black real estate entrepreneurs invested widely in department stores and insurance companies where whites were majority owners.[95] William Sawyer, like other prominent colored people in Miami, would also lend money to whites and blacks looking to start small businesses.[96] Blacks could be white people's landlords from time to time as well. Dana Dorsey, for instance, rented retail space to white businesspeople in Colored Town.[97] He also owned considerable amounts of land in the white sections of North Miami, which he variously rented to white businesspeople or sold on payment plans to aspiring white homeowners, collecting as much as 8 percent interest.[98] Frankly, it was not uncommon for white dollars to turn into black capital.

Perhaps because of the international realities surrounding Miami's young economy, much of the segregation debate was dripping with nativism. White and black Americans both voiced objections toward immigrants who seemingly upset the productive racial order businesspeople were attempting to plant in South Florida. According to local reasoning, it was "British Negroes" from the Caribbean, with their desires for social equality, and profiteering white immigrant entrepreneurs who, in their greed, seemed most responsible for the city's racial tensions. One white member of a local homeowners association summed it up this way: "Most of our negroes and their landlords are foreigners who scorn American citizenship, regarding Miami as a convenient cow from which they milk a constant stream of money into the British possessions."[99] The Colored Board of Trade leveled a similar complaint. "We are over here trying to work out our salvation. But we are being handicapped by the untimely intrusion of foreigners . . . usurping our given opportunities."[100] In the view of the Colored Board of Trade, the variation of black politics that the country's history of property law inspired seemed especially lost on "less informed Bahamians." "In almost everything we say or do, our motives are questioned and too frequently misconstrued by the less informed Bahamians who do not hesitate to spread their misconstructions, broadcast, among their associates."[101]

In other parts of the South and in the urban North, references to "usurping" or "greedy" immigrants stood as thinly veiled references to supposed Jewish profiteering. One finds in the writings of W. E. B. Du Bois, for instance, particularly uncharitable condemnations of southern Jews as "shrewd and unscrupulous foreigners" and as heirs "of the slave baron."[102] In Miami, however, pronounced anti-Semitism was not nearly as prevalent as a more general anti-immigrant, antilandlord sentiment, particularly in the years preceding the large in-migration of Jews in the 1930s.

Pragmatic Solutions

In the fall of 1915, Miami's city council could make no promise that a segregation mandate would keep white capital out of Colored Town. At the news, members of the Colored Board of Trade expressed sharp disappointment. "We trusted your intelligence and integrity to see to it that whatever adjustment was reached, fair and even-handed justice would be accorded to each and all." "To our very great regret we find that has not been done," the board continued, "and we would be unfair to ourselves and unworthy of our place in the body politic, if we did not frankly and emphatically protest."[103]

Protest meant not direct action, but more negotiation. That negotiation included competing propositions for the city to use eminent domain to solve the housing issue peacefully and absolutely.[104] Members of the Riverside Improvement Association argued that the city should use eminent domain to "do away with . . . settlement in that part of the city entirely," and turn black-occupied rental property into a park.[105] The Colored Board of Trade asked, "If the city will go into the real estate business to settle this color-line affair, why not purchase the lots of the white people in the disputed district?" Some white landlords even welcomed the idea. As Henry Griffin, a white landlord and carpenter born in the Bahamas, lamented in the wake of white terror attacks in 1915, "My property is valueless with the negroes frightened the way they are."[106] And Highland Park residents, the colored board advanced, could then take condemnation payments and "purchase homes where there are no colored people."[107]

One is left to imagine the all-white city council's reaction to the idea of condemning white homes on colored people's behalf. Regardless of the deliberations, neither option—condemning black or white housing—became viable. It would have been political suicide for any white politician to knock down white homes for the benefit of Negroes, respectable or no. At the same time, condemning and demolishing black housing through the power of eminent domain would not work because there were too many interests making money from black rentals in Colored Town. Landlords had property rights and often demanded top dollar for their tenements. That, as one newspaper described, made it nearly impossible for "any city council, or any other legislative body" to root them out completely.[108]

There were general logistical and financial matters that Miami's early political leaders could not afford to manage even if they wanted to. When city assessors first tallied up the costs of condemning black-occupied rental property along the western edge of Colored Town, the expense of the land itself exceeded $18,300, or over $415,000 in 2013 dollars.[109] The number of white-owned businesses alone far exceeded the cost of a dozen or so rental houses along the color line. Investigators for the city council concluded that just one white property owner held over $30,000 worth of commercial property and another $8,000 in stock. These figures did not include the potential costs of the various damage suits that recalcitrant property owners—folk like Dana Dorsey—would no doubt level against the city.[110]

The city took the cheapest option, and erected a long fence to hold the perceived color line between Highland Park and Miami's black downtown. City workers painted one side of the fence with black tar. "The district on the black side," one paper explained, "is known as Black Town while the unpainted side is called White Town."[111]

Making Law into Custom

Likely unsatisfied with a simple wooden fence, Miami's white press and its civic leaders looked to other parts of the country for better ways to segregate the races. The most effective means seemed to be a relatively new power in land use regulation and planning called zoning—or more specifically, racial zoning. Unlike neighborhood or deed restrictions, which buyers and sellers ratified through voluntary contractual agreements, zoning was a government power that authorized local officials to restrict people's property rights in observance of state-specified land uses. Zoning would restrict apartments to tracts set aside for multiunit housing, single-family homes to single-family tracts, and so forth. Through *racial* zoning, municipalities and county governments could ensure that black people lived among blacks, and white people with other whites, regardless of a given landlord's or homeowner's desires for potential buyers or tenants. "Although the South invented and made wide use of racial zoning," the historian Christopher Silver explains, "the region relied on Northern planning consultants to devise legally defensible ways to segregate black residential areas."[112] Effective racial zoning promised to prevent both interracial violence *and* high condemnation costs set by litigious landlords. It also proved short-lived. Over the previous fifty years, judges, legislators, and everyday practice had chiseled the defense of property rights deep into the granite of American jurisprudence, and racial zoning, as the attempted regulation of property rights, stood little to no chance.

Miamians followed keenly the invalidation of Norfolk, Virginia's racial zoning ordinance in 1911 and the similar striking down of Baltimore's ordinance, the nation's first, in 1913.[113] The events in Louisville, Kentucky, in 1915 were of particular interest, as the legality of racial zoning, and the impact of such zoning on property rights, continued to move through the courts.[114] "Possibly by following the lines of the Kentucky case," the *Miami Herald* opined, "the authorities of Miami may find that it is possible so to frame an ordinance that neither race can in any way infringe on the separate territory of the other."[115] White officials and homeowners believed that mandated housing segregation, as expressed in the Louisville ordinance, would "prevent conflict and ill-feeling between the white and colored races . . . [and] preserve the public peace."[116] Many remained convinced, however, that "no such segregation ordinance would be able to stand the scrutiny of the higher courts."[117]

White homeowners in the shadow of Colored Town argued that racial zoning did not represent a violation of the Fourteenth Amendment. They contended, further, that only landlords, merchants, and others with a vested interest in violations of the color line would propagate "the heresy that any segregation ordinance will be unconstitutional."[118] The US Supreme Court eventually ruled in the Louisville case, *Buchanan v. Warley* (1917), that racial zoning was indeed unconstitutional, encumbering and in some cases preventing the sale of real estate.

In the aftermath of the ruling, neither Colored Town's landlords nor Highland Park residents respected the city's tar-painted fence. On an early July morning in 1917, white terrorists bombed the largest civic hall in Colored Town, the Odd Fellows Hall. Roused from their sleep, hundreds of black people poured onto the street bearing guns, machetes, and other weapons.[119] On a single summer evening in 1920, Colored Town suffered a reign of terror originating from Highland Park, including several bombings, night raids on black families, and whites spraying black homes with bullets.[120] In this particular string of incidents, a handful of white men barreled down Colored Town's dirt streets and threw a dynamite bomb that exploded near the homes of several families. A reported three thousand blacks came onto the streets with what federal agents described as "a large supply of arms . . . [and] various assortment of weapons [sic]."[121] Police eventually arrived and ordered people back into their houses.

Kelsey Pharr, a black business owner who lived less than a block away from the attack, recalled of the incident some years later, "We lighted my building all around and manned the guns until day-break."[122] The then twenty-eight-year-old Pharr, a mortician and member of the Colored Board of Trade, saw sunrise bring some four hundred white men, all purportedly members of the American Legion, who had been deputized overnight to patrol Colored Town.[123] As soon as the apparent tension subsided, city council members got wind of new white threats "to dynamite one of the three houses . . . occupied by a colored family" on the border of Highland Park.[124]

Miami's business leaders saw their real estate troubles as extensions of the violence sweeping across Chicago and three dozen other cities in the "Red Summer" of 1919. A majority of that summer's conflicts erupted in southern cites, in fact. That seemingly made the Miami Chamber of Commerce's proposal for a racial buffer zone that much more important. Yet again, however, considerations of cost eliminated the prospect of buying out white and black landlords through the power of eminent domain.[125] Moreover, nothing had legally changed between 1915 and 1920. Miami's city officials knew full well that "the city has no legal right to establish a boundary."[126] As a final dissuading factor, any formally created Negro district would likely require a Negro city commissioner to represent it, thereby putting "negroes on an equality [sic] with white people in elections."[127] Segregation, if done "properly," in other words, threatened to *increase* black political power, not diminish it. Any state-sponsored residential measure clearly had to be handled with the utmost care.

In 1921, Miami city commissioners found that care in the spirit of "good government." City officials decided, instead of worrying about US Supreme Court precedent, they would simply assert residential segregation of the races without codifying it into law. Rather than a city ordinance, municipal segregation would be tethered to less overt land use provisions. By the end of the 1920s, most of Colored Town's land would be designated as "industrial," even when it already had apartment houses on it. Any new construction would require written permission from the Miami City Commission. In the short term, municipal officials relied on a vague kind of customary apartheid that, though totally unconstitutional, had the effect of dissuading litigation. In particular, Miami officials successfully ratified a new city charter that, among other things, preserved the white political primary, restructured the day-to-day administrative powers of the mayor, and granted city councilmen the power to "establish and set apart . . . separate residential limits or districts for white and negro residents." The charter also explicitly forbade "negroes" and "whites" from establishing businesses in districts set aside for the other race.[128] No discussion of enforcement, no discussion of legality.

For this simple sidestepping of American law, Miami's civic leaders relied on the principles of federalism and dared anyone to risk litigation in local and state courts. One Reginald Waters admitted the segregation clauses in the city charter were "unconstitutional, but . . . he reproached anyone, especially a white man, for raising . . . an objection."[129] The only thing more remarkable than the baldness of whites in Miami in flouting the law was the widespread tendency of whites across the South to make similar assertions in open defiance of the Constitution. Officials in Atlanta, for instance, followed suit with a similar city charter in 1922, with cities as varied as Birmingham, Orlando, and Charlotte doing the same in subsequent years.[130] In proclaiming the same prohibitions for whites and blacks, city governments hid behind the "separate but equal" criteria upheld in *Plessy v. Ferguson*.[131] It also helped that the precedents of the *Slaughterhouse* (1873) and *Civil Right Cases* (1883) made any civil rights claim, outside of a claim to preserve one's property rights, doomed to the margins of Jim Crowed state politics.

Custom did much of the rest. The fable that one could have segregation without discrimination died hard among whites. And, fearing the broader social and bodily costs of openly defying Jim Crow, few lawyers in the South—black or white—dared to challenge segregation, in principle, for another thirty years. In housing and other matters, they pushed, instead, for a more equal "separate but equal."

Conclusion

One could see the new discourse of southern folkways coming together even as the color line debates played out in the early 1920s. Miami's local papers repeatedly highlighted how the agreed-upon racial boundaries came "by resolution adopted by a joint meeting of colored and white residents."[132] The notion that the color line was the will of "the people" confused the fact that racial apartheid was, first and foremost, an expression of *white* popular sovereignty. Only secondarily did a very small number of Miami's black property owners enter into Jim Crow's Faustian bargain.

For the sake of facilitating Miami's peaceful growth, the city's interracial governing class articulated two kinds of paternalism that would carry on long after the color line debates of the 1910s and early 1920s. One argument advanced the notion that white authoritarianism was permissible as long as white elites worked to minimize white terrorism. A second argument contended that black entrepreneurs had the right to represent their race as long as they maintained their commitment to enterprise and continued to exhibit a predilection for pragmatic solutions to "the Negro problem." "Pragmatic," of course, like "modern," was a fable of urban governance. In this case, "the pragmatic" characterized any solution reached at the ultimate expense of nonwhites. There was also a profound process at play in Miami's frontier era that went generally unremarked: growth, whether people liked it or not, precipitated improvements to the workings of apartheid.

Particularly from the view of the globe's white populations, an entire age, commonly called the Progressive Era, came to be defined by modern nations collectively reaching for efficient, moral, and bureaucratic means to engineer a taller and wider world of sky-high buildings and sky-high profits. This world was to be blanketed in a durable racial peace, or at least so-called Progressives hoped, with explicit racial apartheid, at home and abroad, promising to bring unruly lands to heel. "Order" meant, among other things, protecting white commercial interests under the banners of capitalism, democracy, and modernity.[133]

Miami was incorporated as a city the same year as the US Supreme Court's decision in *Plessy v. Ferguson*, 1896. And while there is no direct causal link between the *Plessy* decision and the establishment of new cities in the United States, *Plessy*, in tandem with broader protections of states' rights, effectively inspired state governments around the country to pass sweeping racial segregation laws with at least three "big-picture" consequences to urban life. First, white ruling interests safely promoted the utility of racial segregation both in governing established cities such as New Orleans or Baltimore and in taming the perceived frontier qualities of undeveloped cities such as Tulsa, Oklahoma, and Miami. Second, expanding land powers, including zoning and eminent domain, promised to give white people fresh instruments for reasserting their perceived social and racial supremacy. Last, in the hands of imaginative urban administrators, racial apartheid had great versatility for imposing a sense of order on potentially chaotic urban milieus. It assisted in chaperoning and at times exploiting women's sexual power, apportioning the scarce resources available to city governments, preventing and justifying interracial violence, and turning at times unforgiving land into profitable real estate. In essence, what W. E. B. Du Bois famously called in 1903 "the problem of the twentieth century" was just as assuredly viewed as *the solution* to a host of environmental dangers and decidedly modern difficulties threatening white popular sovereignty, land- and business owners, and a host of other people constituting South Florida's emergent governing class.

CHAPTER TWO

Bargaining and Hoping

Miami entered the Roaring Twenties with the region's boosters and publicists holding fast to their imaginings of Florida's frontier past. Promotional tracts professed that, "like the early pioneers of the West," the city's entrepreneurs and developers were "winning livelihood from the wilderness . . . America's first frontier."[1] Southern Florida also appeared in serials, books, and pamphlets as the remote and final hiding place for ill-fated pirate treasure, the Fountain of Youth, and Indians unconquered.[2] The state's Seminoles, Florida lore held, never actually surrendered, even after ongoing, bloody "Indian Wars" over the previous century. "The Red Man" on Miami's golf courses and in the bush, "trapping and hunting as they did a hundred years ago," still gave Greater Miami, at once, a modern and a certain timeless feel.[3]

Portrayals of South Florida as untamed and untapped helped inspire a degree of investment and real estate speculation that made the Magic City, in the 1920s, home to new fables about fantastic wealth. "Join the army of wise investors, shrewd businessmen and women, homebuilders and speculators who are buying lots and blocks," developers implored; "these will reap a fortune."[4] Wide-eyed farmhands from South Carolina or librarians from Baltimore or Georgia rode the Florida East Coast Railway southward, swapping tales of crumbling, old robber barons having to make room for the Magic City's nouveau riche. In the first five years of the decade, the number of real estate transactions in Miami had increased tenfold, reaching nearly twenty thousand per month.[5] The population figures leading into the 1920s had already exploded by over 440 percent. And the boom only promised to continue as more and more ships, trains, and Model T Fords pulled into the region. As the *Miami Herald*'s front page pronounced, "How Miami, the Magic City, Grows!"[6]

Growth had a helpmate in the color line. During the segregation debates of the late 1910s, Miami's white business leaders attempted to streamline racial apartheid by making racial violence less necessary and making residential Jim Crowism more absolute. This left Miami's colored population to negotiate not whether but how the color line would be imposed, and how they might benefit from it. Amid white people's own hopes of carving up Miami and its surrounding lands for commercial and agricultural development, Seminoles, American Negroes, and Caribbean islanders found a variety of means, both cultural and material, to grasp at the elusive reins of political power and marginal citizenship. By way of property ownership and, in some cases, overt deference to white political dominance, the region's nonwhite people struck their own deals in a city awash in negotiations and transactions. Whether one was talking about land or power, the result of such bargains was a governing culture that hardened the bond between authority and white racial membership, in the first place, and citizenship and ownership, in the second. The nexus of race, property, and authority would shape, in fact, not just interracial negotiations, but also how colored communities governed themselves.

The Boom

As a region, southern Florida remained beholden to the ability of people to travel to what was, as the start of the 1920s, still a remote corner of the Caribbean. Before the arrival of large passenger trains in the 1920s and the improvement of state highways during the 1930s, southern Florida remained accessible mostly by sea. Even then, ships from anywhere else but the Bahamas were infrequent and often more expensive than most laboring men and women of any color could afford. Thus, before the 1920s, Miami remained something of a small town, and fewer than thirty thousand people called it home. Of that number, 30 percent were colored people, with more than half of that population being Caribbean born.[7] Even "black Miami" as a collection of self-sustaining, year-round communities did not really exist at the start of the 1920s.[8] Instead, in addition to Colored Town, southern Florida was home to a collection of relatively isolated colored outposts that went by names like Kebo, Lemon City, Nazarene, Hardieville, and Railroad Shop's Colored Addition.[9] Outside of the occasional travels of a supply barge, doctor, or postman, Miami's small population and the region's reliance on agriculture and seasonal tourism did little to bring these enclaves together. Both black Miami and what the white chamber of commerce, in 1925, coined "Greater Miami" had to be imagined and cobbled together by real estate developers and political struggles.

What developers labored to sell, in fact, was a dream. In tandem with visions of stately Mediterranean-style homes, a new, modern marvel—aerial photographs—colored by hand, danced across the pages of booster literature in an attempt to bewitch potential investors. "As you look again and again at the picture on these pages you will feel the Miami spell come over you, for it is a spell." The almost hypnotic effect boosters hoped for was the vision of a tropical future, a site that "is now and ever will be the most wonderful place in the world." From a plane's-eye view, real estate developers urged white northerners especially to "let your mind grasp a space covering . . . 135 square miles, all of it divided off into beautiful avenues, built enduringly with coral rock, and lined on either side . . . with palm trees, tropical shrubbery and flowers, with all the colors of the rainbow."[10]

Miamians were, of course, very conscious of the power of color in real estate development. In 1920, the Miami Chamber of Commerce established an independent realty board with five hundred thousand dollars in land and buildings under its control and not a single nonwhite or female member.[11] This board, founded to lobby city-planning initiatives and coordinate real estate transaction standards, ensured that new developers followed segregationist housing practices eventually laid out in the 1921 charter. Through the chamber and Miami's city government, the region's white entrepreneurs attempted to take responsibility for segregation out of the hands of individual whites and homeowners associations. They hoped, instead, to utilize the land itself—as real estate—as an instrument advancing the peaceful prerogatives of Jim Crow. It was important that Miami, as one real estate developer professed, prove to the world its "business aggressiveness and progressiveness." As a city with its face "turned toward the sun," Miami, another developer claimed, was a shelter for "home-loving, intelligent, progressive, [and] honorable people."[12] Keeping unchecked racial violence at a minimum was essential to these proclamations. As a point of fact, early attempts to manage racial peace were inauspicious, as violence in Miami actually increased once more whites and blacks moved into the region. Nevertheless, the growth imperative that first inspired the establishment of both the city charter and the chamber of commerce remained at the center of city governance, as did the driving force behind that imperative: real estate speculation.

Shortly after the ratification of Miami's segregationist charter, the real estate developer George Merrick began his first major land project, breaking ground on what would become his "City Beautiful," the city of Coral Gables.[13] Merrick organized over $50 million of investment from local and out-of-town investors. He then turned around, within three years, and sold triple that amount in real estate—$150 million.[14] As with other sites of the

"City Beautiful" movement of the late nineteenth and early twentieth centuries, Merrick believed that, at Coral Gables, "living may be richer and finer because beauty has been put to its right uses."[15] Hoping to entice those with an affinity for the modern as well, Merrick also attempted to associate Miami with the chief architectural symbol of American modernism—the New York skyscraper. He contended, in fact, that the homes of Coral Gables were to Miami what Manhattan's steel towers were to the Big Apple. Both stood as "great native American architecture." In actuality, the homes of Coral Gables were nothing if not a pastiche of derivations from Spanish, Italian, French, Greek, and even pre-Columbian architectural forms from the Maya and Aztec.[16] Borrowing was, in itself, fast becoming a Miami tradition, and Merrick had no problem borrowing even booster talent from elsewhere. Mindful, especially, that people could be moved by their religious affinities, Merrick paid William Jennings Bryan, arguably the country's most famous orator at the time, $100,000 to talk up Miami's real estate market. Bryan, ever the devout theist, imposed only one condition: that he be allowed to teach Bible every Sunday, which he did in a park near the Royal Palm Hotel.[17] Modern, classical, and divinely associated all at once, Coral Gables was among South Florida's most coveted neighborhoods and, not incidentally, "whites only."

By 1923, dreams of replicating the success of Coral Gables had ramped up national interest in the region. This, in turn, drove booster hopes for finally conquering what remained of the Florida frontier. In 1925, with a new University of Miami chartered in his personal boomtown, Merrick spoke of "The Great Everglade Empire," home to the Seminoles, as the next target of development.[18] Many believed the expansive saw grass prairies and wetlands of the Everglades, which amounted to millions of acres, held the key to southern Florida's future growth. The Everglades' rich soils and open space seemed perfect for agricultural and commercial development. Miami officials were finalizing the city's deepwater harbor project. Access to the Caribbean Sea and the North Atlantic on the east, combined with the unspoiled marshlands to the west, led Merrick and many others to believe that Miami would become "*the* great Pan American port of the Atlantic" and perhaps even the "World's Greatest Winter Resort."[19] Developers began pursuing avenues in Washington and the state capital of Tallahassee to see what could be done to open the Everglades for development.

In the meantime, as one white Miamian remembered, "The Boom did strange things to people." Land speculators began carving up and selling land, often by the dozens of acres. They also sold the same tract of land over and over, sometimes two and three times in the same day, driving up prices artificially. Land prices got so high, so quickly that increased land taxes forced a full third of Miami dairies out of business.[20] In 1925, at the height of the boom, unimproved land in Miami Beach was selling for up to $30,000 an acre.[21] Construction was an equally hot business, exceeding $60 million annually in Miami, $25 million in Coral Gables, and $17 million in Miami Beach.[22] White police officers recently recruited from the fields of rural Florida and Georgia often learned just enough about the city and its burgeoning neighborhoods to turn in their badges for real estate maps and a venture in land speculation.[23] In his run for a city commission seat, Everest Sewell, arguably the greatest of all Miami's boosters during the interwar period, went so far as to suggest that, in ten years, the tourist business increased "1,000%."[24] "Optimism," Merrick remarked, "is the very air you breathe."[25]

Then came the "Big Blow," the Great Hurricane of 1926.

Violent Winds

The sun seemed never to come up on 16 September 1926, as the storm darkened the sky at 6:00 a.m. "It wasn't raining," as one eyewitness reported, "it was simply blowing water from the surface of the ground." Winds of 140 miles per hour and massive storm swells put much of Miami Beach under five feet of water. Coconut Grove, where James Deering and William Jennings Bryan enjoyed handsome homes, suffered bombardment from fifteen-foot-high waves. Colored Town fared better than some of the more exclusive areas because, in their rush to gobble up the best ocean views, whites made sure that black people did not live anywhere near Biscayne Bay or the ocean.[26]

At the first sign of calm, hundreds of tourists and recent arrivals who were on Miami Beach hopped in their cars to flee. They jammed the rapidly flooding causeways that crossed Biscayne Bay. Ignorant that they were only in the eye of the storm, these late evacuees sat stranded in traffic when the back end of the tempest whipped around. Many died right there as winds tossed their vehicles off the bridge and into the water. Counting those drowned, struck by debris, or crushed by collapsed buildings, the storm killed nearly four hundred people and injured over a thousand. A second, smaller storm hit a month later, with winds of seventy-five to one hundred miles per hour. By one account, "The second storm finished where the first storm had failed." It utterly killed South Florida's real estate boom. For several years after the 1926 storms, skeletons were being found washed up and tangled among the mangrove trees off Biscayne Bay.[27]

According to local rumor, Seminoles noticed saw grass in the marshes blooming ten days before the storm, a sign, as newspapers described, "that

the great spirits are displeased and about to strike." "Whites," as one newspaper recounted, "did not follow the lead of the wily natives."[28] After the
storm, believing that they had just experienced God's wrath, many white
Miamians flocked back to church, making houses of worship among the first
structures to get rebuilt. Most recent arrivals cut their losses and fled north
again. Those residents brave enough to stay generously donated time and
money to their ministers, and, in the words of one report, "showed greater
interest in religious activities than ever before."[29] One reporter at the *Chicago
Defender* described the storm as retribution for the city's racial evils: "For that
is Miami—the modern Sodom and Gomorrah!"[30]

Wilhelmina Jennings, a Miamian of Bahamian and American parentage, never forgot the aftermath of the "Big Blow." When the storm passed,
it was around ten in the morning, and Wilhelmina's grandfather, Shaddie
Ward, had climbed on the roof of his house with his three sons to begin
rebuilding. The house, which had six bedrooms and two levels, stood—just
barely—on the corner of NW Ninth Street and NW Second Avenue in Colored Town. Ward was a mason by trade and, by white or colored standards, a
moderately successful landowner. In addition to his family home, he owned
several wood-frame rooming houses, all built on his large Ninth Street lot,
and two Model T Fords. "Tin Lizzies," Jennings remembered of the cars,
"that's what we used to call them." Material prosperity was good in times
of calm weather, but it could be a source of great headache after hurricanes.
Gale-force winds had blown Ward's entire roof off in one piece, tossing it
a block away on NW Tenth Street. Likewise, his Tin Lizzies, while still on
four wheels, had been blown far down the block. The same was true of bits
and pieces of all of Ward's various buildings. Portions of broken window
frames, shards of glass, porch planks, and roofing materials were all over the
neighborhood's muddy, unpaved streets. For Shaddie and his family, days
of work lay ahead.[31]

"That's when the truck came." Wilhelmina, only a young girl at the time,
remembered how armed white National Guardsmen drove their personnel
truck into Colored Town in the hour following that September storm. South
Florida's beachfront was in absolute ruin. The storm had reduced most of the
hotels and boutiques on the multimillion-dollar coast to a heap of beams;
shattered, marooned yachts; and soaked furniture. To meet their immediate recovery needs, the Dade County and Miami City Commission issued
a "negro conscription" order that forced "all negro males of workable age"
to help clear debris on the white side of the color line. In Haiti a few years
earlier, a similar conscription authority, called *corvée*, had empowered US
troops to force Haitian citizens to build roads for infrastructural "improve-

ments." Punishing work conditions and violent enforcement on the part of US soldiers had been among the chief causes for over fifteen thousand Haitians losing their lives during America's presence in that island-republic.[32] Miami's take on *corvée* was not nearly as extensive, but the means and motivations were the same. "They were going through the black areas, getting the black people to go help clean up what happened on the beach because . . . the beach was torn up."[33]

The guardsmen ordered Ward and his three sons to get off their roof and climb in the back of the truck with a dozen other colored people already impressed into service. A proud man of property—property that clearly needed tending—Ward initially held his ground, but he and his sons eventually cooperated when armed whites, to Jennings's recollection, began "getting kind of rough." Once on the truck, Shaddie heard the shouts of his daughter, Mabel, coming from down the street. He looked to see guardsmen dragging her out of one of his smaller family houses. Despite the apparent order to just grab men, "They were making women and men, anybody who was in there, come." Jennings remembered of Mabel, "She refused to go—college student, she wasn't going. She knew her rights."[34]

In short order, Shaddie and his three sons jumped off the truck and, through the mud and over debris, sprinted down the block to assist Mabel. Several national guardsmen gave chase. In the confusion, the dozen or so colored people on the truck jumped off and fled. "Bedlam broke out then." Members of the Ward family retreated into their home, with two guardsmen boxing them into the central hallway of the house, one at the front door and one at the back. According to Jennings, one soldier had discharged his M1 carbine rifle and a single bullet passed through Shaddie's leg and *both* of Mabel's legs. It then, however remarkably, grazed the leg of a second National Guardsman and that of one of Shaddie's sons.

Reports in the *New York Times* described a "shot for shot" gunfight between the guardsmen and two unnamed negro men, "who arrived from Nassau [Bahamas] but a short time before."[35] Other reports described some two thousand colored men and women gathered around the fallen guardsmen bearing arms and shouting. To restore the prevailing racial order, police, deputy sheriffs, and other guardsmen, according to reports, began clubbing "scores . . . unmercifully." Officers arrested some twenty black people who were reportedly "heavily armed."[36] The remaining guardsmen loaded up the truck with all the wounded, colored and white, and drove away.

The whole day and night the Ward family received no word. "We were all scared," Wilhelmina recalled. "That's when Crackers were really bad. . . . They [could] do anything they wanted to you. . . . We thought they had killed them all." Wilhelmina's father later discovered that their loved ones had been taken to the "colored only" ward at Jackson Memorial Hospital nearby.[37] The next day, the aftermath of the conscription order was felt elsewhere. Reports came in of three Negroes lynched ten miles from Miami, their bodies perforated with bullets and burned.[38]

Blood and Property

For something that promised racial peace, Jim Crow required an awful lot of violence. White authorities charged with building—and, in this instance, rebuilding—city infrastructure relied on seemingly exceptional shows of white power, such as lynching or forced conscription. Violence helped hold in place the daily racial indignities upon which American capitalism and its many forms of segregation stood. It fueled the speculation enriching George Merrick and countless others who sought to draw wealth from the Florida territory. Fear of lynching and other acts of racial violence was an integral feature of economic development. It was also, for colored people, part of everyday experience precisely because such incidents were everyday occurrences—not in the sense that they occurred *every single day*, but because they could occur *any given day*, and for reasons totally beyond black people's control. The everydayness and unpredictability of racial violence was the source of its social power and, by extension, one of the many sources of white power.

As the historian and cultural critic Ashraf Rushdy explains, however, these acts were so much more. Racial violence and lynching in particular served as extensions of political traditions and myths governing the transfer and use of property, particularly the management and disposal of slaves as property. When Wilhelmina Jennings recalled how "Crackers [could] . . . do anything they wanted to you," she conjured a history wherein white people, with general impunity, acted out long-held rationales concerning, in Rushdy's words, "the place of collective violence in the service of controlling freedom and slavery."[39] Slaves, as defined by colonial and, later, American law, never suffered murder; they were, as property, only lost to "accidents of correction."[40]

If laws under slavery made black people disposable, then the institution of racial apartheid, in characterizing "the Negro" as only slightly more than property, made black people negligible. Moreover, as the cultural content of Shaddie's experience illustrates, all property—as racialized property—was not created equal. White real estate was, by definition, more valuable than colored property, just as white people were widely understood as more valuable than nonwhites. Following natural disasters generally, as Marian Moser

Jones points out, whites routinely demanded that black people trade their labor for disaster relief.[41] In 1927, one writer from the Associated Negro Press even pointed to Miami to predict how whites would respond to the calamity wrought by a rising Mississippi River. "Blacks will be put to work helping to clear the white man's property." "Mississippi after the flood," the journalist opined, "will simply be a more extensive Miami after the hurricane."[42] As Jim Crow's governing logics went, colored people's natural state was to tend to white people's property, at the service of white people's whims, and, if necessary, at gunpoint. To be sure, in the years between formal slavery and the age of Jim Crow, the myriad uses and forms of property became decidedly different. Yet, there were at least two truisms that connected both moments in history: (1) violence directed at those deemed "colored" carried little to no consequence, for injurious acts against blacks were constitutive of white property rights, and (2) black people could be expected, as a matter of course, to protect and manage white people's property, whether one understood that property as real estate, small children, or, as was often the case, white women.[43]

Speaking to this first continuity—the cheapness of black life—Miami's history during the 1910s and 1920s abounds with all the transgressions against black personhood one might expect. For instance, H. Leslie Quigg, Miami's police chief during most of the 1920s, was, like most white officers in the city, an open and active member of the Ku Klux Klan. The Klan, in fact, served as the civic arm of the Miami Police Department, as it had for other police departments in American cities for most of the 1920s.[44] Not afraid to get his hands dirty, Quigg personally and publicly beat a colored bellboy to death for speaking directly to a white woman.[45] He was also known to single out Negroes for special "interrogation" sessions that included beating the soles of colored people's bare feet with copper-bound rulers or torturing them with makeshift electrical devices, sometimes applied to the genitals.[46] The sexualized violence occurring regularly under the watch of the Miami Police Department was not unlike that commonly featured at the lynching tree.

Around matters of work, whites without badges also resorted to violence against black folk in defense of their perceived entitlements, sexual and otherwise. In a particularly grisly nighttime assault, white musicians, in 1921, lured a Negro band from Ohio into the bush, claiming that the band had been requested by one of Miami's millionaires to perform at a private party. Once isolated on the edge of the Everglades, the assailants beat the musicians within an inch of their lives with wood planks, fence pickets, and other bludgeoning instruments. The band's greatest crime, according to reports, was cavorting with white women in the audience and performing at "whites only" hotels without union membership. Dazed and bleeding, members of the band wandered several hours in the dark before eventually finding their way back to Colored Town's Dorsey Hotel. Dana Dorsey, the hotel's owner, gave the men a place to heal up and offered to pay their train fare out of town. A shrewd businessman to the last, however, Miami's richest colored man made sure to hold the band's clothes as collateral until they repaid him, in dollars, for his kindness.[47]

Black agency in the service of white property—a second continuity—was even more commonplace, as it drove the entire country's employment structure for colored people. Black women experienced this when tending white children in Coral Gables, as did colored people working white people's land on the farms of Dania or Coconut Grove. The laboring black menial, as an integral feature of Miami's tourist atmosphere, owed his or her predicament to whites' ability to hold property and capital. Working-class black people, across the Americas, toiled under conditions of actual or near servitude, certainly.[48] Yet there were also signal moments within the United States when white people expected black people to facilitate even the most brutal defenses of white property against other blacks.

Take the July 1920 death of Herbert Brooks, a black man from the Bahamas. Accused of sexually assaulting a fifty-five-year-old white woman, Brooks took refuge among the shanties of Colored Town. White authorities pursued with bloodhounds. Kelsey Pharr, a representative of the Colored Board of Trade, made, in the words of local journalists, "a personal visit to Mayor [W. P.] Smith and the police station to tender the services of the board" and the Colored American Legion, a black veterans' organization, who decided it was in their best interest to cooperate.[49] Having intimate knowledge of their own neighborhood, members of the Colored Board of Trade and the legion canvassed Colored Town and successfully apprehended Brooks. One group of Americans (black) then handed Brooks over to another group (Miami's white police) on the promise that the accused would get a fair trial. Law enforcement officials agreed to put Brooks on a northbound train to Jacksonville. But the man the press had already labeled "Herbert Brooks, negro rapist" never made it to Jacksonville. According to white witnesses, somewhere in Volusia County, near Daytona Beach, Brooks jumped—while restrained and seated—from the moving train to his death, bashing in his own brains on the tracks.[50]

The Brooks incident highlights the entanglement of property, violence, sex, and race in the city. Vocal members of Miami's West Indian community immediately cried foul in the wake of Brooks's death. They argued that Brooks had been lynched, and they held Colored Town's black American businesspeople principally responsible.[51] West Indian organizers arranged a boycott of all US-owned Negro businesses in Colored Town. Over four hundred Bahamians also threatened to riot and destroy American shops and saloons before US blacks tipped off white authorities and precipitated the deployment of the National Guard.[52] "There is almost a state of war between English and American Negroes," wrote Leon Howe, an FBI agent keeping tabs on the events.[53] West Indians and American Negroes fought in the streets. The Colored Board of Trade called in vain for an investigation of the dubious details around Brooks's death. Meanwhile, forty armed blacks from the American Legion stood guard around American Negro proprietorships to monitor Bahamian unrest.[54]

What appears, on its face, to be a moment of intraracial disunity must be appreciated as steps taken by colored people toward competing visions of racial solidarity and, indeed, competing notions of property.[55] In general, the entitlement under dispute within black communities, particularly among black people of means, was the right to govern and speak for The Race. In the most physical terms possible, individual proprietorships, black churches, and rental real estate evidenced the right to speak. These buildings were the principal means of accumulating capital, and, as a result, they were also a means for building other institutions and symbols of authority within colored neighborhoods. However, businesses and other physical expressions of community building, though celebrated (quite understandably) as markers of black achievement, were often partially, if not principally, funded by white capital.[56]

White property owners with holdings in Colored Town played a critical part in shaping black responses to grassroots white vigilantism. Like the actual buildings of black neighborhoods, the cultural and political content of Negro community building remained tied, quite often, to the interests and prerogatives of white capital as well.[57] Consider West Indians' targeting of American Negro businesses and black businesspeople. These buildings were, simultaneously, symbols of a US-Negro rationale that saw fit to hand over Herbert Brooks *and* representations of a broader white authority that hung over black Miami. What remains important to keep in mind is that this duality does not just capture how many West Indians perceived most American Negroes. It was how American Negroes, particularly those of considerable means, often came to understand themselves.

Like black entrepreneurs and community leaders elsewhere, members of the Colored Board of Trade and the Colored American Legion saw their civic role as policing the Negro race in hopes of crafting common cause and achieving, in the eyes of whites, a measure of political power.[58] But the historian Michele Mitchell takes the point further, highlighting the impact of racial self-policing on gender politics within black communities. She explains how black women, as objects of Negro nation building during the Progressive Era, were often subjected to suffocating and violent forms of surveillance at the hands of black men. Wielding variations of eugenics theory, black men ensured that prohibitions against "interracial liaisons," strict enforcement of "modern notions of hygiene," and black women's conformity to heterosexual norms remained integral features of racial "uplift."[59] Control over women was the mark of any self-respecting "race," and, in the Victorian world of Jim Crow, coming to the defense of white womanhood exhibited civilization of the highest order.[60]

In the context of Jim Crow America, then, handing over Herbert Brooks was a bargain on the part of Miami's Negroes for a fuller slice of American citizenship. Members of the Colored Board of Trade and the American Legion may well have hoped that Brooks might have been justly prosecuted. It seems highly unlikely, however, that, during years of record numbers of lynchings, American black folk could have expected anything other than a bloody outcome. Even if Brooks's apparent murder was, on Negro Americans' part, not intentional, it was clearly contextual and, frankly, foreseeable.

The divide between black Americans and West Indians was by no means absolute. By 1920, a few Bahamians had joined Miami's Colored American Legion and the Colored Board of Trade. Moreover, a considerable number of Caribbean and American blacks intermarried or lived together during this period. The historian Melanie Shell-Weiss reports, in fact, that, in Miami, as many as one-third of black homes with boarders included Bahamian migrants and American Negroes either renting from each other or being married to each other.[61] Still, the high degree of residential congregation meant there were also ample opportunities for ethnic competition. American and West Indian men competed for marriage partners, land, and community visibility, as just a few examples. And, among Colored Town's civically engaged black folk, particularly colored men, there remained a less than amicable climate between West Indian and American blacks.

Statements in the local press and elsewhere suggest that, from the Colored Board of Trade's perspective, shoring up American Negro political power in South Florida required marginalizing Caribbean voices in the polity. Members of the board, for instance, believed in encouraging American in-migration to the region as a means of limiting the sway of West Indians over colored people's politics. As the then twenty-three-year-old secretary of the board, Kelsey Pharr, described in 1915, it was "the progressive negroes *who are citizens of Miami* [who] . . . must be considered as a potent factor in the upbuilding of the city and Dade County" (my emphasis). One impediment to that upbuilding, Pharr repeatedly complained, was the influence of "voodooism" among the city's black population. "It comes from the Bahamas and from Jamaica and especially from Haiti," Pharr explained, "and it holds the Negro because he is naturally a superstitious creature."[62]

At the time he joined the Colored Board of Trade and began making recommendations for Miami's future, Pharr had been in Miami barely a year. Still, it was his own biography as an entrepreneur that made him the ideal spokesperson for the board's vision of acceptable black politics. At twenty-two years of age, Pharr migrated to Miami from Salisbury, North Carolina, in 1914. Working as everything from a life insurance agent to a taxi driver during his teenage years, Pharr landed his first job in Miami as a waiter at the Royal Palm Hotel. As with the many colored maids and Afromobile drivers in the city, Pharr's presence in a servile capacity had the effect of affirming some measure of Miami's racial normalcy. Yet, Pharr was also college educated and envisioned a professional career through which to "serve my people." He got his chance within months of arriving at the Royal Palm. Colored Town's only embalmer died, and Pharr was able to convince three of his fellow waiters to help him pay for a six-week embalming course at Tufts Medical College in Boston. These three men would back Pharr as silent partners in the mortician business for another three years, whereupon Pharr bought out his partners and owned the business outright.[63]

Pharr then went to Roddy Burdine, a wealthy white department store owner who had a history of extending personal loans to both Negroes and whites. Burdine, Pharr recalled, "said I had an honest face, and he loaned me nine hundred dollars without any security except my word. That's the kind of friend he was." The "Burdines" department store that Roddy owned remained racially segregated through the 1950s and would remain something of a South Florida institution until the early 1990s. Few, though, ever knew the history of the chain's chief founder when it came to supporting black institutions like Pharr's funeral home. "He never said much about what he did. . . . I have been successful because Mr. Burdine was my friend."[64]

By Pharr's estimation, leaving behind dark island superstitions and stepping into a modern entrepreneurial age was supposed to right the race and prepare the Negro for fair American competition. "In this advanced age of material progress," Pharr explained, "practically every arable plot of land is held in ownership or sovereignty by a progressive people. It is now our time to . . . open our ears to catch steps with the music of the age and march to the goal of material strength."[65] Before the real estate market even exploded, Miami's American blacks hoped to create their own US outpost in the Caribbean. So determined, Pharr and other members of the Colored Board of Trade publicized Miami in the pages of every national black newspaper, with the expressed intention of "persuad[ing] the best of the colored people the country over to come to our community, buy property, build homes, and help us enjoy this unexcelled climate." Only "the best and respectable colored people" should consider emigrating to Miami, the board warned, and it promised, for the sake of its black and white audience, "to assist the authorities in making it decidedly unpleasant for the low and criminal element of all races."[66] Herbert Brooks learned that this was no idle threat. More, West Indians took such threats seriously and counterorganized accordingly.

Empire and Colony

So culturally diverse was black Miami that the atomized colored communities of South Florida in the 1920s had different geopolitical loyalties. The black section of Coconut Grove, an area populated almost exclusively by Bahamians, had strong ties to the islands and, by extension, the British Empire. African Americans in northern Miami and neighboring Broward County mostly had kin in southern US states. Colored Town was, by all accounts, up for grabs.[67]

What happened to Herbert Brooks was partly a product of that ambiguity. Brooks, it seems, belonged to the Miami chapter of a largely forgotten British expatriates' organization called the Overseas Club, which opened a South Florida chapter in 1919.[68] Britons established the parent organization in London in 1910, and the Overseas Club reached new heights of global popularity during World War I. Organized primarily for Britain's merchant class around the world, the club nevertheless offered a means for British subjects of all classes and colors living abroad to network, to express their shared patriotism for the empire, and to aid Britain's war effort. The Overseas Club reportedly had twenty thousand dues-paying members and boasted chapters as far afield as Tangiers, Morocco, and Yokohama, Japan.[69]

Agents from the Federal Bureau of Investigation (FBI) alleged that the club's Miami chapter propagated views "radical in the extreme" and that it spread "un-American sentiments among the negroes." That meant, in practical terms, that the group offered a means through which Caribbean people living under Jim Crow could identify as something other than American. One member of the club, for instance, Henry Reeves, was a young Bahamian journalist who, in 1923, used connections within the organization to establish a newspaper that would cover events in Miami, the Bahamas, and the broader United States and Caribbean. His publication, the *Miami Times*, in addition to being one of Miami's most successful black businesses during the Jim Crow era, would become the most important black newspaper in the city, a distinction it still holds.[70]

Regrettably, all publications of the *Miami Times* prior to 1948 have been lost to history, making it difficult to discern the club's early activities and, for that matter, to know much at all about everyday black life in Jim Crow Miami. Still, records from government agencies, the *Miami Herald*, and several other publications depict the Overseas Club as an organization that provided a means for black Miamians to espouse a kind of patriotism and civic pride different from the uncompromising Americanism that dominated the activities of the Colored Board of Trade.[71] For one, club members professed that the British Empire, unlike the United States, stood for freedom, justice, order, and good government.[72] John LeMasney, a Haitian national and minister born to Jamaican parents, opened in Colored Town an Overseas Club school for roughly fifty colored children with his Bahamian wife, Mary.[73] For decades, both had worked as domestics for white American employers, but Mary, in particular, according to reports from a then twenty-five-year-old FBI staffer named J. Edgar Hoover, "tells her students that the school is English[,]. . . teaches veneration for things British and teaches contempt for American institutions."[74] Members of the Overseas Club also presided over Guy Fawkes Day celebrations. The 5 November holiday, celebrated across the British Commonwealth, included parades that ended with British subjects, in this case thousands of black Bahamians, hanging and burning Fawkes, a white man, in effigy.[75] Most controversially, Miami's Overseas Club advanced the notion that, because an apparent plurality of the city's black population was born as—or born to—black British subjects, Colored Town was, in fact, not part of the United States at all. Rather, it belonged to the British Empire, and its inhabitants were bound only by English law.[76]

In essentially claiming Colored Town for Britain, the Overseas Club attempted to decouple its neighborhood, as a territory, from the white American violence that otherwise defined and bounded it. It was the Overseas Club that organized the boycotts and protests, perhaps even the physical confrontations, that swept Colored Town in the wake of Herbert Brooks's death. Through its various activities, the organization also encouraged a vision of interracialism that differed from the New South paternalism that framed relations between local whites and the Colored Board of Trade.

One of the Overseas Club's most important leaders was Philip Irwin, a fiery fifty-four-year-old white Irish rector of Colored Town's English Episcopal Church.[77] Irwin used his church to house most of the club's organizing activities, and, as rector, he lived in the Central Negro District with his white wife and daughter.[78] Like other Overseas Club members in Miami, Irwin spoke routinely and passionately about the evils of American segregation, and, as a result, along with John and Mary LeMasney, Irwin remained under close surveillance by the FBI and local police. As was typical of white law enforcement, local authorities believed the Irishman to be leading astray otherwise docile colored folk. Federal agents and police viewed Irwin as "instrumental in fomenting trouble between negroes and whites," and they accused him of using "a great deal of influence among negroes" to encourage black Miamians to arm themselves.[79]

The ongoing animosity between the Colored Board of Trade and the American Legion on the one hand and the Overseas Club on the other inspired a small group of American and Bahamian blacks to open the city's first chapter of the Universal Negro Improvement Association (UNIA). The UNIA, founded by the charismatic West Indian Marcus Garvey, had become the most popular black organization in the United States, and, in major cities especially, the group often brought together black islanders and black Americans. Traveling principally along America's train lines, the Garvey movement worked its way steadily down the Florida Peninsula in 1918 and 1919, but the exigencies on the ground gave the establishment of a Miami chapter particular urgency in 1920. In the words of George Carter, the Miami UNIA's head and a member of the Colored Board of Trade, the association was supposed to serve as a "medium through which the people from the Bahamas and native Americans could support a common cause, and realize that we were children of common parent stock, who were transplanted at different points in America."[80] One of the group's members, James Nimmo, was both Bahamas born and an American army veteran.[81] Nimmo had been radicalized through his service in the Great War and his continued encounters with white supremacy upon his return from the front. As part of the association's militaristic arm, Nimmo drilled UNIA members in battle formations and other methods of armed self-defense.

The group's ideological bent attempted to play up perceived blood ties among colored people. This did not sit well, however, with white members of Miami's Overseas Club, who moved to bar or purge from their membership anyone affiliated with the UNIA.[82] Black nationalism, argued Philip Irwin, was anathema to British pride.[83] These efforts at disassociation, however, did not keep the local press from accusing the UNIA of being "a clandestine branch of the Overseas Club."[84]

The UNIA's leadership in Miami consisted of colored people born in the United States, Haiti, and the Bahamas. And the cultural background of its members, as with the Overseas Club, represented a marked difference from the decidedly American leadership setting the agenda for the Colored Board of Trade and the Colored American Legion. Unlike the Colored Board of Trade, too, Miami's UNIA chapter had unskilled workers, blacksmiths, tailors, and other less moneyed Negroes in leadership roles.[85] The Colored American Legion and the board encouraged Negroes to enlist and to support America's various military involvements in the Philippines and the Caribbean.[86] By comparison, members of the UNIA hosted community meetings denouncing the US occupation in Haiti and other expressions of American imperialism.[87] Officials from the FBI, which maintained surveillance over the UNIA's Miami chapter, reported that the South Florida branch had over one thousand members, but that only seven were American born.[88]

The bureau's attempt to monitor the activities and membership of Miami's Negro organizations folded the UNIA under broad destabilization campaigns that, during much of the 1920s, mirrored the disinformation tactics that J. Edgar Hoover and the bureau used against UNIA chapters around the country, including intercepting and forging correspondence to sow discord among members. Federal law enforcement, through benign neglect, also affirmed the notion that everyday white vigilantes were, in effect, the state, granting Miami's whites impunity to terrorize all "alien" groups of colored people and their white sympathizers. The FBI looked the other way as the UNIA and the Overseas Club suffered from a series of late-night attacks at the hands of the Miami Police Department and unaffiliated white militants.[89] Richard Higgs, a Bahamian Baptist minster and leader in the Miami UNIA, was kidnapped from his home and believed lynched by eight hooded men. Several dozen West Indians poured out into the street, and police responded by disarming twenty-five black bystanders, shooting one, and breaking the guns "over a concrete wall in the jail yard."[90] It was later revealed that Higgs, tied up and fitted with a noose, had been released by his captors with the understanding that he would leave the country immediately. Higgs returned, under threat of death, to his birthplace, Harbor Island, Bahamas.[91] This same group of masked whites lured Philip Irwin, the white leader of the Overseas Club, from his home, beating, tarring, and feathering him.[92] Irwin's white church superiors eventually forced him to leave Miami. They specifically referenced the riot in Tulsa as a preview of what might happen in South Florida if he stayed.[93] "Last night," the Miami Herald reported in late July 1921, "a number of persons, as well as a number of negroes, have received threatening letters signed by 'The Committee that Waited Upon Higgs and Irwin.'" For "persons [and] . . . negroes," the attack on Richard Higgs and the tarring and feathering of Irwin, like the lynching of Herbert Brooks, were meant to serve as proof positive that Miami was "America."[94]

Strategies to undercut both the UNIA and the Overseas Club worked brilliantly. The activities of the Overseas Club diminished substantially without the institutional support of Irwin and the Episcopal Church. The group all but disappeared from the public record shortly after Irwin's departure. And FBI disinformation campaigns helped sow internal discord in Miami's UNIA chapter by the late 1920s. Beset by constant forgeries of correspondence and resulting mistrust, the association's Miami leadership fractured into several splinter organizations. Gunmen shot down a Georgia-born woman named Laura Koffey, one of the group's most promising young leaders, after Koffey broke off to form her own religious sect, the African Universal Church. She was in the middle of delivering a sermon to two hundred people. James Nimmo, the Miami UNIA's military leader, and a second gunman were the alleged culprits. A third suspect, a Jamaican named Maxwell Cook, had been seized by an enraged mob and beaten to death on the spot. The courts eventually exonerated the accused, but Nimmo later told interviewers, "It is my definite belief that someone [from the UNIA] was sent in to kill the woman."[95] As described in one account, "Miami's UNIA chapter died the same night as Koffey."[96]

Trading Land for Rights

By the time of the Big Blow, Miami's lone Seminole schoolboy, known to whites as Tony Tommie, had grown up. In November 1926, a mere two months after the storm, Tommie, had become frustrated with his people's general poverty. He sought an audience with US president Calvin Coolidge in hopes of securing for his people what he called "the rights of an American taxpayer."[97] Seminoles, Tommie contended, "are intelligent, truthful and conscientious, but they are surrounded by a wall. I want to tear that wall away."[98] The young Seminole endeavored to normalize business relationships between whites and South Florida's Indians by popularizing the use of English among the Seminoles. He also wanted to secure access to public school for indigenous children, the same education he had enjoyed.[99] Schooling options for Greater Miami's native peoples were particularly egregious. There were twenty-two public or private white schools in 1920, fifteen schools for colored children, and zero for Seminole children.[100]

For a shot at Seminole education, employment, medical care, and other civic entitlements, Tommie was prepared to offer Indian land, over a hundred thousand acres of it. He also asked that Florida's Seminoles not be forcibly relocated to Oklahoma. Miami's more influential real estate developers—men who hoped, after the collapse of South Florida's real estate bubble, to restart the Roaring Twenties—arranged a meeting between Tommie and President Coolidge on the promise that the Seminoles would forfeit land in exchange for rights.

A student of white people in two senses, Tony Tommie remained remarkably aware of how to move whites through and personally benefit from racial spectacle. He presented himself to local entrepreneurs as the Seminoles' "chief," and he put together a float for the city of Miami's birthday parade in 1926, replete with a dugout canoe and a chickee hut, the standard Seminole dwelling. He also got over a hundred Indians relocated into white-owned commercial villages. The villages were like living exhibits where Indian tenants would simply allow themselves to be observed engaging in daily tasks. Tony Tommie functioned, in effect, as a property manager for white landlords housing Seminole tenants. He fielded complaints and, in place of wages, brought Seminoles groceries bought from the white landlords, their employers. At one point, the men who owned a few of these staged outposts asked their tenants to carve and erect totem poles and other "pan-Indian" artifacts in order to add an air of authenticity to their reservations. This was a request, sources suggest, with which Tommie complied.[101]

Tony Tommie also recognized the complicated ties between sex, culture, and difference, and, even here, he found ways to showcase his entrepreneurship. He started by charging admission to his own wedding with the idea that whites would pay to witness a "real" Indian marriage ceremony.[102] Such weddings, at Tommie's prompting, became a common attraction.[103] Couples who had been married for years—often, in fact, with children— would get married for a second and sometimes third and fourth time in the presence of white tourists, for a fee. Indian weddings, which happened in May, helped lengthen the tourist season, providing a windfall for white businesses throughout the region. These public displays of "native" matrimony also helped affirm Tommie's claim that "no good Seminole ever marries outside his own race."[104]

Miami's Indian weddings were not just a matter of simple theater. When so-called bad Indians got sexually involved with non-Seminoles, especially with Miami's black population, they faced the possibility of being ostracized, or even killed. One Seminole woman, who had a son by a Miami Negro, was killed by a group of Indian women, who then renamed her son Nigger Dick, shaming the boy well into his adult years.[105] A negative opinion of American Negroes, as members of the Overseas Club knew, did not make one any less colored. Still, what was important, perhaps, for Seminoles to exhibit was that they, too, as a civilized, modern people, knew how to keep their distance from Negroes and their women under control.

Frontier Theatrics

In early 1927, the inaugural journey of the Seaboard Railroad, Miami's second rail line, finally arrived. A first-of-its-kind passenger train in terms of its reach into the southernmost corner of the American tropics, the Seaboard carried more than three hundred "Eastern men of prominence" from New York looking to invest in Florida land. As the train pulled into the station at Opa-locka, men atop Arabian stallions, playacting as "Moorish" riders, "rode madly up and down alongside the tracks," the horses kicking up dust among the throngs of waiting white "harem girls." Opa-locka, which had an abbreviated Seminole name, was actually an entire city built during the real estate boom in an imagined orientalist style from *One Thousand and One Arabian Nights*. The city hall, complete with white stucco, minarets, and Moorish domes, sat on Ali Baba Avenue, and was but one building in a town that boasted the largest collection of Moorish revivalist architecture of any city west of the prime meridian. After a stint of sightseeing and a few booster speeches to onlookers, the Seaboard's passengers continued toward Hialeah, which was, at this time, still mostly saw grass, and the easternmost portion of Indian land in the Everglades.

The Seaboard Railroad's trip to Hialeah came just as federal engineers were completing a sixty-five-mile levee on the southern banks of Lake Okeechobee in Palm Beach County to the north. The lands south of Florida's largest lake were prone to tremendous flooding during hurricane seasons, and for the previous seventy-five years the rains consistently thwarted the efforts of farmers to cultivate the land. One hundred people were killed when the lake overflowed during the 1926 hurricane. By the winter of 1927 the new levee presented Miami's business interests with fresh agricultural possibilities.[106] Newly protected by the levees, the Everglades provided the largest contiguous area of organic soils in the world. Over some 110,000 acres, fertile muck or peat blanketed the land, as much as ten to twelve feet deep in some places near Hialeah and twenty feet deep on the southern banks of Lake Okeechobee.[107]

At Hialeah, Tony Tommie ceremoniously opened a makeshift wooden gate that he and a dozen Seminoles built over the Seaboard Railroad's tracks. This symbolic opening of virginal Indian lands to the streaking machines of progress carried, perhaps, certain sexual connotations. And in the words of the Miami Chamber of Commerce, the train's passage through "Chief Tommie's" gate marked the tribe's final relinquishing of "the sovereignty of the muck lands of their former hunting grounds for commercial conquest at the hands of the white race."[108]

As a point of fact, the actual Seminole governing structure allowed for no chiefs; they were governed by a council. And Tony Tommie, if he was anybody at all, could be described more accurately as a press secretary or a branch manager than as some timeless tribal father. Tommie had, in fact, served as a casting director for Native American extras within South Florida's nascent, though ultimately doomed, film industry. He even provided the "Polynesian natives" for a D. W. Griffith film, *The Idol Dancer* (1920), shot near Fort Lauderdale. On this day in 1927, though, Miami's white entrepreneurs cast Tommie in his most important role to date.[109]

"Camera's Grind as Seminoles Turn Over Land": so read headlines in the *Miami News*.[110] Sporting a dark blazer, necktie, light-colored slacks, and two-tone dress shoes, Lon Worth Crow, president of the Miami Chamber of Commerce, spoke from an elevated platform on the Hialeah prairie. The crowd was segregated, mostly white, and numbered some five thousand people. The 5 February 1927 gathering would mark the official date when the last untamed stretch of Florida finally joined America. "You made your peace with the White Father at Washington [President Calvin Coolidge]," Crow told the Seminoles in attendance, "and brought officially to an end that ancient feud between your ancestors and our ancestors, which could have no place in the new Florida." After making statements about the technological superiority of the white man both in America and "in lands across the seas," Crow ended, "Under the unfailing grace of God shall the good muck soil bring to our generation, and to the generations that shall come after us, abundance and the peace that grows through plenty."[111]

For the occasion, Tony Tommie invented a Seminole flag, just so he could surrender it. Standing next to the Miami chamber's president, Tommie then addressed the crowd. He was barefoot and clothed only in the multipatterned, ankle-length shirt of his people. He also sported a Plains Indian eagle feather bonnet for added effect. Though he spoke and wrote in fluent English, Tony Tommie replied to Crow's words in *Mikasuki*, the Seminole tongue, translated by another member of the chamber: "The white man is the child of Destiny . . . the red man is the child of Nature. . . . The child of Nature must allow the child of Destiny his way." "The Chief," as chamber records described the scene, then closed, "My people will watch your people in wonder, but the hearts of my people will be at peace. We are in the care of the Great Spirit. Our fate, like your fate, is in His hands."[112] With that, "Chief Tommie" relinquished his ceremonial headdress, placing it on the head of the now "Chief Crow." The two race men then exchanged a peace pipe that had been provided by a local white collector of Indian artifacts before turning to the final ceremony of the day.

What came next was a pageant to modernity that, like much else from the day, carried no shortage of racial and sexual imagery. Chamber of commerce publications describe "Seminole Indian braves" with wooden spades digging holes. Into those holes "squaws in their wake planted corn as it had been done for 200 years or more." Then, following the row of Indians, came seven tractors, made of rubber and steel, "waiting in a line like race horses at the barrier." In concert, these machines tore across the field, turning up what was described as "virgin black soil," exactly where Indian seed had just been laid. Wooden implements of the past gave way to the instruments of the present and future. Behind the tractors marched a line of young white women, each wearing a sash bearing the name of a different state from the Union and headed by "Miss Miami." In overalls, farmer hats, and red scarves, these symbols of American fertility scattered fresh seeds into what was now newly tilled American soil.

The Closing of the American Frontier

In 1927, with the final Seminole "surrender," the Florida frontier had at last closed. Yet, there would not be any quick bounce back from the real estate bubble's bursting. In October of 1929, Black Thursday rang in the arrival of the Great Depression. That year, the average annual earnings for Miami's 170 manufacturing companies was –$1,372; annual earnings stayed in a deficit for several years to come.[113] The assessed valuation of all Miami real estate dropped from nearly $390 million in 1926 to just under $98 million in 1934.[114] In George Merrick's Coral Gables, the "City Beautiful" was saddled with $8 million in bonded debt, and, in one year alone, defaults on property taxes among this once blue-chip community exceeded $500,000. The scores of foreclosures that swept across Coral Gables, Miami Beach, and Miami gutted that generation of entrepreneurs who, to the last, hoped to become the next Henry Flagler.[115] Merrick lost his entire stake in Coral Gables. And in 1940, as a token to his early vision, the city officials in Coral Gables made Merrick the city's postmaster.

What would be called Miami's "Forward to the Soil" moment drew its name from the agrarian revival movement occurring among Jews in Russia.[116] But this transaction had little to do with abandoning the corrupting force of cities. It was about setting up 21,000 acres of Indian reservation, expanding the Seminoles' slice of the tourist trade, opening the region's first Seminole school, and making 150,000 acres of previously protected "Indian land" available for private sale.[117]

Figure 2.1. Seminoles place custody of land in hands of white men, 1927. Seminole "Chief" Tony Tommie and "Miss Miami," Sara Jane Heliker. (Courtesy of the Charles W. Tebeau Library, Historical Museum of Southern Florida.)

The actual council that governed Seminole affairs censured Tony Tommie for his apparent treason. "Tony Tommie," wrote one high-ranking member of the Seminole council, "has no right to make any arrangements whatever concerning the Seminoles in Florida. . . . [He] is seeking newspaper publicity for his own financial gain, greatly to the displeasure of the other Florida Indians, who absolutely ignore his statements."[118] Despite the protests, Seminoles would lose the land for good. There were fewer than five hundred Seminoles in South Florida by 1930, and the faction that condemned Tommie's actions hardly had the resources to wrest that much land from South Florida's most powerful real estate interests.[119] Seminoles would sue unsuccessfully for proper compensation for their land in 1950. Tommie's actions eventually prompted a group calling themselves Miccosukee to splinter off and attain their own federal recognition in 1962.

What the Seminoles got in return was hardly what Tommie hoped for. When Tommie's Indian school was finally opened in 1927, it had only three students. The Seminoles' self-appointed chief and his white benefactors scared off any potential interest by requiring vaccinations.[120] Seminoles continued to be trapped in spectacle tourism, as alligator wrestling, boat rides through the Everglades, and travelers' desires to view Indians frozen in a forgotten time made South Florida's Seminole villages, by the 1930s, the leading tourist businesses in the whole state. Throughout the growth of the "Indian industry," most Seminoles continued to be quite poor.[121]

Fortunes for the parties involved in the 1927 event could not have diverged more sharply. Lon Worth Crow got credit for saving the Miami Chamber of Commerce and would go on to be a major player in the expansion of real estate programs under the New Deal.[122] The chamber's head of its Everglades committee, Ernest Graham, was responsible for promoting the tract sale of Everglades land once Tommie gave it up.[123] A real estate developer and future state senator, Ernest was father of the eventual thirty-eighth Florida governor and United States senator, Bob Graham. He also worked with these new lands to expand the holdings of his employer, Pennsylvania Sugar, only to be given seven thousand acres of land as severance pay when Pennsylvania Sugar decided to close down what it considered, after a series of cold snaps and hurricanes, to be a volatile operation.[124] The same year Graham received his windfall of land, 1931, Tony Tommie died from tuberculosis at age thirty-two. The wife he married in the presence of several hundred white viewers preceded him in death, also from TB. Tony Tommie and his wife were the only two Seminoles to contract TB over several years. Tommie went to his grave believing that Seminole spiritualists were "fixing medicine" on him in retribution for posing as chief and giving away most of what had been, to that point, hard-fought territory.[125] In contrast, the lands Ernest Graham received made his family multimillionaires for every subsequent generation, first through dairy farming and, later, suburban development and commercial rental property in what would later be known as Miami Lakes. These acres helped launch the Graham family into electoral politics and publishing. Both Ernest and later Bob Graham were elected to high offices, and one of Ernest's other sons, Philip, would become publisher of the *Washington Post*.

Conclusion

With the "Forward to the Soil" ritual, however contrived, Miami's boosters assured entrepreneurs everywhere that South Florida would boom again. And it would, through new technologies and old strategies. The same year the Seaboard Railroad opened and the American frontier finally closed, a new company called Pan American World Airways celebrated its first international flight. Carrying mail by air from Key West to Havana, Pan Am launched the new age of commercial aviation and a new campaign of advertising in which Greater Miami ceased to be "America's First Frontier" and began its new life as "Gateway to the Americas." On the ground, of course, the tried-and-true ways of coercing black labor continued to drive a Jim Crowed vision of prosperity.

The corporations and small farmers who bought Indian land from the Greater Miami Chamber of Commerce used vagrancy laws to conscript colored labor, simply continuing practices common across the South and instituted with particular zeal in the wake of the "Big Blow."[126] "If you didn't have a job," remembered the UNIA's James Nimmo, "they would lock you up. Farmers would come and bail you out. They would take you to their farms and work you for a period of time. The farmers would give you minimum salary. This was common practice."[127] The work of redefining Miami, as during the 1920s, would continue to be decided at the nexus of real estate, racial segregation, and the willingness of Florida's residents to pursue their visions of citizenship within the bounds of property rights. As the Ward family learned after the Big Blow, however, black property rights remained subject to the whims of a white state.

Property, as real estate *and* entitlements, was supposed to solidify whatever modicum of citizenship colored people could achieve. But because pursuits of property remained tied to an economy built on racism, colored people's attempts to gain racial justice and security remained all bound up with the very forms of sexism and white supremacy arrayed against them.

The question facing those aspiring to ownership was not *whether* to endorse white supremacy, but rather *which* white supremacy seemed most likely to provide the desired benefits. The imperialist claims of the Overseas Club, the handing over of Herbert Brooks, or the Seminoles' final "surrender" at Hialeah: the so-called intraracial dimensions of Jim Crow's violence were not aberrations. They proved integral to regional economic progress. Racial and gendered violence maintained order, and order enabled commerce.[128] And Jim Crow's violence, in almost cyclical fashion, made colored people reach even further for something, some property, to hold on to.

PART TWO

Construction

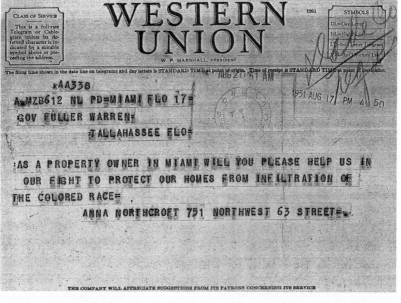

Figure 2.2. A note to the governor, 1951. In a world where landlords and real estate developers variously pushed against and held the color line in pursuit of poor black tenants, homeowners routinely demanded, often quite explicitly, that government officials insulate them from close proximity to black people in general and the black poor in particular. In this telegram sent from one Anna Northcroft to Governor Fuller Warren in the summer of 1951, Ms. Northcroft implores the governor to consider his own property interests in Miami and to take pains to maintain the residential color line. For those politicians governing Jim Crow America, ensuring economic growth and racial peace required fielding such demands on a regular basis. (Courtesy of the State Library and Archives of Florida.)

CHAPTER THREE

Jim Crow Liberalism

Luther Brooks needed a New Deal. Born in 1908, young Luther belonged to a literate white family of Georgia turpentine farmers wiped out by the Great Depression. Like so many men and women in their early twenties, Brooks had been trade school educated and was, by 1930, out of work, inspired to migrate because of economic hardship. He followed a typical migration path, and decided, first, to keep his travels close to his birthplace and extended kin. He moved from his hometown of Iron City, Georgia, just west of Albany, to Gadsden County, Florida, right across the state border. There he began driving a bus for the Florida State Mental Hospital. Gadsden sat in Florida's rural Black Belt, and it differed little from the impoverished countryside Brooks had left behind. Black people made up the majority of the population in Gadsden. Less than 1 percent of them were registered to vote. Like many Americans living in cities and hinterlands, the people of Gadsden also distilled their own alcohol. This, in the midst of Prohibition, helped the inhabitants of Florida's struggling rural communities weather the strain of personal hardship and the wider economic depression.[1]

Brooks's work as a bus driver took him on frequent road trips downstate to Miami. Off and on bumpy dirt roads, he transported mental patients and bootlegged liquor the five hundred–plus miles between Gadsden and Dade counties. While on one of these runs in 1931, Brooks met Franklin Bush, one of Miami's first real estate developers. During the city's frontier years, Bush served as an early drafter of South Florida's color line. Now in his sixties, this onetime piano instructor owned considerable Negro housing in Coconut Grove and Colored Town. The Magic City was still reeling from the mass exodus that followed the 1926 hurricanes, and Bush, by now an aging Miami pioneer, was having trouble finding responsible and honest rent collectors to manage his properties. By the early 1930s, men Brooks's age and younger tended to look to state agencies or, later, President Franklin Roosevelt's Civilian Conservation Corps for work. Bush, however, tried to convince this enterprising twenty-three-year-old that, even during a depression, fortunes could be made in the Negro housing business. Bush attested that, back when he was still a young man and Miami was scarcely more than a few Seminole trading posts, the wisest men did not look to government jobs for help. They made their own destinies in real estate. "Son," Brooks remembers Bush saying, "if you can work for the State of Florida, you're already old enough to work for me."[2] Perhaps fearful of moving so far from home, or perhaps frightened of leaving behind his sweetheart, Gladys, Luther Brooks initially refused Bush's offer. Instead, he went back to Gadsden, and tried his hand at property management among northern Florida's tenant farms. He also got married, and enjoyed the arrival of his first and only child, Margie.

In Gadsden, Brooks collected rents for three white landlords who owned nearly five hundred tenant farms among them.[3] Similar to most white people locked in rural southern poverty, Brooks became a middleman in a system driven by the slow cycles of mule-drawn agricultural production, small-scale agrarian debt, and white racial terrorism. Though better off than the average Negro tenant, Brooks enjoyed little income, and, as a landless white man, his social status reached only as high as the top of the boot pressed down on the necks of Gadsden's black folk.

Through the 1930s and in an attempt to drive up crop prices, the Agricultural Adjustment Administration was offering rural landowners government subsidies *not* to farm. That, combined with new mechanized farming techniques—the kind on full display at Miami's "Forward to the Soil" ceremony—eventually led to thousands of tenant evictions across rural swaths of the Deep South. Both Negro tenant farmers and white rent collectors like Brooks became increasingly irrelevant. Many colored people did not wait long enough to be evicted, though. Spurred by unrelenting penury and frequent white brutality, hundreds and then thousands of colored people fled the Black Belts of Florida, Georgia, and elsewhere for life in America's cities. Facing his own bleak prospects, Luther followed the flow of black migrants into Miami's Colored Town in 1934. He took Franklin Bush up on his offer and sent for his wife and daughter. That June, President Roosevelt signed into law his new National Housing Act.

During the Great Depression and early New Deal, Negro slums stood at the center of political and personal calculations about how best to regulate and profit from Jim Crow. The men and women who built livelihoods and neighborhoods on and around black rental housing played an important part in the development of US politics and economics. They helped harden the color line, for one. Landlords, real estate developers, and even property managers, like Luther Brooks, proved instrumental in making black poverty and segregation an engine of personal and regional economic growth. The same can be said for those who attempted to regulate real estate entrepreneurs. White reformers, politicians, federal housing agents, and an increasingly activist black professional class each had a part to play in tempering or humanizing, but never totally upending, the profitability of segregation. More than a few—as both reformers and entrepreneurs—grew quite wealthy in the process.

Before the age of forty, Luther Brooks would become one of the most important figures in South Florida's housing industry and one of the most successful property managers in the whole United States. He built a fortune over four decades and became a political operative for several Miami mayors and Florida governors. Moreover, he relied almost exclusively on his ability to manage colored rental properties in South Florida's segregated housing market. By the 1960s, many believed Brooks, by virtue of his wealth and political acumen, to be the most powerful man in Miami. That, however, was a future yet to come. During the hand-to-mouth 1930s, Brooks was just one man among scores of people who, in the face of local, national, and international economic collapse, reached for a little of Miami's old frontier magic with help from a rapidly expanding American state.

In political and economic terms, Negro-occupied housing during the Great Depression helped Americans and immigrants alike establish or recover personal fortunes, start new families, and build community. Black slums also preserved and inspired fresh ties between government and capital, as Negro neighborhoods became a cornerstone for how the New Deal actually worked. In the most everyday way imaginable, Jim Crow's ghetto helped shape the lives of ordinary people as they attempted to make meaning under, and indeed out of, racial apartheid and American liberalism.

The unchecked, frontier free-for-all that first pushed work crews into the Florida wilderness at the turn of the century would pale in comparison to the disciplined carving up of racial niche markets that federal and local officials facilitated in the 1930s, 1940s, and 1950s. As historians have recounted elsewhere, New Deal housing programs and other racialized approaches to real estate laid the foundation for postwar prosperity. No less true for the Sunshine State, the New Deal, followed by World War II, became instrumental for what one historian, writing about the postwar period, called "the third Florida land boom."[4] Greater Miami was a place where government officials and their economist friends, through federal housing programs, helped write the color line into national real estate policy. And Miami's residents, like Americans elsewhere, married the programs of the New Deal to the evolving racial politics of the New South.

Yet, Miami's Caribbean geography forced housing to do especially challenging work. The federal state was tasked with underwriting the biracial order that would come to define South Florida's racial landscape for decades to come. Indeed, even as it achieved unprecedented scale across the United States during the 1930s, residential apartheid, in South Florida, was always felt at the level of the individual and the community through Greater Miami's complex ties to the Caribbean. Luther Brooks—like Tony Tommie, Dana Dorsey, and so many others—began his adult life largely unaware of the impersonal processes determining his choices and life chances. What the New Deal moment would teach Miamians of every background, though, is that they could achieve, through the state, new kinds of political and personal power over some of the forces they *could* see.

Harvesting the Great Migration

Of the two million black people who abandoned farm life in the 1930s, only some four hundred thousand—or less than 25 percent—left the South.[5] Most migrated into southern cities and right back into the arms of unfair tenant arrangements and white racism. In Miami's Colored Town, that often meant working as a domestic or other unskilled laborer, making sometimes double what one made on the farm, but remaining dirt-poor. It also meant living in a cramped wooden "shotgun" shack set off a dirt road and without indoor plumbing.

Containing roughly four bedrooms and built side by side, shotgun houses were the most common form of rental property in southern Florida. With many dating back to the days of Henry Flagler, these narrow one-story structures, rumor had it, got their name because a person could fire a shotgun through the front door and have the bullets pass clean through the back doorway without ever hitting an interior wall. Apocryphal perhaps, this explanation reflected a certain folk atmosphere that poor southern migrants created and that rows and rows of these structures evoked as they housed as many as 140 families on one city block. Indeed, while most whites around South Florida lived about 15 people to an acre, in Miami's Central Negro District, up to *600* people lived on a single acre of land.[6] Contemporaneous sources described stretches of Colored Town as "a beehive" of hundreds

Figure 3.1. The shotgun houses of the Central Negro District, 1951. (From Reinhold P. Wolff and David Gillogly, *Negro Housing in the Miami Area* [Bureau of Business and Economic Research, University of Miami, 1951], 13.)

of one-story shotgun shacks. The homes were so close, in fact, that, as one former resident recalled, "somebody could reach out of their window and shake hands with the other person [next door]." Recent scholars interested in artifacts of the black Atlantic have pointed to the structural similarities between Florida's shotgun houses and those in the Bahamas and West Africa as evidence of a truly diasporic architectural form in North America. But shotgun shacks may better be described as artifacts of capitalism. In addition to defining the ghettos of New Orleans, Atlanta, and Tampa, these structures were also built by white capitalists for workers outside of dusty steel plants in Birmingham, Alabama, or crammed onto block after block in Negro ghettos from Houston, Texas, to north Philadelphia, Pennsylvania.[7] Observing Miami's particularly large collection of shotgun shacks, a Public Works Administration (PWA) official from Washington described Colored Town in 1934 as "the most congested slum district that I know of in the country, and that takes into consideration my knowledge of slum conditions in quite a few cities."[8]

From a shotgun shack with no plumbing or utilities on the corner of NW Third Avenue and NW Twelfth Street, Luther Brooks started his first business, Bonded Collection Agency.[9] He paid fifty cents a week rent, and began with seven landlords as clients, 134 tenants under his watch, and a black accountant named Charles Knowles. Knowles was in charge of all of Bonded Collection Agency's early property tracking and bookkeeping practices; he would also be the first of many colored people in Brooks's employ once Bonded expanded in the postwar period. At this early stage of the business, Bonded was still a modest operation that demanded much from its founder. Brooks spent many hours walking Colored Town's streets, familiarizing himself with the landscape and introducing himself to various black and white business owners. Many of the relationships he built in these early years would serve him well during later political conflicts. Brooks also moved his twenty-three-year-old wife, Gladys, and young daughter, Margie, into a small rental home on an all-white block that was within walking distance of Colored Town.[10] Proximity to Negro tenants was crucial, for, with no other employees besides Knowles, it was up to Brooks to knock on the door of each apartment and collect rents personally.[11] Gladys worked as the company's secretary.[12]

During the 1930s, Bonded Collection Agency and other property management companies ensured that the at times brutal economic relationships and folksy indignities that defined agrarian debt peonage translated well into the otherwise impersonal world of big city urbanism. Though many colored people owned rental property in the city, most of the landlords who owned property in Colored Town were absentee whites like Franklin Bush or George Merrick. In the words of one self-described "intelligent, honorable young negro" writing in the *Miami Herald* back in 1912, "We buy a lot; the [white] real estate company buys a half dozen and surrounds you. . . . We are powerless."[13] The real estate explosion of the mid-1920s brought over two thousand wooden tenements to Colored Town, with the boom only increasing white people's rental foothold in the neighborhood. Less than 10 percent of Colored Town's residents owned their own home.[14]

In the estimation of white landlords, crowded tenements and a growing and largely migrant Negro population required the kind of intimate oversight that could preempt tenant organizing while keeping monies flowing back into landlords' pockets. To this end, property managers often got quite creative or downright ugly in squeezing rents and other fees from tenants. Commonly, rent collectors woke up between 4:00 a.m. and 5:00 a.m. to start knocking on doors. "The point was to catch 'em before they went to work," remembered one Bonded employee.[15] Public assistance programs under the Federal Emergency Relief Administration, intended to help America's most destitute families, also served to enrich absentee landlords. Echoing rural practices of exploitation, collectors covered the high costs of rent by sometimes confiscating a tenant's entire welfare check from week to week. The tenant then agreed to accept groceries on credit, creating an almost endless cycle of indebtedness. In cities such as Atlanta, Georgia, and Norfolk, Virginia, where the majority of colored people were on the relief rolls, the federal government was essentially subsidizing the private rental market directly.[16] Other techniques property managers used to defray owners' expenses included making new tenants pay the outstanding balances of old ones.[17] In later years—and after coming under several investigations—Luther Brooks personally denied participating in some of these more egregious forms of profiteering. Yet, even families living in properties managed by Bonded Collection Agency suffered evictions with as little as three days' notice.

From tenants' perspective, the preponderance of shoddy wooden construction, combined with Colored Town's unpaved streets and spotty trash collection, made renting in black Miami an unpleasant and at times dangerous affair. Miami, like most cities in 1940, was one where renters mostly shared bathrooms, and there were over eight thousand apartments in Miami with no private bath (16.5 percent of all dwellings).[18] Of that eight thousand, over five hundred had no bathrooms whatsoever—private or shared. These apartments were the most deplorable in the city, and 82 percent of them were occupied by colored people.[19] A full 40 percent of Negro apartment houses in Miami lacked electricity.[20] During spring and summer months, sweltering, termite-chewed rooms creaked and cooked under the day's heat and the night's humidity. And windows and doorways without proper screens made many mattresses or bedchambers home to any combination of rats, cockroaches, silverfish, mosquitoes, and sand flies. Cases of tuberculosis and dengue fever afflicted many of Miami's black inhabitants as well. Black doctors surveying students at Booker T. Washington High School in 1934 determined that four of ten students suffered from incipient tuberculosis.[21] Death rates from TB among Miami's entire colored population were two and a half times that of whites, in fact.[22] House fires, with their attendant losses of life, were also common. Blazes could rage from house to house as fire engines trudged clumsily up muddy or potholed streets at speeds as slow as five miles per hour.

Colored Town was also home to vice trades that were at times directly abetted by landlords, property managers, and white police officers. Prostitution rings and illegal lotteries proved especially prevalent, as local law enforcement, since the city's founding, intentionally shepherded vice into Colored Town and other black enclaves across Greater Miami. Given the depth of the Great Depression and the remoteness of the Magic City in relation to other corners of the United States, it remained open to political debate as to whether South Florida needed gambling and prostitution to survive.[23] There was little disagreement, at least among whites, however, about where the most unseemly kinds of gambling and vice should be located. Extending police practices begun in the 1910s, Miami's sheriff Dan Hardie, in 1932, made a point of confining underground casinos and brothels to the northwest section of the Central Negro District. "Hardieville," as this area came to be known, served as a center of international vice trades, one that proved quite lucrative to organized crime networks and white police officers on the take.[24]

"*Bolita*," for instance, was an illegal lottery that came to the United States with the nineteenth-century migrations of Cuban cigar rollers to Tampa and Ybor City. The game's name came from Spanish slang for the consecutively numbered "little balls" that handlers used to decide the lottery's winning number. In the 1920s, *bolita* moved north from central Florida into Atlanta and south to Greater Miami on the tracks of the Florida East Coast Railway and Seaboard Railroad.[25] The lottery remained small-time during the real estate boom of the 1920s. By the late 1930s, the near complete collapse of real estate speculation and mass unemployment across the urban South made *bolita* popular among many poor and working people. All you needed was a bag of lottery balls and some money to change hands, and you could set up games almost anywhere. The back porches of shotgun shacks and alleys behind bars tended to be especially popular sites for games. Compared to horse racing or other games at fixed odds, *bolita* buyers tended to make lesser wagers, sometimes as low as a nickel per bet. The game's mobility and small stakes made it ideal for underemployed labor migrants from the Caribbean or small southern towns, the kinds of people who literally had little to lose. A five-cent bet could net a lucky gambler twenty dollars at odds of only one hundred to one.[26]

If the ease of starting a *bolita* outfit made the game commonplace, the game's popularity made *bolita* a prime target for white organized crime. As occurred in Harlem at this same time, Jewish and Italian whites, with the help of white law enforcement officers, wrested control of Miami's numbers game from Cubans, Puerto Ricans, West Indians, and American blacks during the 1930s. Often the same white gambling syndicates from New York and other northern cities consolidated and took over the *bolita* rackets in South Florida. Vice, according to some voices in the Negro press, enabled "those of our race [to] allow themselves to be used for fattening the white man," and, for years, black editorialists across Afro-America called for "the Negro to emancipate himself from being a sucker to white racket operators."[27] To the chagrin of black property owners and others among the Negro middle class, vice rings, when combined with other mechanisms of white privilege, lifted countless Italians, Jews, and other ethnic whites into the American mainstream, even as the violence and sexual exploitation wrought by such crimes seemed only to affirm myths about Negro inferiority.[28] By the 1940s, white mobsters, working largely through Negro proxies, dominated illegal lotteries in black communities up and down the Eastern Seaboard. Less than ten years later, Meyer Lansky and Frank Costello, once child-immigrants from Europe, had grown to become organized bosses of international crime outfits founded in Manhattan and expanded through Miami. By the 1950s, Lansky and Costello were using Miami's hotels and revenues generated in South Florida's black neighborhoods to maintain a controlling interest over almost all illegal gambling between New York and Havana, Cuba.[29]

Not all of Colored Town's landlords enabled vice, to be sure, and some even complained that *bolita* and its related illegalities sapped their revenues. "When *bolita* throwing starts," reported the *Palm Beach Post*, "it takes first place over everything else. The players will gamble any cash they may obtain rather than spend it for food or rent."[30] To the estimation of some landlords, the potential irregularity of rental money seemed justification enough to participate in vice trades. The absence of sound policing in black Miami made this easier still. As Colored Town's population grew, landlords of every color purposefully hired pimps and other purveyors of vice to manage their rental properties in return for kickbacks.[31] Rather than turn to Luther Brooks or some other reputable rent collector, as one candid white slumlord explained, "You can have a colored man operate [your real estate] for you and he can run it as anything he wants. The colored man can make a bundle on the side and you'll get yours."[32] Illegal lotteries would explode with the new tourism and consumer opportunities of the post–World War II economy, and absentee landlords would continue to prove instrumental in expanding what would become, by the late 1950s, a ten-million-dollar-a-year numbers trade in Dade County alone.[33] During the Depression years of the 1930s, *bolita* remained relatively marginal, though. Mostly, like the low-level bootlegging in which Brooks and countless others participated during Prohibition, *bolita* simply helped soften the sting of poverty.

The white press, property owners, and those in law enforcement made sure prostitution also remained largely confined to black spaces. Amid charges from a white Baltimore physician on vacation that Miami was Sodom to Baltimore's Gomorrah, the *Miami Herald* responded indignantly in 1922, "There is no house of prostitution in this city, except perhaps two or three places patronized sporadically by colored people."[34] The attempt to separate Colored Town from "the city," particularly when it came to matters of illicit sex and tourism, inspired the founding of Hardieville. And the strategy generally proved effective in protecting Miami's attractiveness, at least until the "Big Blow" and Depression hit. As happened with black domestic workers, foisting flesh trades onto Colored Town affirmed a notion that proved far more durable than Miami's real estate market. Whites believed in some "natural" association between black women and communicable disease. Black middle-class men and women tried to decouple that association.

Specifically, working-class black women became the principal objects of sexual reform. Incidents of rape against black maids, white men's evident taste for colored prostitutes, and even the occasional account of interracial love among Miami's "lower classes" inspired fears of sexually transmitted diseases flowing freely from black women's bodies across the Florida Peninsula.[35] The black physician and landlord William Sawyer worked with James Jackson, a white doctor, to tackle venereal disease and other sexually transmitted diseases. Jackson, on the one hand, complained that too many white men infected their wives after midnight trips into Colored Town. Sawyer, on the other, used the opportunity to address long-standing inequalities in black women's access to health care. It was in the apparent interest of both parties to focus their efforts on Miami's black women. In addition to directing their testing and treatment efforts toward colored women, Jackson and Sawyer called for the forcible removal of sex workers from Colored Town's streets and organized male escorts for "good women" walking about after 9:00 p.m.[36]

Black women's organizations, which had begun proliferating in Miami during the mid-1920s, also played a central role in trying to disassociate sexual disease from upstanding black womanhood. In the spirit of a prevailing notion of black respectability and uplift, Miami chapters of the Delta Sigma Theta and Alpha Kappa Alpha sororities, as well as various women's study clubs and garden societies, organized to encourage both thrift and upstanding hobbies among young colored women. These included sewing classes and community service. With many members of these women's organizations being property owners themselves, they made a policy of not housing more than a few single black women in any given rental unit, and encouraging others to do the same.[37] Crowded women's accommodations, it was believed, contributed to young girls going astray.[38]

None of Colored Town's interrelated afflictions—housing deterioration, public health crises, or the vice trades—were new to the 1930s. Still, they would serve new purposes in the interest of economic recovery. Negro slums during the booming 1920s were potentially loathsome and unsightly for white people who occasionally braved black spaces. But they represented little threat to Greater Miami's national visibility, its moral viability, or the general profitability the city and its beachfront. "Miami," as one longtime observer noted in 1929, "is a charming place for a frolic. So, in a different way is New York. The undercover conditions are probably much the same in both places—but New York does not pretend morality."[39]

By the mid-1930s, there seemed little use in pretending. The availability of federal housing assistance and other pots of government money provided by President Roosevelt's New Deal gave local authorities the economic means for making dramatic corrections to Miami's landscape. As part of this moment, the need of many white entrepreneurs to rebuild South Florida's reputation as a site of viable investment combined with a list of longstanding black grievances to make Negro housing a front-page issue.

The Spirit of Reform

In September 1934, the *Miami Herald* ran a two-week-long series on slum housing in the Central Negro District. Part of its aim was to generate popular support for newly minted programs of public housing and federal slum clearance. Local editorialists argued that "Colored Town must . . . be cleaned, thoroughly. . . . Arrangements must be made to replace hundreds of the houses [with] modern dwellings."[40] Many landlords worried that any calls for "replacement" housing endangered their rental assets. George Griley, a white man who owned over 230 tenant houses in the Central Negro District, served as president of the Colored Town Property Owners League, a landlords' lobbying group. He complained of "lopsided" coverage in the press and placed most of the responsibility for Miami's housing woes at the feet of city officials and employers who refused to pay black workers a decent wage. "The city," Griley remarked, "has been collecting taxes for which they return nothing except irregular garbage and trash collection." Griley also complained of unpaid rent and theft on the part of tenants who, among other things, sold stolen electric boxes and wiring to scrap dealers.[41]

The *Herald*'s series represented something of a breakthrough in Jim Crow–era media in that it gave Negro leadership a venue for pressing broader concerns about white profiteering and the moral well-being of poor colored people. The series sparked volleys of blame fired between this party and that. Landlords blamed job discrimination and the lack of city services for black poverty. City officials and white employers blamed landlords and the absence of sound Negro leadership. Black leaders cited rampant racism up and down white society. And everyone whose voice seemed fit to publish blamed South Florida's colored tenants. As *Herald* reporters noted, "Colored people who have never lived in a decent house or among decent surroundings cannot be expected to care for the property on which they live in colored town."[42]

As with matters of black prostitution or gambling, many of Miami's black property owners argued that programs of racial uplift would improve tenants' general behavior. The Greater Miami Negro Civic League, of which Kelsey Pharr was president, emerged in this period as a decidedly more civic-minded version of the Colored Board of Trade. The league ventured several attempts to educate black tenants about appropriate cleaning habits and moral uprightness.[43] The Bahamian-born minister John Culmer and *Miami Times* editor and Nassau native Henry Reeves, both members of the organization, used their respective clout as religious and media figures to host revivals and publicize methods through which tenants could "dress up" their tenements and achieve "sanitary perfection." The Race, they argued, depended on it. Miami depended on it. "We owe it," said Culmer, "to ourselves and to our employers to so live that we shall not be branded as germ carriers." "This campaign," Reeves explained, "is the most important in the history of our section." Just a decade removed from open conflict between the Overseas Club and the Colored Board of Trade, the slum reform issue seemed important enough to inspire new West Indian / Negro American alliances.[44]

Ironically, some white observers actually cited Miami's culturally diverse black population as the source of filth and decay in colored South Florida. A local white physician, drawing on his personal knowledge of blacks from Cuba, Trinidad, Venezuela, and several other points south, advanced the argument that Colored Town was a petri dish of seething tropical diseases matched "perhaps no where [else] in the world." "Naturally the coming of parties from all these areas has brought types of disease, racial characteristics and social habits which act and interact upon each other, producing unique conditions for Miami."[45] Others believed that the history of conflict between Caribbean and American blacks was chiefly responsible for the continued deterioration of black civic pride. "Miami's colored town," as one *Miami Herald* columnist explained, "is composed of negroes from many countries outside the United States. This mixture of classes closely herded together inevitably leads to neighborhood controversies and conflicts of a more or less serious nature."[46] Beyond the typical calls among whites for Miami's diverse colored leadership to take more "personal responsibility," some of the reasons given for the conditions of Negro slums bordered on the ridiculous. In perhaps the most outlandish claim, George Griley contended the following about why white landlords kept black people in dilapidated wooden shacks: "The negroes don't want concrete block houses. They won't stand on anything but wood. They object to fireproof construction."[47] Wood planks were, of course, much cheaper than concrete, and for *that* reason, far more than black people's supposed preferences, Griley's Colored Town Property Owners League would make sure that wood construction predominated in the Central Negro District well into the 1960s.

Some Depression-era landlords, especially those committed to complying with the law, feared condemnation or the prospect of demolition under federal slum clearance. In most cases, though, even if a given piece of property was condemned, that hardly meant the end of business. The first problem was the lack of political will on the part of city officials. Short of condemnation, Miami's housing office had weak enforcement powers, and, even with the exposé in the *Herald*, the city's booster politicians remained far more concerned with generating new commercial and suburban real estate than in fighting costly court battles with landlords over run-down Negro shacks. Second, condemned properties quite often were more difficult to remove than standard ones because their owners might have abandoned them, leaving them to be taken over by squatters or managed by unknown third parties. In yet other instances, well-connected landlords simply evaded or openly defied municipal enforcement powers, ignoring notices from building inspectors and continuing to collect rent.

With condemnation generally serving as a weak threat, the real danger to landlords' bottom line was public housing, which was first proposed in 1933 under the establishment of the Public Works Administration. In Atlanta, housing officials razed a shantytown called Tanyard Bottom and replaced it with Techwood Homes, America's first public housing project. Though Techwood was a "whites only" rental project, Miami's landlords knew that similar housing options were being discussed to help slum-clear Colored Town. Rental lobbyists like George Griley complained, quite disingenuously, that Negro rentals had not been profitable since the boom years of the early 1920s. They argued, moreover, that public housing, in addition to being a financial "loss to the federal government," would only worsen the private housing market by entering into "direct competition with property owners" and driving down prices.[48] Across the United States, landlords, looking to prove their point in court or state legislatures, blocked scores of public housing projects, particularly the early projects (1933–35) that promised to serve as instruments of slum clearance. As a testament to their strength, public housing construction during the 1930s, and for decades after, consistently fell short of proposed quotas, sometimes by as much as 75 percent. Mindful of landlord litigation working through state supreme courts elsewhere, PWA officials in Miami decided it was better to sidestep costly litigation altogether. They built South Florida's first black housing project on vacant land far from densely populated areas.[49]

Sweet Land of Liberty

In October of 1936, a dedication ceremony in a remote section of northwest Miami rang in the groundbreaking of Liberty Square, the first black public housing project in the South. Less than ten years earlier, the land under Liberty Square belonged to the Seminoles. Now, in a ceremony carrying different hopes than the "Forward to the Soil" event, a band played "The Star-Spangled Banner," "Dixie," and "America" among its musical selections. The program captured through melody what public housing was supposed to mean for Florida—a victory for Uncle Sam, the American South, and the American people.[50] Officials presiding at Liberty Square's dedication assured realtors and other private housing advocates that government projects would not inject "unfair competition into the legitimate real estate business." Public housing would merely compete in "real estate fields where unscrupulous dealers have been collecting exorbitant rentals [sic] for unsanitary and inadequate accommodations." Liberty Square would prove "proper living quarters can be built for what our negroes can afford to pay." Furthermore, housing bureaucrats mused, "The day soon may come when there will be no slums in Miami."[51]

Managed by the newly formed Miami Housing Authority, Liberty Square was actually one of two public housing projects built for South Floridians. Following the opening of the black project in 1937, the authority opened an all-white project called Edison Courts in December 1939. Despite their being mere blocks from each other, Edison Courts and Liberty Square had been deliberately constructed to stand apart and to expand in opposite directions as South Florida's population grew. Between them, NW Sixty-Second Street served as the color line—whites to the north of the street, coloreds to the south—and a twenty-acre tract between NW Twelfth and Thirteenth Avenues provided an east/west "buffer strip," creating a second border between the two. Black need for public housing quickly outpaced that of whites because colored people's housing options were so limited. Between 1937 and 1940, developers expanded Liberty Square twice. The project grew to nearly 1,000 units compared to some 350 units in Edison Courts.[52] It came to cover sixty-three acres and house 10 percent of South Florida's entire colored population, and there were still thousands of families applying to get in.[53]

Liberty Square's repeated expansion prompted Dade County officials and the project's architects to erect a four-foot-high concrete wall backed by a line of trees on the "Negro" side of Twelfth Avenue. Compromise-through-concrete—in this case, colloquially referred to as a "race wall"—would serve as a model for other builders who, by the end of the 1940s, began including concrete walls as standard features of larger concrete, black-occupied housing projects.[54]

Jim Crow, Reformer

Segregationist politicking enabled the realization of much of the New Deal, and, as the campaign to reform Negro housing illustrates, twentieth-century liberalism and racism were, in large part, inseparable.[55] Two of the most important local players in helping federal officials navigate landlord intransigence were the attorneys John C. Grambling and A. B. Small. Both men had been judges in Dade County, and both knew precisely which city and county commissioners they could count on to break ground on Liberty Square. Their support of the project also reflected paternalistic worldviews common among white Americans of influence. Said Small of his support of the project: "I am one of those, being a true-bred Southern man and a descendant of slave owners, who feel that the negroes are the wards of white people and that we ought to be very scrupulous in trying to see to it that they are given proper living conditions." "This project," Grambling contended, by contrast, "will be one of the greatest blessings that Miami ever had. It will not only eliminate the possibilities of fatal epidemics here, but fix it so that we can get a servant freed from disease [sic]."[56]

As the historian Raymond Mohl describes, Miami's housing reformers "were hardly altruistic in their motivations" when it came to proposing the location of Liberty Square. At Liberty Square, many white civic leaders saw an opportunity to "remove [Miami's] entire colored population," in the words of one 1934 letter. The project, in effect, was supposed to draw the black population out of Miami's downtown and finally help whiten a region that had been black, Indian, and Caribbean since before the arrival of the Florida East Coast Railway. The very same month as the Liberty Square dedication ceremony, journalists at the *Miami Herald* described Colored Town as "a festering sore in what might be one of the best white residential parts of Miami."[57] This medical characterization, which would become common in references to black communities for generations, accompanied a twenty-year plan from the Dade County Planning Council that included "removing [the] entire Central Negro Town to . . . three Negro Park locations." The first of these was to be Liberty Square.[58]

The fertile Native American lands that first lured agribusiness and other investors into the Florida bush in the late 1920s seemed to promise an answer for finally realizing the separation of Colored Town from "the city." Relocating Colored Town, though, required, at minimum, ginning up contrived visions of a Caribbean utopia among those black Miamians principally concerned with racial uplift. Dade's white planners claimed to have conducted "wide personal investigation" in the Bahamas, Cuba, and "through the West Indies" to help conceptualize large green spaces replete with "many pools, bathing, fishing, and other recreational features." White visions of a black Caribbean—far from the sea—also included promises to connect colored people to the land in a productive, agricultural relationship that even Seminoles could never achieve. Two of the three projected resettlement areas purportedly had soil that was either "generally good for tree and vegetable purposes" or similar to "the Bahama Islands, where civilization is quite largely based on tropical fruit trees." In a manner similar to the bucolic reform programs of Franklin Roosevelt's Civilian Conservation Corps, cultivating trees and other agriculture would "in great measure raise the standard of living of our Dade County negroes . . . and . . . tie them to the soil in a more happy manner than they have ever been used to in Florida."[59]

The planning council's tropical vision of "Negro Resettlement," perhaps unsurprisingly, enjoyed much black support. Many of the city's more influential middle-class black folk were deeply in favor of relocating undesirable colored people and putting the state to work in the name of their *own* notions of race progress. Architectural historian John Stuart has located correspondence written by black property owners, dated as early as 1933, wherein members of Miami's colored upper crust ask city and federal housing officials to clear Colored Town of its poorer black families so a better class of Negro could thrive in Miami's downtown. A group claiming to be "the representative business and colored men of Miami" asked white officials, in their words, to "obtain a territory contiguous to Miami where we may segregate some of the best families from the classes of undesirable elements." This committee included Kelsey Pharr, John Culmer, and others who would eventually work with city officials to forward the cause of slum clearance in Colored Town. The "environment in which our children are growing up," these men argued, "is revolting to the educated, well-bred colored people of Miami."[60] These men were also in charge of policing entry to Liberty Square once it was built, helping impose the income restrictions that kept Miami's most destitute colored people out of the project.[61]

In the lead-up to Liberty Square's groundbreaking, members of the Greater Miami Negro Service League effectively deployed the local government as an arm of black-on-black policing. The group's members, as part of the city's informal "fact finding committee," used their neighborhood knowledge to help housing officials go after the weakest or, from their perspective, least favored property owners in Colored Town. In contrast to white landlords,

who often openly flouted the state, black landlords, because of a newly empowered cadre of black housing reformers, experienced greatly increased
state oversight. Among those landlords first targeted was "a wealthy Miami
negro," unnamed in the press, "who claims city hall influence."[62] White city
officials denied any connection to the man, and his properties were summarily condemned. One black woman, fearful of what appeared to be a sweep of
condemnations afflicting black owners in Colored Town, pleaded with John
Culmer, a black minister in charge of designating properties for condemnation, to spare her house. She complained that housing agents had been
denying her application for home improvement loans, causing her home to
fall unjustly into disrepair.[63] The first estate that city officials moved against,
however, was that of a particularly notorious figure named W. D. Davis.

Celebrated by the Colored Board of Trade as a successful contemporary
of Dana Dorsey during the 1920s, Davis went on to compile a checkered
record that included being accused of or serving time for gambling, grand
larceny, the unlawful distilling of liquor, two murders, and incest with his
thirteen-year-old daughter.[64] He also owned over 140 tenements in Colored
Town before dying suddenly in January 1934.[65] When pressed about the horrible condition of much of his real estate, Davis had complained that he was
penniless and that he could not afford to keep up his properties. He could
always afford to fight condemnation in court, however. Reformers were able
to move against Davis's estate immediately after his death. Upon breaking
into his safe—professedly in search of a key to his safe-deposit box—local
authorities pulled out over one hundred thousand dollars in bonds and cash,
most of it in small bills and wrapped in rubber bands.[66] Since Davis left no
will, Miami's probate court split the sum equally among his four children.

A precursor of the urban renewal era to come, Liberty Square and the
attendant antislum campaign represented a kind of spatial uplift facilitated
through black and white collaboration. "Compared to the thousands of old
huts," wrote Mary McLeod Bethune about Liberty Square, "it is a garden spot
for our people."[67] In Colored Town, paper floors or floorboards with splin-
ters or wayward nails were commonplace. At Liberty Square, children ran
across living rooms floored with cheap, but sturdy, asbestos tiles. Colored
families at Liberty Square may not have had the electric refrigerators found
in most white homes, but they were provided with iceboxes that at times
proved hard to come by in Colored Town. In lieu of laundry facilities, builders installed oversized kitchen basins intended to serve for washing clothes
as well as food.[68] This too was an improvement over Colored Town accommodations, which were serviced mostly by well water. And though five miles
from friends, family, stores, or churches left behind in Colored Town, Lib-

Figure 3.2. A from-the-ground view of the Liberty Square Housing Project, 1937. (Courtesy of the Charles W. Tebeau Library, Historical Museum of Southern Florida.)

erty Square residents enjoyed the benefit of buses to take them back to the old neighborhood. As a point of fact, it was the daily commutes of Liberty Square residents traveling "over town" that first helped bestow upon Colored Town the "Overtown" moniker it currently carries. A few pesky inconveniences notwithstanding, the Liberty Square project represented a breath of fresh air from Colored Town's squalor and functioned in no small way as a beacon of pride for many black Miamians. "Anytime people came to Miami, we rode through the project because [it] was so different from the area that we lived in."[69]

According to Liberty Square's administrator, James Scott, the experiment in government housing promised to "inspire and encourage [Negroes] to become good citizens." But, even more than that, Liberty Square helped many American and Caribbean colored folk believe in the possibilities of US citizenship, some for the first time. Scott, for instance, would be the first black housing official in Miami's history—the first Negro to hold any kind of office in Miami, in fact. And his managing of Liberty Square helped give residents and the friends and family of residents hope that colored people could finally expect to achieve greater control over their destinies and their government. Perhaps most important, Liberty Square, despite its detractors among white real estate interests, promised a better capitalism. Landlords in other parts of the city, Scott noted, "have had to tear down and build new apartments and houses, with all modern conveniences, to satisfy the demanding public."[70] George Schuyler, a nationally renowned social commentator and *Pittsburgh Courier* editorialist, wrote that Liberty Square gave black Miami "an air of independence" and the project's co-op store was a stellar example of the kind of progressive black capitalism that "points the way to our next emancipation."[71]

For Schuyler and others, the need to affirm capitalism as part of black people's vision of freedom seemed pressing indeed in the 1930s. Even with so many black people placing their faith in the power of private property, black communists in the North and South were making a persuasive case that capitalism was incapable of delivering racial justice. From the effective communist attorneys arguing on behalf of the "Scottsboro Boys," to the grassroots communist organizing going on throughout the South, to the public declarations of leftist intellectuals like W. E. B. Du Bois and Paul Robeson: communism, in many respects, resonated powerfully among blacks from all walks of life.[72] Miami's James Nimmo, a Bahamian formerly of the Universal Negro Improvement Association, was, by the 1930s, an open communist and a particularly vocal opponent of the vagrancy laws and convict leasing practices that made "coming to Miami . . . like coming into slavery."[73] With both fascism and communism carrying the torch of national progress in Europe during the 1930s, preserving the integrity of American capitalism was, for advocates of the New Deal, part of the point. Black New Dealers, like Mary McLeod Bethune or housing economist Robert Weaver, seemed less concerned about staving off what seemed to be rising European despotism. Jim Crow offered its own despots. Instead, the New Deal's programs, and public housing in particular, represented a way to keep black people committed to American private enterprise.

Liberty Square may best be understood, in fact, as both a product of and an engine for a growing black liberalism that, during the late 1930s, enjoyed profound breakthroughs and suffered frustrating setbacks. For a few brief months in 1937, for instance, black organizations in South Florida secured the appointment of Miami's first black police officer, only to see white locals undo the effort.[74] Mary McLeod Bethune, Robert Weaver, and others within President Roosevelt's so-called Black Cabinet helped ensure that 6 percent of the labor used to build Liberty Square came from Negro workers. That effort, too, fell victim to white counterorganizing, this time through all-white unions.[75] Still, something was indeed changing in the world of "the Florida Negro" post–Liberty Square. The various fleeting victories that seemed to come in rapid succession in 1937 helped inspire Miamians, in an effort to secure longer-lasting gains, to establish their first NAACP chapter that year.[76] Moreover, Democratic senator Claude Pepper opened the door for urban black voting power in Florida when he spearheaded the successful repeal of Florida's poll tax in 1938. Though his aim was to end the adverse effects the poll tax had on working-class white voters, colored people took advantage of the opportunity by pushing several avenues for reform and a never-before-seen electoral power.

Black political power always threatened to expand beyond those who simply owned property. But white terrorism, during the first third of the century especially, kept voting and other forms of democratic political involvement beyond the reach of those without other influential connections. In 1920, whites used intimidation and violence to turn more than one thousand black people away from the polls. In 1931, only twelve black people voted in Miami's municipal election.[77] In contrast, by 1939, Sam Solomon, a savvy and popular funeral director, had become the first Negro to run for Miami's city commission, a possibility previously unheard of.[78] Solomon, the NAACP, and several newly formed black organizations would register seventeen hundred new black voters. They would also openly defy intimidation from the Ku Klux Klan. In the actual 1939 election, both Solomon and a host of "black" issues would lose to white opposition.[79] South Florida's colored population nevertheless began to engage in more proactive forms of political organization.

As inspiring as half victories could be at times, abbreviated justice and partial successes defined the New Deal for blacks in South Florida and, in fact, across the United States. Just as public housing programs helped increase black people's formal political participation, federal dollars also enabled white city and county officials to improve and modernize Jim Crow's built environment. Dade County received a $4 million federal funding package from the Public Works Administration, nearly double that of Duval County, home to Florida's largest city, Jacksonville.[80] Those funds improved Miami's harbors, schools, hospitals, bridges, and waterworks, all in typical segregationist fashion. With $40,000 in government money, whites in Coral Gables built their $54,000 "whites only" Coral Gables Library in 1937.[81] Colored Town got its first library a year later, built entirely from a handful of donations from black property owners.[82] Miami officials built the $320,000 Orange Bowl, originally called Roddy Burdine Stadium, in 1937, with $100,000 from the PWA.[83] It took three years of constant activism for colored people to even be allowed in the building, and, when they finally were, in typical Jim Crow fashion, white stadium officials relegated black visitors to a small "colored only" section behind one end zone.[84]

Perhaps in no other aspect did the New Deal seem more lopsided, and perhaps nowhere were its consequences longer felt, than in the realm of home finance.

Black, White, and Colors

New Deal housing legislation, such as the Housing Act of 1934 and its subsequent amendments, was established with the stated intent of expanding the housing options for Americans during the Great Depression. To this end, federal officials invented and sustained previously nonexistent avenues for real estate speculation through the creation of several unprecedented public/private collaborations, including the formation of the Federal Home Loan Bank Board (FHLBB), the Federal National Mortgage Association (FNMA), the Home Owners Loan Corporation (HOLC), and the Federal Housing Administration (FHA). By designing, managing, and even marketing these new agencies and their products, Washington invited Americans in Florida and across the country to increase their lending and borrowing activity. Liberalizing home finance promised to provide relief for the entire real estate industry by first ensuring new sources of capital for lenders, construction companies, and those who could achieve home equity. Then, the housing sector was supposed to propel the growth of countless small and large businesses that stood to benefit from the expansion of property ownership.

Racism informed every step of this process, and the New Deal state, in both its national and local expressions, made racial segregation integral to America's economic recovery. Working through banks, insurance companies, and city governments, the federal government, for one, helped free up the availability of credit along explicitly racial lines. University-paid housing experts, politicians, and federal bureaucrats cited interracial conflict around housing and argued that, if efforts to drive a depressed economy through housing were to work, local officials and civic leaders would have to remain committed to protecting the principles of racial and class exclusion. Federal officials wrote national housing policy accordingly, and local authorities and homeowners seemed all too willing to confirm their conclusions.[85]

The Federal Housing Administration opened its Miami offices in Coral Gables, which sent the message, right away, whom the administration served. The "whites only" City Beautiful founded by George Merrick became the outpost from which local staffers of the Home Owners Loan Corporation worked with FHA officials to expand white homeownership and, during the 1950s, white slum ownership.

At its founding, though, the FHA had the specific responsibility of improving buyers' access to credit while providing lenders with much-needed legal and financial protection from potential mortgage default. Prior to the establishment of the FHA, banks regularly expected home buyers to make down payments as high as 50 percent and to meet the terms of a five- or ten-year mortgage. The FHA offered borrowers the option of putting 10 percent down on affordable twenty-five- and thirty-year mortgages. Between the program's inception in 1934 and December 1936, four thousand families in Florida received FHA-backed home mortgages; 100 percent of them were white.[86] In 1939, the FHA insured mortgages on nearly two thousand homes. The overall value of the mortgages came to $7.5 million in Dade County alone. And here again, every buyer was a white person.[87] In Chicago and Saint Louis, the FHA actually helped a few American blacks access avenues to property ownership.[88] Mostly, though, the administration was antagonistic, on "economic" grounds, to the prospect of black property ownership. Over several decades (and in spite of the reality of black ownership), the federal government, through its housing wing, played a critical role in linking the right to own property with whiteness.[89]

As in other corners of the country, the Miami HOLC was responsible for drafting "Security Maps," which, through property appraisal, determined which communities represented safe investments for FHA financing and other types of lending. HOLC staffers gave every neighborhood in South Florida a letter grade and an accompanying color: "A" neighborhoods were coded green, "B" neighborhoods blue, "C" yellow, and "D" red. Each grade or color reflected a range of factors, including "sale and rental demand . . . [the] social status of the population . . . accessibility of schools, churches, and business centers . . . and the restrictions set up to protect the neighborhood." Higher-grade communities were more exclusive, better zoned, and, without exception, peopled by whites. HOLC staffers remarked that "A" areas, aside from being "well-planned" "hot spots," were "homogenous," and in demand as residential locations in "good times or bad." The second category ("B" neighborhoods) included homes that were, to 1938 observers, "like a 1935 automobile—still good, but not what people are buying today who can afford a new one." Neighborhoods with a "C" grade were "lacking homogeneity" and suffered from "infiltration of a lower grade population," in addition to being beset by insufficient utilities, "heavy tax burdens, poor maintenance of homes, etc." Last, "D" neighborhoods were characterized by "detrimental influences in a pronounced degree." They housed an "undesirable population" or were imminently threatened by "an infiltration of it." "D" neighborhoods, in short, were "those neighborhoods in which the things . . . taking place in the C neighborhoods have already happened."[90]

In establishing this system, scholars in the emergent fields of urban land economics and what was then called "urban ecology" claimed only to be describing, not creating, segregationist practices. They argued that, even before the establishment of New Deal housing programs, communities invariably declined when black people and other lower-class families moved in. Homer Hoyt, a University of Chicago–trained economist, observed, for instance, that prices in racially transitioning neighborhoods went up briefly because the first few colored families to move in had to pay a premium to cross the color line. Then, prices would drastically drop as whites began panic-selling. By placing emphasis on the fall in prices, rather than on the questionable motivations of whites who felt the need to escape their black neighbors at an economic loss, Hoyt, and the American mortgage industry that he and others influenced, depicted black residents, and not white racism, as the chief cause of residential price decline.[91] Hoyt went on to become the principal housing economist at the Federal Housing Administration in 1934. His uncritical acceptance of housing value being assessed from a white point of view represented a widespread sentiment.

Far from simply reflecting racial truths, government housing officials created them. Indeed, white real estate interests devalued blackness itself by color-coding neighborhoods. White property appraisers helped execute a more ambitious partitioning of South Florida's land along racial lines, and they imposed even stricter biracial rules onto the region's culturally diverse population. One's race in Jim Crow Miami had long been defined by where one lived. Now, though, such exclusion had been formalized. From Miami's FHA offices, one-page area descriptions went out to Realtors and lenders detailing the rationale for the grade given each community. Each description accounted for cultural and national variations in white people while also remaining stridently uncompromising on the black/white divide.

Appraisers, right up front, envisioned two mutually exclusive categories: "Negro" and "Foreign-born." Communities such as Colored Town and Coconut Grove, wherein a majority or plurality of blacks were from Caribbean islands, never received anything other than a "Negro 100 percent" notation. As testament, perhaps, to the failure of the Overseas Club to distinguish themselves from American Negroes a generation earlier, South Florida's colored people, no matter where they were from, could never be "Foreign-born" in the eyes of Miami's housing assessors.[92] Faced with the reality of residents from all over the Americas, and indeed the world, HOLC appraisers in Miami viewed their grade method as a single, "un-segregated" system, and, curiously, a step toward racial progress. "To avoid . . . setting up . . . two grades of residential trends (one for whites and one for negroes), it was decided to approach the city-wide picture from the trend of the desirability of white residential property." For this reason, Miami's appraisers explained, "all negro property in the community was given a D rating."[93]

Assessors, by contrast, allowed for distinctions between "Whites," "Latins," "Cubans," and "Jews," with each group enjoying slightly different privileges in Miami's housing market. "Whites" were Americans, and the measure of residential normalcy. "Latins" were not people from Latin America, but Italians. Theirs were communities largely integrated across class lines, with everyone from laborers to "retired capitalists" making between five hundred dollars and twelve thousand dollars a year. "Latins" always lived in solidly "B" neighborhoods, except for those who lived in Coral Gables, which enjoyed an "A" grade. The reason for "Latin" people's consistently good grade, even with such a variety of incomes and housing values, was "well enforced restrictions"—zoning rules and housing covenants that maintained building quality and kept out Negro "undesirables."[94] Cubans seemed to have no impact one way or the other on a given community's grade. Those who lived in or near the "Negro 100 percent" Liberty City occupied "D" neighborhoods. Those Cubans who lived in high-end homes off Biscayne Bay found themselves in "A" communities.[95] In the state's eyes, they were variously "white" or "Negro" for the sake of bureaucratic simplicity. The southern tip of Miami Beach—the now-legendary South Beach—had sound structures and residents with high incomes, yet it received a "C" grade by virtue of the number of "German & Russian Jews" living there. There is little evidence to suggest, however, that this grade had a negative impact on Jews' ability to access the mortgage insurance market. The Jewish section of Miami Beach was one of only two "C" neighborhoods in Greater Miami to still receive "ample" mortgage coverage from local lenders.[96] In cultural terms, Jews warranted an ethnic distinction ("C"), but given their race-based access to credit, they were white.

Neighborhood grading during the 1930s was hardly a fine science, but the program's scientific trappings helped turn popular racial knowledge into real-world consequences. Moreover, *how* HOLC staffers divided South Florida real estate in the early and mid-1930s may not be as important a question as *who* was doing the appraising. Miami's HOLC appraisers were not disinterested technocrats; there were men like Lon Worth Crow, the "White Chief" from the 1927 Everglades farming ceremony and president of his own real estate brokerage. Six of the HOLC's eight Miami staffers, in fact, were realtors, mortgage brokers, or real estate developers who stood to profit

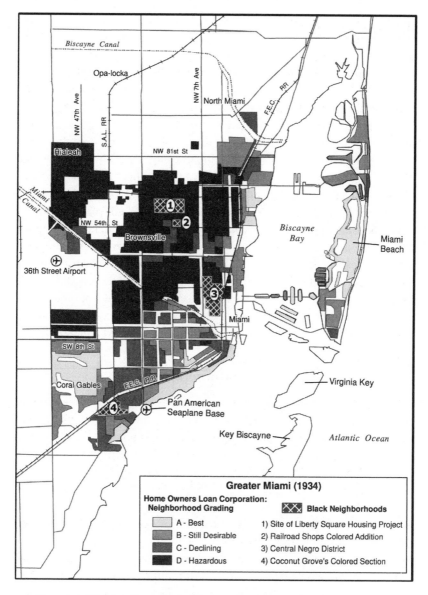

Figure 3.3. HOLC grading and select black neighborhoods in Miami, 1934. (Map by Gordie Thompson.)

greatly by controlling the residential market values around Miami. In the hands of working entrepreneurs, the power to draft HOLC "Security Maps" did not just determine the value of existing homes, it granted real estate developers the security to color-code their profits in red and green—"Negro" and "white"—so they could safely build speculatively and guarantee profit zones on a metropolitan level.[97]

As a point of fact, HOLC's staffers gave "D" grades to tracts of land on which no one even lived. These areas were supposed to serve as sites for a "Negro resettlement strategy" that white housing officials imagined would one day cleanse Miami's downtown of its black occupants. These were the areas that would eventually house all-black Liberty Square and all-white Edison Courts, but they were also those areas that Miami planners hoped would become the center of black South Florida more broadly. Extending "D" grades across select portions of the region's undeveloped land also heightened the relative value of those white communities far from the county's racial frontier.[98] Perhaps most important, by making it difficult to impossible for colored people to secure federal mortgage insurance, even when they opted to live far from Colored Town, HOLC officials ensured the continued necessity and profitability of black-occupied rental property.

Conclusion

In raw economic terms, the city that eventually welcomed Luther Brooks or enriched George Griley was not the site of some pure, free market. As in Chicago, New Orleans, and every other major city in the United States, largely invisible barriers of lending discrimination fenced in Miami's colored population and forced them to consume disproportionate amounts of rental housing. Through the 1940s, colored people in Dade County remained between 20 and 30 percent of the total population. Yet, according to a 1938 report from the Miami Chamber of Commerce, 82 percent of the nearly eight thousand Negro-occupied dwellings in the city were rental properties.[99] It seemingly made little economic sense to build single-family homes or even newer rentals in black communities because of (1) colored people's difficulties in getting loans and (2) the existing demand for black rental property.

Through the 1930s, landlords and property managers continued to cram colored people into rental housing. Across the color line, whites would enjoy the benefit of newer, more spacious options. Colored Town, by 1940, consisted of 92 percent renters, and only 7 percent of the housing stock there was less than ten years old. Nearly a third of black housing in the neighborhood had been built before 1920, compared to less than 2 percent for white Miamians living in working-class communities.[100] White absentee landlords continued to own most of the neighborhood. For, with over four-fifths of colored people renting their homes citywide, Negro rental housing in South Florida was as sound an investment as aviation or tourism, and one that generally required far less start-up capital. Ownership was a complicated *cultural* process as much as an economic one, however. And as South Florida and the nation came out of the Great Depression, a growing black middle class found new ways to assert their property rights, consumer power, and political voice, always with the help of the Jim Crow state.

CHAPTER FOUR

Pan-America

Colored Town grew out of both the Caribbean basin and the American South. And at no time was this more evident than at midnight New Year's morning. Throughout the 1940s and 1950s, those celebrating in bars or hotels and those attending reverent midnight masses at nearby Catholic, Episcopal, and Anglican churches would empty into Colored Town's streets as it wrenched to life with the *Junkanoo* parade, a raucous march of song and dance. Letting loose on horns made of conch shell or brass, whistles, and drums of all shapes and sizes, the musicians, called "Shepherds," wore elaborate costumes and feathered headdresses akin to those of Trinidadian Carnival or Mardi Gras. Accompanying the Shepherds, men and women strode along on stilts and in face paint and masks, also wearing costumes of bright colors and sequins, ringing bells. With the festival itself having originated on plantations in the Bahamas and Jamaica, the celebration commemorated a seventeenth-century, slave-owning African prince, purportedly named "John Canoe." Through his economic and military prowess, John Canoe, it was believed, vexed British and Dutch slave traders off Africa's Gold Coast. *Junkanoo* celebrated Miami's deep connection to the people of the Caribbean and the history of slavery. In the context of Negro uplift, the parade also served as an expression of collective community ownership carried out in the spirit of black material success and hoped-for self-determination.[1]

As the *Junkanoo* parade moved down Colored Town's streets, it provided a showcase of black people's cultural and commercial accomplishments. The procession began on NW Third Avenue near NW Twentieth Street, the northern edge of Miami's downtown colored enclave. It then moved south down Third, slowly and loudly, passing over 150 separate businesses. Storefront dentist and law offices, restaurants of every flavor, laundries, beauty salons, and drugstores each provided marchers with a partial view of the Central Negro District's robust economy. Even more lucrative were the row upon row of wood-frame houses that lined the avenue. In these rental properties resided the colored people who fueled the Magic City's segregated commercial life. Sounds of the *Junkanoo* fished more marchers out of a sea of narrow, one-story wood homes, dirt alleys, and outhouses. Breaking up the architectural monotony were larger, wider brick and stucco homes, some with two stories, large front porches, and, occasionally, two and three bathrooms to spare. These belonged to black Miami's professional class. With something as small as a sash of colored cloth to wave or a spoon and jar to clang together, Colored Town's bystanders—the well off and the destitute—joined the procession. As one participant recalled, "The neighborhood woke up and it was alive."[2]

The procession turned left at NW Fifth Street, Colored Town's southern border, and took NW Second Avenue back north toward the old UNIA Hall on NW Nineteenth Street. In terms of commercial activity, Second Avenue was even more impressive than Third. Known variously as "the Stem," "the Avenue," and "Little Broadway," Colored Town's Second Avenue, with over 140 separate proprietorships, was home to black Miami's most impressive businesses. The *Junkanoo* crawled and crept up Little Broadway past larger, multilevel buildings, many lit up with colored lights. Among the most impressive structures stood the Mary Elizabeth Hotel, the Harlem Square Nightclub, the Lyric Theater, and the massive Mt. Zion Baptist Church. When the procession ended at the UNIA Hall, it was dawn in South Florida. Impromptu marchers and musicians, exhausted from hours of revelry, returned home or filed into any one of the eateries they passed along the way for breakfast.[3]

The *Junkanoo* procession exhibited a truism about ownership more generally: property meant much more than just real estate. In terms of actual deeded property, white people at midcentury owned the majority of Colored Town's homes and many of its businesses. But black people found ways to assert their own claims over South Florida's land through cultural practice and creative appropriations of state power. People of all colors in Jim Crow America took advantage of property as both a physical thing *and* a bundle of rights.[4] For if "real estate," narrowly defined, concerned matters of commerce and law, the *meaning* of land came from how people used it and the claims they made on it through everyday practices and, at times, exceptional powers of state.[5]

This is not to minimize the power of capital. Colored Town's residents saw the impact of white capital in the deterioration of black rental housing. They smelled its fragrance as the Miami City Incinerator burned garbage trucked into Colored Town from Coral Gables or Miami Beach. Yet, even white capital helped set the conditions for black people to negotiate and transact over the boundaries and rules of white supremacy.

The *Junkanoo* parade could not have been such a popular and powerful example of black civic life, for instance, without Caribbean and American people migrating under the aegis of empire over the previous fifty years. The sea surrounding Greater Miami was teeming with English-, Dutch-, and French-speaking islanders—subjects of the empires John Canoe flouted centuries earlier. In addition to these lived and labored the various Spanish- and Portuguese-speaking peoples that populated the hemisphere. At the start of the twentieth century, white officials from the United States, in their own competition with European powers, moved to exert their growing influence on neighboring republics through a combination of military occupation, proxy rulers, and corporate partners.[6] As early as the 1910s, capital from the United States had become so deeply embedded in the commercial and political fortunes of Caribbean and Latin American countries that critics had taken to calling the United States "the Colossus to the North," or, more caustically, the "most powerful and aggressive of imperialist nations."[7]

Conceding that the United States, by the 1930s, had indeed become something of a "bad neighbor," Presidents Franklin Roosevelt and Harry Truman used their respective administrations to advance a so-called Good Neighbor approach to foreign policy. In the professed spirit of Pan-Americanism, Roosevelt ordered US troops to withdraw from Haiti in 1934, following nearly two decades of occupation there.[8] And Truman, in place of direct US rule, promised the wider Americas economic and international security in exchange for solidarity with US commercial and military interests.[9]

The geopolitics of empire and international trade, like the *Junkanoo* parade, would walk the streets and step into the homes of Colored Town and white Miami. For whether embarking for Haiti under a US flag or waving a sash at midnight in Colored Town, ordinary people made sometimes playful, sometimes pragmatic, and always political claims over territory they did not, in a legal sense, own. That was culture's power—land's power—and that's what bound both to politics. By affirming that Miami was still more than America, the *Junkanoo* echoed the antiracism of an Overseas Club that, by the 1940s, had been long gone. It also magnified a powerful and ongoing political condition that still tethered British subjecthood, even for black people, to certain benefits in Jim Crow America.

Building on a related, if distinct, political tradition, Miami's black Americans looked to budding wartime liberalism for their own protection. Citing the apparent success of Liberty Square and the openings allowed by World War II, they fashioned the old, entrepreneurial politics of the Colored Board of Trade (itself defunct by the 1940s) into a half dozen new political organizations, thus laying the foundation for Miami's early civil rights movement. During the 1940s, especially, ownership would become citizenship, as US blacks used their status as property-owning taxpayers to gain Negro patrolmen in 1944, a "colored only" beach in 1945, and, in 1950, a Negro court in which to try their "own people."

Here, too, in the development of black liberalism, the power of capital and racism would be felt. The creation of a kind of "Negro state" seemed, to many, like discernible and uniquely American progress. Yet, in practice, it required full-throated defenses of white supremacy in other corners of society. To demonstrate their fitness for political power, many American Negroes held fast to narrow understandings of property rights and citizenship; they also issued repeated endorsements of state violence directed, to a disproportionate degree, at poor colored people. It was the only message that both black and white observers would accept, it seemed. And in becoming a political force unseen in the South since the days of Reconstruction, Negro liberals in the 1940s helped white Americans preserve practices of indirect rule that remained typical of resource extraction and the colonial predicament facing people of color around the world. Through Colored Town, and through black and white assertions over South Florida's land—in cultural, political, and commercial terms—the region's inhabitants showcased vividly the flexibility and strength of apartheid in the Americas.

A Good Neighbor Moves In

"Good Neighbor" Pan-Americanism, as an expression of midcentury American liberalism, promised to do for poorer Latin American and Caribbean nations what the housing and employment policies of the New Deal set out to accomplish for dispossessed American citizens. It represented an alternative to Nazism and Communism, and, at least in theory, America's "Good Neighbor" approach was supposed to bind the Americas under a spirit of cooperation and collective affluence by way of expanded international trade and more robust political alliances. Those suspicious of the United States' benign intentions pointed to the resources flowing back into the United States through the country's asymmetrical trade relationships with its foreign neighbors. Through depression, war, and postwar, the United States fed its consumer economy with copper from Chile and Peru, sugar from Cuba, bananas from Central America, many thousands of Mexican laborers, and countless barrels of oil.[10]

Pan American World Airways, based out of Dinner Key in Miami's Coconut Grove, proved instrumental to the realization of US Pan-Americanism. During the late 1920s, the company effectively inaugurated the international aviation age through its fleet of boat-bottomed planes, called "Clippers." With their seaworthy frames, Clippers could turn any calm stretch of open water into a runway. The company immediately opened less industrialized countries in the hemisphere to increased US military presence, investment, and, later, island-hopping tourist packages. By 1935, Pan Am, serving as America's "Wings over the World," made Miami the largest airport entry on the globe. Moreover, Pan Am allowed the United States to challenge the imperial designs of aerial powers like Germany and France while initiating a new era of diplomacy built on playing up what one Argentine minister called the "bilateral link between the Anglo-Saxon and the Latin world."[11]

With the onset of world war, Germany tried violently to sever that link. Most international trade, at this time, still happened by boat. Thus, German submarines, in 1942, began targeting Allies' imperial ties to the rich resources of the Caribbean and Latin America. Lurking off the Florida coast, Hitler's U-boats preyed upon British, Mexican, and Canadian oil tankers, as well as any nonmilitary merchant ships bringing war goods along the currents of the Florida Gulf Stream. Between 1942 and 1943, Germans sank over six hundred merchant ships and tankers off America's East Coast. More vessels, by the score, smoked and limped into American ports, with smoldering holes blown out of their hulls and masses of fallen sailors caught and twisted among the debris.[12] It only took a few short months of successful Nazi attacks to leave the formerly "white" beaches of Dade and Broward Counties darkened with crude oil and littered with crates of foodstuffs, mangled oil drums, and other remnants from the cargo holds of downed ships. Local blackout ordinances slowed beachfront nightlife to a crawl. Rumors also spread about midnight Nazi landings on the coast. Axis weapons caches were supposedly hidden in abandoned cabanas, and inside captured German subs American sailors found ticket stubs, soda pop bottles, and brochures from Florida hotels.[13] When federal gasoline rationing and travel restrictions began, it seemed like the final straw. As the president of the Fort Lauderdale Chamber of Commerce recalled, "Florida was cut off. It looked like we were going to starve down here."[14]

In response to the perceived threats that had already left Florida's tourist economy besieged, the Greater Miami Chamber of Commerce and its repre-

Figure 4.1. Squadron B, Non-commissioned Officers Physical Training School, Miami Beach, 1943. (Courtesy of the Black Archives History and Research Foundation of South Florida Inc.)

sentatives in Washington pleaded for the US military to commandeer South Florida's leisure infrastructure. In short order, the nation's armed forces took over local landing strips and boatyards, turning them into modern airfields and naval bases. They also converted hundreds of hotels, both on Miami Beach and on the South Florida mainland. Golf courses became shooting ranges, dining rooms became mess halls, and hotel suites became barracks. The arrival of black troops transformed the beach as well. Never before had colored people, other than domestic servants, slept on Miami Beach. At one new training school for noncommissioned officers, careful negotiations among military men led to the formation of racially integrated squadrons, the first act of explicit desegregation in South Florida's history.[15]

Racial segregation on the beachfront would return after the war, leaving the most lasting changes to the built environment itself. The army spent $12.5 million militarizing and updating South Florida's beachfront. Federal officials granted another $50 million in government contracts to local companies. Pan Am was among those most richly rewarded for its apparent patriotism. In addition to training thousands of pilots, navigators, and mechanics, the company flew over ninety million miles for the US government

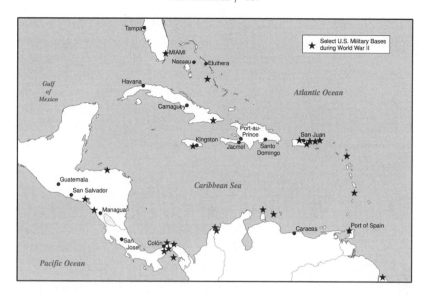

Figure 4.2. The Caribbean during World War II. (Map by Gordie Thompson.)

and built fifty airports in fifteen different countries. The millions of dollars Pan Am gained from federal business funded an array of innovations, including, just two years after the war, the development of nonstop and all-cargo flights to Buenos Aires and nonstop passenger service as far as Johannesburg, South Africa.[16] Locally, the dramatic spike in federal investment would whet the appetite of Florida boosters and countless entrepreneurs for at least another generation.[17]

The military provided the principal means for inter-American collaboration during wartime. White army officers stationed at or deployed from Miami worked with the Greater Miami Chamber of Commerce to strengthen South Florida's ties with the governments of Brazil, Colombia, and, before fascist sympathizers took power in 1944, Argentina. One Colonel Mettler, for instance, on a mission to Brazil, conveyed to South American officials the Miami Chamber's talking points about the "excellent conditions he had found here [in Miami]." Mettler then worked his Washington connections to sell Miami as "the ideal spot in the United States for the development of the Pan American program on a large scale."[18]

The Color of Pan-Americanism

Between 1938 and 1948, southerners dominated the US government's most important foreign affairs posts. Decades of black disenfranchisement made southern congressional seats some of the safest in the nation; this, in turn, made white southerners disproportionate beneficiaries of seniority rules in the US Congress. Multiple secretaries of state, ranking members of the Senate Foreign Relations Committee, and holders of a number of important foreign affairs posts in the House of Representatives all came from southern states.[19] It was therefore not surprising that American foreign policy tended to advance explicit segregationist values abroad. "Americans have carried American hatred to Haiti," James Weldon Johnson charged in 1920.[20] Perhaps more accurately, American boots (or dollars) on the ground in Cuba, Panama, Trinidad, and elsewhere strengthened white supremacy already in force abroad, bringing to the region greater degrees of racial violence, sexual exploitation, and harder color lines in hotels and other public places.[21] All responsibility did not rest with the Sons of Dixie, however. President Roosevelt and member of Congress showed little aversion to racist statecraft. Roosevelt, in particular, cooperated intimately with British imperialists in the lead-up to World War II. He and other liberal politicians also collaborated widely with more conservative southern legislators to bring the New Deal in line with Jim Crow.[22] So it went with Pan-Americanism, as well.

Domestic spending on "Good Neighbor" infrastructure privileged southern cities and segregationist urban development within those cities. White officials used new welcome centers and cultural exposition pavilions to further modernize Jim Crow, either by keeping nonwhites away from other amenities or by displacing colored people during their construction.[23] In 1941, for instance, Miami's city planners proposed a "Negro Slum Clearance Project" that was supposed to raze over 350 black-occupied houses in order to make room for a new train station, white-occupied apartments, and a Pan-American Trade Mart Plaza.[24]

In many instances, projects like these ran into organized clusters of property owners who were mostly white and whose own interests trumped any consideration of big-picture Pan-Americanism. The plaza, which was supposed to house exhibits "from all states in the Western Hemisphere," never got past Colored Town's landlords; they killed the project in court.[25] A group calling itself the Pan-American League, in 1942, proposed the construction of an inter-American hospitality center, meant to serve as a place where Latin travelers could congregate separate from Negro accommodations. Here, however, white homeowners living near the slated site of the project stopped the measure, citing the possibility of race mingling and an accompanying threat to property values.[26] And "Interama," a permanent exposition for the Americas—approved in 1939 with the backing of US senator Claude Pepper—suffered decades of setbacks, including insufficient financing, recalcitrant white homeowners, and failure to meet the standards of "public use" at various proposed sites.[27]

The difficulties Miami had initiating many of its "Good Neighbor" projects proved especially frustrating as competitor cities advanced their own Pan-American growth agendas and threatened Miami's status as "Gateway to the Americas." Nearly a year before the events of Pearl Harbor drew the United States into World War II, *Time* magazine anointed Miami as the vanguard city for inter-American commerce. "The United States will face South for the next 50 years," *Time* claimed in January of 1941. "The Caribbean will become an American lake, [and] Miami sits on the front door step of tomorrow's big business."[28]

At this time, it was New Orleans, not Miami, that did the bulk of America's business with its southern neighbors. Through its contacts in Congress, southern agribusiness sold half its cotton, two-fifths of its tobacco leaf crops, and a third of its rice to foreign markets, with most of it traveling via New Orleans to and through the Caribbean.[29] In 1944 alone, New Orleans exported nearly eleven million dollars in goods to Rio de Janeiro, twenty six million to Buenos Aires, and twelve million to Valparaiso.[30] "Partly to prevent New Orleans from monopolizing . . . the trade of the Caribbean countries," wrote one observer in 1946, "the people of Miami . . . believe they should act before New Orleans goes too far with its plans."[31] Galveston, Texas; Tampa and Jacksonville, Florida; Mobile, Alabama; Norfolk, Virginia: the competition for the most global southern city was stiff. Hoping to finally make good on South Florida's potential, the Miami Chamber of Commerce created a Pan-American Committee tasked with reaching out to the nearly 150 different chambers of commerce conducting business in Latin America.[32] The city of Miami's News Bureau, in 1942, established a fifty thousand–dollar publicity budget strictly for the purposes of courting Latin American and Caribbean investment. By the time America came through World War II, Miami's News Bureau was up to publishing some fourteen million words in nearly one thousand newspapers throughout the Americas and Europe every year.[33]

With words came ideas. Much of what lay subtly communicated in Pan-American boosterism included racial arguments about the desired complexion of international brotherhood. On a scholarly and civic front, federal authorities funded academic research projects and the erection of monuments aimed at reimagining and celebrating Northern and Southern European history as part of a single great, white tradition. Federal authorities invested in the establishment of Latin American Studies departments at southern universities, such as the University of Texas, Austin (1940), and endorsed

Pan-American research projects conducted by independent scholars, university professors, and think tanks. Much of the work produced in this era uncovered and played up the cultural and political commonalities of "Anglo" and "Latin" America while also downplaying the African and Indian foundations of Latin American identity. Founded in 1931, Miami's Pan-American League, in 1944, unveiled the first of many monuments to Simón Bolívar, a man whom, with no shortage of racial implication, they referred to as "the George Washington of South America." Five years later, the mayor of Havana, Cuba, Nicolás Castellanos, received the go-ahead from the Miami City Commission to erect a similar monument of Cuban national hero José Martí in Miami's Bayfront Park. Tellingly, General Antonio Maceo, a black national hero equal to Martí in his importance to Cuban independence, received no such honor.[34]

The imaginings and hopes for a white Pan-Americanism did not preclude many nonwhites from taking considerable advantage of the moment. Actual numbers are hard to come by, but the chatter in the press and in organizational records of local Pan-American civic groups suggests that darkskinned Spanish speakers routinely arrived at Miami as workers, investors, or tourists. The president of the Pan-American League, local clergymen, and airline executives from several companies all complained of "Florida Crackers" who belittled colored foreign travelers. Often, more affluent white men and women in favor of inter-American travel made arrangements for more swarthy visitors to stay at the University of Miami or in people's homes in all-white suburbs, such as Miami Shores. In addition, the continued push to slum-clear Colored Town or to create hotels specifically for black and brown sojourners seemed necessary both because tourists from Latin America could happen upon unsightly Negro shanties and because racist white hoteliers routinely forced dark-skinned tourists into local YMCAs and "colored only" lodgings. "Hotel accommodations are a ticklish point," wrote one travel writer from the *Chicago Defender*, "and dark-skinned Puerto-Ricans or Cubans are apt to be sent over to the Mary Elizabeth, the acknowledged stopping place for Negro travelers."[35]

As the historian Millery Polyné explains, "African Americans idealized . . . Pan-Americanism," as well.[36] Particularly in their outreach to Haiti, American Negroes of means saw themselves as part of a traveling black governing class that had analogues in place to one day run the first independent governments in postcolonial Africa, Jamaica, and elsewhere.[37] Black advocates of state-sponsored US internationalism, like Claude Barnett and Walter White, acted explicitly in the name of "Good Neighbor" outreach and promoted black capitalism and nation building in the "dark" countries of the

Antilles. Their Pan Am or Eastern Airlines flights southward almost always stopped at Miami on the way.[38] In Colored Town's hotels—and, even more often, in the homes of Miami's black elite—an emergent black internationalism that was procapitalist, proproperty, and, often, pro–United States of America found a sympathetic ear and a place of overnight respite.[39] While on a junket abroad, W. E. B. Du Bois, an unapologetic radical, might reconnect with William Sawyer, his old assistant at Atlanta University. Far more often, though, it was black liberals and entrepreneurs, such as Mary McLeod Bethune or the Virgin Islands' governor, William Hastie, who, between flights, made time to address groups of black socialites at Colored Town's Mt. Zion Church or in the dining rooms of fraternal organizations like the Adelphia Club.[40]

Claude Barnett and Kelsey Pharr were especially close, and letters between the two are full of invitations extended, regrets of travel canceled, and references to care packages sent between them from Accra, Orlando, and various points in the Caribbean. Of the two men, Barnett traveled more internationally, to be sure.[41] Yet both shared insights and broke national news stories about their experiences with white cab drivers or which train companies or airline carriers were most amenable to black business. "The ticket sellers [at the Florida East Coast station]," Barnett relayed to Pharr, "were over nice to me."[42]

Travel corporations could be especially fickle beasts when it came to building inter-American ties in the age of Jim Crow. Usually, whether or not one got the "Negro" treatment coincided with one's status and direction of travel.[43] In 1939, executives at Pan Am, in collaboration with US State Department and Miami city officials, helped Haiti's president, Stenio Vincent, circumvent the potential degradations of having to stay in "Negro" accommodations. Vincent had come to the United States as part of a series of meetings with President Roosevelt to hammer out the terms of a postoccupation, Good Neighbor trade relationship between Haiti and the United States. Pan Am executives, however, were forced to put Vincent on a train out of town because not a single white hotel in Greater Miami would take him.[44] Only months later, Kelsey Pharr reported to the *Baltimore Afro-American* that Pam Am was charging American Negroes an extra two hundred dollars to *leave* the United States and enter Cuba. There, Pan Am was trying to make it easier for its Cuban colleagues to keep hotels in Havana segregated by reducing the number of black American travelers going to the island. Bad press and the war emergency soon halted the practice, as Pan Am, in 1946, became the first airline to sign nondiscrimination contracts with black-owned travel agencies.[45] Even in the postwar period, though, foreigners, as a rule, enjoyed better treatment from travel corporations because of their potential to turn any racial slight into a matter of international diplomacy. This would prove similarly true in matters of housing, urban commerce, and labor. In contrast to "civil rights," international relations, like property rights, offered a much more powerful vocabulary through which to seek state protections, it seemed.

Picking Politics

In 1943, the War Food Administration entered into contract labor agreements with British Caribbean colonies, similar to the bracero deal brokered with the Mexican government a year earlier. The point was to ease wartime food shortages being felt in both the United States and Great Britain.[46] Like Mexicans, Caribbean workers had their own motivations for wanting to come stateside. Low wages in the islands and the high cost of food imports brought new waves of hunger and hardship to Caribbean people in the 1940s. Europe no longer had the need for bananas and other luxuries from the tropics; a reduction in the consumption of Caribbean exports thus helped worsen already difficult labor arrangements across the region.[47]

Migration raised new questions about the value of foreign citizenship in Jim Crow America. A web of international protections and local lobbying groups eventually allowed Mexicans and Mexican Americans in Texas to pursue and attain what were then called "Caucasian Rights."[48] In a similar manner, layers of contracts gave Caribbean migrants the diplomatic and institutional leverage to pursue rights not enjoyed by the average American Negro working in a wartime economy. The most important provision, binding in a contract signed between the governments of the United States and Great Britain, stated that "the Worker shall be entitled to freedom from discrimination in employment because of race, creed, color, or national origin in accordance with the provisions of Executive Order 8802 of the President of the United States."[49] No such protection whatsoever applied to Negro janitors cleaning up after troops in hotel bathrooms, or to the two-thirds of all black women who worked as domestics in Miami.[50] A second contract struck between American employers and the Department of Agriculture's War Food Administration promised that planters, too, would honor antidiscrimination laws governing war labor. A third contractual bond existed between Caribbean migrant workers and every white party involved: their employers, the War Food Administration, and their colonial home governments of Jamaica and the Bahamas. These bound black Caribbeans to engage only in lawful behavior.[51]

To help all parties honor their various agreements, the Labour Department of Jamaica issued a pamphlet to West Indian guest workers, warning them to "guard against loose talk" and not to be offended when supervisors in the United States referred to them as "Negro." "Remember," reminded British war authorities, "in the United States the word 'Negro' is not used to offend but is used and accepted in the same way as the word 'coloured' [is] in Jamaica."[52] Wisely, most workers paid far more attention to their contracts than to this pamphlet, for laborers had agreements outlined in President Roosevelt's executive order, point by point, and employers routinely ignored them. Black migrants, having been provided with a hard copy of their rights, often spent the long trips across the Caribbean straits committing their labor contracts to memory, later quoting chapter and verse when inevitable disputes with their white bosses emerged.[53]

Some twenty-five thousand West Indians traveled to the United States as part of the wartime migrant labor program. Initially, they worked in frigid labor camps, tending wheat, potatoes, and other staples for the war effort in northern states. While considerably fewer than the fifty-three thousand Mexican workers participating in the bracero program at the very same time, West Indian migrants were widely regarded as a nuisance far greater than their numbers.[54] Citing various labor protections in their contracts, Caribbean workers of color registered consistent complaints about white racism, insufficient pay, the unavailability of Caribbean food, the lack of nearby Anglican churches, and even the cold weather.[55] Jamaicans, especially the ones from Kingston and surrounding areas, seemed to be the most troublesome.[56] "Nothing was ever quite right with them," remarked one white labor supervisor from Ohio.[57] When compared to Mexican braceros, Jamaicans and other West Indians, in the eyes of white employers, seemed to argue louder than Mexicans, work less than Mexicans, and want more money than Mexicans.

Perhaps most frustratingly for whites, West Indians often broke the sacrosanct social codes of deference that should have accompanied their new status as "Negroes." In May of 1943, an overcrowded boatload of some four thousand Jamaicans bound for New Orleans rioted against military police when army officials and agents of United Fruit Company did not provide the Caribbean cuisine, medical attention, and separate bunks they had promised.[58] Another ship en route to Norfolk, having been chased by a German submarine, had its cargo of seasick and hungry Jamaican workers erupt with enough discontent to force white officials to seek Claude Barnett's intervention to placate black unrest.[59] Caribbean folk, as one federal administrator noted, appeared less "amenable and [accepting] of traditional local racial differentials" than American colored people.[60]

In response, federal labor officials sent West Indians south for the winter. Responding to promises from white growers that Jim Crow would leave West Indians "more closely controlled and looked after," the Department of Agriculture sent 75 percent of the wartime West Indian workforce to cut sugarcane, pick mangoes and snap beans, and harvest Florida citrus in Goulds, Dania, and other agricultural pockets dotting the old Seminole landscape.[61] But before migrants picked anything anywhere in Florida, they passed through Miami's Colored Town. To the estimation of immigration officials and growers, Miami's Central Negro District was supposed to serve as the site of informal "racial education" for workers awaiting immunizations, work assignments, or personal effects from the British Caribbean.[62] Some growers of exceptional means built tent cities for their workers near or on farm labor sites. "There would be no Cesar Chavez in the Sunshine State," explained one historian about the lack of labor organization among West Indian agricultural workers during this period.[63] And creating work camps far from urban areas served a broader strategy to keep migrant island workers docile. Several thousand West Indian migrants remained in Colored Town, however. They lived in a neighborhood that, by name and definition, was supposed to teach Jamaicans and Bahamians how to be "coloreds" in America. Black folk had other ideas.[64]

Bill Sawyer, a well-to-do American Negro, marched down the dusty, unpaved stretches of NW Second Avenue trailed by dozens of West Indian migrants in the fall of 1943. Sawyer had recently graduated from Fisk University and was the son of William Sawyer Sr., Miami's most highly reputed black physician and, after the recently deceased Dana Dorsey, its wealthiest Negro real estate investor. Bill had planned on following in his father's footsteps at Meharry Medical College, but his side job, at least during the harvest season, was to knock on door after door in black Miami in hopes of finding food and beds for his regiment of itinerant workers. Independent farmers and agricultural corporations employed well over four thousand Bahamians and Jamaicans in South Florida the last two years of the war. That made Sawyer's job of bed hunting as time consuming as it was financially rewarding.[65] "All day long, all night you would see me walking up and down the streets with crowds of people lined up behind me. I was . . . placing them in different places. . . . That's how I made so much money."[66] Immigration and Naturalization Services paid Sawyer to make sure workers' living conditions approached something close to standard—no mean task in Colored Town. Bill was also supposed to ensure that Caribbean colored people stayed off Miami Beach, out of Coral Gables, and far from other decidedly white spaces. "White people," he noted, "have always didn't want nothing to do with Negroes. So all these Negroes is coming in from Jamaica, from Nassau and different places in South America. I had to house them." But Sawyer, recognizing his importance in preserving the boundaries of racial apartheid, proved ever resourceful. He noted that he "had enough sense" to know that, if whites "gonna treat me like that, I made up my prices for doing this. . . . I told them this bill comes to $400 or $500, $600[;] well only half of that went to the [expenses] and the other half came to me because [the government] wasn't hardly giving me anything."[67]

While Sawyer was unique in his status and novel in his approach, his ability, as an American Negro, to take advantage of Colored Town's bumper crop of Caribbean workers was not uncommon. Pool halls, lounges, and shotgun shacks in the Central Negro District were places where American workers learned the details of Caribbean people's various contractual arrangements.[68] Across wartime South Florida, in fact, white employers began noticing that American Negroes had a striking familiarity with the labor contracts and accompanying protections afforded Caribbean blacks. US blacks, too, had committed the contracts to memory. Dozens of white employers, within and outside the defense industry, were soon forced to give black laundresses and stevedores wage increases and overtime protections similar to those outlined in West Indian work contracts. Some workers threatened increased absenteeism; others took even more days off once their pay improved to play *bolita* or meet with family and friends.[69]

New Apartheid

Southern Florida's coastal cities existed under threat of Nazi U-boat attack for only a short period of time—roughly a year, if that. Still, the anxiety and rumor wrought during the war made new forms of Jim Crow policing among the many updates the Magic City experienced. Miami's police chief Leslie Quigg warned the Miami City Commission that, in light of German submarines prowling off the Florida coast, "The war is not far from our front door." The police department, according to Quigg, needed six new submachine guns, lots of ammunition, "tear gas bombs, gas masks, etc." Nazis were not the only threat, it seemed. "Should we ever be called upon to quell a race riot, we should find ourselves unfairly handicapped by a lack of proper arms." "In fact," Quigg continued, "the knowledge that we are armed properly would go far toward eliminating the possibility of such riots." One unanimous city commission vote and eight hundred dollars later, Quigg got his arsenal.[70]

In addition to more weaponry, police officials helped reinstitute a work pass ordinance that had become popular on Miami Beach during the 1930s. The ordinance, which passed not just in Miami, but in nearby Hollywood and Fort Lauderdale as well, called for the creation of work pass cards bearing the photo, thumbprint, and address of any person working in the service, entertainment, and tourist sector. Caribbean agricultural workers got no such cards. The work pass program tracked the employment of nearly sixty thousand black and white Miamians during the 1940s, and the program itself lasted well into the 1960s. With the threat of Nazi invasion largely gone by 1943, the passes, in practice, functioned mostly as instruments for an evolving Jim Crow.[71]

Work passes fit nicely with existing protocols about "Negro curfews." As part of the same batch of negotiations the Colored Board of Trade made in the late 1910s, white officials helped initiate region-wide prohibitions against colored people being outside of designated black districts after certain hours. Municipal governments in Dade and Broward Counties systematically policed racial borders to be sure colored people were off "white" streets after select hours, usually sometime between 6:00 p.m. and 10:00 p.m. Black South Floridians who broke curfew could expect any combination of arrest, harassment, police questioning, or violence. Any white citizen immediately gained police power over any Negro caught on the wrong side of town after the appointed hour. "It was made known to us in no uncertain terms," recalled Joe Wheeler, a resident of Hollywood, that "you shouldn't . . . be caught in [the white part of the city] after dark. . . . That's the way it was. . . . We knew this."[72] Peggy McKinney recalled that, as an eighteen-year-old black laundress who worked at the Tides Hotel on Miami Beach, she always had to carry her work pass in case the police caught her outside of Colored Town after 10:00 p.m. "If you was stopped by the police, you had to show this card, that you were coming from work or whatever."[73]

The work passes and curfews functioned with other forms of discrimination to make people of diverse history, language, and culture into "coloreds."[74] Any dark-skinned tourists, unfamiliar with the laws, found themselves in danger of suffering white violence as well, unless they could quickly muster a foreign accent or some other kind of "permission." On the fly, members of the Pan-American League were repeatedly forced to designate special venues to entertain foreign travelers "because dark-skinned Latin American visitors have run afoul of Miami's Jim Crow . . . curfew."[75] Being "colored" meant, among other things, occupying "white" spaces for the purposes of work, and occupying "Negro" spaces for everything else. It also meant maintaining the racial integrity of the region's most lucrative consumable: the beach.[76]

The Nation Builders

Up and down Florida's Gold Coast, whites generally barred blacks from experiencing the Atlantic shore in anything other than a servile capacity.[77] "Negro maids," as reported by the *Chicago Defender*'s Miami correspondent,

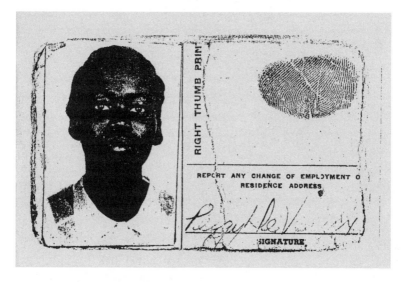

Figure 4.3. Peggy McKinney's identification card. (Courtesy of the Black Archives History and Research Foundation of South Florida Inc.)

"were permitted to carry their charges onto the public white beach and can do so on the exclusive hotel beaches, but the unwritten law is that they must not muddy the water by bathing in it."[78] If they wanted to go swimming, young Negro men and women had to hazard the crumbling edges and debris of rock pits filled with runoff. Or they ventured across the color line and risked white harassment to recreate among the manatees and water moccasins that frequented South Florida's inland waterways. Drowning deaths were common, as was the accompanying grief visited upon colored parents at the loss a son or daughter to a rock pit or snakebite.[79]

On the streets of Colored Town, a jumping nightlife and the general condition of Negro poverty carried different dangers. The same antiblack discrimination that kept colored people un- or underemployed ensured that many would continue to resort to gambling, prostitution, or theft as a means of blunting the edge of poverty and property-based racism.[80] Sometimes numbering two or three a week, murders in front of nightclubs could result from drunken disputes over illicit sex, *bolita* games, or other matters tied up with interpersonal conflict, gender power, and basic personhood.[81]

The strengthening of Miami's vice industries, *bolita* chief among them, seemed to exacerbate the social pressures that raw population increases brought to Miami's cramped Negro neighborhoods. During the 1920s, the dice games and small *bolita* outfits that had occasionally emerged in the alleyways of Colored Town had exploded to the point that, by the middle of the gainfully employed 1940s, crap games and numbers runners literally occupied more corners than streetlights in Colored Town. Religious leaders in Miami's Central Negro District, by the end of the decade, charged that "bolita operations . . . drain the Negro cash into the pockets of White operators and authorities," to the tune of "$4,000,000 per year."[82] This increase in vice, moreover, brought an increase in violence. The Federal Bureau of Investigation reported in 1942 that Miami led the nation in homicides, and that did not count the dozens of police killings that occurred in the Central Negro District.[83] Apart from violent incidents on Colored Town's streets, acts of domestic violence were common occurrences in the neighborhood. Men and women used everything from guns and knives to pots of boiling water as weapons in deadly homebound killings.[84] And many women about town, committed to not becoming victims of violence, frequently wore switchblades taped to their thighs or razors hidden in their hair.[85]

On matters of simple leisure, the personal and existential costs colored people bore under Jim Crow served as clear reminder that, for them, there was not one Miami, but two: Miami and Their-ami. "Their-ami," as one young woman pined in the pages of the *Crisis* in 1942, "is the 'ami' that the vacationist dreams about—miles and miles of beautiful Atlantic Beach . . . towering coconut and royal palms, majestic hotels and apartments." "Their-ami," she continued, "is the 'ami' I can only imagine and dream of."[86]

From the standpoint of Miami's black civic leadership, the life-and-death difference between Miami and "Their-ami" was fundamentally about an unresponsive and uncaring state. Police, at street level, ran gambling operations in Colored Town for white mobsters holed up in hotels across town and as far off as Havana.[87] The Miami City Commission repeatedly ignored pleas for Negro parkland and better zoning enforcement. There was also the problem of white paternalism in the judiciary. "White judges," explained the minister and storeowner John Culmer, "are inclined toward leniency because they feel Negroes are irresponsible." "I believe," Culmer continued, "our people have taken advantage of that."[88] "Frankly, I was a little more lenient," admitted Cecil Curry, a white municipal judge. He added, "You are not going to stop [black Miamians] from fighting, craps, cards, and the like. . . . I took into consideration that they were uneducated and have to shift for themselves from a very early age."[89] Curry's leniency included sentencing anyone convicted of killing a black person to only twelve months in the county jail. By contrast, if a Negro even attempted to rob a white man, the mandatory sentence was five years in the state prison.[90]

What was the value of Negro life in an international city? Kelsey Pharr, as an undertaker, had heard the wailing of grief-stricken families and had seen firsthand how violent and preventable deaths tore at the social fabric of Miami's Central Negro District. He told *Atlanta Daily World* reporters that he could hear young colored men threaten each other outside his office window, saying, "I can kill you and get out for $100." "Decent people of the community," Pharr lamented, "fear for their lives."[91] A white cop chased a black suspect into Pharr's own backyard, beating him nearly to death.[92] Kelsey witnessed the whole thing. Other black leaders, however, had no trouble arguing for even greater violence against black people. "Examples should be made," remarked the head of Miami's largest black Baptist church. "There should be some hangings or electrocutions, or whatever they do," he continued. "Life is too cheap in our section of the city."[93]

There was no Pan-American League or airline executive pleading publicly for the residents of Colored Town. Instead, as in previous decades, advocacy work on behalf of black people continued to flow primarily through entrepreneurial and civic organizations run by black property owners. For a community of over forty thousand, no one organization could bring all of "the Negro's" issues to white elites' negotiating table. John Culmer, Kelsey Pharr, and other Negro leaders from Miami's frontier years continued to be persuasive and important voices, until the Colored Board of Trade fizzled out in the 1930s. Many of its members, like Dana Dorsey, had died or had grown weary through their years of fighting for Negro civil rights and property rights. "I've been in so darned many tight places here over 25 years," Pharr confided to Claude Barnett in 1939, "that I'm inclined to 'let George do it,' in order that I may eventually get out of here alive."[94] Pharr and his contemporaries cultivated, and in some cases hotly debated, a newer crop of black businesspeople. These included the dentist Ira Davis; the attorney Lawson Thomas; the radical mortician and newspaper publisher Sam Solomon; the Reverend Edward Graham; and Annie Coleman, a volunteer nurse and minster's wife. Miami's second generation of "Race Men and Women" arrived during the Great Depression, and, like their predecessors, they used their new organizations to push for race reforms primarily through the discourse of respectability, entrepreneurship, and taxpayers' rights.

Groups like Sam Solomon's Citizens' Service League, Ira Davis's Adelphia Club, and Coleman's Friendship Garden and Civic Club found different pressure points at which to poke and prod concessions from white officials. Through them, Pan-Americanism in Miami became two things at once. It was state building of the kind on display in decolonizing republics abroad, and it offered yet another expression of a broader, Jim Crow governing approach that one historian called "separate-but-equal liberalism," also known as "equalization."[95] On the promise of making "separate" more equal, the same southern politicians driving Pan-American development directed millions in government dollars to aid private enterprises in segregationist economy building, improving everything from black hospitals to schools. Equalization was perhaps best articulated by George Smathers during his successful 1950 Senate campaign against ardent New Dealer Claude Pepper. Before a Saint Petersburg, Florida, audience, Smathers promised that he would continue to provide "better homes, enlarged schools and improved health facilities . . . to our negro citizens" without compromising "the progress we have made on a local basis to improve racial relations."[96] Equalization generally remained an issue-by-issue, fight-by-fight proposition, however.

Indeed, the attempt to "get things done" at the local level offers direct contradiction to binary depictions that cast Caribbean politics as predominantly militant and American Negro politics as primarily accommodationist and obsequious. Negro efforts at equalization, for one, could include disruptive direct action tactics.[97] At the very same time, propertied blacks from the Caribbean, such as John Culmer and Coconut Grove's Ebenezer Stirrup, were among those most stridently opposed to stepping outside established channels of Jim Crow negotiation. The difference was not one of culture. It was one of property. And that included, as in the case of Caribbean migrants, the bundle of rights and entitlements that accompanied labor contracts and British subjecthood in the United States. The point of equalization movements was to strengthen the contractual bond—writ large—between American Negroes and their government by exhibiting black people as having held up "the Negro" side of the bargain.[98]

Here again, the bond between property and politics was hardly abstract. Rather, that bond hardened and became even more discernible in the 1940s, as America's class of black professionals began expanding, as local avenues to political power began opening, and as the rhetoric for American democracy became increasingly lofty in the midst of World War II.[99] Particularly after the gradual abolition of the poll tax and the outlawing of white political primaries in 1944, the urban black vote slowly grew, and with it Negro businessmen, clubwomen, and ministers across the South fought racial exclusion in the labor and consumer marketplace. Turning exclusion into segregation, they set about the hard political work of pursuing "colored only" seating and bathrooms built into stadiums, "colored only" swimming areas, the appointment of "Negro police," and other markers of (separate) equality.[100]

In Miami, older, propertied black professionals bargained with white officials for improved access to public services, and when that failed, they bankrolled younger Negroes, without property, to carry out activism on the streets. The Adelphia Club, for example, kept two full-time community organizers on payroll. If rebuffed during negotiations with the city's political elites, the group promised any obstructing white politicians that it would swing the Negro bloc vote toward the club's chosen candidate during important elections. In reality, no group could claim such singular power, given the diversity of Miami's black cultural tapestry—islanders and sharecroppers' kids, local-born business owners and Bahamian domestics. That, however, was hardly the point, as long as whites outside of Colored Town believed that the Adelphia Club spoke for "the Negro." The city's most influential black minister, John Culmer; arguably its most powerful Negro labor organizer, Charles Lockhart; black Miami's most renowned attorney, Lawson Thomas; and several colored real estate brokers and professional leaders were members of the Adelphia Club, and met every week to help set "the Negro's" political agenda.[101]

The group's head, Ira Davis, was an especially well connected dentist who worked for years as a political operative for George Smathers. A forty-year-old World War I veteran, Davis would trade dirt on Smathers's political enemies in exchange for favors.[102] Smathers, in return, would talk up Davis and other Adelphia Club members among his white colleagues and even quote them on the stump if they took "favorable" positions on preserving southern localism and the like.[103] Referring to the Adelphia Club, staffers for Senator Claude Pepper remarked in 1949, "In [Miami's] Negro community, a group of businessmen have perfected . . . political organization."[104] Pepper would learn this all too well, as information from Davis allegedly helped Smathers red-bait Pepper into his most humiliating political defeat, and the loss of his US Senate seat, in 1950.[105] Similarly clandestine actions helped modify Miami's engagement with the Atlantic world.

A Black Atlantic

In 1940, Miami's activist entrepreneurs ramped up the push for a public Negro beach on the Atlantic Ocean. Representing a handful of new organizations, Sam Solomon, Lawson Thomas, and others claimed they were not interested in integrating white beaches per se. Rather, they merely wanted access to the parks, oceanfront, and leisure amenities for which they, as taxpayers, had already paid.[106] This argument for taxpayer rights provided the foundation for Jim Crow's evolving racial contract. When city officials continued to delay, black organizers threatened white South Florida with the prospect of racially integrated beaches.[107] Two young colored women and five men, respectable and unpropertied, descended on Baker's Haulover, the region's most popular white beach, and initiated a "wade-in." Like the more famous sit-ins to come, this premeditated act served as the final stage of a meticulous plan to force whites to defend segregation in the courts. A local union representative for colored longshoremen, named Judge Henderson, called the county sheriff, Dade County commissioners, and, most important for publicity purposes, the *Miami Herald*. Lawson Thomas, a member of the Adelphia Club and one of only two black lawyers in Miami at the time, followed the seven black protesters to the beach with five hundred dollars in his pocket. This was bail money from an NAACP fund. The point was to get arrested.[108]

There would be no arrests that day. Despite the countless threats and acts of physical violence that had kept Negroes off the beach for nearly fifty years, no one had gone to the trouble of writing a segregation statute that actually banned colored people from South Florida's beaches. The simple assertion of segregation that appeared in the 1921 city charter, as unconstitutional as it was, only applied to the location of black and white homes and businesses. In the face of direct legal challenge, all that could be mustered by the million-dollar cities of Miami and Miami Beach, according to eyewitnesses, was a blustering deputy yelling, "You niggers come out of the water!" When the protestors finally did come out, they did so with guarantees that Dade County would provide a safe swimming space for colored people to gather and picnic.[109]

To placate black demands, city officials gave colored people access to an island three miles from the Miami mainland called Virginia Key. As early as 1918, white officials allowed a "Negro Dancing Pavilion" on the key as part of the city's early attempts at Jim Crow. But since the island was thick with mosquitoes and sand flies and beset by terrible riptides, few used it for swimming. Given its remote location, the island was an out-of-the-way place. As part of the broader geography of black leisure in America, it sequestered the leisure demands of Miami's Progressive Era black population, but proved utterly impractical without some serious investment.[110] That investment came with World War II, when the US Army took over Virginia Key for the purpose of drilling Negro troops, conducting demolitions exercises, and carrying out other training programs best done far from Miami's locals. At the end of major combat operations, the army imposed harsh "public use" restrictions on the island. Miami City and Dade County commissions found themselves saddled with a property so heavily regulated that they could neither sell real estate on it nor generate revenue from it. It made sense simply to give it to the Negroes.[111] White officials notified the black

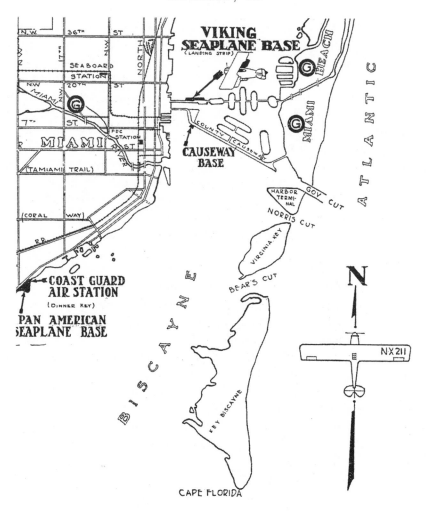

Figure 4.4. Virginia Key and the surrounding area. (Courtesy of the Charles W. Tebeau Library, Historical Museum of Southern Florida.)

community of their decision through Miami's Negro entrepreneurs. William Sawyer's daughter, Gwendolyn, remembered, "A group of well-intentioned, white citizens came over to daddy's with the astonishing information that we were going to be allowed to use Virginia Key for bathing in the surf. The only catch was there was not [a] way to get to it."[112] Sawyer and a few of his colleagues organized a ferry.

The beach officially opened on 1 August 1945, to almost universal praise. To black leaders, Virginia Key Beach was evidence of their growing political power. The city even hired security guards to keep whites out. For West Indian travelers, the beach perhaps offered a more material connection between their lives in Miami and their memories of home. The "colored only" beach, moreover, kept blacks sequestered and helped prevent what the white owner of the "whites only" Urmey Hotel called "a blight on the entire Gold Coast."[113] The mosquitoes, sand flies, and seaweed were still, at times, overwhelming. The riptides remained treacherous. But these features did not dissuade more than two thousand colored people from packing up and picnicking on Virginia Key on any given Sunday. Slightly lower numbers visited throughout the week, and as many as fifteen thousand came to enjoy sunrise services on Easter Sunday.[114]

Black people from as far afield as Baltimore, New York, and Monrovia, Liberia, came to experience Miami's black Atlantic. The urban North, South, and global South sent some three hundred thousand nonwhite vacationers to Florida every year in the early 1950s, and Virginia Key Beach was among their favorite destinations.[115] According to the recollections of Leah Sands, who remembers traveling to the beach as a child after church, "the Key" was a place where Bahamian and American heritage mixed in the form of food, song, and dance. Black dollars—local, national, and international— helped fund a parking lot for over twelve hundred cars, and build a carousel and a miniature railroad for children. It built cabanas and installed cold-water drinking fountains. Maids and laundresses, who poured their sweat equity into making white Miami shine, finally had a safe place to bring their kids. As Joyce Dent recalled, "They had entertainment for the kids and I was happy to see [my mom] happy, for a change. . . . Nobody ever told me that the other beaches were restricted," Dent continued. "I just thought that's where we went, anyway."[116]

Colored Nation, Negro State

The appointment of black police officers was a trickier business, for here Negroes were asking whites to compromise their monopoly on state violence. Miami officials tried repeatedly to meet the demands for black policemen, going back to the turn of the century.[117] But each time, white residents organized against the attempt. Black Miamians, with their eyes on the globe, made their request for colored police by noting the Magic City's visibility on the world stage, and by drawing explicit parallels between Miami's racial climate and empires and colonial arrangements elsewhere. The Adelphia Club's Lawson Thomas pointed out, for instance, that "the darker people of the world [watch] us . . . [with] Hitler and Russia throwing their fingers at our faults. They are throwing a scorching light on the Negro in America."[118]

Figure 4.5. Mounted Negro patrolmen, ca. 1945. (Courtesy of the Black Archives History and Research Foundation of South Florida Inc.)

Like the liberalism to come, black nation building often required shaming whites into action, and giving American Negroes access to the benevolent and putative power of the state.

White people's only condition was that Negroes use that power solely on themselves. When city officials appointed the city's first five black cops on 1 September 1944, they did so using an emergency war provision for military police. The men also trained in secret. Only American citizens could be officers, and the city relied on Ira Davis to screen each candidate personally. Even more crucial, white city officials prohibited Negro police from ever arresting whites who wandered into Colored Town. Instead, black law enforcement had to detain white offenders and call in the incident so that white officers could formally take the accused into custody. Colored cops could also not be called "police officers"; that, too, was a privilege reserved for whites. Instead, their official title was "patrolmen," a military designation reflecting their status as "war emergency" workers. Regardless of their second-rank title, though, Negro patrolmen enjoyed the same twelve-hour shifts as white officers, and the same pay. Black officers also wore badges and could carry guns. Armed colored people had consistently responded to threats against their community in previous years. Now it was legal.[119]

On the day the first five patrolmen took their oath, hundreds of children, men, and women—foreign and American born—gathered to see the event. As if following the *Junkanoo* procession, a crowed marched NW Second Avenue, led by the new black patrolmen as they walked their first beat. The visible reality of respectable Negroes in uniform seemed to place black Miami, in the words of one local businesswoman, "on the threshold of a new era." One young onlooker who attended the swearing-in ceremony remembered, "They were like our saviors."[120]

It soon became evident that these "saviors," like white policemen, were not above illegal search and seizure or a little excessive force.[121] Nor did every Negro in Miami welcome or even respect colored patrolmen's newly bestowed authority.[122] Stop and frisks were standard. And it was not uncommon for a traffic stop or a moment of questioning between black patrolmen and a citizen to turn into some form of physical violence.[123] Edward Kimble recalled that, for his first five days on the beat, his authority came not from his badge, but from his fists. Alleged lawbreakers, he intimated, "wouldn't take the idea [that] you could arrest them like white cops. . . . Just ask for an ID and you'd have to fight. . . . I was young and strong, and I'd bust your ass—they found out in a hurry."[124]

In cities as varied as Louisville, Baltimore, and Charlotte, blacks took strong "law-and-order" positions to gain black police officers, and black businessmen and businesswomen, in every one of those cities, led this effort.[125] Even as antivice campaigns North and South targeted colored people's nightclubs and other sites of "race mixing," many black Americans appropriated these campaigns to articulate and partially achieve their own visions of American citizenship.[126] More specifically, the discourse of crime prevention offered black entrepreneurs—doubling as race reformers—an important vocabulary about morality and the integrity of property, one that helped them circumvent whites' personal feelings about black people and secure important alliances with white business interests, politicians, and power brokers. To talk about black criminality, rather than white supremacy, was to demonstrate your "reasonableness" as a Negro leader. It was a way into accessing other state powers in the name of reform.

Luckily, perhaps, for Miami's black business elites, the experiment of using black patrolmen worked better than many expected. Negro law enforcement, in its first year, made over four thousand arrests, generated over fifty-six thousand dollars in fines, and helped lower the violent crime rate in Colored Town by almost 50 percent. Four years later, the number of black officers increased from five to twenty. The number of violent crimes held flat and juvenile delinquency declined by some 60 percent.[127] Black patrolmen had become so effective that, just two years after their arrival, city attorneys noticed "an organized campaign on the part of *bolita* operators to dispense with the Negro police force."[128] Perversely, Lawson Thomas also credited black-on-black police brutality as facilitating civic-mindedness among Negroes. "Today we find that Negroes are more willing to complain about any infraction of their rights if Negro officers take advantage of their position. Before they were afraid."[129]

Six years after appointing black police, city officials appointed Thomas to the bench, making him the first Negro since Reconstruction to serve as a judge in a southern state. Thomas, like black patrolmen, was subjected to several limitations on his authority. City officials denied him the power to hear cases involving whites and initially made him convene court without an actual bench and without wearing robes. Thomas could only try cases involving misdemeanor offenses or violations of municipal ordinances. Any felonies committed in the Central Negro District remained beyond his jurisdiction. These limitations, in the eyes of some, made Thomas only "half a judge," or in the words of one northern newspaper, "Judge Jim Crow."[130] Still, Thomas appreciated his new post as "a tool [that] gives us a measure of self-government within the bounds of segregation."[131]

Greater "self-government" in America, as in various colonies and, later, postcolonies abroad, meant expanding the black ownership class's authority over "the Negro Race," and not just in a vague moral or aesthetic sense. Indeed, in very material terms, Lawson Thomas became the legal arm of a mostly American black leadership class who sought to tether their own aims to postwar reform movements in South Florida. Integral to Greater Miami's popularity and growth through the city's Depression years, racial terrorism, vice, burlesque shows, and gay entertainment came under direct fire once international business picked up and once the military began dumping millions in "clean" capital into Greater Miami's hotels and travel infrastructure.[132] No longer the "wide-open town" of its youth, Miami, in booster accounts, was supposed to offer moral, year-round living.[133] The "New Miami" included everything from campaigns against gambling and strip joints, to prohibitions against the distribution of "lewd and indecent literature," crackdowns on white supremacist hate groups, and raids against any establishment offering homosexual entertainment.[134] The local press, powerful white hotel owners, and other reputable entrepreneurs looked the other way as detectives and beat cops ramped up urban "reform" with crackdowns on suspected homosexuals, Ku Klux Klan members, and the poor.[135] Cleaning up their particular corner of Pan-America, Negro patrolmen rounded up "female impersonators," women engaged in "unnatural relationships," and black men discovered in "compromising positions." The officers brought these "offenders" before Judge Thomas to share the Negro court's docket with petty thugs and *bolita* peddlers.[136]

The Mary Elizabeth

Young Bill Sawyer—our seasonal real estate broker for Immigration and Naturalization Services—would never become a doctor. As the Sawyer family returned from visiting relatives in West Palm Beach, their car was blindsided and thrown on its roof. Bill, only six years old at the time, suffered horrible head injuries, and William, himself hurt, performed roadside surgery on his son. "He operated on me right on the highway." White passersby eventually came to assist.[137] The operation likely saved Bill's life, and he spent a year in a body cast. Complications over subsequent years included a degenerative eye condition that eventually forced the younger Sawyer to leave Meharry and pursue a business degree at Northwestern University. Upon returning to Miami, Bill followed his father into the world of real estate development and hospitality.[138]

William Sr.'s chief real estate achievement, as of the mid-1940s, was the Mary Elizabeth Hotel. Similar in size to many of the hotels on Miami Beach and widely considered to be the finest black-owned hotel in the southeastern United States, the Mary Elizabeth was an uncharacteristically expensive and ambitious Negro enterprise. In 1921, Sawyer's three-story hotel cost forty thousand dollars to build. It boasted eight storerooms on the first floor and twenty-two guest rooms on floors two and three. In the words of one reporter, the hotel's concrete frame made the Mary Elizabeth, without question, "the best construction yet in that part of the city." Following the wartime migration of black troops, Caribbean workers, and the opening of Virginia Key Beach, the Mary Elizabeth enjoyed a string of prosperous years that allowed Sawyer to add sixty new rooms, all with private baths, and a brand-new roof garden. Once William, in 1949, put his thirty-year-old son in complete charge of the operation, it was left to Bill to update, expand, and introduce the Mary Elizabeth to a younger, hipper postwar clientele.[139]

The Mary Elizabeth served as an important link in a chain of leisure and politics that ran from America's great urban centers into the tropics and back again. Like their activist counterparts, high-society Negroes from Atlanta, Chicago, and other American cities stayed over at the Mary Elizabeth on their way to Haiti, Cuba, and elsewhere in the Caribbean. When wealthy white northerners came to Miami to vacation, their black servants, who were often well educated, would also stay at the Sawyer family's increasingly popular accommodations. Paul Silverthorne, a white designer who built his renown crafting the lounges at the "whites only" Belmar, Albion, and

Figure 4.6. The Mary Elizabeth, at the corner of NW Seventh Street and NW Second Avenue, 1953. (Courtesy of the Black Archives History and Research Foundation of South Florida Inc.)

Sherry Frontenac hotels, also worked as the interior designer for the Mary Elizabeth's famous "Zebra Lounge." "Oh geez," he recalled, "the lines and the screaming, the fights. People were fighting to get in. . . . It was a privilege to be there." The Sawyers paid Silverthorne thousands of dollars, always in hundred-dollar bills, to outbid wealthy whites seeking the services of the city's hottest designer. "This was the best contract I ever had," Silverthorne admitted. "The best cash I ever made in my life."[140]

The hotel's barbershop was Cuban run and quite popular with a number of that country's migrants and travelers during the late 1940s and early 1950s. Remembered one Colored Town resident who rented a room to Cuba's nascent revolutionaries, "Every year when they would have these uprisings in Cuba, these Cubans would come over and they . . . stayed a while." Discussing every topic from baseball to Karl Marx, young Cuban men would converse in the Mary Elizabeth's barber chairs by day and grace the hotel's dance floors by night. One young, particularly articulate Cuban named Fidel Castro was, in fact, a fixture at the Mary Elizabeth. "Castro used to be there all the time," Bill Sawyer recalled. Even through his degenerating sight, Sawyer could recall of Castro, "He had a beautiful sister." Juanita Castro, like

Figure 4.7. The Zebra Lounge, Mary Elizabeth Hotel, 1950. (From John A. Stuart and Paul Silverthorne, "Pragmatism Meets Exoticism: An Interview with Paul Silverthorne," Florida theme issue, *Journal of Decorative and Propaganda Arts* 23 [1998]: 381.)

many white Cubans meeting across town with Miami's chamber of commerce, would part ways with her brother over politics and eventually work for the Central Intelligence Agency. Both brother and sister, however, knew the Mary Elizabeth as a place that drew Puerto Ricans and Cubans to watch the retirement announcement of boxing champion Joe Louis, and, in 1950, the Miss Latin America beauty pageant.[141]

In addition to Cubans and other islanders, white locals and tourists frequented the Zebra Lounge and many of Colored Town's more popular clubs. Ironically, much of the neighborhood's popularity had to do with the zoning laws that made "whites only" Miami Beach such an exclusive city. Whereas white hotels on the beach had to stop selling alcohol at 1:00 a.m., city of Miami officials allowed black tavern owners to continue selling booze until 5:00 in the morning. The Central Negro District, as a result, enjoyed a host of "after-hours" white business. "My club was packed," Bill Sawyer recalled, "jammed [with] . . . nothing but white people. . . . White and Colored would be in there all night long and all day long." Racial custom also required that all the topflight Negro talent that played on Miami Beach had to travel back to Colored Town once their sets were over. "They couldn't stay on the Beach," Silverthorne later explained, "because segregation wouldn't allow them." The combination of racist mores and city zoning law made Colored Town's nightspots hotly integrated into the wee hours.[142]

Conclusion

I came back to Miami from Jamaica in need of American doctors and American food.[143]

—Ramona Lowe, journalist, 1948

Something about Miami was indeed American—and Caribbean. The *Junka-noo* parade and other markers of Caribbean and black American congress in Colored Town never made it onto the travel pages of the *New York Times* or into the advertisements of Pan American Airways. And, yet, those in the know learned quickly that many of the so-called tropical spaces and exotic cultural trappings that comprised the average "Pan-American" depiction of Greater Miami lay beyond the borders of the region's white hotels and bars. As postwar prosperity brought more tourists to South Florida, it became increasingly known, mostly through word of mouth, that if a bona fide "Caribbean" or even "southern" culture existed at all in South Florida, it was to be found in and around Colored Town. White visitors would jam Miami's black churches to enjoy colored folk's choirs.[144] And after 1947, as many as eighteen thousand white people would pack the Orange Bowl to watch Miami's annual Negro college bowl game—the Orange Blossom Classic.[145] As was customary, white travelers also came to Colored Town to participate in more private activities behind closed doors. In a case that made national headlines, two white women from New York, seen with a black male desk clerk and a musician at the Mary Elizabeth Hotel, were arrested, fined $250, and sentenced to thirty days in jail. Their punishment came down even though, as papers reported, "there was no evidence of the improper conduct [prostitution] for which they were charged."[146] Black patrolmen held them, nonetheless. White police officers made the arrest.

The wartime and postwar United States stirred colored people into an already swirling black Atlantic. While fresh boatloads of Jamaicans landed in southern port cities during the 1940s, workers from Barbados wound up conscripted to US plantations and bases in Trinidad. England's "coloured clubs" saw white Londoners, black Britons, and West Indians having to make room for Negro American troops looking to share the dance floor.[147]

Greater Miami, as at the turn of the century, remained part of this perpetual world in motion. And like the other locales, the city itself—in its violence and possibilities—provided a site at which to negotiate white supremacy's rules.

As part of that negotiation, South Florida's residents and business leaders nurtured notions of collective ownership. "'Colored Only,' meant something," Dorothy Graham, a longtime Miami resident, explained. "It was yours."[148] The process by which "colored only" came to mean something requires understanding how US-born black people in Miami asserted "America," if only to claim rights from it. It also requires appreciating how colored people attempted to create space for racial progress in Pan-American Miami by working through established political channels, on behalf of taxpayer rights, and in deference to the designs of property owners and the pragmatism of the color line. Regardless of black or white American assertions, South Florida remained a land with a stubbornly Caribbean geography and culture. Yet it would not need the development of nonwhite tourism, new networks of West Indian labor migration, or international trade during and after World War II to ensure that the meaning of land would continue to be up for grabs. Homeowners, landlords, and the racial complexities of postwar real estate did that well enough on their own.

CHAPTER FIVE

Knocking on the Door

The police arrested Felton and Willie Mae Coleman for allegedly mishandling their garbage.[1] The Colemans, a Negro couple, had recently relocated from a shack in Coconut Grove to the emergent Miami suburb of Brownsville when Dade County sheriff's deputies, in the fall of 1945, knocked on their door. After taking both husband and wife into custody, officers also arrested Jack and Claudia Wilson, a second colored couple who lived nearby, for the same offense. The arrests came as the latest in a string of harassments the families suffered at the hands of white neighbors and Dade County officials. In the wake of black in-migration, Brownsville became the site of repeated cross burnings, Klan marches, and other threats of white terrorism.[2] County authorities, at the behest of all ninety-nine of the neighborhood's white families, also withheld building permits and sparingly collected black families' trash.[3] When that failed to repel colored buyers, Dade's county commission, in August 1945, decided to zone Brownsville as a "whites only" community. "People of the white race," the commission decreed, "should not be permitted to encroach upon the areas which have been designated for Negro occupancy, nor should Negro occupancy be extended into areas heretofore designated for White occupancy."[4] In doing nothing, the Wilsons and Colemans were suddenly in violation of the law. And their trash was piling up.

Nearly thirty years had passed since the US Supreme Court had deemed racial zoning unconstitutional. That ruling had not stopped the city of Miami in 1921 and countless other local governments across the South from simply asserting "mutual segregation" ordinances as part of their broad powers to ensure the "public good." During the 1930s and 1940s, most of these same local governments had taken advantage of massive federal infrastructure projects. The hand of the New Deal provided jobs by the thousands and poured concrete by the millions of tons, transforming the South and indeed the hemisphere.[5] Dade County commissioners, as they had at Liberty Square and Edison Courts, used their slice of federal funds to erect a cement wall between Brownsville's white and Negro sections. As a none-too-subtle confirmation of the wall's purpose and inspiration, they painted a broad "red line" streaking the length of the barrier.[6] In Brownsville's wall, the redlining "Security Maps" of New Deal housing agencies took vivid, concrete form. The wall also buttressed earlier practices within local government that helped keep Brownsville white. Well into the 1940s, if black people owned land in Brownsville, white staffers at Miami's building permit office made sure Negroes never built dwellings on it.[7] Asserting racial zoning anew with aid from Washington made local practice federal practice. And it exhibited the degree to which whites in Greater Miami understood land segregation as a centerpiece and core value of American liberalism.

The true source of Brownsville's race trouble, many believed, was a white real estate developer named Wesley Garrison. In 1943, Garrison had begun moving through the area buying up empty tracts of land and purchasing houses from white residents. He combined certain pieces of property and subdivided others.[8] Through his various investment companies, Garrison financed mortgages for colored folk living around Miami, and moved them into Brownsville. In addition to the Wilsons and Colemans, Garrison sold to a Puerto Rican minister, Bruce Torres, and family. The Torres clan, though fairer skinned, was equally viewed by whites as part of Brownsville's downward turn. The Torres kids attended the colored-only Dorsey High School, named after the late Dana Dorsey, Miami's most renowned black real estate developer during the Progressive Era and one of Garrison's early business partners.[9] Like their black neighbors, the Torres family suffered cross burnings on their lawn and several nights of white terrorism.[10] They, too, thanks to Garrison and the whites of Brownsville, lived as colored people.[11]

Garrison's real estate practices fit the description of those derisively called "blockbusters." However, unlike the image of the scheming realtor who disappears once money changes hands, Garrison did not abandon his buyers to white harassment and unlawful arrest. He, instead, bailed the Coleman and Wilson couples out of jail, and he helped secure their attorney, E. F. P. Brigham, widely considered one of the most savvy real estate attorneys in the state of Florida. "It is understood," reported the Miami correspondent for the *Pittsburgh Courier*, "that Mr. Garrison has spent huge sums fighting local restrictive laws."[12] Garrison, who had been the chairman of the Republican Party in Dade County and a landlord on Miami Beach, called in his white connections to advance his case through the courts and the press.[13]

Several of Garrison's fellow white landlords threw money at the cause. Garrison had also been known as something of a political instigator when it came to his dealings with white segregationists. During an early hearing on the case, he nearly came to blows outside the courtroom with one of Dade County's white attorneys.[14]

In their joint effort to fight unlawful racial zoning, both the developer and his clients benefited from older notions of black property rights. Over the years, Garrison had developed strong relationships with several black civic leaders, most of whom held on to their status as "Lincoln Republicans" through the age of Franklin D. Roosevelt.[15] One of his friends was, in fact, Lawson Thomas, Miami's most respected black attorney. Only years from becoming Miami's first black judge, Thomas demonstrated the deep memory of black property rights discourse by filing an amicus brief invoking the Civil Rights Act of 1866. "All citizens of the United States," read the act's most quoted passage, "shall have the same right, in every State and Territory, as is enjoyed by white citizens thereof to inherit, purchase, lease, sell, hold, and convey real and personal property."[16] It was a passage black people would cite again and again in their pursuit of property rights over the course of the twentieth century.[17] Miami's best-known black activist, Sam Solomon, also a friend of Garrison's, rallied support for the colored residents of Brownsville.[18] A small group of black landlords, the Negro Property Owners League, added their voice to the chorus.[19] Undoubtedly, civil rights, for the colored parties involved, was synonymous with property rights. Yet prior to Garrison's involvement, according to research conducted by the National Urban League, "Negroes have heretofore felt it unwise to violate local custom."[20] As a *white* real estate developer and landlord, Wesley Garrison enjoyed a special kind of authority to orchestrate an interracial coalition and fight on behalf of the Wilsons and Colemans, and to do so in the name of "birthright" and their "constitutional privilege of pursuing happiness by hard work and saving [their] money and purchasing a home."[21] Garrison et al. defended Brownsville's colored homeowners all the way to the Florida State Supreme Court, which, in 1946, deemed Dade County's racial zoning ordinance a violation of the Fourteenth Amendment.[22] By the time of the ruling, the whites of Brownsville had already begun moving out.

Much about American liberalism was decided, quite literally, on the doorsteps of black people. In the immediately postwar period, as occurred during the first color line debates of the 1910s, South Florida's residents fought bitter struggles over tangled questions of housing, "the Negro problem," and

the uses and abuses of government land policy. Conflicts between white homeowners and white real estate developers, in particular, continued to revolve
around the economic pressures that white tenants and white property owners faced, even in an economy built on the marginalization and exploitation
of "the Negro." Through the person and property of colored people, white
Americans acted out their respective senses of entitlement, their racial ideas
about property rights, and their contradictory appropriations of state power
in defense of those rights. Not infrequently, white Americans confronted one
another over issues where colored people played no immediate role (such
as when white tenants and their landlords debated the merits of rent control after World War II). But even in those moments, because of America's
economic and social dependence on apartheid in real estate, conflicts *within*
Jim Crow's white world remained as racially inflected as any fight over, say,
restrictive covenants or "race walls."[23]

Much of what was at issue was how white Americans could reconcile two
foundational, if competing, tenets of American democracy—white popular
sovereignty and property rights. In most white people's estimations of effective liberalism, it was government's job to preserve what was, in effect, the
ideological foundation of lynch law—namely, that white Americans, not
the state, were sovereign.[24] Real estate served, for many, as one expression
of that sovereignty; a white man's home, after all, was supposed to be his
castle.[25] At the very same time, the ideas about property rights upon which
white power stood—ideas that continued to hold a privileged position in
American culture and law—seemed increasingly bound, by the 1940s, to
emergent discourses and interracial understandings of *black* civil rights. As
in the case of Wesley Garrison and his black clients, a growing movement
to make the state defend the rights of black Americans coalesced with an
increasingly organized group of white real estate developers, landlords, and,
occasionally, even white homeowners. Interracial alliances for housing reform ran up against a similarly organized movement of white property owners looking for the state to defend their rights to exclude or contain black
people.[26] Federal, state, and local politicians caught at the center of these
struggles saw it as their responsibility to ensure economic growth and racial
tranquility while preserving America's "separate but equal" society. For both
white citizens and those in a position to govern, the riddle of postwar liberalism was how best to square expanding state powers while ensuring that
white Americans would still accept government's legitimacy.

Part of the solution to this problem was infrastructure. What one historian described as the state's "infrastructural power" included decentral-
ized and discreet government authority to draft and enforce land law, build

roads, provide government services, and carry out other largely overlooked or seemingly benign expressions of state largess. In matters of housing, infrastructural power included everything from guaranteed mortgages from the Federal Housing Administration to rent control to public housing, slum clearance, and other uses of eminent domain.[27] Infrastructural power was what colored people were after when they assumed control over tenant selection at the Liberty Square housing project, when they pushed for black patrolmen, or when they called in vain, in 1915, for Miami city officials to expropriate white homes for the sake of "mutual segregation." These and similar efforts would be ongoing in the 1940s. Even before the end of World War II, it remained clear that infrastructural power would mostly protect and extend the reach and longevity of white power. Moreover, in a postwar period in which the United States would assume its role as democracy's defender around the world, infrastructural power over real estate, in particular, proved instrumental to maintaining the racial peace, to holding the color line, and to monitoring South Florida's, and indeed America's, economic growth.

The fact of white supremacy's evolution was not lost on black folk. Burning crosses illuminating dark lawns or hooded white men marching down the street could be frightful sights. Still, for many, one of the most terrifying sounds in the postwar, Jim Crow South was an unexpected rapping at one's front door. It might not be a lynch mob, as it easily could have been during Miami's frontier era. But a knock on the front door could be the police coming to serve a warrant for "permit violations" or officers and city officials there to carry out an eviction with a writ of possession. Just as surely, it could be the landlord or a property manager coming to collect or raise your rent. White supremacy's more ancient expressions were never far away, of course. White violence often preceded *and* precipitated state action, and it was the foreseeable consequence of state inaction.[28] There was nevertheless an increasing professionalism to white racism in the 1940s—an expanding infrastructure—that changed the terms of black protest and the face of South Florida.

The Price of War

During South Florida's war years, the military conversion of the beachfront put a serious squeeze on accommodations for tourists and tenants. The US Army commandeered over 100 apartment houses and 250 Miami Beach hotels, nearly 75 percent of all the hotels in the city. Across Biscayne Bay, on the Miami mainland, military officials repurposed meeting halls, metal shops, and every manner of rental or commercial real estate. Even the prestigious

Biltmore Hotel, a Coral Gables establishment that cost ten million dollars to build in 1926, became the region's Veterans Hospital. Taking advantage of the tightened housing market, many hoteliers and rooming house owners in Greater Miami increased already steep boarding prices from fourteen dollars to forty dollars per night. Some seasonal apartments even went for the outrageous sum of thirteen hundred dollars per month. In nearby Fort Lauderdale, winter housing options had gotten so tight that travelers took to renting couches in people's living rooms.[29]

The gouging that immediately followed militarization made South Florida, in 1943, one of over six hundred regions in the country to come under regulation by the Office of Price Administration (OPA).[30] Established in 1941, the OPA was supposed to stave off inflation that might have followed near full employment and increased government consumption during wartime. The administration promised to stabilize Americans' cost of living through rationing, rent control, and consumer price controls. Some eighty thousand apartments in and around South Florida fell subject to OPA oversight as a result of the wartime and postwar housing shortage. War's end brought the end of rationing. And by 1946, corporate lobbying and popular concerns over the price of meat helped pit organized labor against the OPA, bringing an effective end to wartime price controls.[31] Still, rent control continued, governing everything from rent costs to the conditions necessary for landlords to evict tenants.[32]

As in other corners of the economy, real estate industry lobbyists fought federal rent regulations relentlessly. The National Association of Real Estate Boards (NAREB), which, through its local affiliates, combined landlords, realtors, and other real estate interests, complained that rent controls kept new housing from being built and kept current owners from selling or investing in their properties. NAREB drew a direct line between rent control and the proliferation of slums, in fact. Slums existed, NAREB contended, because "the existence of federal control, especially on rents . . . [has] prevented even greater production [of new housing]."[33] In opposition, proponents of rent regulations argued that, without government protection, war demobilization would actually worsen the country's wartime housing crisis by causing rampant price gouging, particularly against returning veterans and minorities.[34]

Both those advocating for landlords' property rights and those fighting for tenants' consumer rights framed their positions as matters of civil rights. In so doing, they hoped to take advantage of an increased capacity for civil rights enforcement emerging within the Truman administration. Staffers at the National Association for the Advancement of Colored People (NAACP) directed letter-writing campaigns at US senators and representatives. NAACP members also helped craft the Taft-Wagner-Ellender housing bill, introduced in 1946. If passed, the bill promised to go far beyond even rent control in forcing landlords to provide safe, standard housing. Real estate interests had on their side Charles Wilson, chairman of President Truman's Committee on Civil Rights and the chief executive officer of General Electric. Among his first acts as America's highest-ranked civil rights officer, Wilson asked South Florida's civil rights officials to start dismantling rent control. He tasked the Dade County Civil Rights Council with investigating "just what civil liberties and constitutionally guaranteed rights are knowingly and deliberately denied [to] that *minority group* of US citizens[,] . . . landlords who are subjected to 'rent control'" (my emphasis). Landlords, in Wilson's estimation, were a "minority" whose complaints were "concrete, direct and easily ascertainable." Their grievances, moreover, were a direct contrast to "a very large proportion of the complaints of other un-named minorities [which were] largely imaginary, visionary, abstract, and unfounded."[35] Property rights were apparently civil rights for white people, too.

Wilson's understanding of landlords as an aggrieved minority served as part of an increasingly capacious notion of rights developing during the mid- and late 1940s. Indeed, the time of the late New Deal was a moment when Americans began imagining what President Franklin Roosevelt described as the "Second Bill of Rights." Whereas the first ten amendments to the US Constitution guaranteed certain liberties—rights the government could not impede—Roosevelt, in 1944, articulated a range of entitlements befitting American citizenship. Americans, above all, had the right to a job. They had the right to good wages and to quality food, clothing, and shelter; to recreation even. Americans also had the right to protection from unforeseen calamity.[36] But these rights, as Roosevelt had become so effective at communicating, were not abstractions. People heard them, understood them, and pursued them in the context of their lived experience. Sometimes that experience came as a property owner. Other times it was the experience of being a tenant farmer or tenement dweller. Following World War II, as the historian Laura McEnaney explains, "The majority of urbanites experienced the demobilization years not as homeowners, as we may imagine, but as renters, subject to the will and whim of landlords."[37] Freedom from those whims thus stood among the positive rights Americans sought for themselves as well.

Race and Postwar Rent

After a series of debates and stopgap measures moved various rent control powers from the federal government to states and municipalities, Congress allowed national rent regulations to expire finally in 1953.[38] A few cities, such as Chicago and New York, responded along the way by enacting stronger rent control ordinances at the local level. Miami and Miami Beach did not. As early as 1947, Congress effectively defanged enforcement of national rent control when, after continued lobbying from real estate groups, it eliminated criminal prosecutions for noncompliance.[39] That same act of Congress allowed landlords to raise rents a flat 15 percent, or whatever could be "negotiated" by landlord and tenant. In most cases, the continued modification of rent control further shifted costs to tenants.[40] Responding to cries of unfairness from tenant advocacy groups, many landlords cast these reforms as a fitting restoration of private property rights transgressed during wartime. "Other property has been returned to its owners since the war," argued the chairman of the Greater Miami Apartment House Association, "and rental housing should likewise be immediately returned."[41]

Whether one owned dozens of properties on Miami Beach or just a duplex in Colored Town, the change in rent control law caused already harsh landlord practices to worsen, and tenant hardship became a fundamental feature of Greater Miami's postwar tourist economy. On all-white Miami Beach, rents immediately doubled on 20 percent of apartments.[42] Miami Beach also boasted a slightly prettier sibling to the notorious "kitchenettes" confining the poor in northern ghettos like Chicago's Black Belt. Kitchenettes were jerry-built apartments that landlords carved up two and three times over, and that novelist Richard Wright so gravely described as "the funnel through which our pulverized lives flow to ruin and death on the city pavement, at a profit."[43] Landlords on Miami Beach would routinely seal off kitchens and turn one apartment into two, charging "beachfront" rents on both.[44] Miami Beach was hardly a slum, but public parkland remained scarce and working-class whites were increasingly hemmed in by private golf courses and a growing number of overpriced hotels.[45] Employment, like hurricanes, was also violently seasonal, further leaving colored and white renters similarly vulnerable to high housing costs.

Even those with more regular, well-paid employment on the Miami mainland, such as white policemen or firemen, faced constant threat of eviction due to high housing prices. Often, white law enforcement officers had to shack up with relatives or completely separate families just to make ends meet.[46] It was not a reach to consider police brutality as linked to the precariousness of many officers' living situation. Naturally, though, the threat of white police violence, combined with the general "colored" condition of overpaying for slum housing, made Negro lives in Miami the closest comparison to what one could find on Richard Wright's South Side. But, no matter where one lived, how one experienced being "white" or "colored" remained relationally bound both to one's own living quarters and to that of one's supposed racial opposite.

It was indeed a fact of urban America that the color line helped set housing costs, and that residential prices were lived in racial terms.[47] In 1949, it could cost colored slum dwellers a $100.00 deposit and $18.00 a week to move into a two-room shotgun shack that likely suffered from inconsistent electrical service and lacked indoor plumbing. Across the color line, tourists from Cuba, Chicago, or New York paid *$17.50* a week—with no deposit—to stay at a hotel with a private beach, turndown service, and a TV and telephone in every room.[48] It was access to those cheaper, better amenities that made many of Miami's tourists, in a fundamental sense, white. White hotel rates were especially attractive if one came to the Magic City "off season." By contrast, being colored, in addition to experiencing employment discrimination and widespread state neglect, meant paying more and getting less. Certainly, lodgings in most Colored Town slums were not the same price as hotel rooms. However, the average substandard dwelling in the Central Negro District cost $33.00 a month, while the average two-earner Negro household made just under $63.00 a month.[49] Part of being Negro, in effect, meant paying more than 50 percent of your household income on shelter, or, as was far more often the case, shacking up with family, friends, coworkers, or total strangers in even smaller accommodations than your white counterparts. Black city trash collectors, who by all accounts had relatively good government jobs, made so little money in relation to what they had to pay in rent that, according to Miami's mayor, "a great number of them just wander around sleeping where they can." Some even slept on the grounds of the city's trash-processing plant.[50]

Because postwar housing shortages impacted white Americans as well, South Florida's poor and working-class white tenants suffered Jim Crow exploitation of an altogether different kind. They had the distinct misfortune of living in apartments that landlords knew would be attractive to white tourists, precisely because of their distance from Colored Town. One white World War II veteran made $170 a month working as a clerk for the city of Miami, a job no black person could even get. His landlord asked for $140 a month in rent, or over 80 percent of his wages. That amount was scheduled to double once the winter tourist season began. To defray his housing costs, the clerk moved in with his mother, father, and nephew. Another clerk with roughly the same salary lived with her husband in a $200-a-month apartment. Come the start of "the season," the landlord scheduled to evict the clerk and every other tenant in her complex to clear the way for "whites only" tourist rentals.[51] The economic frailty of many landlords, particularly the white elderly, adversely affected white tenants as well. "The landlady worries us to death," explained one Mrs. Goessling. "We have been in our house for 5½ years. . . . [Now] she wants it for her own use. She is elderly . . . but where are we to go?"[52]

Around the country, the white housing experience was, in a word, mixed. For one thing, in terms of total numbers nationwide, more whites than blacks lived in slums. A 1946 study of over forty American cities showed that the *overall* number of white inhabitants in substandard housing (1.2 million) was more than double that of nonwhite slum dwellers (495,000). Yet, only 19 percent of all white people, compared to 58 percent of nonwhites, lived in substandard units. White slums, moreover, tended not to be as condensed as black housing. They remained relegated mostly to rural areas, or, if in urban areas, white slums were scattered among more middle-class housing. White slums also tended to be occupied by their owners. By contrast, a full 80 percent of black slums across the South were occupied by tenants. That number leaped to 90 percent when one considered the Negro housing stock in northern and western US cities.[53] As in the 1930s, black rental housing in the immediate postwar period tended to be in tightly packed quarters and overcrowded. White terrorism, racist housing policy, and landlords' ability to maximize profits all accounted for "the Negro's" unique immobility.

White tenants thus had a rent problem, and colored tenants had a race problem. A rent problem meant that rent was too high, and that you had to pay it because, being poor, your options were limited. A race problem meant that rent was too high and that you lived in a structurally unsafe dwelling because white developers, city officials, or racial terrorism left you confined to one "colored quarter" or another. The chief differences between white and black renters, in short, were (1) the power to choose, and (2) the ability to have state actors and white residents respond positively to that choice.[54]

Greater Miami's white renters had more options than colored tenants— more than colored homeowners, in fact. And this reality did not just shape the complexion of Greater Miami and other cities; it shaped white politics and American liberalism fundamentally. One of the many accomplishments of price controls during the 1940s was, again, how they empowered Americans to protect perceived consumer entitlements to an affordable and high standard of living. However, even as black and white people pursued the same entitlements, particularly the Rooseveltian entitlement to a home, the fullness of those privileges remained bound to white racial membership.

Push, Pull

The end of rent control in Miami Beach further transformed an already transforming South Florida. A mass of so-called "rent refugees" included over four hundred white households who abandoned the beachfront in search of affordable living quarters and the possibility of FHA-insured home mortgages inland. "The working class," Burnett Roth, a public advocacy attorney, complained, "is being eliminated from the Beach."[55] Tributaries of white outmigration from Miami Beach flowed into a broader stream of arriving white migrants who spurred suburban development throughout South Florida. From the rural South, the metropolitan North, and even from the wider Americas they came, taking jobs in new office buildings, commercial districts, and schools, and increasing Dade County's white population 97 percent between 1940 and 1950. (The "nonwhite" population increased by a relatively slight 31 percent over the same period.) Colored people, who had comprised 30 percent of Dade County's total population in 1920, had fallen to only 17 percent of the population by the end of World War II.[56]

The arrival of more whites precipitated the emergence of new all-white municipalities incorporating around Dade and Broward Counties. With every Oakland Park, Miami Shores, or Lauderdale Harbors came new shopping centers and planning and zoning ordinances that privileged parking, fueling stations, and other accoutrements of the automobile age.[57] Realtors, real estate attorneys, and even a few wealthy farmers all began buying up tracts of land and breaking ground on new subdivisions. They made South Florida the most explosive postwar housing boomtown in the country. By 1950, thirteen of every one hundred homes in Greater Miami were new construction. Miami's home-building rate was double that of Los Angeles, California, its nearest competitor.[58]

Eminent domain took on new and important value as a result of this growth. To meet the basic infrastructural needs of the white population, planners began initiating new public works projects all over the region. New schools, hospitals, roads, and airport runways all opened to receive Greater Miami's new residents. The Pan-American project also marched apace, as city planners continued their race with New Orleans and other coastal cities to become the "Capital of the Caribbean." By 1945, white Americans generally defined appropriate state action as that which allowed government officials to compensate for capitalism's flaws without interfering with the fundamental workings of the market economy.[59] Eminent domain in South Florida fit precisely that need, helping whites balance Jim Crow segregation and capitalism in the postwar period.

Through eminent domain, feverish development on behalf of whites consolidated and cropped what little black housing existed outside of the black downtown or Coconut Grove. Just as the war mobilization in the region ramped up, the city of Miami confiscated twenty black homes in Sanford's subdivision, located just north of Coconut Grove, to build a park for whites. In the Negro outpost of Nazarene, white homeowners and city planners chipped away at dozens of black-owned homes, building a park here and there.[60] Decades before incidents of so-called Negro removal became part of American urban lore in the urban renewal era of the 1960s, white people wielding eminent domain forced the dispersal of black folk whose individual and collective property rights, and likely firearms, might have made them otherwise difficult to move. Not simply the consequence of benign or incidental forces, racial segregation in the 1940s continued to be the result of white people's active deployments of the state's power over the land. And perhaps nowhere in Greater Miami was that power more dramatically felt than in the black enclave of Railroad Shop.

Growth Pains

In 1898, colored railroad workers began purchasing property in a designated wooded area northwest of the city center, an area called Railroad Shop's Colored Addition, or "Railroad Shop" for short. The community grew quickly in the 1910s, becoming a flourishing semirural settlement that, even as its population increased during the 1930s, suffered from none of the density problems that made Colored Town such a social concern. According to Edward Braynon, a former resident of the neighborhood, Railroad Shop was "completely crime free . . . even though it was in the City of Miami." The child of a Bahamian father and an Alabaman mother, Braynon remembered his neighborhood as one of large, close-knit families. For the first few decades of the community's existence, some 95 percent of the families owned their own homes, but population pressures and the cycles of racial exclusion around Dade County reduced the homeowner-to-renter ratio to roughly fifty-fifty by the late 1930s. As in Colored Town, Railroad Shop's residents made daily investments in their neighborhood that reflected a heritage and culture drawn from both Caribbean and American elements. Much of their food was southern or Bahamian cuisine prepared fresh from what they raised around them. "People had chickens and everybody had vegetables and fruit trees," Braynon remembered.[61]

Abutting Railroad Shop, across the color line of NW Twelfth Avenue, was a whites-only community called Allapattah, and it, too, had expanded greatly during the 1920s and 1930s. With the growth of Allapattah came the promise from Miami city officials for a new whites-only school. The Dade County Board of Public Instruction purchased sizable tracts of real estate within the white community to fulfill this promise. But by 1942, less than six months after America's entry into World War II, still greater population increases among the area's whites prompted Dade's school board to propose a new and much larger Andrew Jackson Allapattah School for white children. The proposed property line stretched into Railroad Shop.[62]

The influx of rural white families to South Florida and the broader wartime housing shortage created an ever-encroaching ring of white-occupied homes around Railroad Shop as the war went on. In the words of one former resident, "It was a black island in a sea of white."[63] White Allapattah, by the assessment of the Home Owners Loan Corporation, was a "C" area of fifteen hundred–dollar to thirty-five hundred–dollar homes. About 10 percent of its population was Cuban. The only downside to the community, according to HOLC's appraisers, was a "lack of zoning restrictions" and its closeness to "undesirable areas." Railroad Shop, being the so-named "undesirable area," was, of course, a "D"-grade community, yet, not surprisingly, it was also listed as having Cubans as 10 percent of its population. In the late 1930s, whites noticed that Railroad Shop residents had begun to buy across the color line, on the east side of NW Twelfth Avenue.[64] In response, Allapattah's residents began organizing into neighborhood, civic, and benevolent associations. They rapidly incorporated the Seventeenth Avenue Manor Improvement Association, the Northwest Improvement Association, the Allapattah Lion's Club, and the Exchange Club of Miami. Allapattah's whites then demanded in April of 1942 that the five-member Miami City Commission use the authority of eminent domain to have "the negroes in this addition removed," their homes leveled, and their property turned into a park, playground, or other municipal property for the exclusive benefit of Allapattah's white residents. Miami's commissioners unanimously supported the initiative. But with municipal coffers strapped by other wartime development projects, city officials could only promise to acquire Railroad Shop after the war, when the funds necessary for purchase and condemnation proceedings became available.[65]

As the municipal treasury slowly grew and black people continued to trickle across Twelfth Avenue, city officials made inexpensive preparations to condemn Railroad Shop. First, as was done to the Colemans and Wilsons in Brownsville, white officials denied colored residents permits to make basic home repairs. This would reduce black property values and drive down the impending costs of condemnation. Some sources even suggest that city planners had in their offices a big map of the area, whereon they placed a large X on every property tract owned by a black resident. Over the X read the phrase "Issue No Permits," even though, up through 1946, nearly every city in Florida, including Miami, had far exceeded any previous record for building permits issued. Nature inflicted the second blow. Large hurricanes in 1944 and 1945, in addition to the standard wear and tear brought by yearly subtropical thunderstorms, began taking their toll on a number of homes in the neighborhood. Then came enforcement. Any colored residents caught performing home improvements or doing more than the most basic repairs, even after the storms, would be arrested by Miami police and sentenced to jail time for violating the city's building ordinances. These residents who suffered arrest, unlike the Colemans and Wilsons nearby, had no white developers to bail them out. Black folk in Railroad Shop took to doing their construction work by lamplight at night, hearkening to how their predecessors built Colored Town a half century earlier.[66]

A year after the war ended, Miami city officials accelerated their efforts to push out Railroad Shop residents. They offered colored residents between $100 and $800 for each house depending on the size, or $150 per lot. The market price for empty inland lots just north of Railroad Shop was a *minimum* of $1,000 apiece. Blacks with legal representation, including colored veterans who reached out to Burnett Roth, tended to get more compensation, those without got less, but most received nowhere near the cost of a new home in a war-tightened housing market.[67] Getting new housing proved all the more difficult with the Coral Gables office of the FHA still encouraging blanket rejections of American and Caribbean blacks who sought home mortgages.

Unable to stay anywhere near their old neighborhood, several black homeowners negotiated to have their physical house moved to another location in order to defray some of the costs of starting over, but that would also require that residents pay their own relocation costs.[68] Other residents tried resisting relocation and city officials' discriminatory permit policy by enlisting the legal aid of Lawson Thomas. Yet, it seemed, even Thomas saw little that he could do because of the far-reaching authority eminent domain granted for building schools, parks, and other discernible "public goods."[69] Residents waited for word on when they were supposed to be out.

Moving Day

Ruby Pierce's parents bought eight lots of land in Railroad Shop back in 1916, when she was just two years old. It took another two years of saving and work to finish building the family home. Now, facing displacement on a date to be determined, Ruby was in her midthirties, and stood on the corner waiting to catch a bus down into Colored Town to look for a new apartment. It was the morning of 1 August 1947. Ruby needed to get an early start because the day was warming up quickly and weather reports predicted afternoon showers. As the bus approached, she noticed a dozen or so police officers congregating at the end of her street. "I thought [the officers] were out there to raid the *bolita* house," she recalled. But unbeknownst to Ruby or anyone else, the cops had come to evict Ruby's seventy-four-year-old mother, Eliza, and many of the other families in the neighborhood. By 10:00 a.m., with the late summer air already steaming with moisture, patrols of motorcycle police moved into Railroad Shop. They were flanked by representatives of the Dade County School Board.[70]

Officers began combing the four blocks between NW Forty-Sixth Street and Forty-Eighth Street, from NW Twelfth to Fourteenth Avenues, knocking on doors. In a frenzied two hours, during which the rains began falling heavily, officers carried out a court-ordered writ of possession, legally authorizing the execution of eminent domain. Delores Johnson McCartney, who was thirteen years old at the time, remembered sitting on the couch with her mother and six-month-old baby sister when the police and school board officials darkened her doorstep. "Then came this man. He told my mother we had to move out." Because it was the middle of the day, most of the neighborhood's adults were not even home when the evictions started. The preparations for condemnations would be handled, by and large, by Railroad Shop's elderly and by neighborhood teenagers who were home from school for the summer. Ruby Pierce got news of the eviction while apartment hunting some forty blocks away. Hysterical, she rushed to take the bus back to Railroad Shop. "I cried all the way home." By 1:00 p.m., officers had forcibly evicted thirty-five families from their homes, casting them and their property out into the storm. To minimize water damage to their possessions, kids, expectant mothers, unemployed men, and old folk struggled to move couches, dressers, and other furniture under mango and avocado trees. City officials even condemned the fruit trees; these would be ripped up from the ground and sold to local growers at a discount.[71]

While tending his fish market in nearby Brownsville, George Kilpatrick heard of the police raid from an out-of-breath customer who had run to tell him the news: "Your wife and three kids have just been put out in the rain!" Kilpatrick rushed home to find everything he owned, including his brand-new refrigerator, dumped out in front of the house. "We had no place to go. We slept out in the rain all that night. A lot of other people did too."

According to one black publication, residents, regardless of age, were put out. Many stood bewildered with "tears streaming down their faces." Some families, in defiance, ripped up the checks city officials offered them and elected to stand their ground against what they called an "inhuman" and "unfair" removal. Police, threatening violence and arrest, muscled any resisters into the street. Officers dragged the aged Eliza Pierce right from her home. One evicted black couple had eleven sons, all of whom had served in the United States military. Many of the families that had not been evicted, those from Forty-Eighth to Fiftieth Streets, took in whom they could. A few others called the Red Cross seeking shelter. Not a few families, among them the Kilpatricks, chose to remain outdoors, under tarpaulins, in tents, and in the storm to watch over their now rain-soaked belongings.[72]

City officials declared all the homes "condemned," padlocked the doors, and boarded up the windows in preparation for the building of the Andrew Jackson School. Signs outside the doors read "No Trespassing." "If you went back in," recounted James Bendross, a teenager at the time, "you were trespassing." "They did not need those schools," remembered Edward Braynon. "The schools were practically unused for years but that was the only way they could legitimately get those black families out of there."[73] Ejected families looked, among other places, to the services of Luther Brooks's Bonded Collection Agency. As the most well-connected rental agent in South Florida, Brooks could help families ease the difficulties of finding an apartment.[74] This white son of Georgia held the keys to that most elusive thing in 1940s' Miami—a vacant, "colored" rental unit. Some Railroad Shop residents, by virtue of their now-immediate housing needs, were forced to buy land they had never even seen.[75]

Those homeowners from Railroad Shop who fought for and won the right to keep their physical house had their dwellings relocated to Carver Ranches in neighboring Broward County. The land set aside for relocated homes was far from public transportation, sewerage, and, for many, as far as fifteen miles from the family, jobs, and churches of Colored Town. As a procedural matter, the city arranged for work crews to cut the electrical wires to a given house, dig out its foundation, and drag it onto the back of a flatbed truck. Bumping and bouncing slowly north along US-1, the trucks would then drop off the houses, with most having been structurally compromised in transit. Homes were placed directly in the dirt or sometimes on concrete slabs or blocks. Only a month after the whole ordeal, it did not seem to matter at all. The now-rootless homes of Carver Ranches stood no chance against the 155-mile-per-hour winds of what would simply be called "the 1947 hurricane." As recounted by one witness of the ensuing destruction, the storm "tore down all those little houses they had transferred from Railroad Shop."[76] Entire families were ruined.

The Blockbusters

The accomplishment of Railroad Shop as a black suburban community, and the pain of whites' attempt to erase it, must be appreciated in the context of black people's struggles to overcome near constant restrictions on their housing options. In much of the nation, colored people's power to choose their place of residence remained greatly limited because of racially restrictive covenants—contracts that kept white homeowners from selling their houses to nonwhites. In California, restrictive covenants variously barred all "non-Caucasians." That included Armenians, Hindus, Mexicans, Jews, and "descendants of former residents of the Turkish Empire."[77] In most cases, by the late 1940s, restrictive covenants had become largely irrelevant, or at least were redundant. They provided a measure of personal security to a white buyer perhaps, but, as the historian Arnold Hirsch notes of Chicago, "restrictive covenants . . . served as little more than a fairly coarse sieve, unable to stop the flow of black population when put to the test."[78] Whites frequently performed their most effective acts of segregation at the level of credit, well before there was ever a transaction. And, often, black folk simply avoided areas where they knew they would have trouble taking out a mortgage or would suffer threats. In a given neighborhood that might be priced out of most colored people's reach, restrictive covenants served as window dressing to make that particular community feel "exclusive." Mostly, through practices that continue into the present, white property assessors around the country so structured the housing market in racial terms that, it was believed, selling your house to a black person immediately had adverse effects on all your neighbors. Residential "race mixing" flew in the face of simple, economic common sense.[79]

There was, however, a second, competing imperative that also made perfect economic sense: actively challenging the color line. In many American cities, the legality of restrictive covenants and lingering, if illegal, practices of racial zoning came under constant attack from landlords and developers looking to open up new black housing options at a profit. St. Clair Drake and Horace Cayton point out that in 1940s' Chicago, for instance, "some of the larger white real-estate companies with an eye for business began to break the covenants." A new opening did not lead to the dissolution of segregationist real estate practices per se. It led to more price gouging in most instances, in fact. As Drake and Cayton note, white developers "moved

Negroes in one or two apartment buildings, immediately raising the rents from 20 to 50 percent."[80]

So it was in postwar Miami. When a particular rental market seemed maxed out, white developers sought to open new markets. Black in-migration would create new tensions and new opportunities for Floridians to organize on behalf of both colored and white people's property rights. Restrictive covenants were particularly ineffective in South Florida because developers were buying up land so quickly. White home buyers could not enter contractual agreements fast enough to keep up with the pace of postwar speculation. Thus, in addition to Wesley Garrison, other white developers such as John Bouvier, Malcolm Wiseheart, Julius Gaines, Harry Markowitz, and Floyd Davis bought up land at a rate that hearkened to the robber-baron hopefuls of the George Merrick and Carl Fisher generation. "There are many colored veterans who can qualify [for] and are entitled to . . . home benefits," explained Harry Markowitz. A landlord and eventual owner of Miami's most illustrious black motel, The Hampton House, Markowitz would fight to build a subdivision of over 150 homes, financed by his own development company, Markel Industries Inc., and mortgage-insured by the Federal Housing Administration and the Veterans Administration.[81] Many of the tracts white developers bought for black housing remained vacant, though, as city and county officials attempted to block development with one zoning requirement or another. Whereas developers from Miami's frontier era could generate sales by the dozens per day, postwar entrepreneurs pushing for black housing faced color lines hardened by the millions of dollars in federal mortgage and construction subsidies that made up Jim Crow's infrastructure. The need to break down apartheid's less visible barriers made developers' acts of obvious self-interest—as in Garrison's organizing on behalf of black Brownsville—serve as a kind of civil rights capitalism.

Landlords or developers who, to placate white observers, built concrete walls around one black project in one part of the city could serve, in a different part of town, as enemies of segregation, challenging white homeowners or zoning boards to improve their bottom line. It was, indeed, a defining feature of American apartheid that white capital could both break down and harden the color line in the name of "free market" practices. When encouraging colored home ownership, some developers took advantage of the climate of antiblack lending discrimination by offering more precarious forms of credit, such as contract sales that included balloon payments.[82] Others, in concert with white realtors, snapped up white homes by the handful to spark panic selling among white residents. These entrepre-

neurs would then ask black buyers to pay a premium to live in neighborhoods realtors still framed as "exclusive." Still others bought up land for the
sake of creating new black rentals, hoping to take advantage of the high rents
black people generally paid in the postwar period. "Slum property owners and race restrictive covenant manipulators," wrote the housing reformer
Robert Weaver in 1945, "are two sides of the same coin."[83]

Making Deals

In 1946, two white developers, John A. Bouvier and Malcolm Wiseheart, purchased some eighteen acres in a colored section of Coconut Grove. Known
as St. Alban's, the land belonged to the Episcopal Diocese of South Florida.
On the promise that the men would develop new Negro housing, the church
sold Bouvier and Wiseheart the acreage for twenty-five thousand dollars, an
amount well below market value. Coconut Grove, like Railroad Shop and
Brownsville, was not nearly as congested as Colored Town, and the young
black priest who helped broker the deal, Theodore Gibson, wanted to keep it
that way. Gibson wanted, in fact, to improve black people's general housing
condition in Miami. He therefore encouraged the sale with the understanding that Bouvier and Wiseheart would build single-family homes for colored
families.

Gibson's life history captured the complexity of black Miami itself. The
then thirty-year-old reverend had graduated from Colored Town's Booker T.
Washington High School in 1934, and he was a student there when public
health officials began combing Colored Town's shotgun shacks for the environmental causes of child tuberculosis.[84] Gibson was also born in Miami
to Bahamian parents and raised, in part, in the islands before moving back
to Colored Town and, later, furthering his education in Virginia and North
Carolina. In his travels, Gibson had seen and experienced firsthand the difficulties landless poverty visited upon colored families in both the Caribbean and the American South. He also came to believe, as a result, that
homeownership was the principal means through which to continue the
good work of racial uplift. To Gibson, selling precious Miami city acres at a
discount was fine, if it advanced black property ownership.

Once the land changed hands, Bouvier and Wiseheart had other ideas.
The developers planned to build duplexes to rent, not single-family homes.
Moreover, they were going to partner with other white developers to begin
adding even more rental units to Coconut Grove. This transaction came as
part of a $500,000 development plan for Bouvier, Wiseheart, and their busi-
ness partners to own and manage over one thousand units of black-occupied

rental housing across Dade County.[85] The pair began immediately selling off smaller pieces of St. Alban's property to other white developers as a way to recoup their original investment. They first sold two and a half acres for $18,000, immediately recouping nearly two-thirds of their initial costs. They then sold another two and a half acres for $12,500; that gave Bouvier and Wiseheart a $5,500 return on their investment with over twelve acres still in hand. One of the buyers, Julius Gaines, was a white real estate developer and part owner of the Casablanca Hotel on Miami Beach. Through his connections on the Miami city zoning board, Gaines got approval to build thirty-two new rental units in the St. Alban's section right away.[86] In no time, congestion in Coconut Grove's colored section seemed likely to get worse, not better.[87]

Since the years that Franklin Bush and Walter de Garmo first began selling lots in Coconut Grove, the community was one where the old tensions between island blacks and southern Negroes simmered in the midst of affluent white neighbors. "A cruising police car," noted one observer from the Works Progress Administration in 1939, "keeps peace between the American Negro and the numerous West Indian Negroes who call themselves British, speak with a different accent, and act superior to their American cousins."[88] Part of West Indians' perceived cultural chauvinism, such as it was, came from the fact that Coconut Grove's mostly Bahamian population had a 25 percent rate of homeownership—more than double the rate found in the increasingly "Yankee" slums of Colored Town.[89] Even if some considered Coconut Grove home to a "higher class colored" from the Caribbean, the neighborhood suffered from the same climate of employment discrimination that forced blacks into servile labor. Bahamian maids and yardmen numbered greatly among the Grove's black homeowners, and most tended the homes and gardens of their wealthier white neighbors.[90]

Most blacks in Coconut Grove wanted standard, single-family homes. Most white Grove residents did not mind Bouvier and Wiseheart's proposed expansion of black housing in principle, so long as the number of colored units remained kept to a minimum. Tolerable developments included, perhaps, a few houses to accommodate a handful of Negro maids and their children, but little more. The developers promised to build the necessary "race walls" and a 250-foot-wide "buffer zone" between colored and white housing. When the scale and character of the development became clear, however—all rental property, and lots of it—Coconut Grove's white homeowners and its black residents expressed a shared sense of betrayal and found common cause in opposition to the St. Alban's project.

The Door to a Movement

In August of 1948, members of an all-white Coconut Grove Civic Club met with black Coconut Grove residents at the neighborhood's American Legion Hall. This was the only building in the neighborhood where whites and coloreds were allowed to meet together. Most of the whites there came to protest the threat Negro rental expansion posed to their otherwise exclusive community. A few of the more vocal white attendees exclaimed that the St. Alban's tracts should have been reserved for a white elementary school or more affordable "whites only" housing. Theodore Gibson, who was at the meeting, then rose to speak. He addressed the mostly white crowd passionately about the gravity of the Negro housing situation. He recalled his youth in Colored Town. He also described how deplorable conditions and high rents still forced Miami's colored poor to cram into one-bedroom shotgun shacks. "My people are living seven deep," he lamented. The phrase *seven deep*, popular among the city's black housing advocates, reflected the math that placed forty-nine thousand Negroes in Miami's seven thousand colored tenements.[91] The priest then offered a point-by-point condemnation of the lack of trash collection, the outhouses, and the general sense of abandonment that overshadowed the black Grove.

In the audience that evening sat a petite white woman named Elizabeth Virrick. During the real estate boom of the mid-1920s, Elizabeth moved to Miami with her husband, Vladimir, a Russian architect who worked on designing Liberty Square and Edison Courts. Elizabeth and Vladimir spent part of the early 1940s in Haiti while he finished some development work there following the US occupation. The couple also owned an apartment building for white occupancy in Coconut Grove. Well-off, traveled, and Ivy League educated, the two were typical Grove residents, but Elizabeth was never the same after she heard Gibson speak. Perhaps she saw a frightening connection between the degradation of an occupied Haiti and the world Gibson described. Whatever it was, Virrick later admitted that Gibson's words turned her toward a life of housing reform. All night, she claimed years later, the young priest's words stayed with her. She decided to knock on the clergyman's door the very next morning.[92]

When Gibson opened his door to Virrick, the two of them stepped into a whirlwind of political activity. Together, they would establish the Coconut Grove Committee for Slum Clearance. Peopled by both blacks and whites, the committee provided yet another moment of interracial activity in the age of Jim Crow. It was also the closest thing Miami had seen to a black tenants'

Figure 5.1. Elizabeth Virrick of the Coconut Grove Committee for Slum Clearance. (Courtesy of the Charles W. Tebeau Library, Historical Museum of Southern Florida.)

rights group in the city's history. Interest in the committee among Negroes was obvious—improve colored housing, improve colored life. White involvement in Grove slum clearance was slightly more complicated. Most white sympathy came from concerns over the adverse effect of slum conditions on the health of Negro children and expectant mothers, the kinds of colored folk who often crossed into white spaces as domestics.[93] There was also a concern among white Coconut Grove residents that their homes might eventually be overtaken by rental speculators, as occurred in Brownsville.

Less concerned with drafting a manifesto than with addressing specific problems, the Coconut Grove Committee for Slum Clearance used a combination of federal, city government, and voter authority to make small, manageable gains that helped bring discussions of race and space out of local chambers of commerce and into the public discourse. The committee's first line of attack was the black Grove's plumbing problem. There were nearly five hundred outhouses in the black area of Coconut Grove. These were irregularly emptied by a city sewage truck known, somewhat comically, as the "Honey Wagon." Using her connections among white homeowners and local banks, Virrick raised over seventy-six hundred dollars to install new plumbing and toilets to replace each of the outdoor commodes.[94] Gibson used his growing influence to encourage the formation of colored block clubs, community pride parades, neighborhood cleanup drives, and the assignment of a Negro police officer to the Grove's black section. Black and white Grove residents descended, as a group, on the Miami City Commission, prompting commissioners to pass an ordinance requiring running water, septic tanks, and flush toilets in every apartment. With mixed results, white members of the group also used their access to local media to pressure landlords into lowering colored people's rental costs. The hope, there, was to get black rents to mirror more closely those paid by white renters.[95]

Concurrent with these events, the US Congress finally passed the Taft-Ellender-Wagner bill, making it the Housing Act of 1949. The measure, after some three years of debate between property rights and consumer rights advocates, enabled local governments to apply for federal funds to pay for eminent domain actions against areas formally designated as "slums." These monies could also be used to build public housing, and to shepherd the broader execution of eminent domain for the purposes of urban redevelopment.[96] The Coconut Grove Committee threatened to use this new instrument against the St. Alban's project. It promised a new school, or perhaps a park, that would preempt potential slums. What the committee demanded, in keeping with Gibson's vision, was that Bouvier and Wiseheart build only single-family homes.

Part of the point, which was quite novel for the period, was to expand black people's access to property by threatening real estate developers with land taking. Just as important, in the estimation of the Grove's white residents, a set-aside community of homes, properly bounded by concrete walls, would preserve the low-density residential pattern that many saw as key to keeping disease and crime out of the community. Yet again, preserving sound race relations required possible use of eminent domain. As the slum committee's attorney, Abe Aronovitz, explained to the Miami City Commission: "If you sit back and do nothing, [slums] will destroy the fine relationship that exists between White and Negro residents."[97] In a chance meeting on the streets of Coral Gables between Malcolm Wiseheart and Aronovitz, Wiseheart assured the committee's chief counsel that he and Bouvier "had no desire to have the ill will of anybody in the Coconut Grove area." Further, he wished to resolve the conflict with Grove residents in as "amicable" a fashion as possible.[98]

The reality, of course, was that landlords fought the slum committee's wave of organizing every step of the way. Using arguments about property rights and prominent real estate attorneys, developers and landlords—black and white—thwarted the slum committee's more ambitious goals. Efforts to rezone the black section of the Grove for single-family homes failed, as did efforts to draw on federal funds and to lower the cost of rent across the board. Perhaps most critical to property owners' counterorganizing efforts was Luther Brooks of Bonded Collection Agency. Bonded's owner represented nearly two hundred different landlords at the time, some of whom were the most powerful property owners in the state. One of his clients, for instance, was the brother of then US congressman George Smathers. Another was a district court judge. Then there were the many hotel owners, lawyers, and physicians for whom Brooks managed properties. By virtue of his chummy relationships with members of Miami's all-white, all-male city commission, Brooks weakened one initiative after another, crying "socialism" at nearly every federally funded solution.[99] Brooks kept Miami's first slum clearance committee from clearing a single slum, in fact. Apart from gaining improved garbage collection and sanitation—reforms for which Brooks later took credit—Miami's housing reformers changed little about the profitability of black poverty.

With Friends Like These . . .

As they would for several years to come, opponents of slum clearance in the late 1940s and early 1950s walked a fine line of trying to make "free market" arguments while remaining sensitive to the lingering question of segregation and inequality. Echoing earlier arguments against rent control, Miami's real estate interests argued that claims of Negro destitution were overstated and merely provided a "sentimental smoke screen" to close the eyes of the American people "while socialism takes over the country." Targeting black voters, real estate lobbyists took out anticommunist ads in the city's black newspaper, the *Miami Times*, and pointedly criticized the use of government funds in housing as a program that would foster black dependence and ultimately betray Negro slum dwellers. They argued for black self-help and the integrity of private property. In perhaps the most racially insightful—if politically disingenuous—indictment of the white Grove home-owners' position on slum clearance, FHA commissioner Franklin Richards suggested that what might look like liberal benevolence actually functioned "to eliminate minorities from specific areas under the guise of a slum clear-ance program."[100] Claiming to represent Miami's "colored and white land-lords of Negro homes," Luther Brooks accused any Negro in support of slum clearance as having been "duped" by white liberals who simply wanted to distance themselves from the black poor.[101] All they had to do was point to Railroad Shop.

The same year that Virrick and Gibson's committee began threatening eminent domain against the Grove's white developers, there came a second wave of evictions at Railroad Shop. Dade County's government pushed out fifty additional colored families who lived between NW Forty-Eighth and Fiftieth Streets and Twelfth and Sixteenth Avenues. In place of black homes, county officials built Allapattah Junior High, a fire station, and a park—all declared "whites only." According to a *Miami Herald* report issued some thirty years later, the egregiousness of the 1947 ouster had so shocked the remaining households that many residents simply "gave up and refused to fight."[102] Still, over twenty home and business owners sought the assistance of E. F. P. Brigham, the same attorney Bouvier and Wiseheart used to fight off eminent domain in the Grove. Brigham fought for higher condemnation awards than the first group of black homeowners received. Neal Adams, a black grocery store owner, Railroad Shop resident, and owner of rental property in Colored Town, had secured Brigham's services and played no small part in a handful of residents gaining over seventy thousand dollars in damages.[103]

For Virrick, Aronovitz, and other whites who purportedly advocated for black rights, making the case for broad slum clearance across Miami required sidestepping, or at least downplaying, the reality of Negroes' serial displace-ment. Thus, in addition to claiming slum clearance as a form of civil rights, the Coconut Grove Committee stuck to populist, progrowth arguments in the press. "If Miami were in danger of having an atom bomb dropped on it," wrote one editorial in favor of slum clearance, "no one would object if the federal government loaned us the money to set up defenses. . . . [With slums,] potentialities for destruction . . . are just as great."[104] How could the Magic City market itself as a landscape of bathing beauties, sunshine, and tropical leisure, went another line of argument, if deteriorating black slums kept getting all the national and international attention? Slum clearance, in the political calculus of growth, promised to protect that which remained

Figure 5.2. "Let's Do Some Erasing Tomorrow!" *Miami Herald*, 26 June 1950. (Courtesy of the Charles W. Tebeau Library, Historical Museum of Southern Florida.)

best about Miami and its surrounding municipalities. Only by literally erasing the Negro slum from the face of South Florida could the region rest assured of a profitable and progressive future.

Grove activists also argued that the proliferation of Negro slums hurt the country's broader claims for moral superiority in a well-stoked Cold War. Of slum clearance, Virrick would later recall, "We felt that this [was] a wonderful way to counteract Red propaganda." In fact, "Voice of America," the international broadcast service of the US State Department, trumpeted the slum-clearing efforts of Virrick and the Coconut Grove Committee into

Germany, Russia, and across the Americas in an attempt to counter some of the bad press generated by white terrorism and racial injustice.[105]

In the short term, Grove homeowners, it appeared, successfully claimed the Cold War's moral high ground. In their attempt to rezone the Grove for single-family homes, the Coconut Grove citizens' committee collected over eleven thousand signatures and got the housing issue moved to the November 1950 ballot. On Election Day, Miami voters from across the city voted in favor of Virrick and Gibson's efforts, even though most were in no way affected by the building of Bouvier and Wiseheart's St. Albans's project. Eminent domain proceedings were swift, liquidating the developers' assets in a matter of months and leading to the groundbreaking of a new "public good"—the St. Alban's Nursery School, built specifically for the children of black domestics working in the Grove's white section. No developer would build black residents the single-family homes they originally sought. City planners rezoned the entire St. Albans tract as "public" infrastructure.

Conclusion

Greater Miami's early postwar years affirm the notion that interracialism was often a political strategy, not a moral aim.[106] The myriad nationalities and histories—the people—crammed into categories of "white" and "colored" displayed a fullness of landed politics that nurtured several emerging assumptions about the appropriate role of the postwar state. One of those assumptions was a palpable, if still soft, consensus that condemnation and deployments of eminent domain represented the most fitting responses to substandard Negro housing. If poor Negroes were the problem, government land action seemed to offer the solution.

In the lead-up to the displacements at Railroad Shop, the National Urban League described that neighborhood as just "another slum area within the city limits," citing the neighborhood's lack of sidewalks and unpaved streets. League members heard tell of the permit discrimination black folk suffered and demanded an investigation. But in 1943—a full four years before the first displacements—the league also justified white petitions for Negro expulsion as the expected response of property owners faced with a "40-acre Negro subdivision . . . in the heart of an area of attractive moderate priced homes." Even though there was no Miami chapter of the Urban League, the report's dismissal of Railroad Shop relied on local knowledge. Urban League staffers interviewed nearly forty black and white Miamians, including Ira Davis, William Sawyer, and the black labor organizer Charles Lockhart.[107] The league's conclusions suggest a certain disregard for Railroad

Shop among Miami's more elite blacks. So do contemporaneous reports from local journalists. Writing about the troubling displacements at Railroad Shop, the *Pittsburgh Courier*'s Miami correspondent, John Diaz, drew readers' attention to the fact that, despite the long history of careful negotiations between "prominent Negroes and whites . . . some members of the community have expressed the opinion that [Miami's civic leadership] . . . should be augmented with persons, representative of the masses, who are more familiar with the true conditions of the slums."[108]

The attorney Lawson Thomas fared particularly badly in the political fallout around the Railroad Shop evictions. He had been out of town on business the day of the first mass displacement, a fact that some suggest may have determined the unspecified day of the police raid. Some also believed that Thomas may have been complicit in the forced ejection of Railroad Shop's residents on the promise that he would later be named to the South's only black judgeship, which he was. Correlation, of course, is not the same as causality. However, reports described people shouting as they were being ousted from their homes, and in possible reference to Thomas, "We were sold out!"[109] Thomas denied charges of his complicity or possible incompetence. "I did my best, but I am not God."[110] In the flood of hurt and blame left in the wake of Railroad Shop's evictions, Thomas and many residents of the neighborhood would not reconcile for decades.[111] Without a smoking-gun document outlining a possible quid pro quo, Thomas's role in the particular displacement suffered in 1947 remains today mostly a matter of community rumor.[112]

The apparent victory of the Coconut Grove Committee for Slum Clearance, less shrouded in hearsay and speculation, would be Pyrrhic, nonetheless. First, despite its interracial face and seemingly altruistic aims, the campaign by the Coconut Grove slum committee affirmed a white supremacist discourse that treated black housing, and by extension black people, as a direct threat to the economic destiny of white families and a tourist-dependent South Florida. Second, antislum advocates gave eminent domain a racially progressive veneer that would remain in place once South Florida entered the highway-building era of the 1960s. Third, in the still ill-formed discourse of postwar racial justice, Miami's early slum clearance campaigns set white developers alongside violent segregationists as the greatest enemies of progress and equality, thus saving more liberal forms of white supremacy—such as affluent homeowner politics and the coming fever of growth liberalism—from any meaningful racial critique. Fourth, Bouvier and Wiseheart ultimately won. Not only had they made many times their initial investment, but the Miami City Commission, in November of 1950, would vote to keep *all* federal slum clearance funds out of the city, thereby insulating landlords around the city from the possibility of mass land expropriation. Expelled from Coconut Grove, Bouvier and Wiseheart simply picked up their profits and continued work on two new developments, Carver Village (black) and Knight Manor (white).[113] Fifth and finally, Theodore Gibson, having once cut a poor deal with white developers, traded a short-term, zero-tolerance position on residential segregation for the promise of long-term housing reform. A new political player in the Jim Crow city, he introduced himself to white Miami as a savvy and pragmatic political operative. And the role Gibson played in casting displacement as the progressive response to housing reform would be the first of many political deals he would strike in his long career as a civic leader.

Around the country, the walls of Jim Crow continued to harden. After the passage of the 1949 Housing Act, it took no time at all for whites in Jim Crow cities like Aiken, South Carolina; Nashville, Tennessee; or Baltimore, Maryland, to use the new federal slum clearance powers to bulldoze black homes and replace them with "whites only" developments.[114] Yet even as cases across the country rolled in about slum clearance projects furthering segregation, racist uses of eminent domain coalesced with a rising movement for black housing reform. As the 1940s turned into the 1950s, America would continue to see white property owners—developers, homeowners, and landlords—variously casting themselves as friends to "the Negro," even as they advanced their own property interests. As was clear from black people's relationships with Wesley Garrison or E. F. P. Brigham, white capitalists could, at times, be natural allies. This proved all the more true as white developers and landlords drew from their own corner of the New Deal state—the Federal Housing Administration—to protect Negroes and their own economic foothold in Jim Crow's ghetto.

CHAPTER SIX

A Little Insurance

In the summer of 1950, only a few months removed from completing the biggest real estate development of his life, Bill Sawyer's father, William, was dead from complications following a heart attack. Back in January, William opened Alberta Heights, a concrete-block development of eighty separate two- and three-bedroom apartments. Reporters at the *Atlanta Daily World* and the *Pittsburgh Courier* celebrated the new building as a great achievement for the race, and the *Miami Times* lauded William as the "only colored man we know of to build such a project in the South."[1] In July of that year, Miss Puerto Rico was crowned "Miss Latin America" on the patio of Sawyer's Mary Elizabeth Hotel.[2] By August, the ailing doctor was interned at Jackson Memorial Hospital, the very hospital he helped found and the one where white physicians had barred him from practicing medicine in 1924. William's obituary described him as "reputedly Miami's wealthiest Negro," and a man who had "amassed his wealth from real estate holdings and [a] lucrative medical practice."[3] Perhaps realizing the substance of his legacy, William did not pass without giving his son Bill, principal heir to his fortune, a last important lesson. "When my daddy was dying," the younger Sawyer recalled, "he had me come in and gave me a long talk. He said, 'Bill, try to be as careful as you can with your developments and your monies and stuff like that because you are a nigger and I want you to know that for the foreseeable future you are going to be a nigger.'" "For a long time," Bill concluded, "I found that to be very true."[4]

Thirty years earlier, as Caribbean migrants and black Miamians traded barbs and played checkers on the front porch of William's doctor's office, one could imagine the elder Sawyer delivering similar admonitions to the men of Colored Town. When young Bill's degenerative eye condition worsened, it destroyed William's hopes for Bill to achieve, as *he* did, success through medicine. Real estate no doubt figured prominently in a father's amended dreams for his son. Bill had four hundred apartments and two hotels to manage as proof of that.[5] The meaning of citizenship, for colored people like the Sawyers, as for the whites who often marginalized them, remained tied not simply to the right to buy or to consume. Citizenship meant the right *to hold*—to make that which one consumes into property— and to be able to pass that property safely from one generation to the next. This had not changed from the age of South Florida's frontier through the years of depression. Nor had this changed through the events of world war or the ensuing American peace. Maintaining the integrity of black property, in fact, became all the more pressing as whites got increasingly efficient at taking colored people's real estate through the expanded powers of the postwar state.

The meaning of being colored in America remained bound to the relationship between state and real estate. For William Sawyer and so many others, the substance of being a "nigger," in landed terms, meant, in great measure, having to protect your property rights against whites who wielded state police powers of conscription, lawful murder, and, increasingly, eminent domain. William's death came only three years after the unsettling expulsions at Railroad Shop. And that event was nothing if not an echo of what happened to Shaddie Ward following the Big Blow, or to Herbert Brooks as he plummeted to his death from a train outside Daytona Beach. The trials of Ruby Pierce, of Bruce Torres, or of Felton and Willie Mae Coleman, replicated countless times in the US South and beyond, served to shape the kinds of folk wisdom parents passed down to their children. At the same time, in the eyes of many black people, ending the condition of being a "nigger" meant freedom from cramped housing conditions. The Sawyers, incidentally, had dozens of Negro tenants living in apartments that were half the size of what was required by law.[6] For the Sawyers' black tenants, their landlord was likely the problem. And for housing advocates concerned with the fate of tenants, ending "nigger" living conditions required wresting eminent domain and similar police powers from the exclusive grasp of exclusionary white homeowners and the engineers of growth in order to put land taking to some "progressive" end. Indeed, in what was, at that time, a great leap of faith, colored folk—like Theodore Gibson, members of the Adelphia Club, and others—reached for their own infrastructural power in an attempt to end deplorable slum conditions or simply to improve the everyday value of black life.

Much of colored people's hope for reforming and eventually ending apartheid flowed from a growing belief that one could use the state to uplift the race. Folk commitments to hold and preserve real estate ran headlong into this swelling reformist ethos. Progressive uses of eminent domain seemed, in part, the path to civil rights. But, just as Jim Crow law and order required meting out violence against colored people, a vision of civil rights tied to eminent domain required compromising black property rights through condemnation and demolition.

With regard to real estate and so many other markers of citizenship, it would be a mistake to think of colored people as espousing well-defined "free market" approaches on the one hand and "statist," or "interventionist," approaches on the other. What were seemingly competing approaches to land were, in fact, deeply complementary. Most expressions of black people's land politics shared not only an indignation toward white supremacy, as an idea, but also a willingness to punish the black poor, thereby affirming white power, in practice. Equally important, black people of property in the postwar period often articulated their vision of freedom by trying to claim the kind of infrastructural power that had largely been the sole privilege of white Americans. Being a black landlord was not that different from being a black liberal, in other words. At times these people were, in fact, one and the same. The long-term ends were certainly the same—to abolish the uncertainty and fear meant to accompany one's imposed status as "nigger." Only the means, depending on the context, were different, and they differed dramatically.

This chapter continues exploring the integral role colored communities and black property culture played in the development of American liberalism in the immediate postwar period by exploring the overlapping political visions of white and black landlords. In particular, it explores how Jim Crow's rental owners and property managers made use of the hard power of the state and the soft power that came from building community in the colored neighborhoods of the late 1940s and the early 1950s. White rental entrepreneurs drew great social and political power from their investment in black communities. But such power was only possible because of the racial structure of rental capitalism and the role played by landlords and property managers. In particular, real estate entrepreneurs who had their livelihoods rooted in Jim Crow's ghetto served as powerful intermediaries between apartheid's white and colored worlds. Through savvy practices of racial uplift and paternalism, Luther Brooks, Ira Davis, and countless other capitalists effectively tied black people into the Jim Crow state. How well real estate interests managed the slums determined, in effect, the degree to which urban land reform and Negroes' visions of racial uplift would remain beholden to the authority of property owners.

As discussed in the previous chapter, Theodore Gibson, Elizabeth Virrick, and the Coconut Grove Committee for Slum Clearance were largely stymied in their first efforts at housing reform, thanks, in no small part, to Luther Brooks and other well-connected real estate interests in South Florida. Yet, the slum committee's activism, like that of concurrent movements elsewhere in the United States, helped change some important features of rental capitalism in Greater Miami's Negro neighborhoods. Chiefly, the actual building material that made up Jim Crow's ghetto underwent a slow, but important transformation under the pressures of interracial housing reform. Miami's nascent urban reform movement, combined with new and threatening provisions of the Housing Act of 1949, prompted landlords to utilize the federal loan programs of the Federal Housing Administration. Their goal was to replace sloppily maintained wood construction with concrete housing, and, in the process, to keep both black militancy and federal "intrusion" at bay. In one of the most dramatic and overlooked transformations of American housing, the move from wood tenements to concrete apartments would serve as an integral feature of landlords' take on postwar liberalism. And by apparently proving that Miami did not need public housing, the move to make Miami's housing more concrete would provide a potent expression of the kinds of "free market" alternatives that effectively allowed real estate interests to set the liberal state against itself.

Valuing Colored Town

As the slum clearance debates of the late 1940s raged on, Luther Brooks was becoming a rich man. His company, Bonded Collection Agency, had grown into the undisputed juggernaut in the business of managing colored living accommodations. The key to Brooks's business model, particularly as South Florida's colored population continued to grow, lay in his insistence on building and managing, but never actually owning, Negro-inhabited dwellings. Brooks offered what one might call "full-service" management packages, or a kind of Negro rental franchise, perfect for white absentee landlords from Miami Beach or elsewhere seeking minimal entanglements and maximum profits. Brooks, indeed, made slum housing a "clean" investment for white landlords, as Miami's black ghetto fueled prosperity in faraway corners of the country. Vacationing whites from Illinois or New Jersey could pick up several units with the ease one would now experience acquiring a time-share. Once tourists returned home, deeds in hand, weekly checks would simply arrive in their mailboxes. Based on Brooks's own statements in the press, 60 percent of his white clients had never even seen the rental property they owned.[7] Bonded Collection paid the mortgage, taxes, and insurance on a landlord's investment property. It also made repairs, handled tenant complaints, and collected the rent. In return, the property owner, who in more than a few instances bought a house or apartment building built by Bonded, agreed to give Brooks's company between 8 and 9 percent of the total rent collected from tenants each month. This was a favorable rate, to be sure; properties managed under Bonded generally secured the highest available profit margins in the Negro housing game.[8]

It is hard to overstate the profitability of slum housing in the Jim Crow era. In our present-day economy, rental properties considered profitable yield between 4 and 6 percent net annual return. Slumlords in Baltimore, Maryland, according to the geographer David Harvey, enjoyed remarkable returns hovering between 10 and 15 percent annually during the recession years of the 1970s.[9] By comparison, the owners of Negro rentals in Greater Miami, according to Bonded's own bookkeeper, enjoyed an astounding *27 percent* return on their investment every year.[10]

Making money on the front end through construction and on the back end from property management, Brooks gained handsome profits. Of the nine collection agencies managing rental properties in the Central Negro District, Bonded was by far the most successful. By the mid-1950s, Brooks had made enough money to buy several thirty- to forty-foot Chris-Craft deep-sea fishing boats and homes in the Florida Keys, the exclusive suburbs of Miami Springs and Bay Point, and the sleepy town of Sopchoppy in the Florida Panhandle.[11] The 1950s would also see Bonded Collection Agency boast ten satellite offices, and over fourteen thousand units under its management. In 1959 dollars, the company secured more than $640,000 in annual revenue.[12] At the company's height, Bonded managed the tenants for six of the city's fifteen largest property owners. And, at midcentury, nearly half of all the black people who rented apartments in Dade County lived in a unit managed by Bonded Collection Agency. The company was, by Brooks's own account at least, "the largest private housing rental and management agency in the South."[13]

When asked in 1975, after nearly forty years in property management, how he would fix what was, at that time, Miami's still deplorable slum problem, Luther Brooks remarked, somewhat glibly, "Somebody as smart as me has to give it a lot of study."[14] As smart as Brooks clearly was, his success depended chiefly on layer upon layer of racial apartheid. White vigilantism held the color line in some corners of South Florida; discrimination from white lenders held it in others. In Miami proper, as occurred in cities as varied as Birmingham, Alabama, and Detroit, Michigan, planning officials and city commissioners used a variety of zoning techniques to maintain the city's myriad color lines.[15] One especially effective tactic was to use "industrial" zoning designations to keep white and black families separate. Whites lived on "residential" land, Negroes mostly on "industrial." Where city officials *had* allowed for "residential" designations in black communities, developers routinely secured variances, or exemptions to zoning law, which allowed more cagey entrepreneurs, such as John Bouvier and Malcolm Wiseheart, to build duplexes on plots zoned for single-family housing, or to open liquor stores or bars mere steps from family homes and churches.[16] Combined with the Home Owners Loan Corporation's system of neighborhood grading, the patchwork zoning designations of colored neighborhoods made most black property patently ineligible for federally insured mortgages. Moreover, Jim Crow's web of residential color lines made Miami's Central Negro District an especially fertile hotbed of substandard housing and white profiteering, both of which buoyed Bonded's bottom line.

In 1947, wooden shotgun shacks still made up nearly 80 percent of all the homes in Colored Town. Other kinds of wood construction continued to house black folk throughout Dade, Broward, and Monroe Counties. Colored Town's "Good Bread Alley" was a notoriously packed section of the neighborhood, with 178 different one-story apartments, a theater house, a church, and several stores all on a single block. When testifying before the US Congress about the need for real estate reform, Edward Graham, the popular pastor of Mt. Zion Baptist Church, specifically highlighted Good Bread Alley's density as evidence of the cramped and dire housing situation in Colored Town.[17]

Lots in black communities tended to be small, allowing as many investors as possible to get a piece of colored housing. Individual landlords also crammed as many buildings as they could fit onto a single lot in order to maximize their return on investment. As shown in the accompanying illustration, lots south of NW Fourteenth Street, which included Good Bread Alley, remained built up almost exclusively with rental units. In keeping with the notion that greater density equaled greater profits, these tightly packed blocks were valued higher than the lots north of NW Fourteenth Street. Those particular lots, with their mix of large single-family homes, rental units, and commercial property, further evidenced the city's ad hoc approach to zoning in black neighborhoods.

One paradox of colored housing in the postwar United States was that, while often in bad physical shape, black homes were usually on what city planners and commercial real estate developers were increasingly imagining

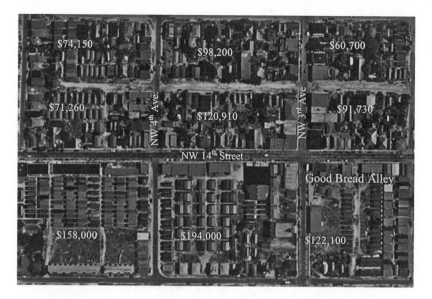

Figure 6.1. Good Bread Alley and vicinity, 1948. (Courtesy of the Metro-Dade Planning Department.)

to be some of the most valuable land in American cities. The country's old colored towns—vividly rendered in dance, as was Detroit's "Black Bottom," or at times entirely fictionalized, as in Ann Petry's *The Narrows*—served, for years, as very real "servants quarters" for Negroes servicing white privilege prior to and immediately following World War II. In the expanding cities of the 1940s and 1950s, neighborhoods bursting with black workers seemed less like an asset than a hindrance. They ran up against blossoming downtown business districts featuring "whites only" hotels, department stores, and universities.[18] As a second paradox, unique to the urban South, the residents of Dixie's colored enclaves were, by the sweat of their brows, supposed to man the material emergence of the modern New South city. They also represented, through their very bodies, the kinds of colored servility most whites deemed a southern tradition or, in Greater Miami's case, an added perk of Caribbean vacationing. A central tension of the postwar period, thus, was that colored neighborhoods were both racially necessary and, increasingly for many, economically expendable.

Planners viewed Colored Town as having some of the most valuable land in Florida. The Central Negro District lay less than one mile west of the hotels of center city. It was also three and a half miles from the hotels of Miami Beach, six miles east of the Hialeah racetrack, and six miles northwest of the

Figure 6.2. Greater Miami, 1949. (From City Planning and Zoning Board of Miami, *Dwelling Conditions in the Two Principal Blighted Areas, Miami, Florida.*)

exclusive white city of Coral Gables. Few areas enjoyed such spatial proximity to South Florida's most lucrative locations. "Miami's life pulsates from this heart," Miami's City Planning Board explained, using an anatomical metaphor typical of the day. Hoping to encourage the total slum clearance of Good Bread Alley in 1941, planners remarked, "A healthy heart with adequate arteries is greatly needed to provide for Miami's unhampered sturdy growth."[19] City officials hoped to replace Good Bread Alley with a new train terminal in 1941, but the outbreak of war and several lawsuits from black and white landlords thwarted the effort.

In Coconut Grove, close proximity between black tenants and white homeowners helped give birth to the Coconut Grove Committee for Slum Clearance. Yet that same proximity between colored property owners and the assets of white landlords made slum clearance and other government redevelopment programs a bitter pill. In part the result of Brooks's business acumen, white landlords owned over 70 percent of the housing in Colored Town during the 1940s and 1950s. They had a history of successfully fighting off redevelopment schemes going back to the days of Franklin Bush in the 1920s. By comparison, Caribbean and American blacks owned some seventeen hundred rental units, or roughly 20 percent, of the apartments in Colored Town. The remaining portion of the neighborhood's residents consisted of black homeowners. For colored folk, the cost of redevelopment looked like what happened to Railroad Shop. Liberty Square was, by this time, at capacity, and teachers, preachers, and much of Miami's fragile black middle class still lived amid the low-grade rooming houses and shotgun shacks of the Central Negro District. Landlords' defense of their own property interests over several decades protected the black homeowners crammed among the tenements, and white businessmen like Luther Brooks made sure to let them know it.[20]

Of Power and Paternalism

One of the most important characters in the story of the Negro in Miami is a white man.

— *Miami News*, 2 March 1962

In a real estate industry increasingly defined by mathematical models of property assessment and expert city planning in downtown offices, Luther Brooks understood the power of street-level politics and the cultural value of collective "colored" ownership. From Bonded's main office, he operated a radio show on Negro affairs. Called *The People Speak*, the interracial program addressed problems such as black voter registration, domestic cleanliness, and race relations. Other radio programs put black rental owners in touch with those lenders who would grant Negroes loans for building or renovations. Much of the show's content actually flowed from the activities of the Greater Miami Colored Research and Improvement Association. This was an advocacy group that Brooks, as president, founded in 1950 and staffed with black and white notables, including Lawson Thomas, Ira Davis, and politicians sympathetic to Brooks's political positions. Through this association, Brooks compiled important allies and favorable public relations in black Miami; the group gave, in essence, an organizational name to the philanthropic and political efforts of the city's black and white landlords. The association, for instance, made a one thousand–dollar donation to a local colored nursery and made regular contributions to colored social clubs and church auxiliaries. Brooks, as the group's public face, even sent promising Negro students from Booker T. Washington High School to college and, eventually, medical and professional school. From the late 1940s through the late 1960s, Brooks could be seen helping out with something

Figure 6.3. Luther Brooks, ca. 1965. (Courtesy of the Black Archives History and Research Foundation of South Florida Inc.)

as small-scale as sponsoring a local colored boys' softball team or making more substantial commitments, such as his long-term role as benefactor and board member of William Sawyer's Christian Hospital, the only hospital serving Negroes in all of South Florida.[21] "Leading citizens of the Negro," wrote one black editorialist in the *Miami Herald*, "hold a very high regard for Brooks, as well as the many fine community contributions and services that he has rendered."[22] Of his apparent generosity in Miami's black neighborhoods, Brooks explained, "I get my money from Negroes. I owe it to them to help them."[23]

In economic terms, Brooks also kept money, goods, and services churning through Colored Town. He made a point, for instance, of hiring only Negro maintenance men, and, in 1951, he had a total of forty such men in his employ. Bonded sent these men to repair jobs about town in a fleet of thirty-four brand-new cars, each tied to Brooks's main Third Avenue office by radio dispatch. And he always made sure to buy a brand-new fleet of cars and trucks every year from local colored salesmen. Through the wages he paid his workers, Brooks injected more than thirty-eight hundred dollars a week into the local economy. As with his apparent philanthropy, Brooks made sure to publicize all these efforts through various annual reports on the state of Negro housing. And these publications, like his other company advertisements, all ran through the press of the Reeves family's *Miami Times*, providing further evidence of his support for black business.[24] Brooks's associates, who included US congressman George Smathers, helped bring black college football to Miami in 1947. Yet again, even small things, like gifting Christmas dinners to black tenants, came as the result of Brooks's careful management of the relationship between white capitalists and black tenants.[25]

Much of the point of this largess was to turn popularity into political power. Brooks understood the power of the black vote, both in its presence and, as in the rural Black Belt communities of his youth, in its absence. A string of voting reforms, including Florida's banning of the all-white primary in 1933 and the abolition of the poll tax in 1938, had emboldened Florida's urban Negroes to pursue voting power earlier than blacks had in other corners of the South. In 1939, Sam Solomon, a thirty-four-year-old Negro mortician from Albany, Georgia, seized the chance to put his name on the ballot for city commissioner. His defiance of Jim Crow custom inspired nearly two thousand blacks to register to vote for the first time.[26] Solomon and other black Miamians suffered the expected death threats in the lead-up to the election. Members of the Ku Klux Klan marched through the heart of Colored Town at midnight, hanging a black voter in effigy and planting burning crosses on street corners. But when white-hooded protesters reached the corner of Third Avenue and Twelfth Street, a mob of irate black residents snatched the burning cross from the Klansmen and trampled it underfoot, shouting defiant threats. Though Solomon lost the election, Langston Hughes immortalized the moment in his poem "The Ballad of Sam Solomon."[27] In short order, Luther Brooks hired the now-famous Solomon as Bonded Collection Agency's public relations director.[28]

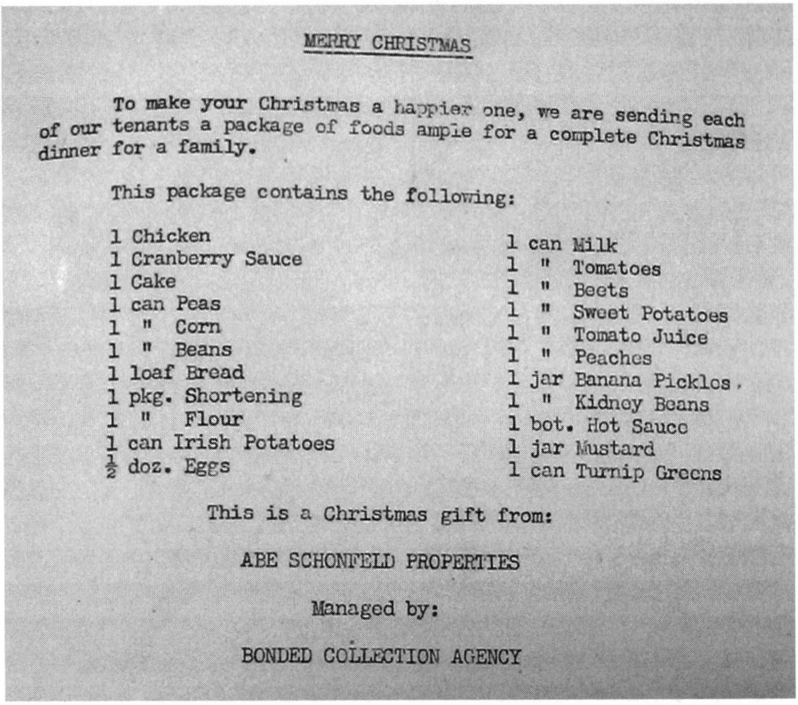

MERRY CHRISTMAS

To make your Christmas a happier one, we are sending each of our tenants a package of foods ample for a complete Christmas dinner for a family.

This package contains the following:

1 Chicken
1 Cranberry Sauce
1 Cake
1 can Peas
1 " Corn
1 " Beans
1 loaf Bread
1 pkg. Shortening
1 " Flour
1 can Irish Potatoes
½ doz. Eggs

1 can Milk
1 " Tomatoes
1 " Beets
1 " Sweet Potatoes
1 " Tomato Juice
1 " Peaches
1 jar Banana Pickles
1 " Kidney Beans
1 bot. Hot Sauce
1 jar Mustard
1 can Turnip Greens

This is a Christmas gift from:

ABE SCHONFELD PROPERTIES

Managed by:

BONDED COLLECTION AGENCY

Figure 6.4. Merry Christmas, 1956. Luther Brooks encouraged Abe Schonfeld, a Jewish Miami Beach attorney and a Bonded client, to donate an entire holiday dinner to each resident of his over one hundred apartments, a gesture intended, in the words of a Bonded employee, "to make [their] Christmas a happier one." (Courtesy of the Black Archives History and Research Foundation of South Florida Inc.)

Between 1939 and 1957, Brooks fought to keep eminent domain weak or to oppose the restructuring of local government to expand the regulatory powers of municipal or county government. And in each effort, Negroes voted heavily with landlords, sometimes by margins of two to one. In a 1953 push to strengthen Miami's powers of land expropriation, for instance, Miami's black voters opposed the measure 67 percent to 33 percent, even though the primary argument in favor of stronger land expropriation pointed to improved slum clearance.[29] Similar voting habits marked elections in the early 1940s and again in the late 1950s.[30] With carefully chosen words, Brooks warned black voters in 1951 to pay attention to "how elections are controlled in slave countries. . . . It can happen here." "Always vote against public housing," he admonished, because "tenants who rent, and all homeowners pay a part of the rent of each dweller in public housing."[31] It's difficult to know the degree to which such arguments resonated with black

Miamians, and black renters in particular, on a person-by-person basis. In a 2006 interview, however, one black Miamian plainly expressed the trend of black people voting against expanded land powers for the local state: "We just didn't trust what those white folks were doing."[32] Clearly, some white folk were more trusted than others. In his political fortunes, Luther Brooks was not just the beneficiary of segregationist policies and practices. He was the beneficiary of America's racial history.

Politics from the Past

The withdrawal of federal troops at the end of Reconstruction, the longtime absence of a federal antilynching bill, and decades of similarly benign neglect from the federal government did little to encourage black people to believe that government, in the abstract, would act on their behalf. As the famed historian C. Vann Woodward explained of black politics at the end of Reconstruction, "When Northern liberals and radicals began to lose interest in the freedmen's cause and federal protection was withdrawn, it was natural that the Negro should turn to the conservatives among upper-class Southerners for allies."[33] When Woodward wrote those words in his now-classic book *The Strange Career of Jim Crow* in 1955, his description of black southern politics remained largely true. If whites controlled the state anyway, particularly in the South, it led to reason, why not deal with whites directly rather than leave matters as important as real estate or community building to impersonal, bureaucratic chance?

At midcentury, governing in the South was a matter of intimacy and the interpersonal as much as it was a matter of votes and policy.[34] The author Zora Neale Hurston spent several years in Miami collecting folklore and working as a domestic in the home of George Smathers's father, Frank, a retired judge. In addition to helping Mrs. Smathers keep house, Zora regularly got into fiery exchanges with the family patriarch, routinely letting "the old cuss," Mr. Smathers, "have it with both barrels."[35] Few played as direct a role in the preservation of racist state practices as a white judge and his son, a southern congressman. And yet, the kind of intimacy Hurston describes as existing between herself and members of the Smathers family—with both its playful and heated exchanges—typified the complicated ties that bound white people to colored people under Jim Crow.[36]

From her room in the Smathers home, Zora wrote letters and articles that remained sharply critical of groups that asked Negroes to trouble local channels of black political power. It made little sense, it seemed, to place one's hope in outsiders who picked fights with white business leaders or who sought civil rights protections from the federal government. "To H— with [the NAACP's] Walter White" or the Congress of Industrial Organization's Political Action Committee, "which had invaded us," she wrote in 1952.[37] In Hurston's view, pragmatic and successful Negro leaders at the local level should avoid civil rights celebrities who flew in and out of cities and rural communities, endangering "the benefits we have been able to achieve through the years since the Emancipation Proclamation."[38] Out-of-town radicals, again in Hurston's telling, stirred up racial strife, led marches, and reprimanded local activists before invariably pulling up stakes. The hometown folk left in their wake would then be forced to repair any fractures that sprang up between black civic leaders and their white counterparts.

Instead of professional organizers, Hurston and many of her contemporaries believed it took commonsense entrepreneurs to hammer out the deals and build the communities that made Jim Crow work in daily life. Respected property owners like T. R. M. Howard and Amzie Moore in Mississippi, Wilbur Gordon of Los Angeles, and Ira Davis, a friend of Hurston's and Smathers's in Miami, were the kinds of people who, years earlier, had built Hurston's hometown of Eatonville.[39] They were also reflected in the interwoven way that Hurston depicted intimacy, money, and power over her years of writing about black life.[40] "The wife of the Mayor," Hurston explained about Janie, the protagonist of her 1937 novel *Their Eyes Were Watching God*, "was not just another woman as she [Janie] had supposed. She slept with authority and so she was part of it in the town mind."[41] For black people, a measure of power came from proximity to power, whether that power was white, male, or both. And though Hurston spent a lifetime challenging cultural aspects of both patriarchy and white supremacy in her folklore and literary work, she espoused a view of politics that required working alongside rather than against local white elites.

Critically, Hurston's views were not the exception, but rather remained widespread among black Americans, particularly propertied Negroes, who understood what Hurston's Janie had learned as part of their own fraught attempts to master pragmatism, paternalism, and property.[42] In fact, Colored Town's civic life, in general, only rarely lent itself to bottom-up organizing. Most Negro activism in South Florida occurred in ad hoc fashion around questions of labor or in the wake of violence or threats of violence, as happened with the formation of Miami's UNIA or in the massive voter registration drives preceding Miami's 1939 election.[43] Even seemingly "bottom-up" organizations, including colored labor unions, worked on the "Race Man" model of charismatic, almost Victorian leadership that one found in old-time colored groups, such as the Colored Board of Trade or the Overseas Club.

During the early 1930s, for instance, communiqués about voting discrimination in Miami, sent to the NAACP headquarters in New York, circulated only among a loose collection of doctors, reverends, and real estate investors in Colored Town. The city's "List of Prominent Race Members" consisted entirely of men who owned property, with several "large property owner[s]" named among them.[44] The Negro patrolmen policing Colored Town in the 1940s, or the various groups that aspired to curtail vice and remove "immoral women" from the streets in the 1910s also owed *their* existence to black property owners who sought to assert greater control over their poorer black neighbors.[45] There, a degree of authoritarianism was justified as necessary for racial progress—making the neighborhood "ours." Women's groups, such as Annie Coleman's Friendship Garden and Civic Club, exerted similar influence, affirming links between bourgeois femininity and political voice. Likewise, the various heads of the local longshoremen's union, such as Charles Lockhart or Judge Henderson; Otis Mundy and Sam Solomon of the Citizens Service League; or the cluster of black men who met regularly as part of Ira Davis's Adelphia Club all assumed the authority, at various points, to speak for the Negro masses as a practical matter of political course. These were the men and women who founded Miami's first NAACP (1937) and Urban League (1952) chapters and who set these groups' respective agendas, from the top down, for years to come.[46] Similar leadership structures governed black communities elsewhere in the United States and under white supremacist regimes abroad.[47]

Regarding the problem of housing across the urban South, specifically, black tenant organizing was conspicuously absent within the range of colored people's political activity. In most cities, any Negroes of discernible organizing talent would be violently subjugated, as occurred with Laura Koffey in 1928, or, more commonly, as occurred with Sam Solomon and Lawson Thomas, they would be folded into some aspect of the white governing structure. The rent strikes one found in Baltimore, Chicago, or Detroit, which often came as part of a broader sweep of interracial activism under the Popular Front of the 1930s, did not happen in Durham, Atlanta, Richmond, or Miami, nor would they for another thirty years.[48] Communists, in fact, had much greater success in organizing tenants in the urban North and colored sharecroppers in the rural South than they had in mobilizing black renters in southern cities during the late 1930s and 1940s.[49]

Landlording the Race

Seeking to explain a perceived narrowness of radical vision among American Negroes, the sociologist E. Franklin Frazier derisively described the black political imagination in Jim Crow America as wrapped in a "World of Make-Believe."[50] Frazier, quoting the economist Abram Harris, explained how "the Negro masses . . . were led to place increasing faith in business and property as a means of escaping poverty and achieving economic independence."[51] According to Frazier, black civic leaders, beginning in the nineteenth century, institutionalized a commitment to property through the black church, business leagues, and the Negro press. Abram Harris went even further, explaining how black tenant organizing, when it did occur, often degenerated into misplaced nationalism and, usually, unfocused anti-Semitism. "If there is exploitation of the black masses in Harlem," Harris wrote in 1935, "the Negro business man participates in it as well as the Jew, while both the Jewish business man and the Negro are governed by higher forces that are beyond their control."[52] Both Harris and Frazier argued that the institutional power of propertied Negroes and the promise of American consumer culture prevented the wide espousal of anticapitalist sentiment among colored folk. This resulted in what the two considered ironclad myths about the fortitude of Negro business, false beliefs in the possibilities of racial progress by way of entrepreneurship, and the misguided hopes of Negroes achieving elevated status through the acquisition of property and acts of consumption.[53]

Black people frequently opposed racist real estate practices by trying to move or buying their own home, when able, or, occasionally, by destroying or stealing a landlord's property. Still, there was a certain truth to Frazier's claims insofar as *formal* black politics, especially as reflected in southern cities, included a pervasive preference among propertied and aspiring blacks for interracial negotiation over protest.[54] By Frazier's estimation, Durham, North Carolina, was the capital of this approach.[55] Home to C. C. Spaulding's North Carolina Mutual Life Insurance Company and scores of other black businesses, Durham served as a beacon of "productive" and "pragmatic" black politics. Black Durham helped give rise to Georgia's Atlanta Life Insurance Company, Central Life Insurance Company of Florida, and countless clusters of elite urban blacks around the South. The engines of rental real estate, small business, and a general commitment to respectable civic associations and behaviors drove the political and material fortunes of many thousands of black people.[56] Black people across the South were not only consumers of North Carolina Mutual's insurance products and mortgages. By way of the Negro press and an emergent network of professional organizations, they widely adopted the entrepreneurial common sense that Durham and the New South exemplified. The southern "city Negro," put another way, embodied a modernism markedly different from that of her northern cousin. It was one that helped colored folk, in the words of one historian, "manage white supremacy" both before and after the post–World War II period.[57]

In a more practical sense, the prevalence of black entrepreneurial culture gave Negro tenants less freedom than their white counterparts to organize against landlords. "Whites only" Miami Beach, not Colored Town, for instance, became the most vibrant center of tenant activism in the immediate postwar period. In response to rent decontrol after World War II, Max Goodman, Burnett Roth, and other Jewish leftists pushed for basic tenant protections, housing improvements, and greater oversight of landlord abuses. A middle-aged Jewish Marxist, Goodman brought together some fifteen hundred tenants to protest decontrol on the beach. He also organized a march for tenants' rights across town in Hialeah, and even testified before the US Congress about the problems facing Miami's white tenants.[58] Roth, an attorney and an ally of Goodman's, proved adept at using arguments about veterans' rights to link justice in housing to broader moral questions about American democracy. Though Goodman and other communists among Greater Miami's tenant organizers rarely organized openly *as communists*, the city's white tenant organizers made critical arguments about the harshness of rental capitalism, arguments that had the potential to help black Miamians.[59] Roth even acknowledged before a congressional hearing that, while housing conditions for white veterans were bad, "the condition of the Negro is absolutely unbelievable."[60]

The problem in Jim Crow's top-down, conservative political culture was, in part, how entrepreneurship set the terms for black leadership. In contrast to their white Jewish counterparts, most of black Miami's most civically engaged community leaders did not encourage tenant organizing; they actively subverted it as part their general "probusiness" political commitments. In regard to the broader governing culture of the South, Edward T. Graham, pastor of Colored Town's Mt. Zion Baptist, remarked that "most Southern Negro leaders are willing to go along with the status quo because they gain from it. This is an old problem with the Negro in America. His sense of values is not rigid enough. His standards are soft." Graham noted the predilection for compromise among many of his propertied colleagues and added, "This attitude may be all right in business dealings; you may have to compromise. But not when it comes to justice. Certain principles cannot be compromised."[61]

In the late 1940s, Graham joined Goodman in an effort to organize Colored Town's tenants, but when a heart attack took Goodman's life in December of 1949, Graham lost one of his most influential and important white allies.[62] White radicals who tried to carry on Goodman's work after his death ran into serious opposition from well-organized segments of Miami's middle-class black leadership. One white communist organizer, Matilda Graff, had been among the many Jewish leftists who came to Miami from New York and other parts of the Northeast in the early postwar years. She recalled that, as of 1951, the nominal leaders of the black community "were three persons—a dentist, an attorney, and a minister—who owned much real estate." Ira Davis, Lawson Thomas, and the Reverend John Culmer, Graff explained, "represented the 'Uncle Toms' of the black churches and the professions." These men, in Graff's words, "were referred to as the 'unholy alliance.' They listened with closed hearts, minds, and pocketbooks."[63]

Graff's dismissive labeling of black property owners as "Uncle Toms" echoes the frustrations and accusations of false consciousness Frazier and Harris lobbed at the black bourgeoisie as a group. Overlooked by most critiques from the Left, however, was the fact that black property owners had a long history of softening Jim Crow's indignities, if only slightly, by working through political channels opened by white businesspeople. Interracial philanthropy became an especially rich site of black/white political collaboration. And while most black leaders had little use for white activists—and certainly not communists—they welcomed white entrepreneurs bearing gifts and building community in the spirit of uplift.

Well-connected whites also promised black property owners access to some of the infrastructural powers that federal and local agents had used to expand white housing options, to displace black residents, and to reinforce the color line in the New Deal and postwar period. In that sense, they, too, could be "liberals."

Keeping tenants under control, in other words, served as but part of a broader effort among "responsible" Negro leaders to protect their community power and to claim, through powerful white allies, new state authority, new state power. On the housing front, specifically, that included taking a federal agency that had historically been the enemy of black self-determination and repurposing it for the sake of preserving the profitability of Jim Crow.

Welfare for Landlords

Since the 1930s, mortgage insurance, as part of the New Deal state, served as Jim Crow's social insurance. And in that vein, the Federal Housing Administration was likely the most effective vehicle for racial segregation in American history. Still, housing officials within and affiliated with the administration did not enforce discriminatory housing policy uniformly across the country because actual social needs for preserving apartheid's racial peace played out

Figure 6.5. Luther Brooks donates one thousand dollars for nursery, 1951. *Left to right,* Edward Graham, Luther Brooks, W. C. Pinkston (treasurer of the nursery), and H. E. S. Reeves (editor in chief of the *Miami Times*). (Courtesy of the Black Archives History and Research Foundation of South Florida Inc.)

differently on the ground from one context to the next. In the early 1940s, the race relations director for the Chicago FHA assisted black people in their efforts to undo restrictive covenants.[64] Similarly, the FHA made adjustments to and improved equal protections in various programs in response to constant pressure from civil rights organizations, white developers, and highly educated black bureaucrats within the federal government. In Los Angeles, California, the need to keep minorities confined forced the local FHA to expand the availability of mortgage insurance to Japanese and Chinese Americans.[65] The FHA, in brief, was hardly a monolith. It had a lot of moving institutional parts and myriad programs. Furthermore, its agenda changed as the legal and political environment changed, locally and in Washington. That the FHA's segregationist impulses lasted as long as they did—from the 1930s into the 1970s—does not evidence the existence of a single agency of single mind. It speaks, rather, to the suppleness of apartheid and to the pervasiveness of Jim Crow rationale across several different populations, debates, and historical contexts.

In Miami, one critical feature of the FHA, and indeed one that has gone widely overlooked as a national practice, was the way landlords and rental developers used FHA mortgage insurance to maintain both the profitability of Jim Crow and the integrity of black real estate in the face of purportedly racist applications of eminent domain. As part of a nationwide effort to keep out public housing and slum clearance after the passage of the Housing Act of 1949, landlords changed the face, though not the complexion, of Jim Crow's ghetto.[66]

Almost immediately following the passage of the 1934 Housing Act, real estate developers around the country began seeking federal mortgage insurance for building tenements. Initially, FHA officials in Washington and regional offices mostly rejected such requests, and, for the agency's first three years, it insured mortgages on a total of only twenty-one rental properties nationwide. In the eyes of the FHA's early administrators, rentals carried too many risks, including high maintenance costs, delinquent tenants, and the possible burden of rent control from state to state. Rentals, it seemed, promised very little in the way of short- and medium-term profits. Most landlords, moreover, were unwilling to meet the FHA's building requirements lest they cut into their rate of return. Shotgun shacks made plenty of money on their own without the burden of the FHA's building requirements.

During the 1930s, as part of America's first attempt at federal housing and slum clearance, Miami's developers joined a swelling chorus of rental capitalists around the country. They argued that rental housing in general and black housing in particular could fetch high returns, thereby serving as a safe investment of FHA-backed loans. In 1936, Miami's George Merrick, the founder of the University of Miami and its restricted surrounding community, Coral Gables, boasted, "Personally I have handled several Negro towns and know there is money in it!" Merrick, like Carl Fisher and many fellow speculators, had been all but wiped out by the 1926 hurricane and the ensuing market downturn. But investing in Negro rental property helped him get back on his feet. The money Merrick made from black housing kept his experiment at Coral Gables alive. It was thus with great conviction that he explained how no monopoly provided higher profits than control of Negro housing in "just one State of the Southeast." Merrick promised real estate boards "Woolworth-Ford-type volume[s of] money." All the government needed to do was provide "unit loan facility on [a] sound long time basis." With a little loan insurance from the Federal Housing Administration, Merrick argued, any entrepreneur or real estate board would come to appreciate the "millions that are available in this [Negro housing industry]."[67]

Several factors finally brought the FHA squarely into the rental business. The first was the threat of competition from another government agency.

The United States Housing Authority (USHA), which Senate Democrats had included in the Housing Act of 1937, emerged with the power to develop local housing authorities across the country and, through them, more public housing projects. By offering government housing options and increasing the oversight of landlords more generally, the USHA threatened to drive down rents and, landlords claimed, slow down the country's economic recovery.[68] This prompted the second factor: coordinated attacks on public housing from landlord lobbying groups. Members of the National Association of Real Estate Boards and its local affiliates peppered Washington with complaints that, among other things, public housing cost too much, did not actually help the poor, smacked of socialism, and did not clear slums.[69] Pressure from them, combined with America's entry into the Korean War, prompted President Harry Truman and members of Congress to scale back greatly the country's public housing program.[70] Developers in localities around the country, as a third factor, began working with black civic elites to push the massive rezoning of black communities, so that America's old colored towns could finally be eligible for some form of FHA loans.

As it concerned South Florida, the effort to rezone black communities brought together black and white housing reformers, but it also galvanized yet another instance of opposition from both colored property owners, tenants, and their landlords. Bearing news from members of the Miami Chamber of Commerce and the city planning office, several black neighborhood leaders, including Lawson Thomas and Ira Davis, held a town hall meeting in Colored Town to explain the city's plan to rezone nearly 150 acres of the neighborhood for the purposes of new single-family homes and concrete apartment buildings.[71] The plan was to facilitate the demolition of the worst housing in Colored Town and to open more of the neighborhood to "better-class homes" for the Negro professional class.[72] Part of the plan included the displacement of over 190 colored families from Colored Town's Good Bread Alley.[73] At the meeting, black tenants vocally opposed forcible eviction. Several black landlords promised to sue. Ultimately the matter was left to Good Bread's primarily white owners, and most of them had no interest in upgrading their wood housing in pursuit of government-backed loans. What the 1949 rezoning *did* do was open up the prospect for new concrete development in areas surrounding Good Bread Alley.

Coming of the "Concrete Monsters"

At the start of the postwar period, Greater Miami received relatively little federal mortgage insurance for Negro rentals. In 1946, the city had only sixty-two units of black rental housing backed by the Federal Housing Administration. By comparison, FHA-backed apartments numbered in excess of twelve hundred in Jacksonville, two thousand in Chicago, and four thousand in Washington, DC. In response to black people's postwar housing needs, a paltry six hundred new apartments went up in Miami's Central Negro District in 1947, mostly of the cheaper, shotgun variety.[74] As the *Pittsburgh Courier's* Miami correspondent, John Diaz, reported, "Negroes in Miami . . . are worse off now than they were ten years ago."[75] Then, just a year later, in 1948, Miami's FHA commitment to black rentals increased tenfold. That number then tripled again the following year to reach a total of over nineteen hundred apartments. This was, by far, the most rapid expansion of FHA rental underwriting anywhere in the United States, and it sparked a proliferation of privately owned black rental housing in Miami matched by only the largest American cities.[76]

Noting the sudden increase, the FHA's southeast US zone commissioner, Herbert Redman, encouraged mortgage-insured lenders to give further priority to those rental developers targeting the Negroes of Miami's Colored Town. The aim was to outpace local public housing authorities. Continued FHA help would allow, in Redman's words, "substantial housing [to be] provided profitably by private capital for a number of tenants in the area."[77] That same year, 1949, Miami's landlords received nearly ten million dollars in federal mortgage insurance to complete construction of almost two thousand new black-occupied tenements. This doubled, yet again, the number of FHA-backed apartment units for Negroes.[78] During all this, by every measure of property appraisal, Colored Town never stopped being a "D" neighborhood.

Miami's transformation was but the tip of the spear in a remarkable movement that landlords and real estate developers around the country advanced in response to the lifting of rent control and in opposition to local public housing and slum clearance campaigns. In 1950, an astounding 99 percent of the 159,000 new rental units purchased in the United States received mortgage insurance from the Federal Housing Administration. The following year, that proportion fell to a still substantial 89 percent.[79] Between 1935 and 1953, fully half of all multifamily dwellings built in the United States were backed by federal mortgage insurance, and 54 percent of those units were built between 1949 and 1951, immediately following the Housing Act of 1949.[80] Electing to conform, finally, to FHA building guidelines, developers in Miami built concrete housing in Colored Town and dramatically expanded the reach of black-occupied rental property across South Florida.

What most developers built would later be called "Concrete Monsters," a colorfully pejorative term coined by Elizabeth Virrick.[81] By the standards of rental units in much of the urban North, "Concrete Monsters" were small, two- to three-level apartment buildings, with little of the charm that made Liberty Square so attractive. Miami's new concrete tenements were often short on green space, offered no off-street parking, and, because of high rents, were still quite crowded. The ceilings were low, shade trees were rare, and interiors were cheaply outfitted.[82] Perhaps most important to both housing reformers and landlords, rent collection practices in these apartment buildings went entirely unregulated.

Many of the same abuses that defined tenant life in shotgun shacks continued under concrete roofs. Repair crews could be unresponsive, and as early as 5:30 in the morning the rent man could come rapping on your door. Most of Bonded Collection's maintenance men were black, but all of the company's rent collectors, at this time, were white men. Their occasional brashness and their not uncommon use of racial epithets, particularly in the wee hours, could feel like a particularly cruel form of mistreatment. Still, at a basic architectural level, Miami's new "Concrete Monsters" seemed to mark the (delayed) closing of the frontier age in Miami's colored communities. The buildings were certainly more resistant to fire and storm damage than wood-frame housing.

Symbolically, they also marked an invitation for black Miami to join the wider, more modern tropics. Recall that in 1947, the *Pittsburgh Courier*'s John Diaz had lamented the lost decade that had beset black housing since the opening of Liberty Square. By 1957, the paper struck a markedly different tone, making sure to cite the good work of Luther Brooks. "Any person who has been away from this tropical playground 10 or more years would never recognize it today—for a miracle has been wrought in Miami[:] . . . absolutely new, streamlined housing with an architectural design which has turned a once-blighted slum area into a tropical delight to the eye."[83] "Let us be proud of our modern buildings," wrote one columnist for the *Miami Times* in 1955. The paper pointed out the better behavior of tenants from "other parts of the city" (i.e., white Miami), and the *Times* asked renters to "PLEASE ASSIST . . . [those] who are interested in the welfare of the tenants" by tending to trash, minding where one hung one's laundry, and keeping "the children [from] running on everyone else's front porches." Noting all the new concrete construction, Miami's largest black newspaper encouraged renters to trust their property manager and reminded its readers, "The landlord has a heart, too."[84] Attempting to prove the point, Brooks made sure to paint ribbons of two-tone colors, pastels, and heavy tropical hues around the buildings he managed—the colors of Art Deco Miami Beach brought to

Colored Town.[85] Photographs of Brooks's projects accompanied articles in both the *Courier* and the *Miami Times*.

For those who lived outside the Central Negro District, the arrival of concrete tenements seemed to wall in colored people's suburban dreams. Black Liberty City residents noted the "rapid construction" of three-level buildings in the neighborhood. Trees were cleared; open fields were fenced off, dug out, and built up. Miami's white residents noticed the expansion as well. The Dade County Commission and Miami City Commission remained too tied up in procedural wrangling to monitor the size and layout of the new projects. Developers, instead, showed their talent for segregationist self-regulation. They tended to build only on clearly demarcated "colored" or "white" sites, or to erect the requisite concrete walls around projects built in racial "border" zones.

In 1940, some 60 percent of Dade's black housing was in Colored Town. By 1950, that percentage dropped to 40 percent. However, because concrete apartments could literally stack black folk on top of one another, the overall number of black-occupied dwellings in Miami's downtown neighborhood actually doubled. Black Miami was growing just that fast. Opa-locka and Brownsville, areas that had barely any black inhabitants during the 1930s, saw, by 1950, the arrival over some thirty-five hundred units of black housing, much of it in new concrete rental properties. One "Concrete Monster" at a time, real estate speculators scattered Greater Miami's colored population to areas far outside the old Central Negro District.[86]

Landlords and Liberalism

The FHA's massive underwriting of black rental housing, though a national phenomenon, served as Jim Crow's social insurance against black unrest in southern cities such as Miami. Like the hiring of Negro patrolmen or the opening of Virginia Key Beach, the FHA's new engagement with black rental housing served as a critical piece of the equalization movement sweeping across the South. For tenants, it took black housing and made it look more like what whites had long enjoyed. For Ira Davis and other black leaders, broadening the availability of FHA loans for Negro rental housing represented a step toward expanding colored people's access to FHA funds more broadly, also a benefit largely reserved for whites. Davis was himself a landlord. He married Louise Beatrix Stirrup, youngest daughter of Ebenezer Stirrup Sr., Coconut Grove's most successful—and some would argue most notorious—black landlord. Bonded Collection Agency managed the rental properties from which Ira and Louise secured their nest egg. Louise, inciden-

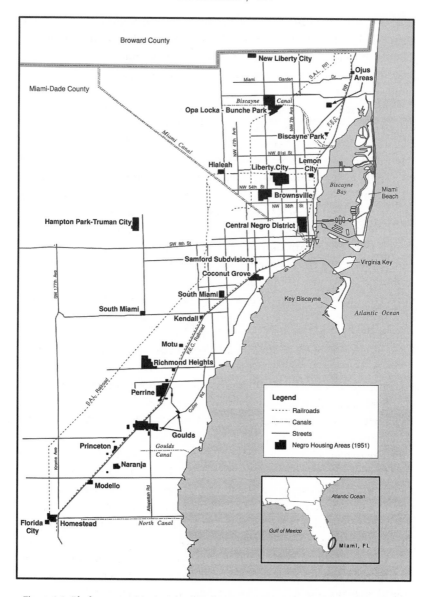

Figure 6.6. Black communities in Miami-Dade County, 1951. (Map by Gordie Thompson.)

tally, was also Theodore Gibson's history teacher at Booker T. Washington High School, and Gibson credited "Miss Stirrup" with "[beginning] me on the subject of civil rights."[87] Once Louise Stirrup became Mrs. Ira Davis, she proved instrumental in getting young Theodore plugged in to early uplift campaigns being run by her husband.

Most times, Ira's vision of politics was the backroom, face-to-face kind that so often raised hackles with more militant reformers and activists. After all, local leftists, according to Matilda Graff, considered him a member of the "Unholy Alliance." When it came to matters of housing, though, Davis had no trouble asking for increased federal investment and oversight. Trading on his political connections, Ira Davis, until 1949, was the only Negro in Greater Miami to have gotten an FHA-backed loan for a single-family home.[88] Speaking, as he often did, for the colored collective, he told federal housing officials in July 1948, "We want our own homes." "Others," he continued, "need rental houses, apartments, duplexes and some need low-cost housing. I hate to think that because of our color we are going to be denied ownership of our own homes."[89] As part of the same movement that tried to liberalize the FHA from several levels (and ultimately succeeded) Davis and many of his contemporaries, Robert Weaver and Frank Horne among them, had vested interest in seeing black landlords participate in the FHA rental movement.[90]

By the same turn, black landlords were critical to the arguments, advanced by Luther Brooks and others, that private enterprise was the best remedy for apartheid's hardships. William Sawyer was sixty-three years old when, in 1949, he bought the three-acre stretch of Brownsville land that would serve as the site for his Alberta Heights project. The six-building concrete development, which he named after his wife of forty years, was among the first financed by an FHA-backed mortgage. The same was true of John Culmer's Francina Apartments, which had twenty units and was located in the Central Negro District.[91] Culmer, who had been quite effective at using the government's slum clearance power to rein in the abuses of black landlords in the 1930s, was also very critical of the administration's discriminatory practices toward colored people. He often cited FHA racism as evidence of black people's need to look for help beyond the state.[92] Yet he, like white developers, clearly did not oppose state programs in the abstract. Continuing black traditions of *spatial* uplift, both Culmer and Sawyer used the FHA's favorable loan terms to outfit their apartments with modern accents and amenities, including aluminum blinds, gas refrigerators, stoves, and water heaters.[93] Citing "well-appointed" units and "the latest conveniences," local FHA officials, white property rights advocates, and the local black press celebrated these and other new black FHA developments as evidence of racial progress secured by the "free market."[94]

Striking the Right Tone

"Free market" arguments helped landlords profit openly from racial segregation while concealing the government's role in breathing new life into Jim
Crow's ghetto.[95] The Miami Chamber of Commerce, in 1950, developed a
special subcommittee, calling it the Committee against Socialized Housing,
or CASH. Alongside other groups, such as the Property Owners Development
Association and the Free Enterprise Association, CASH was one of several
landlord lobbying groups in Florida to recruit state politicians, engineers,
and attorneys in an effort to keep government mortgage insurance coming
in and government land expropriation and public housing out. As evidence
of their success, the state of Florida received over seventy-six million dollars
in monies earmarked for welfare between January of 1949 and June of 1951.
Not a dime of it went toward filling the nonmilitary public housing vacuum.
In fact, thanks to white homeowner intransigence about the location of
public housing sites, and landlord lobbying at both the state and municipal
levels, no government housing would be built at all in Dade County between
1940 and 1954.[96] This was roughly the same period during which landlords
received ten million dollars in mortgage commitments from the FHA.

The Cold War arguments that developed in the battle between the Coconut Grove Committee for Slum Clearance and Greater Miami's developer
community continued to govern the political debate over the state's role in
the housing market. Rental lobbyists, still crying "socialism," argued that,
rather than subject businesspeople to undue government competition or
regulation, landlords should have the freedom to self-regulate. In 1950, Miami's mayor, William Wolfarth, granted rental owners the necessary latitude
by passing weak, almost token, slum clearance oversight, with no federal
funding.[97] The measure did little to quell activists in Coconut Grove and
other observers, who continued to advocate for federal slum clearance and
public housing. One columnist at the *Miami Herald*, a paper sympathetic to
slum clearance advocates, noted that "the socialism epithet was not raised
when Federal money went into our International Airport." Neither was it
raised when "Federal money financed the Orange Bowl, [or when] Federal
guaranteed mortgages touched off the building boom here."[98] At issue, it
seemed, was the *kind* of liberalism South Floridians should accept.

So it was on the race question as well. In spite of the federal government's
impressive record on maintaining racial segregation, the US Supreme Court,
in 1948, ruled that racially restrictive covenants were unconstitutional (*Shelley v. Kraemer*). This, combined with the apparent liberalization of the FHA's
position on single-family homes in 1950, seemed to uncork the triple threat

of integration, miscegenation, and white downward mobility. "Obviously," wrote CASH representatives, "recent supreme court rulings [mean] . . . the federal government cannot permit race segregation in its own public housing projects. . . . We wonder what effect these things are going to have on property values." But it was other and more traditional racist "values" that CASH would employ in its race-mongering publicity campaign. Citing a 1948 congressional investigation of public housing in San Diego and Los Angeles, CASH exposed the discovery of a "Negro Communist leader living in the project with a White woman employee of the [housing] project." "Are the Communists for Public Housing?" asked the members of Miami's most powerful real estate lobby. "You Bet They Are!"[99]

Though he came of age as a white man in the Depression-era South, Luther Brooks was never recorded engaging in overtly racist rhetoric. He instead used the weight of his wealth and reputation as a businessman to drive his corner of a landlord movement, protecting his clients' interests in various ways. "What he did was behind the scenes. He was a silent lobbyist," remembered his son-in-law and business partner, George Harth.[100] Congressmen, US senators, and even a few Florida governors found themselves guests on one of Brooks's Caribbean fishing excursions.[101] A day of deep-sea angling—and, with luck, a marlin strike—would sometimes be all it took to remove a few troublesome lines from proposed legislation. Brooks openly paid the way for city commissioners to take trips out of town.[102] And later, he even got his son-in-law placed on the Miami City Planning Board, again, just for a little insurance.[103]

But the debate over postwar housing was hardly an intellectual one, or even one strictly about political favors. It was about the location and profitability of black housing, and it drew from the basest politics driving American apartheid. Newspapers reported that CASH, in addition to spending perhaps as much as one hundred thousand dollars in its campaign against "socialism," "spread vicious rumors" and resorted to "intimidation of the Negro population."[104] Luther Brooks denied being a member of CASH.[105] Still, rumors surfaced that maintenance men in properties managed by Bonded Collection Agency were turning off the electrical service to the apartments of any black tenants known to vote for federal slum clearance or public housing. In search of white voters in the 1950 referendum against federal slum clearance, Miami's real estate developers touted their support of segregation as a public service. CASH asked those white citizens pondering slum clearance to consider, "Where will the displaced colored families go?" It then pointed out, "More than 3,500 home units, exclusively for colored, are now under construction by Free Enterprise."[106]

Miami's real estate interests knew they were playing with potentially incendiary materials. Even as developers used race baiting to limit government involvement, they were actively expanding black housing right up against white enclaves. In 1951, any claims about the free market's progressive gifts seemed undone by the age-old problem of Jim Crow's violence.

Still the Frontier

When Elizabeth Virrick, Theodore Gibson, and other housing reformers in Coconut Grove repelled John Bouvier and Malcolm Wiseheart from their neighborhood in 1949, the developers simply moved their money to what they imagined would be a less troublesome section of South Florida. In a neighborhood called Edison Center, the two men broke ground on two FHA-financed housing projects—Knight Manor, which was for whites, and Carver Village, named after George Washington Carver, which they designated for colored people. Because whites had so many more housing options than Negroes, Knight Manor remained only half full. Blacks, meanwhile, were on waiting lists to get into Carver Village. Rather than have potential rents rot on the vine, the two developers converted Knight Manor to a majority-black apartment building, renaming the whole project after Tuskegee's famed botanist and inventor. The few white residents of the building, and many more from the surrounding Edison Center community, responded immediately.[107]

In a dizzying array of organizing, Edison Center's whites first formed the Dade County Property Owners Association, a group that quickly rose to over two hundred members, some of whom were, in fact, renters. White residents then organized a one hundred–car motorcade that paraded past Bouvier's and Wiseheart's family homes with megaphones and protest placards. Following that, Edison's homeowners asked that the city of Miami invoke "emergency police powers" so it could forcibly evict all Negroes from Carver Village without waiting even for a court ruling or condemnation proceedings. Given the police action that had purged Railroad Shop of colored families just four years earlier, a mass eviction of Negroes was, frankly, what state reform and regulation—what liberalism—looked like for troubled white homeowners. Edison residents flooded then governor Fuller Warren's office with letters, telegrams, and petitions seeking a swift and decisive correction to what was an obvious transgression of Jim Crow's residential rules. In one letter, a Mr. and Mrs. Hammack condemned Bouvier and Wiseheart's influence on city housing policy, leveling what was becoming an increasingly popular charge. "Would you help us in this fight [against] discrimination against whites," they pleaded. "John Bouvier . . . being a member of [the] zoning board in Dade County," the letter

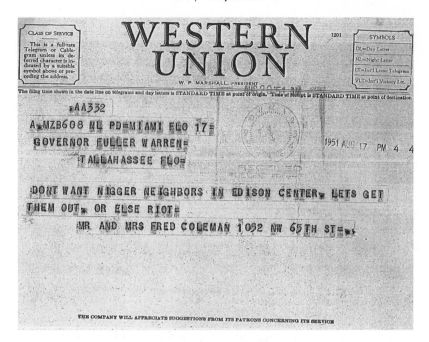

Figure 6.7. Western Union telegram (17 August 1951). (Courtesy of the State Library and Archives of Florida.)

continued, "is rezoning our area for his own benefit." Other correspondence was far more direct in its pleadings and proscriptions: "Don't want Nigger Neighbors in Edison Center. Let's Get Them Out. Or Else Riot."[108]

As a final form of community activism, a small cadre of Edison residents deployed more familiar means of expressing white power. They organized night rides around Carver Village, shouting warnings and epithets from moving cars in an attempt to expel black residents through intimidation.[109] Then, in the predawn hours of 22 September, whites with training in explosives ignited over three hundred pounds of dynamite outside of a vacant apartment at Carver Village. As far as fifty blocks away, Miamians felt concussive waves from the blast, as the bomb shattered hundreds of windows and destroyed or damaged ten different rental units.[110]

Fearful of further race agitation from the white grass roots, members of the Miami City Commission proposed using eminent domain. Though they had previously supported the building of St. Albans, the commission broke ranks with Bouvier and Wiseheart and agreed, four to one, to enter condemnation proceedings on the project. Louie Bandel, a politically moderate city commissioner and ardent supporter of pragmatic Jim Crow solutions, including the Negro police force and court, spoke in particularly strong favor of the move. The city of Miami should, in his words, "condemn the buildings at Carver Village . . . and . . . acquire them by eminent domain for municipal purposes." Commissioners tossed around ideas for a playground, a water treatment facility, or swimming pool: anything other than Negro housing would apparently do.[111] As a multibuilding, concrete housing project, however, Carver Village carried a $1.3 million price tag, far more than the Miami City treasury of $700,000 could afford. Carver Village, despite all its potential racial problems, was simply out of the city's price range.[112] In what seemed like an almost cyclical problem returning from the Progressive Era and the war years, segregation by condemnation was just too expensive. The consequences were predictable.

White residents detonated a second batch of dynamite on 30 November. This one generated an explosion strong enough to toss hunks of concrete debris over fifty yards from the initial blast site, causing twenty-two thousand dollars in damage. Miraculously, no one had been killed in either the September or the November attack. Local people nevertheless understood the attacks in the context of violence elsewhere on the globe, renaming Carver Village "Little Korea."

The project's developers used the event to shore up the point that private capital was always friend to "the Negro." John Bouvier condemned the bombing as "a dastardly act of professional murderers," and vowed to use the power of his dollars to counteract the blatant racism he had witnessed in South Florida's housing market over the previous decade. Talking to black reporters, he linked the history of racial violence to the violence of eminent domain abuses in Greater Miami. He also communicated what he knew to be true about the link between residential segregation and real estate profits, because he himself had grown rich off Jim Crow. "We [whites] have taken from Negro use and converted to white use all the Railroad Shop areas formerly reserved for [the] Negro," Bouvier told reporters. "As a result . . . a lot in the Negro district of Miami will bring from $6,000 to $10,000 . . . but a similar lot in a white residential district will cost around $800 to $1,000." Bouvier and Wiseheart, in spite of the constant criticism they received from white and black housing activists, claimed to be "working to relieve an injustice." Bouvier then warned—in a statement that collapsed Miami's violence with recent mob action directed against blacks a few months earlier in Chicago, Illinois—"There will be no Cicero here."[113] In the Windy City that previous July, white home- and business owners, among other things, bought explosives in bulk and simply handed them out to neighborhood teens to terrorize black tenants indiscriminately.[114]

Figure 6.8. Carver Village bombing, 30 November 1951. (Courtesy of the State Library and Archives of Florida.)

To be black, in part, was to potentially be bombed. Indeed, it's likely that trepidations about Soviet invasions or the atomic bomb espoused by white people nationwide paled, for colored people, in comparison to more everyday fears about bombings at their churches, homes, and apartments. The Southern Regional Council, a group of white progressives, noted that, between 1951 and 1952, white terrorists in eastern North Carolina bombed the homes of more than forty black families, and that figure only counts those bombings that were reported.[115] The city of Birmingham, Alabama— infamously known as "Bombingham"—was particularly beset by white terrorism, even by southern standards. It suffered fifty reported bombings between 1947 and 1966.[116] The most militant fringe groups also targeted the growing Jewish and Catholic populations migrating into and fanning out across the white suburbs of the *new* New South. Some seemingly more progressive southern cities, such as Atlanta and Miami, tried to preempt the violence by banning the trappings of white supremacist groups, such as the wearing of hoods or neo-Nazi paraphernalia.[117] Most of these efforts, though, simply drove terrorist groups underground, where those with military experience could more safely conspire with seemingly more respectable homeowners, employers, and religious leaders.

During a dangerous six months in Florida in 1951, there were twenty successful or attempted bombings against black or Jewish property. Each one in the Sunshine State, as elsewhere, had to do with white Americans trying to control a geography that, through the buying and selling of land, threatened to get out of their control. "Jews outside of Miami Beach will die," came one threat from a group calling itself "The Confederate Underground."[118] Just days after the second blast at Carver Village in late November, a third blast erupted there, this time in concert with similar attacks against a Catholic church and the Miami Hebrew School and Congregation.[119] In a particularly notable incident, Harriet and Harry T. Moore, two teachers and NAACP activists from the central Florida city of Mims, died after white vigilantes detonated a bomb placed under their house on Christmas Day 1951.[120]

The concurrence of anti-Semitic, anti-Catholic, and antiblack violence greatly threatened South Florida tourism, the region's chief industry. "We . . . urge every decent American throughout the country to conduct a boycott of the winter resorts of the State of Florida and of its big orchard citrus products," signed a three hundred–person assembly from Brooklyn, New York, in a letter to Governor Fuller Warren. Wrote another observer from up North, "Every decent American recognizes . . . a chain of events that has made Florida a hunting ground where fascist bigots can feel free to bomb Negro housing projects, Jewish synagogues and Catholic churches while the authorities sit idly by." As letters from everywhere between Indiana and Connecticut poured in, one of Governor Warren's aides noted, "The State of Florida in the North was receiving the worst publicity imaginable."[121]

The threat of lost revenue and Florida's sullied reputation prompted decisive action from state officials. Governor Warren traveled personally to Carver Village to inspect the damage and later assigned an investigator to work with federal, county, and municipal law enforcement on the case. Their investigations yielded three white, male army veterans and one white woman, Helen Russell, a fifty-five-year-old Sunday-school teacher who had also been vice president of the Edison Center Civic Association. All four had their indictments eventually dismissed in federal court in August 1955, the judge citing lack of evidence.[122] As a more lasting response, Miami's city commission immediately changed Carver Village's zoning designation from "residential" to "industrial," thus preventing Bouvier and Wiseheart from financing any new developments. Black and white housing reformers pointed out that the new zoning designation enabled the building of a vocational school that, unlike the one built at Railroad Shop, Miamians actually needed.[123] The seemingly reckless placement of privately funded apartments for Miami's black population also opened the door to public housing, which many considered a much sturdier form of residential segregation.[124]

Taking One for the "Public Good"

Ongoing intransigence from landlords, on the one hand, and white homeowners and Dade County commissioners, on the other, left only one site for Greater Miami's first black public housing project since Liberty Square—the colored community of Para Villa. The government's project was slated to displace over one hundred black residents in the name of providing housing for one thousand. Several of Para Villa's residents were New Deal success stories who had graduated from Liberty Square to buy their own homes. When city assessors and property surveyors started knocking on black families' doors to begin condemnation proceedings, Para Villa's residents, recalling Railroad Shop, flatly refused to admit them. Others organized into the Para Villa Homeowner Improvement Association and met with federal officials to increase pressure on local authorities to find an alternative site for "colored only" public housing. They even arranged a public hearing on the matter, attended by nearly nine hundred people in protest of the development.[125]

In 1953, Luther Brooks and E. F. P. Brigham were among several white property rights advocates who helped Para Villa's black homeowners tap FHA funds and raise nearly $10 million to carry out their own "private enterprise" slum clearance project. Brigham was considered by members of Miami's development bureaucracy to be a "tenacious and unscrupulous jurist." He also carried a hefty price tag of some $6,000 by the time he tallied his final billable hour. The residents of Para Villa accepted some of Brooks's financial assistance and also built an informal economic collective that pieced together $25, $50, and $100 donations to pay for Brigham's services.[126] As the group's paid spokesman, Brigham argued that the private Para Villa project would "become a model for the entire South with Negroes gaining self-respect in a movement to clear their own slums instead of letting others [the government] do it for them."[127] *Jet* magazine celebrated the effort. Ultimately, though, a collection of federal housing officials and local housing reformers, including Elizabeth Virrick, Theodore Gibson, Ira Davis, and Frank Horne, pushed the project past grassroots opposition. A neighborhood of blackowned homes, many made of pinewood, became the James E. Scott housing project.[128]

Conclusion

As black Miami's old wooden homes and slums became more concrete, so did the wall between South Florida's colored folk and the tree-lined streets of Coral Gables, the swaying palms of Miami Beach. The FHA, in the hands of landlords, would continue to facilitate the profitability of racial segregation. So, too, would public housing, resurgent in 1953 as the answer to both slum conditions and racial violence. In the nearly twenty years between Liberty Square and Para Villa, white housing officials and landlords maintained their faith in residential segregation as a social balm and a source of profit. Black folk's knowledge of that faith—and of violence suffered by bulldozer or bomb—drove the kind of organizing carried out at Para Villa. It haunted black people's collective narratives about serial displacement. And it animated the stories, in the case of the Sawyer family, exchanged between father and son.

Because of the reality of white violence, the belief in property as power remained critical to black visions of civil rights. But Jim Crow's property politics also gave white capitalists and homeowners the opportunity to preserve one of the most destructive and foundational myths of racial segregation—namely, that apartheid and the free market, at their best, were mutually beneficial, so long as everyone had the chance to own and improve their assets. As landlords continued to fend off slum clearance and public housing, their particular version of liberalism in the late 1940s and 1950s seemed to offer proof positive that American capitalism, with a little insurance, could meet "the Negro's" needs.

Among the many instruments of racial segregation in postwar Miami, FHA mortgage insurance became critical to how landlords governed within Jim Crow's political culture. The administration, as an advocate for "free enterprise," allowed rental developers and their lobbyists to cast themselves as friends of black homeowners threatened by urban redevelopment, public housing projects, and other uses of eminent domain. FHA programs also enabled landlords to generate support among white voters in opposition to "socialistic" government housing and slum clearance programs, which, real estate lobbyists argued, threatened to encourage "race mixing" and drive down white property values. The FHA, in short, became critical to arguments about the *social* benefits of "free enterprise." It helped harden the notion that "the market" could somehow bring about racial justice without compromising white pursuits of private property.

"Our economy promises all equal access to consumer goods in a free market." So said Robert Weaver, a black economist and federal official, to a roomful of Urban League activists in 1948. "But for minorities," he added, "the housing market has not been and is not free. We must take steps to make it so."[129] The free market, from Weaver's perspective, was liberalism's promise. And colored people's broad commitments to private property as a source of power inspired the kind of liberalism that would propel black activism in the 1950s and 1960s, even as many black people fell victim to more—and more dramatic—incidents of state-sponsored displacement.

PART THREE

Renovation

Figure 6.9. "City of Miami Welcomes You." (Courtesy of the Black Archives History and Research Foundation of South Florida Inc.)

CHAPTER SEVEN

Bulldozing Jim Crow

"Negroes . . . had to fight for what they got. . . . You are going to meet tremendous resistance."[1] With these words, E. F. P. Brigham, Miami's most renowned real estate attorney, warned Miami city commissioners to leave Virginia Key Beach alone. In the late summer of 1953, planners and politicians had been eyeing Virginia Key as a site for a new airport, a Pan-American welcome center, or possibly an expanded sewage-processing plant for Miami Beach. Brigham, by this point, had acquired an impressive résumé fighting for colored people facing displacement. He joined a chorus of white reformers, including Coconut Grove's Elizabeth Virrick and the conservationist Marjorie Stoneman Douglas, to help preserve the Key's beach as a "colored only" institution. The hope of many black Miamians and their white allies was, actually, to expand the city's black beach to accommodate, in Douglas's words, "the people who are partly negro, or entirely negro, who come up from [South America]."[2] Improving the quality of nonwhite tourism was not simply a matter of black people's personal amusement, or even international brotherhood. It was a question of welcoming colored consumers and black small business that had commercial and political consequences for the entire state of Florida and, perhaps, the hemisphere. The following year, 1954, Miami's mayor, Abe Aronovitz, obliged those seeking to improve the quality of Jim Crow tourism by adding sixty-plus acres to the "colored only" section of Virginia Key. Aronovitz had been the attorney from the Coconut Grove Committee for Slum Clearance. Now, as Miami's mayor—its first Jewish mayor—he promised "a recreational facility . . . that will serve our Negro population for many years to come."[3]

The trick to keeping apartheid viable was to preserve the kinds of meetings at which the Key's fate had been decided. What one might call the "conference approach" to racial and spatial management was at least as old as Jim Crow itself. It remained predominant around the country, and it gave a very small range of property owners and politicians tremendous power in shaping interracial governance and metropolitan development.[4] Over the previous half century of building South Florida, politicians, local chambers of commerce, and loosely affiliated white real estate interests each had to account for "the Negro" in their respective visions of growth. Over those same years, colored property owners used their own political and social importance, as contributors to Jim Crow's order, to work their way into Greater Miami's governing class. In the 1953 Virginia Key case, which turned the threat of black displacement into an expansion of Jim Crow's infrastructure, Miami's black leadership spoke through white proxies. Nearly a decade after World War II, white friends still mattered greatly in the transactional world of apartheid. Yet, black Miami's middle-class spokespeople also had the ability to speak for themselves (and many "colored" others) by virtue of their status as businesspeople, professionals, and taxpaying property owners. Their voices had been integral to Jim Crow's functioning.

By the 1950s, the version of white supremacy that operated in the constitutional world of *Plessy v. Ferguson*—the version that inspired political transactions between blacks and whites over housing, law enforcement, and leisure—had advanced a very narrow definition of civil rights. Jim Crow's political culture was the political culture of property owners. It dictated that segregation was not anathema to civil rights, and that civil rights, conversely, did not necessarily mean ending segregation. Civil rights, instead, were synonymous with property rights, broadly understood. Civil rights meant the equalization of government entitlements, such as black and white beaches of roughly the same quality.[5] It meant the protection, not always realized, of black people aspiring to accumulate wealth.

Within such a vision, it seemed natural that black activist-owners would hold the figurative keys to Jim Crow's conference room. Such had been the case since the days of the Colored Board of Trade. But as more people, in the 1950s and 1960s, committed themselves publicly to dismantling Jim Crow, many people without property moved to kick open the door to the conference room and take a seat at the negotiating table. White landlords, politicians, and propertied black community leaders each tried, in their own way, to keep the unpropertied out of the conversation because of the dangers, frankly, that increased democracy presented to their respective sources of authority. In an economy built by and for landlords, it was in nobody's interest to give tenants, especially colored tenants, increased political voice. Tenants and tenant organizers, naturally, would have other ideas.

For Floridians—black and white—managing desegregation required fighting to hold the political center for property owners. It required continued uses of the conference table and placing an even greater faith in real estate and infrastructural development as instruments of racial reform. It required, perhaps most of all, hardening a political culture that accepted as natural two longtime traits of segregationist governance: (1) property owners as the voice of "the Negro" and (2) "the Negro" as an acceptable target of violence carried out in the name of the "public" or "common" good.

Enter slum clearance, urban renewal, highway building, and other uses of eminent domain. Greater authority over land development provided owner-activists, white businesspeople, and growth-minded politicians with the means to maintain a workable political order, to expand Florida's economy, and to minimize, in the meantime, the kind of violence that occurred at Carver Village. "Tourists don't take vacations where there is blood shed," remarked one astute member of the Greater Miami Chamber of Commerce. "Birmingham can have violence and open the steel mills the next day. Miami would find its hotels empty."[6] Infrastructural power facilitated what one University of Miami political science professor called in 1965 the "quiet revolution in Miami."[7] And it empowered Jim Crow's governing class to preserve a political culture built on keeping seemingly reckless, unproductive politics at the margins.

In the case of black people, in particular, many Negro leaders understood eminent domain or urban renewal the same way earlier generations had understood Negro-assisted lynching or police brutality carried out by Negro patrolmen—means, if properly handled, to improve the reputation of "the Negro." Certain black leaders, such as Theodore Gibson and Ira Davis, placed a faith in land expropriation that remained strong at midcentury. In some cases, that faith grew as the size of land projects grew, despite those many moments when land liberalism divested black property owners, here and there, of their real estate. Indeed, concerns about the increased political voice of the black poor and, as explored in the next chapter, black people's broad commitment to suburbanization set the bounds of "pragmatic" racial politics and made the homes of less connected black people, especially black tenants, acceptable casualties in a postwar parade of "progress." Across the country, in fact, key sectors of America's black propertied class, including the black press and probusiness civil rights organizations, accepted eminent domain as part of a necessary, if at times unfortunate, grammar of state violence, liberal violence.

Rather than simply treat the decade after World War II as the seedtime for what we recognize today as the civil rights movement, events in South

Florida show these to be the years in which Americans began decoupling white supremacy from Jim Crow, slowly and haphazardly, to allow white power to survive without apartheid. In the changing world of a Pan-American city, however, the political calculations that had held black property owners in good stead for decades would break down as the 1950s turned into the 1960s. Population growth and ongoing black poverty in Miami inspired increasing black militancy. Expanding the uses of eminent domain, even in the name of civil rights, ran up against an existing culture of black ownership and community building, advocated mightily by Negro landlords and landlord lobbyists, such as Luther Brooks. Tenants, in addition, would start to have their own ideas about citizenship, separate from middle-class black spokespeople. And the arrival of more than one hundred thousand exiles fleeing the Cuban Revolution dramatically changed who would indeed sit at the conference table going forward.

Revising Miami's Image, One Conference at a Time

Men—Reservados Para Hombres Blancos.

—Men's bathroom sign, Miami Bus Station (1958)[8]

For boosters looking to sell the city abroad, "Magic Miami" remained a decidedly white destination in the 1950s. Airline and railroad corporations, as reflected in the Delta-C&S Airlines advertisement shown in the accompanying illustration, celebrated Miami as a "Caribbean stepping stone" where white travelers promenaded in front of modern skyscrapers and high-end boutiques on their way to the islands. The imagined globe-trotter who landed at South Florida stood in stark contrast to the dark exotics peopling the tropical destinations of the Caribbean Sea. What travel companies often sold in such advertisements were primitives abroad and segregation at home, minus the apparent ugliness of the New South's caste system. Call it "exclusivity" or "luxury," it was left to Greater Miami's business leaders to bring a picture-perfect and marketable segregation in line with reality.

At the time of this 1954 advertisement, Miami was well on its way to taking down the most overt markers of Jim Crow apartheid. Some segregationist signage remained, certainly and, at times, in Spanish for the foreign colored travelers who needed a little help with local custom. But the 1950s were also a period when white businesspeople outside of designated colored enclaves began appreciating the purchasing power of black locals, "dark gentlemen from the South, the islands," and what one white vendor

Figure 7.1. Delta-C&S Airlines advertisement, 1954. (Courtesy of the Duke University
Advertisements Collection.)

called the "rich Negroes" from Chicago and other points north.[9] Beginning
with the recession years of 1952 and 1953, many of Miami Beach's white
hotels struggled to make their mortgage payments, especially during summer months, when tourism, as a rule, slowed down. Seeing an opportunity,
one white Miami banker, likely John B. Turner of First National Bank, called
Colored Town's Rev. Edward Graham and gave him a list of which hotels
seemed in most dire straits. It was in Turner's interest to have his debtors
make their payments, and many believed it was in black Miamians' interest
to leisure, finally, on Miami Beach. The most needy hotels on the beach
tended to be smaller operations, and they were often run by Jewish families
less committed to protecting some vague notion of southern "tradition."
The famous contralto singer Marian Anderson, honoring her own commitment never to perform in front of Jim Crowed audiences, also went a long
way toward easing Graham's efforts. A mere month after the December 1951
bombing at Carver Village, Anderson performed at the Dade County Auditorium before some two thousand people, the largest mixed-race gathering in
city history.[10] Graham pointed out Anderson's success to white hotel owners.
He also offered the hoteliers on his list the chance to tap the black spending
power that large organizations would no doubt bring when they came to
Miami for their next conference.[11]

That summer, several white hotel owners accepted Graham's offer, and Miami quickly became, in subsequent years, a premier destination for all-black and mixed-race conventions. In August of 1952, the Southern Tuberculosis Conference brought Miami white and black delegates from Washington, DC, and cities across the South. The following July, the National Education Association convened, with white and Negro delegates spending their dollars at some of Miami Beach's best hotels. The National Baptist Convention, in September of 1953, attracted some twenty thousand delegates to the city, with a dozen white hotels opening their doors to Negro travelers for the first time. More came from the AME Church, the National Negro Florist Association, the National Negro Insurance Association, black Greek organizations, and many other groups.[12]

When Abe Aronovitz became Miami's mayor in 1953, he immediately began sending Ira Davis, Annie Coleman, and other more prominent black Miamians with letters of invitation to attract even more black tourism to Miami. This, in turn, increased travel from parts north into Colored Town's hotels and homes, and then into the Caribbean. Black Caribbean sojourners moved in the other direction, up from the islands, through Jim Crow Miami, and along rail and bus lines to Washington, DC, New York, and even Canada.[13] For colored people, too, Miami was a "Caribbean stepping stone." The national black press covered the conferences and the international travel that Negro celebrities launched from South Florida. And through their respective organizations, Graham, Coleman, Davis, and several other black Miami notables provoked even more favorable publicity for the city, laying the institutional groundwork to welcome black travelers. Their expansion of commercial networks, first established during the 1940s, enabled desegregation in South Florida's hotels to *precede* the 1954 US Supreme Court decision in *Brown v. Board of Education*. One *Pittsburgh Courier* report perhaps captured it best in 1953: "Miami is tightly jim crow, except when it comes to taking colored folks money [*sic*]."[14]

Conferences of a different kind—namely, those between black and white power brokers—led to new breakthroughs. But usually black access came on a business-by-business basis and at the behest of only the most "persuasive" spokespeople. This proved especially true in the intervening years between the *Brown* decision and the Civil Rights Act of 1964. Real estate developer Wesley Garrison was booted out of the "whites only" Urmey Hotel in 1955, for instance, for trying to host a racially integrated Republican Party event that included Lawson Thomas and Sam Solomon.[15] As late as 1963, it took nothing less than one of America's most famous celebrities, Frank Sinatra, to lower the color bar at the Eden Roc, among the ritziest hotels on Miami

Beach. Sinatra convinced hotel management to accommodate Sammy Davis Jr. and Harry Belafonte on the promise that both men would take the service elevator to their rooms and remain relatively out of sight. Belafonte, who had been staying at Miami Beach hotels since 1955, paid little heed to the conditions. Sammy spent every evening entertaining guests in the hotel lobby, loudly.[16]

Most black people had to rely on less star-studded negotiations. Within *Plessy*'s legal context (the years before *Brown*), savvy political operators like Edward Graham or Ira Davis continued to be valuable instruments of racial reform because they dealt directly with Miami's white governing class. Sometimes sympathetic whites initiated the discussion, as in the case of South Florida's hotels in 1952, and sometimes Negro property owners encouraged a little direct action, just to get the conversation started. Direct action, as a strategy, though, carried some inherent dangers because it required that Miami's elite property owners move Negro politics, if only temporarily, out of the conference room.

Boycotts offered one case in point. Boycotts had been anathema in Miami for years because they risked alienating white allies within the chamber of commerce and on the city commission. Starving white businesses of black dollars worked better in northern cities, where white entrepreneurs had less political clout among black professionals and working people. In Chicago and New York during the 1930s, for example, "Don't Buy Where You Can't Work" campaigns had been used to great effect in opening black employment options. Activists in Montgomery, Alabama, in an epic yearlong stand against segregated buses between 1955 and 1956, provided the first successful example of boycotting in the urban South. There, black domestics and other working people allied with an emergent group of community organizers to keep white employers from subverting the movement. Today, the success of Rosa Parks, E. D. Nixon, Martin Luther King Jr., and so many others is largely credited with sparking the modern era of the black freedom struggle. In Jim Crow Miami, however, the events in Montgomery greatly unsettled "the Magic City's" propertied Negro leadership. Lawson Thomas, John Culmer, and other members of the Adelphia Club issued the following directive in the *Miami News* during the bus boycott's summer months: "1) Join no boycott movement. 2) Obey state laws regarding segregation until they are changed. 3) Support all legal moves by Negro organizations to end segregation." Respected organizations, not unruly agitators, they argued, should guide racial progress. "Our situation here unlike that in Montgomery," explained one resolution from Sam Solomon's Citizens Service League, "does not warrant putting our people who ride the buses to such inconvenience."

The *Miami Times*, owned by the Bahamian publisher H. E. S. Reeves, echoed these sentiments. Reeves explained in print that, regardless of boycotts' effectiveness elsewhere, "We can't see it for Miami. It might hurt the very people it is intended to help."[17]

In place of boycotts, black Miamians conducted the occasional sit-in, for at least there, Negro business owners could have a better handle on who showed up. In the case of Jim Crowed buses, carefully conducted sit-ins orchestrated by Theodore Gibson and Edward Graham in 1957 forced the Miami Transit Company to conference with Ira Davis and other Adelphia Club members, who, in turn, demobilized the Miami chapter of the NAACP and reinstated racial equilibrium.[18] After bus desegregation, the task at hand was to preserve a workable political climate for ongoing discussions of other issues.[19] The costs of the direct action strategy could be high for a city in constant need of outside investment, and especially high for blacks at the forefront of such actions, as Gibson and Graham learned. In 1957, both men were dragged before anticommunist inquisitors in the Florida state legislature for refusing to turn the NAACP's membership lists over to white segregationists. It took a full five years of litigation, going all the way to the US Supreme Court, before their names were fully cleared of any criminal charges.[20]

Skillful direct action could occasionally pay quick dividends, and at less personal cost. In 1959, black Miamians desegregated all of Dade County's beaches within just a few hours thanks to several phone calls, a fistful of tax receipts, and an afternoon swim for some of the city's more respectable Negro young people.[21] A group of swimmers, including Athalie Range and Garth Reeves, son of *Miami Times* owner H. E. S. Reeves, descended on Miami's premier all-white beach, Crandon Park. "My dad was far more conservative than I was," Garth Reeves admitted about his father many years later.[22] Still, it is likely that Garth's father schooled him on how best to get concessions from Miami's white civic leaders. "We brought along our [property] tax receipts," the younger Reeves recalled, "[so everyone] could see that we were freeholders [property owners] and we had paid our taxes." Police and their superiors, who might have wished to arrest the protesters, "said not a word," perhaps because they had "nothing to say" to citizens whose property taxes paid their wages.[23] It would take several more years before folkways caught up with stateways, as racial conflict on Miami's beaches remained a threat well into the 1960s.[24] Nevertheless, as was true during the early postwar years, it was hardest to deny black people access to public amenities, at least officially, when they owned property and remained current on their taxes.

Members of Miami's black governing class made a distinction between direct action—wade-ins, sit-ins, and such—and boycotts because, since the mid-1940s, direct action had been an acceptable weapon *within* an agreed-upon repertoire of interracial negotiation. Direct action could also bring otherwise unpredictable youth under the shelter of brick-and-mortar institutions, like black churches, and under the tutelage of more established organizers, as illustrated by Ella Baker's work with the Student Non-violent Coordinating Committee in Greensboro, North Carolina, in the early 1960s. Still, during the 1950s, even direct action held the danger of alienating sympathetic white people. No matter what black Miamians demanded, white business owners and politicians needed investors and tourists to view Florida as a progressive and exceptional beacon in an otherwise intolerant South.

Something in black politics was changing, though, even under carefully monitored activism and the occasional success in desegregation. For decades, taxpayer rights arguments helped black representatives access an important vocabulary about property and political entitlements, one that allowed them to circumvent whites' personal feelings about "the Negro" and secure, instead, important alliances with white business interests, politicians, and power brokers. H. Leslie Quigg, as just one example, was a man who, during the 1920s and 1930s, admitted to torturing and even murdering black people as Miami's police chief and as an open member of the Ku Klux Klan. Yet, in 1953, as a Miami city commissioner, Quigg voted to approve a proposal from Ira Davis to publicize the city in "some National Negro Magazine." "The Negroes," Quigg explained, "[are] taxed just like anybody else for these publicity funds and they should be entitled to some benefit from them."[25] Quigg's apparent conversion notwithstanding, taxpayer rights arguments, by the end of the 1950s, seemed increasingly ineffective in an expanding suburban world of private clubs, government subcontractors, and discriminatory realtors and homeowners associations.[26] The close of the decade saw the racial headway made at beaches and hotels met by failed efforts at desegregation elsewhere.

As hope for desegregation grew, a fundamental contradiction about property politics seemed thoroughly exposed. Property rights—that bedrock of American citizenship—also included the right to discriminate. Yet black property owners, if past movements for racial progress offered any indication, were somehow supposed to spearhead the end of racial segregation. Conferencing among black and white elites may have worked to equalize certain institutions. It may even have worked in those areas where black dollars seemed of increasing value, such as in beachfront hotels or on municipal golf courses. But what about housing or, for that matter, schools?

Here, the "conference approach" proved consistently and utterly ineffective. Around matters of segregated schools, in particular, white residents, planners, and the courts kept the benefits of education bound to real estate and "whites only" neighborhoods. To fight for better schools was to fight for better homes; that meant breaking the resistance of white homeowners associations that cropped up seemingly overnight. When formal school desegregation finally got under way, white flight, the demotion and transfer of black school principals, and teacher-imposed segregation within classrooms routinely resulted.[27] Orchard Villa, which was just east of the black suburb of Brownsville, was the first school successfully desegregated in South Florida in the fall of 1959. By Christmas of that year, it was 100 percent Negro.[28]

In the wake of the US Supreme Court's ruling against Jim Crowed institutions in *Brown v. Board of Education*, property rights, as an idea, became an increasingly sturdy shield for segregationists. White judges generally responded to challenges against racial segregation by affirming the right of individual home- or business owners to discriminate.[29] Only real estate developers and realtors in search of black buyers cared to point out that Jim Crow practices, such as restrictive covenants, actually served to regulate private property rights. Southern moderates, such as Florida's governor LeRoy Collins, preferred to set the Constitution's property protections in opposition to its equal protections clauses. "Under our free enterprise system and under our laws," Collins told Floridians in 1960, "a merchant has the legal right to select the patrons he serves. And he is certainly going to be protected in that legal right."[30]

The Good Governor

LeRoy Collins, Florida's governor between 1955 and 1961, was among the first southern politicians tasked with dismantling Jim Crow segregation as a means of ensuring regional economic growth. Famously, he used his inaugural address to set the tone for what would be his administration's official approach to the race question. "Boycotts, ultimatums and preemptory demands," he told Floridians, "can never achieve what persuasion, peaceful petitions and normal judicial procedures can do for the Negro race." "I believe," he said further, "[that] we can find wise solutions . . . if the White citizens will face up to the fact that the Negro does not now have equal opportunities; that [the Negro] is morally and legally entitled to progress more rapidly."[31] Collins's characterization of racism as a moral problem, not an economic or political one, seemed at once courageous, in the context of white supremacy, and apathetic, in that it asked little of white Americans from a legal or policy standpoint. Outside of his public pronouncements, however, Collins did not believe in leaving race reform in the hands of some hopefully moral citizenry. He believed in a much more hands-on approach backed by one of the most ambitious economic and infrastructural powers available to American politicians—eminent domain. As a centerpiece to his administration, Governor Collins attempted to engineer race relations and modernize Florida through the forceful applications of bulldozers, federal funds, and strengthened powers of land expropriation.[32]

Transforming the Jim Crow cityscape remained central to Governor Collins's vision of modernization and racial peace. Not unlike Miami's Negro business leaders, Collins feared that black pursuits of racial justice would, in the words one of his advisers, be "banged out on the street corners by the worst educated sections of the population." Racial hostilities, moderates like Collins argued, originated from an unmanaged citizenry and drove up police costs, polarized neighborhoods, discouraged investment, and stimulated incendiary demagoguery. Sensing Florida to be keenly susceptible to such problems, Collins believed that urban planners and statewide interracial committees could deliver a "professional educational approach" to race relations wherein responsibility for Florida's progress rested "on [the] shoulder[s] of community leaders."[33] Collins, as the literature in his personal papers attests, had also been receptive to ideas about housing and morality bandied about by progressive white groups like the Southern Regional Council (SRC). "The wretched slum dwellings of our Southern cities," wrote SRC members in 1952, "do us incalculable harm, morally as well as materially."[34] Using slum clearance to remake the southern city, the council believed, would, by extension, remake southern politics and society. There's every indication that Collins shared this sentiment.

By placing hope in urban renewal as a *social* program, LeRoy Collins affirmed the legal and cultural power land liberalism held over many who aspired to govern postwar cities and nations in the 1950s and 1960s.[35] Urban renewal in the United States was, on the one hand, a narrowly defined federal program established in 1954 through which federal officials offered to pay two-thirds of an eligible city's expenses for multiblock slum clearance projects and infrastructural developments. On the other hand, urban renewal functioned as *a discourse of progress*, greatly preceding and far outliving the formal parameters of the program.[36] That discourse, especially in the Jim Crow South, included the notion that urban renewal would improve race relations.

Urban redevelopment's perceived connection to the race problem was perhaps most evident in the institutional barriers standing between the state of Florida and federal redevelopment monies. As on explicit questions of civil rights, white state politicians used arguments about federalism and "states' rights" to obstruct the advocates of urban redevelopment. By 1959, it had been over a decade since the 1949 Housing Act had expanded cities' condemnation powers, and, still, Florida had yet to access federal slum clearance funds. Governor Collins tried and failed, repeatedly, to amend the Florida State Constitution and to work urban renewal enabling legislation through committee.[37] Years later, Collins complained publicly about how Florida had "one of the worst apportioned legislatures in the country." The state's twenty smallest, rural districts contained only 13 percent of Florida's total population, yet they elected over 50 percent of seats in both the Florida House and Senate. Safely, legislators in these seats—also called "pork-choppers"—protected the agrarian roots of their power by routinely blocking tax, reapportionment, and spending initiatives that would have tipped state power toward metropolitan regions such as Greater Miami. "Pork-choppers" also adamantly opposed urban renewal as part of a suite of arguments that included antiunion rhetoric, celebrations of localism, and, of course, openly antiblack sentiment. As Collins later described, "The uglier [the] things [a rural legislator] said . . . the stronger it made his position in the little domain he came from."[38]

Downstate in Dade County, as in other parts of the metropolitan South, property rights and state's rights arguments against urban renewal already helped replace Jim Crow's more incendiary language. As Miami's own segregationist state legislator David Eldridge complained about urban renewal, "Federal funds are used and therefore federal control will come into a purely local situation." Urban renewal also, he added, "eliminates a very basic human right . . . for an individual American citizen to own, possess, and dispose of private property."[39] "They talk about urban renewal as the answer to clearing slums," Luther Brooks remarked in 1961. "I say it is not the answer. The answer to slum clearance is still . . . the local people who live in the slums, from education and your local law enforcement agencies."[40]

Property rights and localism arguments against urban renewal made the Sunshine State similar to states across the southern and southwestern United States at this time. What contemporary observers now recognize as "the Sunbelt"—a sprawling network of southern and western metropolitan regions defined by "probusiness" growth policies—began, in fact, as a collection of local real estate interests and employers committed to bottom-line concerns, such as hindering the ability of tenants to sue their landlords, of workers to collectively bargain, or of local governments to expropriate land through eminent domain.[41] Often en route to highly visible national political careers, white attorneys and small business owners, such as South Carolina's Strom Thurmond or Arizona's Barry Goldwater, established their conservative bona fides by winning contests broadly framed—and bitterly fought—against slum clearance advocates in city governments and state legislatures. Miami's own Luther Brooks was cut from the same cloth. Unlike Thurmond or Goldwater, he had no desire for a political career with national visibility. He did, however, help galvanize a set of property interests that, throughout the US South and West, left cities saddled with massive slum districts and left state legislatures often beset by gridlock when it came to urban redevelopment. "Because of legal impediments," Collins bemoaned in 1959, "Florida has sadly lagged in this whole field of slum clearance and urban renewal."[42]

The Road to Civil Rights

Collins was fortunate to be in the governor's mansion when President Dwight Eisenhower signed the 1956 Federal-Aid Highway Act. Through the modernization of Florida's roads, ribbons of concrete expressways promised to provide important renovations to the state's economic infrastructure while connecting Florida's various metropolitan regions. Most important, the federal government would cover nine-tenths of any condemnation, demolition, and construction costs. The *Miami Herald*'s editorial page connected the dots immediately: "Slum Clearance in Miami will start with the building of the proposed highway system."[43]

Collins and Florida's urban mayors had every intention of using the interstate system to raze Negro slums whenever possible. But, to the surprise of some, many white residents living in Greater Miami's bedroom communities balked at the plan, including Miami's former mayor Abe Aronovitz, who had resigned from his mayor's post after only two years, citing health concerns. As one of his last public acts before his death in 1960, Aronovitz echoed the consternation of white suburbanites who worried the highway would destroy many fit suburban homes and render whatever real estate it left behind worthless in the shadow of the expressway. What would emergency vehicles do with so many local thoroughfares cut off? And contrary to the governor's own designs—indeed, perhaps worst of all—the highway, they argued, would "cause dissatisfaction and dissention between the races" by driving Negro slum dwellers "into other areas."[44]

In response to these challenges, Governor Collins and those city commissioners who supported the plan pointed to the $193 million in construction contracts and condemnation payouts the project would bring, being sure to highlight, as well, the boost expressways would give South Florida's long-term economic growth.[45] Apart from its ability to bind Miami more tightly to the rest of the nation, the highway would connect South Florida's growing suburbs, its center cities, its beaches, and its airports. It also gave planners the authority and capital to circumvent the landlord lobby's cadre of shrewd and well-financed lawyers and state politicians who were driving up public service costs for everybody. In the face of such arguments, echoed often in Florida's major news outlets, most dissent on the expressway was short-lived and feeble.[46]

The final route for South Florida's leg of the interstate had yet to be determined when plans for the highway were first announced. Still, every proposal included some version of Interstate 95 connecting to one or two east-west expressways running right through the Central Negro District.[47] Support for this plan came much more quickly from blacks than it had from whites. For, after meeting with the necessary business leaders and state representatives, black liberals widely endorsed the highway as an instrument of progress and a continuation of earlier attempts at spatial uplift. In razing slums, the highway was, in fact, an instrument of civil rights, many argued. The Greater Miami Urban League—which, at this point, was run by the so-called Mayor of Black Miami, Ira Davis—believed the demolitions to be "necessary for the continued progress of our city."[48] H. E. S. Reeves of the *Miami Times* conceded, "The expressway, will, perhaps, cut into our already limited living space displacing some people. Happenings of this kind are regrettable, especially for poor people, but with the expansion and progress of a city, there is little you can do about it."[49] The hope for most black residents, affirming white fears, was the continued opening up of Greater Miami's suburbs, which had continued in earnest since Wesley Garrison opened up Brownsville in 1946.[50] The *Miami News* put it perhaps the most bluntly for residents of the Central Negro District: "Somebody has to be unlucky."[51]

Road officials estimated that the highway would displace only some five thousand people.[52] The black neighborhood "over town" contained more than forty thousand. Some journalists expressed concern that, even after the proposed highway was built, the bulk of Miami's downtown Negro slum area would remain "in full view of the tourist hordes . . . driving on the expressway." The Central Negro District, all 136 blocks of it, had been, in one *Herald* reporter's words, "a blight on the glittering metropolis of Miami . . . the resort capital of the nation." And many feared that one, two, or even three highway interchanges might not be enough to give Miami's downtown the fresh start it needed.[53] No matter where the highway ultimately went, the future of Florida, it seemed, still needed urban renewal.

Governor Collins finally caught a break in 1959 when the Florida Supreme Court ruled that the Tampa urban renewal agency could expropriate and sell off for redevelopment the Negro rental property of one Phillip Grub-stein. Tampa's city planning officials argued that Grubstein's apartments, re-gardless of their actual condition, lay within "The Scrub," a forty-acre section of Ybor City, which was itself a community of Cuban and black American ci-gar rollers and *bolita* peddlers going back to the late nineteenth century. "The Scrub"—like its sister in Miami, Colored Town—had become a financial burden to city government. It soaked up disproportionate amounts of police and fire services while generating little tax revenue for municipal coffers. Florida's justices ruled that condemnation and redistribution of all rental properties in such a burdensome neighborhood would represent a "public good" under Florida's narrow eminent domain guidelines. The court ruled, in effect, that any designated "slum" area could be condemned and sold off en masse with little regard for individual properties within a designated urban renewal zone.[54]

Empowered by *Grubstein*, Governor Collins quickly advanced urban re-newal, in tandem with continued interstate building, as the best means for the wholesale modernization of Florida.[55] In fact, he appointed the very same people who fought on behalf of the city of Tampa in *Grubstein* to di-rect the state's advisory committee on racial relations. Chief counsel for the city of Tampa, Cody Fowler, became head of the "Fowler Commission," the governor's official commission on race relations. The governor staffed his commission with corporate airline and oil executives, city journalists, and bank presidents, including Miami's John B. Turner of First National Bank.[56] These were the entrepreneurs who, in tandem with local "Race Men," would be charged with helping to build both the economy and the productive race relations of the new Florida. Collins then used federal funds provided for such commissions under the Civil Rights Act of 1957 to publicize the benefits of urban renewal to Florida's city governments and to encourage, in 1959, the formation of local "biracial relations" committees for every city in the state.[57] Because of continued landlord resistance, actual demolition of slums would not occur in Miami for several more years. Instead, the biracial committees would serve as the first social consequence of Florida's new poli-tics of urban redevelopment.

Activism Stuck in Committee

The establishment of the governor's race relations / urban renewal com-mittees dovetailed with ongoing efforts in the summer of 1959 to deseg-regate lunch counters and other amenities in Miami's downtown depart-ment stores. Most department stores in the city had sit-down dining service labeled "whites only," combined with stand-up counters where black and white people could eat together. Black shoppers could also not try on clothes in store dressing rooms, but were allowed, occasionally, to buy garments and take them home to try them on. Shoppers could then return the clothes if they proved ill fitting.[58] Black people from Latin American countries could take advantage of practically any feature of downtown shopping.[59] "Such," one Miami historian explained, "were the idiosyncrasies of the Jim Crow system."[60]

These and other daily indignities prompted fifteen black and Jewish activists to establish the city's first chapter of the Congress of Racial Equality (CORE) in 1959. A pacifist group founded in Chicago in 1942, CORE had a commitment to nonviolent direct action that seemed well suited for the conference approach to race reform already in place in Greater Miami. Each of the Miami chapter's black members, moreover, also belonged to the local NAACP and counted among their mentors Theodore Gibson, Edward Graham, and other more established civic leaders from Coconut Grove and the Central Negro District. South Florida's CORE chapter, consequently, continued with the timeworn strategy of using sit-in demonstrations to spark negotiations of the color line between black and white businesspeople.[61]

During protests, groups of fifteen to twenty activists would move from store to store, followed by television news crews or reporters. Initial actions in the summer of 1959 lasted less than a half hour, but as news of CORE's activities spread, "more Negroes kept arriving," and sit-ins went from lasting minutes to lasting five-plus hours. "We ended [one protest] with a group of about 50," one activist recalled.[62] As charged, Miami's Bi-racial Relations Committee moved to make its meetings the principal site of negotiations between CORE activists and department store owners. John Turner, the bank president, represented white business interests at the table. Dr. John Brown, an ophthalmologist and CORE's primary spokesman, sat alongside Theodore Gibson and Edward Graham of NAACP leadership, accompanied, too, by sympathetic white journalists and white CORE members. CORE's more radical white members, particularly its Jewish Marxists, resented constantly halting the group's actions, "[calling] on the nominal leaders of the black community for help," and effectively turning the group into yet another arm of elite politics. As Matilda Graff, one such member, described, "There were always top level meetings with the 'leaders' of the community, white and black—the clergy and professionals, plus the board of the local NAACP branch. . . . We never had the feeling that average people would be welcomed at such events."[63] It took a year of conferences and negotiations before, as one source described, "Business Leaders led by John Turner desegregated stores *en masse* on August 1, 1960."[64] Entrepreneurs, not activists, it seemed, largely got credit for the demise of Jim Crow shopping.

Publicly, Theodore Gibson took pains to allay fears among more militant activists that the NAACP or the biracial committee intended to co-opt CORE's activism. "We are all interested in the same goals," he pledged to CORE members in the fall of 1959. "There is no competition."[65] Yet, in correspondence between Edward Graham and Gibson following the 1960 resolution on lunch counters, it remained clear that NAACP leaders, in conjunction with their white allies, aspired to keep CORE in check. "I am sure not any of us desire to disturb so serene an accomplishment," Graham warned Gibson. "However, there's many a slip between the cup and the lip. Please don't let this happen." "I am leaving on Tuesday for a small vacation," Graham explained. "The fate of the future is in your hands." Graham then closed with a parting shot at Miami's more upstart activists: "CORE is now convening their seminar. The chances are, they would get happy. God forbid!"[66] Considered something of an upstart in the late 1940s, railing against Negroes prone to compromise, Graham, by 1960, had unquestionably become a civil rights insider.

Before leaving town, Graham gave assurances to Miami's white business leadership that, even in his absence, the NAACP would keep things calm— "A promise was made."[67] John Turner accepted that promise on behalf of Miami's Bi-racial Committee and his allies in the Greater Miami Chamber of Commerce. He wrote in response to Graham, "I . . . was happy to get your assurance that the CORE institute [*sic*] would not precipitate nor stir up any demonstrations. . . . So much progress has been and is being made and it would, in my opinion, be a tragedy . . . to alienate those who are beginning to work together toward the solution of our problem."[68]

Summarily, the city of Miami "dissolved" its Bi-racial Relations Committee "after lunch counters [were] desegregated." Turner and Miami's latest mayor, Robert King High, then reestablished, on Governor Collins's orders, a new committee dedicated to facing what seemed like a more pressing matter—the Cuban Revolution.[69] "We are aware," Collins's staffers noted, "that Miami and Dade County are dealing with problems not just of race relations but with minority group relations in general, particularly those related to increasing Latin populations." The plan was to change the "race committee's" name and, by extension, its political commitments. "We would therefore suggest that wherever bi-racial committees appear, it might be well to substitute 'Committee on Intergroup or Community Relations.'"[70] Apparently, in a "metropolitan area with broad, rather than limited economic horizons," biracial politics would no longer do.[71]

The Cuban Revolution jolted a commitment to Pan-Americanism that dated back to the years of Franklin Roosevelt. And in Robert King High, Miami had its own charismatic and visionary Democrat who seemed primed to turn the nascent multiculturalism of Florida's conference approach into an instrument of social and political transformation. High had been a protégé of Abe Aronovitz, and had risen quickly as a brilliant and ambitious lawyer. He boasted fluency in Spanish, had been well traveled in Latin America, and, quite remarkably, ascended to Miami's mayoralty at only thirty-two years of age. High was, in many respects, the energetic Pan-American mayor the city had been waiting for. And while Miami's new mayor recognized racial desegregation as an important issue, his progressive stand on the race question included growth liberalism (i.e., slum clearance and urban renewal) for blacks and a much more robust civil rights liberalism for recent arrivals from Cuba.

"Them Damn Cubans"

A Negro minster remarked that perhaps the American Negro could solve the school integration problem by teaching his children to speak only Spanish.

—Juanita Greene, *Miami Herald*, 1961[72]

Mayor High viewed the "committee" approach to race relations as one step in the establishment of a larger web of social services and security measures being provided Cuban exiles by the federal government. He appointed a Cuban-exile attorney of Pan-American Bank, Nestor Morales, as the chair of what would now be called Greater Miami's "Community Relations Board" (CRB). The mayor's office explained the change as necessary to reflect Dade's destiny as "a growing cosmopolitan center . . . composed of numerous and differing social, racial, religious, linguistic, cultural and economic groups."[73]

Even with its new orientation, the CRB, in conjunction with city planners, continued to endorse urban renewal. Observers still saw slums and threats of racial violence as imperiling Pan-American growth. As one Dade County official explained, "Miami is the center of inter-American trade. . . . Tourism is the life blood of our economy, yet all these have suffered because of the race issue."[74] "No great city," the Miami City Planning Board argued, "can afford to tolerate slums, least of all one that purports to be a paradise."[75] Decades of race-based urban development, as a point of fact, made

Figure 7.2. Aerial view of downtown Miami, ca. 1959. (Courtesy of the Charles W. Tebeau Library, Historical Museum of Southern Florida.)

it possible for Caribbean or American travelers to see the color line from the window of a passing airplane. On one side of the Florida East Coast Railway tracks stood a modern downtown built of white concrete, with stucco finishes, marble accents, and fresh paint. On the other side, a less bright city, still largely made from wood, represented an earlier age. Reflecting the midday Florida sun, Miami's downtown literally shone "white" next to its darker neighbor.

Apart from encouraging the city's urban redevelopment needs, Miami's new take on "community relations" immediately reduced black people's voice at the city's proverbial conference table. The CRB hoped to appeal to white people's hearts and minds during the "baby steps" of desegregation. The board thus continued to favor "voluntary and persuasive" measures, such as polling Dade County residents on their racial beliefs or arranging meet and greets between different racial groups.[76] More meat-and-potatoes concerns, particularly those questioning special government benefits granted Cuban exiles, hardly made it onto CRB agendas. The city of Miami's Community Relations Board, in the words of one black leader, seemed "not worth a dime." Its proceedings were often doubly preoccupied by the establishment of a communist republic next door and a need to reaffirm the deliberate pace of Pan-American city building. Theodore Gibson, perhaps beleaguered from his role in monitoring militancy among the city's young people, warned CRB members in 1963, "The young Negro men and women coming back from college are not willing to let us old people . . . keep dragging our feet." As proof positive of the board's general ineffectiveness at initiating race reform on a metropolitan scale, every one of the all-white municipalities around Miami avoided forming "race relations" committees entirely. "In as much as we do not have any colored population within our [city] limits," wrote the mayor of Bal Harbor, an exclusive coastal community in north Dade, "it would be impossible to form such a committee."[77]

The frustrations black activists felt about the CRB further diminished the value of the "conference" approach to race relations, to be sure. For the average black man or woman, though, any disappointment with the old conference politics was likely overshadowed by the anger many felt toward newly arrived Cubans. Indeed, "If it wasn't for the Cubans . . ." became a common phrase opening any number of stories black and white Miamians told about jobs they used to have or, in Negroes' case, especially, jobs seemingly promised in the context of civil rights reform.[78] Some reports claimed that, in the first four years following the 1959 revolution, roughly twelve thousand black people alone "lost jobs" to Cubans.[79] Two hundred–dollar supplements from government relocation programs, combined with an additional one hundred–dollar federal allowance a month, enabled Cuban men and women to sell their labor sometimes for as little as half the wage asked by black yardmen or domestics. In some cases, Cuban schoolteachers and judges, believing their return to the island was imminent, worked as janitors, dressmakers, and in other jobs once reserved largely for poorer Negroes, Jews, or Puerto Ricans. They also undersold unionized white workers.[80] The National Labor Relations Board, in 1961, received scores of complaints about whole garment factories, or "runaway" shops, shutting down their operations to follow cheaper Cuban labor into Hialeah.[81] "We are becoming guests in our own house," argued Art Hallgren, the white vice president of the Florida branch of the American Federation of Labor. "Instead of the Cubans adjusting to our way of life," Hallgren believed, "we are having to adjust to theirs."[82] Whites, who made up 94 percent of the garment workers in 1960, would fall to just 18 percent of the garment-producing labor force in less than ten years; black numbers decreased from 6 percent to less than 4 percent.[83] Even the underworld economy that had buoyed certain sectors of black Miami over the previous decades seemed turned on its head. A perceived Cuban takeover of Miami's numbers game by 1963 prompted the *Miami Times* to wonder aloud whether "refugees had taken over . . . the game that originated in their country."[84]

The year 1963 represented the point when Miami's Cuban problem seemed worthy of national attention. Stories in the *Wall Street Journal, New York Times*, and even national black publications like *Jet* magazine began highlighting the racial and economic pressures the revolution had brought to the Magic City. By the end of 1963, failures at the Bay of Pigs and repeated botched assassination attempts against Fidel Castro ensured that, for Cubans, there was no "going back." "It is easy for us to see we are no longer wanted," remarked Leopoldo Abard, one of one hundred thousand refugees in Miami in 1963. "You feel the ill will on the streets. They even give us dirty looks now for speaking Spanish on the bus." No less of a friend to "the Negro" than Governor Farris Bryant, LeRoy Collins's successor and an unapologetic segregationist, conceded that the state had failed black Americans, especially when comparing black people's experience to the sustained welcome granted Cubans. "I think the Negro people in Miami and surrounding areas who were being booted out of their hotel and service jobs by Cubans really conducted themselves very well," Bryant argued. "I think under similar circumstances they might have been forgiven for a pretty violent reaction."[85]

As someone who worked black communities at street level, Luther Brooks perceived the so-called Cuban problem well in advance of the national media. He also seemed, in many ways, to be a more effective advocate for black rights than the CRB or other offices from civil rights arms of the federal government or the state of Florida. Brooks first became aware of the economic impact of the Cuban exodus through the spike in vacancies that hit Colored Town. In search of work, many black tenants began fleeing the Central Negro District for nearby Broward County, regularly leaving their rents unpaid. Just two years after the revolution, Bonded Collection Agency lost 20 percent of its tenants.[86] In response, Brooks converted a few of his collection offices into employment agencies doubling in property management. He also paid two hundred dollars for spot ads on local radio targeting black Miamians who needed jobs.[87]

Flanked by Charles Lockhart, his black public relations director, Brooks, in December 1961, testified before Congress on behalf of what he viewed as the racial double standard being suffered by South Florida's colored people. After offering federal lawmakers his routine claims about how well and how long he had known "the Negro," Brooks explained that, in addition to the government subsidies underwriting cheaper Cuban labor costs, a separate set of state policies actually encouraged black male wage earners to leave their families behind. "When work ran out and there was no more unemployment compensation," Brooks explained of Colored Town's men, "[many] picked up their hats and walked out on their families. . . . As long as [the father] stays, no one in the family is eligible for welfare."[88] Those mothers who opted into welfare, he explained, "are left to live on less welfare than is available to Cuban refugees."[89] Many Negro women actually decided to avoid government welfare altogether because of "suitable homes" guidelines that forced welfare recipients to be subject to invasive and often degrading examinations by white social workers. Even inconsiderate rent collectors, with their predawn calls at the door, were not so troublesome. And Cuban exiles, by contrast, suffered no home inspections in order to receive government aid. "Relief agencies," Brooks flatly remarked, "are more responsive to the pleas of Cuban refugees who ask for supplemental aid than they are to the pleas of colored [people]."[90]

Slum housing remained one of the gravest dangers facing black families, of course. As government bulldozers slowly cleared a path downstate for Interstate 95, some 60 percent of black women domestics, most working in Miami Beach hotels, remained tethered to the slums of the Central Negro District.[91] Three-fourths of Miami's rental housing stock still consisted of some kind of wooden shack built *before* 1939.[92] This was the Miami that urban renewal was supposed to fix. It was the city that boosters, in their publicity campaigns, effectively concealed. Yet, many believed that because of political players like Luther Brooks, the hardships of Jim Crow would continue to plague black citizens and Miami in spite of all the changes foreshadowed and promised by desegregation and massive Cuban in-migration.

Slum Politics

I know what the colored man is thinking.

—Luther Brooks, 1961[93]

If the conference approach to civil rights depended, in part, on reformist politicians and activists reaching common ground, then dislike for Luther

Brooks provided a great starting point. Brooks, by the late 1950s and early 1960s, had developed all the connections and political brilliance one might expect from a first-generation millionaire with a fourth-grade education. And he used every bit of it to make urban paternalism the lifeblood of Miami's Jim Crow ghettos. Any hope Florida had for modernizing race relations, many had come to believe, required rooting out the man widely considered most responsible for slowing down housing reform and disempowering black voters from street level up. "This man," Edward Graham charged of Brooks in 1953, "comes over here and handles all the collections. . . . He's just milking us dry [in what] amounts to millions of dollars a year."[94] "If we ever are to get rid of slums and give these citizens in the Negro areas a decent place to live," Robert High charged during his 1957 mayoral campaign, "we should not have a mayor who is obligated to Luther Brooks."[95] "Luther Brooks," another city commissioner claimed in 1961, "lines up the Negro vote through [Bonded] Collection Agency."[96]

Year upon year, issue after issue, it seemed Brooks enjoyed a power few could accurately define or measure. That, in effect, was part of its potency. Complaint files against Brooks's clients would, inexplicably, collect dust in Miami's slum clearance office.[97] Brooks's immediate relatives wound up on the City Planning Board.[98] Obligations to pay city property management licenses went away without explanation.[99] And tenant organizing in Colored Town, even when encouraged by Graham and other more radical activists, remained conspicuously absent. Repeatedly, Elizabeth Virrick, Edward Graham, and Theodore Gibson demanded grand jury investigations of Brooks's various spheres of influence.[100] "As far as I am personally concerned," Brooks responded to one such charge in 1958, "a grand jury investigation . . . would help clear the air of a lot of things, including my so-called political influence" and other "accusations and innuendos."[101]

Rumors swirled, in particular, around Brooks's black public relations director, Charles Lockhart, who, according to one political science professor at the time, enjoyed distinction as Miami's "most influential Negro leader."[102] A Bahamian, a longtime member of the Adelphia Club, and a labor leader in the city's only black union during the late 1930s, Lockhart, the professor maintained, enjoyed greater political standing than the whole Miami chapter of the NAACP, any one of South Florida's black ministers, or even the *Miami Times*.[103] Through Lockhart, hearsay had it, black tenants who refused to vote Brooks's way in critical elections suffered harsh reprisals. Lockhart would allegedly send Bonded's maintenance men to the homes of wayward voters to disconnect electricity or threaten evictions. Little documentary evidence exists, however, to substantiate suspicions of direct political coercion, as Bonded Collection Agency routinely circumvented litigation and tenants rarely testified.[104] To any accusation of personal wrongdoing, Brooks would simply point out, "I've been all over the colored sections, night and day, for nearly 30 years. . . . I've never carried a gun, and I feel as safe in Colored Town as a baby in its mother's arms. I don't think it would be that way if Negroes believed I'd done them wrong."[105]

Occasionally, Brooks, to great fanfare among black residents, threatened to block initiatives slated to improve white areas "until something is done for colored children" and Negro areas "long neglected."[106] The long-term source of Brooks's strength, though, came more from the way he affirmed the very political culture upon which the whole city ran. Greater Miami—like the rest of the urban South before the Civil Rights Act—was a city where (1) race relations remained best handled through personal relationships rather than through state enforcement, and (2) civil rights remained secondary, among blacks and whites, to property rights. Brooks offered Negro schools, churches, and civic organizations cash donations and gifts in amounts Lockhart described as "thousands [of dollars] annually." And when Brooks did these and other acts of community building, he was providing proof positive "that peaceful negotiation is the best method of obtaining lasting and valuable objectives."[107]

Brooks's politics, in effect, were Negro politics; they were landlord politics, American politics. Thus, when investigative journalists derisively referred to Bonded's owner as "General Brooks," "Slum Baron," or the "King of the Tenements," it would be black editorialists and property owners who most often came to his defense. Many would point out Brooks's philanthropy or the number of respectable black leaders who left their property in Bonded's care.[108] Wrote Eliot Pieze, a black freelance journalist in 1958, "Leading citizens of the Negro area hold a very high regard for Brooks as well as the many fine community contributions and services that he has rendered during his more than 24 years in the area."[109] John Culmer, who, somewhat ironically, had been a legendary public housing advocate during the 1930s, praised Brooks as "a genius at making money" and "a man of high Christian character." Said Ira Davis, a similar advocate of land liberalism and a landlord, "This community can justly be proud of Mr. Brooks and hope others will follow his example."[110]

Brooks and Davis were, in fact, quite close and served together on several committees associated with black tourism and improving "colored only" health-care facilities. And, as Davis did against Claude Pepper in 1950, Brooks and his company were quite effective at derailing the political aspirations of those whom Brooks considered self-righteous liberals. Mayor

Robert King High, for instance, had aspirations of being Florida's next great governor, and comparisons were often drawn between him and the highly popular LeRoy Collins. Both High and Brooks could be found at the same dinners and social events in the Central Negro District, working the room and shoring up their respective bases of support among black ministers and business owners. High, however, refused to be photographed with Brooks, a man he considered the beneficiary of "gutter politics."[111]

Evidence from a 1964 internal memo at Bonded suggests that Brooks sent Charles Lockhart to work in the campaign of Haydon Burns, who was High's opponent during that year's Democratic gubernatorial primary. Lockhart was supposed to give Burns insights into the source of High's popularity, particularly as it concerned the mayor's ability to "[gain] the Negro vote without alienating the White vote." Lockhart armed Burns with statistics about High's black support, particularly the 90 percent of black votes that apparently made up 60 percent of High's total vote in his last mayoral victory. Burns then used this information to antagonize and visibly agitate Miami's mayor in televised debates. He dubbed High "the NAACP candidate." During the campaign, Burns's supporters also harped on the mayor's ties to both Robert Kennedy and polarizing Negro leaders such as Martin Luther King Jr.[112] One particularly salacious advertisement depicted a pregnant Negro woman in a rocking chair claiming, "I went all the way with Robert King High." With High encircled in a storm of race baiting, Miami's notoriety as being out of step with the rest of Florida on the "Negro question" cost him the 1964 contest.

In exchange for Lockhart's help, Burns, now governor, appointed Brooks's public relations man to the chief consultancy for Florida's statewide War on Poverty Program, the Office of Economic Opportunity in 1965. There, Charles Lockhart—the former union leader—used tactics he learned while working for Bonded in Miami to demobilize tenant organizing across the state.[113] In Goulds, for instance, a tiny migrant farm and meatpacking community located twenty-five miles southwest of Miami, tenants, in 1966, complained of high rents and slow repairs. Though the rental units in Goulds were handled by Brooks's management company, tenants lived so far from the center of Bonded's philanthropic presence that few tenants even knew Brooks's name. They only knew the signs—"Managed by Bonded"—plastered on the outside walls of their apartments. "We have asked for back doors and never gotten any answer . . . but Mr. Bonded has never listened to us before we organized. . . . We can't trust Mr. Bonded or Mr. Lockhart . . . So that is why we the people's have taken things upon our self's [sic]."[114] Upon arriving in Goulds, Lockhart, according to one tenant, "introduced himself as a consultant for [OEO]," but then proceeded to "[argue] the rental agency point of view."[115] "You can't expect $20 worth of housing if all you can afford to pay is $10," charged Lockhart. He brushed off tenant demands and then blamed out-of-town radicals for getting tenants "all riled up." "Even though he's being paid from anti-poverty funds," one local OEO organizer remarked, "he came to our meeting in Goulds and did everything he could to ruin our efforts to organize these people." Though technically a part of the Great Society's administrative structure, Lockhart endeavored to weaken tenants' legal protections and affirm instead a paternalistic relationship between black tenants and their rental agency. "After a few minor improvements were made," Johnson said, "the rent was increased and the residents just gave up."[116] That tenants were able to organize at all in 1966 had been the result of several new developments that, over the previous six or seven years, had begun transforming Florida's politics at street level.

Street Politics

Brooks was a political creature of Jim Crow. Thus, as Jim Crow's spatial, political, and social contours began to shift, cracks started forming in the edifice of his power. The most dramatic threat was the impending interstate highway. I-95's path within Miami's city limits seemed constantly in flux between the late 1950s and early 1960s. It changed almost from year to year, depending on who occupied the governor's mansion, who held the state's most important bureaucratic posts, or which major captain of industry cared to exert his influence on the expressway's path. LeRoy Collins's successor, Farris Bryant, reevaluated the path of the highway in 1961, likely at the request of a major campaign contributor named Ed Ball. Ball, who ran the DuPont Corporation, sought to lessen the disruption that a proposed off-ramp posed to his downtown Miami property, DuPont Plaza. The reevaluation apparently included moving the highway's path west from the Florida East Coast Railway corridor to a path much more residentially disruptive to the city's Central Negro District.[117]

Brooks learned of the plan immediately and began making preparations to reorient the center of his business beyond the borders of Colored Town. He also made sure to let his clients know. John Culmer's wife, Leome, recalled how Brooks told her husband about the city's plan for the Central Negro District long before politicians and planners ever revealed it to the public. Brooks had been the Culmers' property manager for several years. "My husband asked Luther Brooks, 'What are you going to do with all these people, you talking about doing this and that?' [Brooks] said, well the plan a long time ago was [that] you'll be going to Carol City, you'll be going to Opa-locka and you'll be going here and there."[118] John Brown owned property as well, thanks to his earnings as a popular physician. And even though he was CORE's chief spokesman, he was also a property owner who did business with Luther Brooks. "Luther Brooks," Brown recalls, "came to us to tell us about what some of the plans were for Overtown and the black community. And he brought his maps of everything and showed us, this was about 1959, 1960."[119] Brooks's black clients were among the first to sell their properties "over town" and begin reinvestment in northwest Dade County.

In the legal arena, *Baker v. Carr*, a landmark 1962 US Supreme Court decision on reapportionment in state legislatures, undercut a crucial piece of landlords' and property managers' influence. Rural legislators would no longer dominate the Florida state House. *Baker* came down too late for Governor Collins to benefit; he had already left office. The ruling nevertheless shifted political power in Florida and the rest of the South from rural districts to metropolitan areas, thereby ensuring that "pork-choppers" would no longer control real estate regulations, civil rights enforcement, or how federal money was spent in the state. *Baker*'s impact seemed only to magnify the changes Cuban immigration brought to Brooks's business—increased vacancies and the like—by making it easier to get state redevelopment projects approved.

Recognizing the futility of trying to fight back several waves of change, Brooks elected to diversify his investments and to endorse urban renewal, as a result. As long as the program gave his clients "full cash value" for their property, Brooks believed that "urban renewal might be the answer to completing the job which I fought so hard to see done."[120] He gathered money he saved and three hundred of his wealthiest clients and ventured to invest in a new enterprise, a freshly incorporated city off the Atlantic Ocean called Islandia. Islandia was thirty-three different islands seventeen miles south of Miami's city hall. Brooks became Islandia's first mayor: chief executive of a city boasting only twenty-seven residents and eighteen eligible voters. The city's estimated real estate value was forty million dollars, however. In lieu of an actual city hall, Brooks governed Islandia from his property management office at 4150 NW Seventh Avenue, a nondescript storefront in black Miami.[121] When questioned about the venture, Brooks replied candidly, "Got to keep something boiling in the pot all the time. . . . Sure I made a lot of money, but you got to keep planning ahead."[122]

Tenant organizing represented perhaps the least foreseen and most sweeping threat to Brooks's power because it tore, brick by brick, at the very foundation of Jim Crow's political culture. It was one thing for physicians or the scions of black Miami's wealthiest families to try to force conversations about piecemeal negotiations or Jim Crowed leisure. Tenant organizing undercut the paternalistic relationship between renter and property manager. It also lent itself, as the 1960s wore on, to more strident racial critiques of white landlords, racist politicians, and so-called Uncle Tom property owners.

We Still Talking?

In Fort Lauderdale, the largest city in Broward County, black tenants, in 1959, began to organize in response to the typical winter rent increases. Bonded Collection Agency managed fewer than fifteen hundred apartments in Broward compared to the ten thousand units it managed in Dade County. There was also a much less sizable and organized black property-owner class in Broward. Both those conditions made Broward fertile ground for organized tenant unrest. The urban paternalism Brooks and the black bourgeoisie had practically perfected in Miami had the power both to defuse activism and, at times, moderate landlord abuses in the Central Negro District. Without that political scaffolding existing in Broward, conditions and profiteering were often worse in Fort Lauderdale than they were in the dankest corners of Colored Town. From laundresses and janitors, landlords demanded as much as $25.00 a week, plus utilities, for a one-room apartment. White renters in Miami paid less than $23.75 *a month* for similarly run-down accommodations.[123] One hundred dollars a month was also equivalent to the mortgage on the three-bedroom house or a Cuban refugee's entire government relief check.

Nathaniel Wilkerson, a black college graduate who could only find work as a chauffer, organized a mass meeting of over four hundred tenants at a Fort Lauderdale Baptist church. He explained to media, black community leaders, and, later, city commissioners how the city's colored tenants "have no protection." Leases, when renters got them, were one-way documents that bound tenants to pay rent, but let landlords off scot-free. Tenants already paid between half and two-thirds of their income in rent; when they refused to pay more, landlords responded with a wave of evictions. One sixty-year-old white landlord, Ben Biegelsen, filed forty eviction notices in immediate response to black demands for repairs. "If they force us out," one tenant warned, "they'll have to evict every Negro in Fort Lauderdale."[124]

Ultimately, Fort Lauderdale's tenant activists suffered widespread evictions and received only weak assurances from city officials to expect more public housing. Broward's activists, while generally disregarded, nevertheless garnered media attention that helped propel a glacial leftward lean on what should be done about Negro slums. Events in Broward also exhibited a political evolution that was being catalyzed by protest elsewhere. In the late 1950s, popular depictions of globe-trotting celebrity activists, such as Kwame Nkrumah or Martin Luther King Jr., made the front pages of black newspapers—windows into what was possible, even in small towns like Fort Lauderdale. As summed up in the title of an address honoring Wilkerson and the efforts of Broward's tenant organizers: "They Can't Keep Us Down Now That We Have Been Places and Have Seen Things."[125]

Few would have imagined that Negro slums also made for good prime-time television. In the summer of 1961, WCKT, the Biscayne Television Corporation, broadcast two exposés on Negro housing conditions at the 7:00 p.m. hour—"Miami Condemned" and "Condemned: 65 [days later]." Both highlighted the abysmal housing situation in black Miami. Reporters named names of the city's worst landlords—black and white—while cameras conveyed the deplorable state of their properties. Luther Brooks, Robert King High, Elizabeth Virrick, and a host of city and county officials were suddenly beamed into the living rooms of South Florida homes. So, too, were the scurrying roaches, gaping ceilings, and small Negro children forced to play on garbage heaps. The series won a Peabody Award for journalistic excellence in 1961. More important, Miami's embarrassment gave Mayor High the latitude to clean out numerous dusty corners of the city's municipal bureaucracy. The mayor orchestrated several firings of housing officials, many with links to Brooks. High arranged, in addition, a first-of-its-kind telecast of the proceedings of the Miami City Commission as officials passed the first minimum housing code in the city's history.[126] In a review of the program, the *Miami Times* professed, "We are now paying for our prejudices and the immature thinking of the past."[127]

Television greatly impacted the content of housing policy and of how people started talking about housing. Slum housing, just a generation earlier, seemed a necessary, if regrettable, feature of private enterprise and "mutual segregation" in a region starved for investment and visibility. By the early 1960s, slums carried an association with apartheid itself, which was increasingly considered, if not a clear evil, an at least commercially unfavorable set of laws and customs. Most Negroes in Greater Miami went without a television in their tenements. "Miami: Condemned" was not for them; it featured practically no tenant voices, in fact. One instead can safely compare "Miami: Condemned" to the efforts of the Community Relations Board or, better, *How the Other Half Lives*, a late nineteenth-century account of life in New York's tenements compiled by Jacob Riis, the muckraking Danish journalist. The point of "Miami Condemned," like Riis's account, was to tug

on the heartstrings of white audiences—in this case, an increasingly subur-
ban white audience—and inspire them to action. "From Hialeah, Miami
Beach, Homestead and points between," wrote members of the Coconut
Grove Committee for Slum Clearance, following the broadcast, "many interested people . . . urged that our group become a countywide operation."[128]
Naturally, suburban interest did not necessarily turn into positive change.
Even after the passing of a new housing code was televised, enforcement
continued to be nonexistent. Black residents of Coconut Grove registered
their ongoing discontent in a Calypso song printed on the pages of their
community newsletter:

> July brought us a law, which gives
> A Force for Sanitation
> They'll act against illegal trash
> There'll be no hesitation
> But not a man is on the job
> Observe the eager petitioners
> Three months ago you passed the law
> Wha' hoppen, Messrs. Commissioners?[129]

Marginalizing Militancy

The National Urban League's executive director, Whitney Young, described
Miami in 1965 as "the one city in the nation where Negroes regard poverty
as paradise."[130] As the playful critique of tenant calypso conveyed, locals
knew better. Miami, as the 1960s wore on, produced a growing cadre of
militant activists who, through leaflets, marches, and rallies, tried to circumvent the political players and institutions managing urban paternalism. These activists openly condemned what they perceived as employment
discrimination at white-owned companies, and, like Luther Brooks, they
often drew specific and hard-hitting comparison between the prompt assistance being offered Cubans and the enduring poverty and racism facing
the black poor.[131] Brooks was no ally of Miami's organizers, of course. In
fact, ongoing negative associations between Luther Brooks and rental profiteering compelled Miami's most prominent property manager, in 1962, to
change the name of his business from Bonded Collection Agency to Bonded
Rental Agency. Brooks also decreased the frequency with which his picture
appeared in Bonded advertisements in the *Miami Times*. He instead ran ads
featuring pictures of and quotes from happy black employees.

New organizations, such as the All People's Democratic Club, joined more established groups, such as the NAACP, the Urban League, and CORE, to call attention to police brutality, merchant price gouging, and many of the lingering markers of black second-class citizenship. Yet, tenant discontent and radicalism remained conspicuously absent from the black press. Instead, older moderates, like Theodore Gibson, continued to argue that "Urban Renewal is the best tool yet devised to eliminate slums."[132]

In tandem with white officials, more-established black leaders continued to sell urban renewal as a route to social justice, particularly as landlord intransigence weakened and as "$200 federal relocation payments" all but guaranteed displaced residents a home beyond the slums. "Everybody was excited," remembered Sonny Wright, one former resident of the Central Negro District. "They had all these pretty pictures, renderings of how the area is going to look. It's going to tear down this and build that." Gibson, bearing promises of FHA mortgages and an end to the stigma of "Negro business," stood among those black leaders who, in Wright's words, "sold us on Urban Renewal. That was supposed to be the big savior."[133]

Donald Wheeler Jones, a charismatic twenty-eight-year-old attorney, was the more militant successor to Gibson in Miami's NAACP. Rather than push urban renewal, Jones placed emphasis on poverty and the increased police brutality among Miami's white cops in the wake of the Watts rebellion in 1965. Jones pointed to the dangerous cocktail that new "stop and frisk" laws made when combined with simmering black frustrations about unemployment. "The average Negro citizen," he explained in a letter to Mayor Robert King High, "has, by and large, borne his burden in silence as a sacrificial lamb for the extension of freedom and democracy to refugees from another land."[134] Citing, yet again, unequal treatment between Cubans and blacks, Jones described black Miami as brimming with "seething hatred" that would "[make] Watts look like a picnic."[135]

Even in an age of increasingly sharp black rhetoric, the conference approach to race reform continued, for many, to be preferable to boycotts and more confrontational forms of direct action. And those who failed to follow Miami's unspoken political conventions were pushed by more conservative black leaders to the city's political margins. Cecil Rolle, a Miami native born to Bahamian immigrants, was among those who repeatedly attempted to boycott white merchants who sold cheap goods at high prices and restricted black consumer credit. With Jimmie Chatmon, a local Southern Christian Leadership Conference member, Rolle called for a march on city hall to force greater regulation on landlords, including mandatory extermination services and an end to the practice of shutting off tenant utilities. They organized black Miami's first rent strikes. This was in 1966, seventy years after the first clapboard shacks were built in Colored Town. Chatmon and Rolle also demanded employment quotas for black people in civil service jobs. With almost every call for justice, the pair threatened that South Florida's black population would "take to the streets" if their demands were not met.[136]

The pushback they suffered came from the top as well as from the grass roots. One black Miamian wrote the following in rebuke of Rolle's 1963 boycott of a white ice cream shop: "Mr. Rolle does not realize the many wonderful friends white businessmen make in Negro communities."[137] The *Miami News* reported that, in response to the proposed city hall march against landlords, "Dade Negroes followed their old leaders in ignoring [the] call. . . . Only four persons showed up." John Brown of CORE, Theodore Gibson, and Athalie Range were among those who condemned the demonstration. It did not fit how politics were *done* in Miami, they argued. Tenant issues, in the meantime, would continue to be handled by property managers like Luther Brooks.[138]

In the absence of formal political power, tenants tended to express their frustration through what observers sometimes called "wanton destruction." Bonded's repair crews commonly found plumbing and drains jammed with everything from mayonnaise jars to shag rugs. "How they get them in there," one Bonded employee remarked, "I'll never know."[139] Bernard Dyer, a tenant organizer who came to Miami from Harlem in 1966, explained that seemingly destructive tenant behavior came from a people "so socially scarred that they strike out at society."[140] To Dyer and others versed in what was becoming an emergent vocabulary of Black Power, denigrating tenants as agents of "wanton destruction" failed to appreciate black rental housing as an expression of white supremacy. It failed to see slum housing and the tenant practices it engendered as an extension slavery, peonage, and segregation, or as what Stokely Carmichael and Charles Hamilton termed in 1966 "institutional racism."[141] Substandard apartments were not tenants' "own" homes, activists argued; they were monuments to white people's power, to "the psychic damage of white racism." They represented white people's infrastructural power.[142] Dyer argued, in fact, that the increasingly inward forms of violence and ruination carried out by poor Negroes in ghettos across America originated among less visible economic factors that forced black people to sustain themselves on the black market. "When I say a 'black market' I mean it literally," Dyer explained. "When it is a 'black' market, it seems the size of the rooms can be decreased . . . amenities can be removed, and even housing inspectors can look the other way."[143] Still, to most observers, the thousands of dollars tenants ran up in repair costs provided little evidence of broader social problems. It only affirmed black people's cultural deficiencies. Wrote one white Miamian to the *Miami Herald*, even if Negroes "did suddenly acquire some money, whether through welfare or better paying jobs and moved into better housing it would soon look the same. . . . It is a substandard people who create substandard housing."[144]

Again, it fell to black moderates in positions of leadership to dispel such characterizations. Athalie Range was Miami's first black city commissioner, appointed by Robert King High in 1966. Shortly thereafter, she became, under Reuben Askew, the first black appointee to the cabinet of a Florida governor. In her role as commissioner and through masterful use of the conference approach, Range made several of what the *Miami News* called "middle of the road" recommendations for housing reform.[145] In January 1967, she helped write the city's strengthened housing code, which, among other things, made it illegal for landlords to force an eviction by shutting off utilities and banned the use of stoves and ovens for the purposes of heating apartments. Range also fought white landlords who tried to refuse the applications of black renters.[146]

Within her first year as commissioner, Range established, in conjunction with the Urban League, a "tenants court" specifically set up to try renters accused of "wanton destruction."[147] With the housing code in place, Range remarked, "The property owner should be protected."[148] Purportedly modeled on a similar court in Baltimore, wherein tenants brought landlords up on charges of negligence, Range's tenants court focused on curtailing the damage ghetto blacks were doing to both private property and "the race."[149] "When I saw the need for a minimum housing code, I went after it militantly. Now I'm doing the same for a tenants' school." Range promised that the court would "protect those tenants . . . who need protection from that minority who persist in maintaining unwholesome and unsanitary conditions that cannot be attributed to hardship."[150]

The real estate reporter for the *Miami News* remarked that, in Range, "landlords have some strange support."[151] Yet it was likely that Range's own status as a landlord, and the chronically poor condition of her rental properties, had a part to play in her political centrism. Just three months before her tenants court recommendation, in fact, Athalie Range appeared in the pages of the *Miami Herald* as the owner of a wood-frame rental house cited for several violations, some over three years old. Her tenants were living in a house with damage substantial enough to require demolition.[152] Miami's newest and most visible housing reformer, in other words, stood in violation of her own housing code. Renters, if found guilty in tenants court, had to go to a "homemakers school," which included mandatory instruction in proper domestic skills and basic home repair.[153] In the meantime, punishments for landlords, other than an embarrassing news story or two, continued to be much slower in coming.[154] Range moved her own tenants to a house up the block, only to be profiled several years later as a negligent, absentee landlord in an investigative televised news report.[155]

Range's tenants court brought Jim Crow's political logic—the logic of Lawson Thomas's old Negro Court, really—into the postapartheid city. It placed considerable responsibility for poverty on the behaviors of the poor, and poor black "homemakers" in particular.[156] It also privileged the ability of middle-class blacks, through the power of the state, to uplift the race while making what many considered minimal disruptions to the racial status quo. The tenant organizer Bernard Dyer and other observers suspicious of landlord power wondered aloud, for instance, if the court merely "raises in the imagination of slum dwellers a frightening picture of a new weapon wielded by property owners."[157] In affirmation of the concern, Range, according to reporters, admitted that "she had talked to a number of landlords who had agreed to set up the [tenants] school at their own expense."[158] She also spoke directly to Dyer and other new arrivals who, to her mind, threatened the "cool" race relations that the tenants court and the conference approach helped preserve. "Right here and now, I'd like to serve warning on outside agitators that their activities will not be tolerated in Miami."[159] Like most efforts to improve slum conditions, Range's tenants court would be short-lived; tenants simply wouldn't participate to an extent that kept it viable. The abiding assumptions the court reflected and maintained, however, echoed the kind of "pragmatic" race reform that Zora Neale Hurston, Charles Lockhart, and so many others believed in and advocated.

Negotiating Celebrity

Black property owners, beyond even Athalie Range, continued to wield great influence within civil rights circles. And that condition, combined with the deeply embedded and paternalistic counterorganizing networks long developed by white rental interests, continued to make antilandlord activism one of the hardest forms of protest to organize. Frankly, even with black rental housing in such terrible shape, it was still easy to dismiss less well-connected activists like Jimmie Chatmon or Bernard Dyer as impractical if not irrational. As was often the case in politics driven by personality and influence, however, the power of celebrity proved harder to dismiss. For this reason—the luster of charismatic black leadership—the highly publicized frustrations of Martin Luther King Jr. in Chicago in 1966 provided perhaps the most important boost to black tenant activism in South Florida and elsewhere.

With the country seemingly beset by increased black aggression in the mid-1960s, more conservative black newspapers, such as the *Miami Times*, clung to King as a model of acceptable Negro politics. This was especially true before his "controversial" 1967 denunciation of the Vietnam War. Over a year before King described the US government as "the greatest purveyor of violence in the world today," he moved his family, in the dead of the Chicago winter, into a run-down tenement on that city's West Side. King hoped to call national attention to the hardships of black renters. He also endeavored to prove the suitability of nonviolent direct action in advancing the cause of civil rights in the North. "Many ministers," one Chicago reverend recalled, "had to back off [from supporting King] because they didn't want their buildings to be condemned or given citations for electrical work, faulty plumbing or fire code violations."[160] Lack of support among Chicago's black middle class, political maneuvers by Mayor Richard J. Daley, and white animus in response to protest marches contributed to thwarting King's efforts to spark an open-housing movement in the city.[161] For many observers, the depth of black poverty and the hateful whites King encountered in Greater Chicago's Cicero neighborhood, in particular, demonstrated the limits of the famous reverend's protest vision and exposed the futility of nonviolent direct action more generally. Nevertheless, King, even in ostensible failure, brought the desired media attention to Negroes' housing woes.

After Chicago, neither King nor Negro property politics, broadly understood, would be the same. Shockingly, but perhaps as a testament to the sheltered upbringing of the black elite even under Jim Crow, King admitted to becoming aware of the condition of slums in his own Atlanta only *after* his Chicago experience. He remarked in 1966, "I had no idea people were living in Atlanta, Georgia in such conditions."[162] Following King's apparent realization, SNCC organizers took to reforming rental housing in Georgia's capital city. Moreover, black newspapers around the country began publicizing more moments of tenant organizing. Max Goodman, a white Miami Beach organizer, and Edward Graham tried to organize Colored Town's tenants as early as 1949, yet, based on the available issues of the *Miami Times*, the first explicit mention of tenant organizing ever reported in the city's flagship black newspaper likely came in 1966, *after* King's "Awakening in Chicago."[163]

Martin Luther King's actual organizing efforts in Miami, as in Chicago, proved largely unsuccessful and marginal. Just following the Cuban Revolution, more militant black activists widely ignored his admonitions that Negroes should build common cause with Cuban exiles.[164] King then came to Miami in June 1966 hoping, in his words, to "meet with local leader-

ship and begin working on . . . the whole situation of slums, rent gouging, unemployment, and underemployment." He found a receptive ear in
Mayor Robert High. But, as in Chicago, "Miami's Negro leadership," as only
the satirist George Schuyler could capture, "was cold as Antarctica."[165] King,
an apparent "outside agitator," had no local source of ongoing support.
He nevertheless remained symbolically valuable to those property owners
and business leaders who governed black Miami. An often beleaguered and
frustrated pacifist, King, like Malcolm X or Claude Barnett, came to Miami
mostly to enjoy ocean fishing and other South Florida amenities. The Magic
City, it seemed, was a place to escape more stressful intrigues elsewhere.

Less than six months after Martin Luther King left Miami in 1966, King's
office in Atlanta received several letters from SCLC organizer Jimmie Chatmon seeking financial support. Miami's SCLC chapter, headquartered in
a Central Negro District apartment, was about to be evicted, having fallen
two months behind on its rent. SCLC organizers had built little political
capital among West Indians and American Negroes of any note. As a result,
the local SCLC was literally being starved out of existence, failing to meet
its basic operational expenses. As Chatmon explained, "It takes [a] long
time to become accepted as a spokesman for . . . the Negro people. We have
put [in] a lot of sweat, energy, and time. Some of us have lost our [own]
apartments, jobs and income and have been harassed and intimidated."
Chatmon never named the source of their political trouble explicitly, understanding, perhaps, that King's recent visit would have given him a sense
of who was to blame for the group's difficulty. Chatmon only noted, "The
middle class Negroes in Miami are still sweeping the ghetto problems under
the rug." "The idea with them," he continued, "seems to be that there may
be problems in Mississippi, but no mistreatment or malnutrition here. They
are making believe no problems exist here. So we have been forced to meet
all expenses by ourselves."[166]

Across the country, white Americans were citing property rights as justification for keeping black people locked in rental housing, out of white
schools, and out of suburban communities. Nevertheless, the politics of
property—when in black hands—could also be an effective weapon against
dissident black voices, it seemed.

Dave Bondu, a sharp-witted entertainment and political commentator
at the *Miami Times*, also worked as a photographer and publicist for Luther
Brooks at Bonded Rental Agency.[167] Commenting on the sweltering political
atmosphere of the summer of 1966, Bondu explained the proper place of
street protest in a city usually governed by cooler heads. Referring to King's
Chicago failure and attempting to dissuade local upstart activists like Jimmie

Chatmon, Bondu warned, "If anyone is thinking of asking our young men and women to go out into the streets and demonstrate, he is making a big mistake. . . . For if anything goes wrong, it might be your child or you who gets killed or wounded for life." Then, "after the march is over, we still have to go to the conference table to make sure of the 'demands.'" Conferences, after decades of negotiation and increased frustration about the Community Relations Board, still seemed eminently preferable to disruptive marches in 1966. Perhaps more important, money and merit, not white supremacy, are what appeared to matter in America after the Civil Rights Act. "If you have the money, you can buy a home in any section of town you desire; if you are qualified, you can get any type of job you want." If there was marching to be done, "the only place I'm going to march is behind that little white ball on the golf course."[168]

Conclusion

In spite of the radicalism most often remembered in reference to "the sixties," there was also an abiding conservatism within black politics during that decade that had everything to do with how Negro politics had developed over several preceding generations. Bondu's words, for instance, echoed those of Kelsey Pharr, who contended more than a half century earlier, "On the battleground of life, men succeed or fail, rise or fall, solely on merit."[169] For years, targeting the markers of merit—objects of consumption, largely—meant understanding hotels, beaches, and other kinds of real estate as symbols of power and citizenship. Whites, through decades of ongoing disfranchisement, violence, apartheid, and still-vibrant arguments about the sanctity of private property, ensured that access to objects would, indeed, define citizenship. And after tremendous political, cultural, and economic investment over several generations of compromise—albeit racially asymmetrical compromise—that belief in property was not going to disappear.

Fighting to line up black property rights with black merit, in fact, is what prompted Negro businessmen and white city officials, in 1957, to desegregate Miami's municipal golf course in the first place.[170] Elmer Ward, a wealthy black landlord and pharmacist, brought suit and started a conversation.[171] Property continued to be both things *and* entitlements. Yet, there were clear costs to making hotels or golf courses the measure of equality. As Matilda Graff, of CORE, pointed out, "The Miami NAACP was fighting for the right of blacks to use public golf courses, but its relevance was not exactly appreciated in a community that still lacked electricity and sanitation services."[172]

Colored Town's residents needed many things more than golf courses, to be sure. When it came to appreciating the benefits of ownership, however, there would sometimes be no contradiction at all between what most black Miamians felt they needed and that for which the most prominent black political voices were fighting. Talking to reporters for the 1961 documentary "Miami Condemned," one young black mother pointed reporters to the wooden, dingy shack barely standing behind her. "I had accidents in that house. . . . I fell through the bathroom floor when I was [pregnant with] my last baby. . . . Evidently, I must of hurt him, one side of his face is disfigured. One ear's larger than the other." City housing officials, this tenant believed, "don't seem like they're gonna do nothing else . . . for the colored people, too well." "The only way you can kind of manage, if you have any money at all," she admitted, "is to move out to the suburbs."[173]

The suburbs—this tenant's sentiments about where hope was to be found provide an echo of conversations swapped over clotheslines or in Colored Town's churches or barrooms. They were the stuff of black visions of freedom at the top and at the very lowest rung of Jim Crow's hierarchy. Truly, at least as it concerned real estate, black people believed what most Americans had come to believe in the postwar period, perhaps only more so. Out there, somewhere in the suburbs, much more than their dream house awaited. Their very rights as citizens were waiting there for them, too.

CHAPTER EIGHT

Suburban Renewal

"This will sound strange coming from me," Rev. Theodore Gibson admitted
in 1962, "but somebody ought to protect the white people." Talking to local
reporters about how to solve South Florida's race problem, Gibson noted the
"cases where the white people in [suburban] neighborhood[s] get along with
the first Negroes who move in, but then are driven out by the riff raff." "That,"
the minister maintained, "shouldn't happen." Head of Miami's NAACP chapter at the time, Gibson had great faith in the inevitability of desegregation,
and he believed that white homeowners, with exposure, perhaps, to the right
kind of black people, would soon make their neighborhoods available to upwardly mobile people of color. The coming end of Jim Crow beckoned a
world where there would no longer be a "colored only" anything—no more
"colored only" beach, no more "Negro Court," no tension between liberalism and property rights. Instead of blackness being a kind of collective property, there would only be *private* property in its deeded and freely transferable
forms. Yet, Gibson, like other racial moderates, had come to realize in the
wake of widespread resistance to open housing and school desegregation that
white homeowners, ever spooked, he thought, by the black poor, had no
interest in allowing black people to shed so easily the apparent stain of being
"Negro" under Jim Crow. To bring about his vision of democracy, the man
many called "the Martin Luther King of Miami" advocated for white realtors
to run stricter background checks as a means of weeding out black "riffraff"
who might otherwise inspire white flight or, worse, racial violence. "Instead
of just thinking of Negroes as Negroes," Gibson pleaded, "homeowners and
real estate people [should] treat them as individuals."[1]

Belief in black people as individuals, rather than as a single "Negro"
monolith, stood at the heart of Greater Miami's "conference table" approach to race relations. It also remained central to how Gibson ran Mi-

ami's NAACP and to how black property owners and racial moderates were coming to frame civil rights more generally around the country. Notions of the black individual, in fact, shaped how postwar liberals envisioned urban renewal as a civil rights program. Gibson and other housing reformers imagined that relocation monies from the Federal Housing Administration and public housing developments might help separate the suburban Negro "wheat" from the "chaff" living in the projects. Racial liberalism, after all, counted on the ability to associate desegregation with refashioning "the Negro" into a better, "American" property owner.[2] Reflecting a broader civil rights vision, Gibson believed that South Florida's suburbs, if properly managed, could serve as sites of interracial consensus between persons autonomous, moral, and, ideally, creditworthy. "If he doesn't fit in," Gibson remarked of the imaged black buyer of diminished character, "don't sell him a house."[3]

Not unlike the taxpayer rights arguments first made by colored property owners at the turn of the century, or the push for Negro tourism in the 1940s and 1950s, belief in the social power of suburbs offered a jumping-off point for the building of interracial common cause because it left certain foundational elements of white supremacy—such as the right to exclude and white fears of the black poor—free from critique. Haines Colbert, a white reporter at the *Miami News*, for instance, praised Reverend Gibson's levelheaded and empathic approach to real estate through a telling choice of words. "The Dade County chapter of the National Association for the Advancement of Colored People has turned its guns around and trained them on the Negro." Colbert, like reporters at the *Miami Herald*, applauded Gibson and his organization for keeping the door open to compromise, for appreciating white anxiety, and for "[putting the] shoe on [the] other foot."[4]

Sure, housing had served as an ever-broadening shield of white people's privileges in the twilight years of Jim Crow. But that was kind of the point. Racial progress—as imagined by Governor LeRoy Collins, Athalie Range, or Luther Brooks—meant determining which black people were deserving of opportunity and gently increasing equality for *those* people, without compromising whites' generally acceptable and widely distributed privileges.[5] As the historian Wendy Wall points out, "The language of consensus—a consensus built around individual freedom—could be deployed to extend civil rights to individual black Americans[, but it] was much less successful at reversing the economic and cultural legacies of . . . group-based oppression: white supremacy."[6]

"Protecting" white people, to borrow Gibson's language, had been critical to achieving Miami's "quiet revolution." It paced the opening up of beaches, downtown lunch counters, and golf courses.[7] Still, as it concerned housing, it would prove impossible for Gibson, or anyone else, to unmake the idea, by this time a half century old, that freedom from Negro neighbors was, in itself, a political and social privilege. Few white homeowners cared to split hairs over which black people apparently lowered property values and which ones did not. *All* black people were a potential threat to property values insofar as any one of them could become the one-too-many that inspired fearful whites to panic-sell and send home prices plummeting.

Inside the creaking, cramped apartments of the Central Negro District or on neighborhood streets during the *Junkanoo* parade, Miamians absolutely created moments of recognizable opposition and struggle. Greater Miami indeed belonged to a laboring Negro South that, in the words of the historian Robin Kelley, fought white supremacy at every turn, "despite the appearance of consent," through theft, foot-dragging, the destruction of property, and, at times, even open attack on "individuals, institutions, and other symbols of domination."[8] Miami also belonged to a world, however, wherein Caribbean migrants, black Americans, and many once known as "colored" seemed far less committed to destroying property or attacking symbols of domination than with *acquiring* property and *appropriating* such symbols. The patently *un*progressive rules of urban and suburban real estate—built on the principles of rent seeking and racial and class segregation—demanded of colored people, even working-class colored people, not just a radical, but a *capitalist* imagination, one arguably as old and complicated as black slave ownership and the promise of landownership after Emancipation.[9] As colored people became Negroes, Afro-Americans, and more, they remained as interested in the problem of governing as they were committed to resisting, perhaps even more so.[10] As personally edifying as everyday forms of resistance could be—as heroic and courageous as public standoffs against white supremacy often were—the exigencies of property ownership created an equally quotidian and arguably more potent power that many colored people were up against and after: infrastructural power.

Since before Miami's frontier days, black people cared deeply about distinctions between "riffraff" and more "upstanding" folk. And if they hoped to keep white supremacy from erasing those distinctions, many black people, by the 1950s and 1960s, sought the same kinds of privileges, protections, and instruments of exclusion that seemed like a commonsense entitlement for white homeowners. The process of keeping black communities free from the burdens of white profiteering and racist state action, in other words, moved many black people to try their hand at weapons invented, explicitly, for advancing white supremacy. Blacks in the suburbs formed homeowners associations, attempted to control zoning, and bitterly opposed public housing, often citing the same cultural and policy arguments against poor black people that whites had used against them.[11] Black suburban homeowners, moreover, would link their defense of property rights to the institutional foundations laid by landlord lobbying groups. Many would remain landlords themselves. And in allying with what had become a robust set of ideas and practices meant to protect the integrity of rental profits under Jim Crow, black suburbanites issued a direct rebuttal to practices of displacement that colored people suffered through the state's repeated deference to white homeowners.

Suburbanization would encourage unprecedented kinds of black militancy, no doubt. Homeownership represented an escape from tenantry, the attainment of stronger legal voice, and emancipation from the undue influence of slumlords. For all that suburbs promised, though, they affirmed, in their very structure, a set of assumptions about nonwhites that adversely impacted black suburbanites themselves, leaving them uniquely vulnerable and facilitating the preservation—indeed, the modernization—of Jim Crow's racial double standards.

In order to appreciate the hardening of a political culture that continued to make black people the bearers of difficult and unpopular policy choices, one must understand the hopes placed and frustrations found by black people in suburbia during the 1950s and 1960s. Black people's endorsements of urban renewal, their complicated relationship to landlords and growth liberalism, and the constancy of black downward mobility all served as processes that can be explained, at least partly, by how colored people experienced suburbanization. Even the story of America's suburbs—for everybody—must begin in Jim Crow's slums, in other words. For whether American born or immigrant, widespread belief in suburbs at all originated *within* the Jim Crow urban context, and remained deeply informed by the kinds of property politics that enabled so many to profit from black poverty.

The End of Colored Town

During the 1950s, no matter how hard residents tried, it seemed Colored Town, as a neighborhood, could not shake its reputation as "notorious" and "unhealthful." Back in 1942, the *Crisis* magazine ran an entire special issue highlighting the businesses, civic, and social life of the Central Negro District. Photographs of black-owned homes and apartment buildings accompanied lists of Negro social clubs and articles profiling the professional achievement of the Race.[12] But, ten years later, Colored Town's middle class remained largely overshadowed by the neighborhood's deplorable housing conditions, saloons, and general infrastructure of white profiteering. On one of his many trips to Miami en route to Haiti, Claude Barnett admitted, "Second Avenue is terribly depressing to me with its smoke shops and grog joints and white people reaping harvests." Barnett was happy to "get out" among the city's growing black suburbs "and see good living[;] it gives a different impression."[13] Another black journalist, Carl Thomas Rowan, had visited Miami near the end of the war, and, like Barnett, he returned in the early 1950s to a disquieting continuity. "I had to hold my nose there in 1945, for the slum shacks were the worst that I had seen anywhere in America. . . . Many of these shacks still existed—in a more dilapidated condition than ever."[14] Life "over town" brought certain cultural charms, such as the *Junkanoo* and Orange Blossom Classic parades. Yet, living there seemed increasingly synonymous with street crime, windows without mosquito screens, and a rickety roof over your head during hurricane season.

Suburban communities, such as Brownsville, promised something different. When one had as options life in Colored Town or living in Miami's concrete suburbs, for many, it hardly seemed like a choice. One resident of the Central Negro District, feeling perhaps compelled to clarify what had become the dominant narrative of tragic displacement in Overtown, stated in 1997, "I didn't have to move [from Overtown]. I moved because I wanted to, because I was renting and wanted to buy my own home." Sometimes it was as simple as the explanation offered by Andrew Robinson, a retired lab technician: "A man wants his own home, his own lawn, and maybe a pool. Where in Overtown could you have a pool?"[15] Recall the name of the community was pronounced as two words, not one—"over town." The Central Negro District, as the 1950s became the 1960s, was supposed to be "over there," far from the black suburbs in which people long known as "colored" were supposed to become something else entirely.

If not mostly a suburban people, black folk in Jim Crow America mostly aspired to be. According to a 1948 report from the National Urban League, three out of four middle-class black families desired suburban living. The US Supreme Court's ruling against restrictive covenants in *Shelley v. Kraemer* that same year seemingly made suburbs a real possibility for colored people.[16] In response to the legal opening offered by *Shelley*, white politicians and developers around the country began stoking existing black demand for suburbs. They recognized the ability of all-black subdivisions to serve as instruments of racial containment, high profits, and peaceful residential growth. By the early 1950s, brand-new neighborhoods such as Pontchartrain Park in New Orleans and Richmond Heights, fifteen miles south of Miami, emerged as part of a cottage industry that would see capitalists and open-housing advocates around the country jointly marketing suburbs as symbols of economic self-determination, political participation, and equal education for upwardly mobile black people.[17] As conveyed in Lorraine Hansberry's *A Raisin in the Sun* or in the policy recommendations of longtime housing reformer Robert Clifton Weaver, suburbia stood, in many respects, as the "End of History" for an emergent civil rights movement.[18]

In South Florida especially, new subdivisions at Richmond Heights, Carver Ranches, and Bunche Park promised tens of thousands of people freedom from the Central Negro District's Jim Crow slums. Such freedom, however, had to be fought for, even in suburbs. For, if acres of detached single-family homes and green spaces constituted a vision of ownership free from rent collectors, dirt streets, and crime, making that vision a reality demanded that black people organize into homeowners associations, parent-teacher associations, and other clusters of democratic action committed to preserving and advancing black property rights.

Assuming Infrastructural Power

Athalie Range and her family were the first to buy a single-family home in Liberty City in the early 1950s. Prior to that, she lived in the Liberty Square housing project. When she finally moved into her own home, her chief concern, common among black "frontier" families in more remote suburban communities, had less to do with white homeowner violence than it did with assuming power over the "colored only" infrastructure they experienced on a daily basis. Range and her husband, Oscar, had four children, which meant the Ranges remained acutely concerned about the condition of Liberty City Elementary. That was the single Negro school serving Liberty City homeowners, Brownsville, the Liberty Square housing project, and the remaining black families in Railroad Shop. With a total of twelve hundred students, the school had no lunchroom and no trees or grass anywhere on the grounds. The buildings were all portables, which meant all the water fountains were outdoors. And, because white school builders cut corners in even the smallest details, the pipes to the water fountains ran aboveground. Under the Florida sun, fountain pipes cooked and boiled the water, making it practically too hot to drink.[19] Still, children were so thirsty, as Range later recalled, they "began lining up at about 10:30 in the morning . . . to get a drink before lunchtime."[20]

In what would be her first act of organizing in a political career spanning over fifty years, Athalie Range, already in her midthirties, became head of the Liberty City Elementary Parent-Teacher Association. She organized over one hundred black families to descend on a local school board meeting and demanded improvements in the most basic school conditions. A roomful of agitated black parents, especially in what were usually all-white suburban school board meetings, generated enough surprise and anxiety among white school officials to secure immediate improvements for colored students. In 1952, the board built an entirely new building for Liberty City Elementary, indoor water fountains and all. From her position in the PTA, Range pushed for other improvements in trash collection and transportation services, before eventually joining the ill-fated effort to desegregate Orchard Villa Elementary in 1959. As in school desegregation cases elsewhere, expressed concerns over the moral and in some cases psychological well-being of children provided an effective argument for securing concessions from whites.

At an even deeper, spatial level, though, black suburbs nurtured a particular understanding of democracy that linked the postwar subdivision to existing beliefs among colored folk about moral uplift and taxpayer, consumer, and property rights. A demonstration of actual ownership was supposed to give one access to other entitlements. In particular, black suburban homeowners fought constantly for the right to control the location of schools, churches, and other zoning measures, mostly because proprietors in the saloon and leisure business tended to follow black migrations into the suburbs.[21] Churches, in fact, became particularly important tools of black suburban development and preservation because Dade County zoning stipulations mandated that bars and saloons had to be at least twelve hundred feet from religious buildings. A few well-placed churches could keep an entire community bar-free.

Black residents protected their zoning power to great effect in Richmond Heights, a black suburb opened by a white Pan American Airways pilot named Frank Martin. Martin and his wife, Mary, had been impressed with the verdant colored communities they saw during their many flights into the Caribbean. And initially they worked with Ira Davis to make Richmond Heights the preeminent location for black World War II veterans and their families, often on terms as favorable as twenty-five dollars down.[22] Quickly, saloon owners in Miami recognized a new market. They would be turned away, however, when over six hundred black homeowners, organizing as "RESIDENTS, HOMEOWNERS, TAXPAYERS, and CHURCHGOERS," signed a petition intended "to better our way of life and . . . increase our standard

Figure 8.1. Richmond Heights, 1951. (From Reinhold P. Wolff and David Gillogly, *Negro Housing in the Miami Area* [Bureau of Business and Economic Research, University of Miami, 1951], 22.)

of living physically, morally, and spiritually." As consumer-citizens, the residents at Richmond Heights successfully kept their neighborhood "free from the dens of iniquity foisted on the Negro citizens of this County in other areas."[23] Richmond Heights' residents knew that, far off, in the northwest corner of Dade County, black suburbanites in Bunche Park had failed to insulate their community from the influx of white-owned bars. At Bunche, a savvy white saloon owner circumvented the county guidelines by simply buying the two black churches on opposite sides of his bar.

Owing partly to the organization of its residents, Richmond Heights became a particularly attractive destination for black city dwellers. The *Miami Herald* called the neighborhood, which sat on twenty-two hundred acres, "Shangri-la for Negroes." It had paved streets and sidewalks and homes made with the same concrete construction found in white communities. Thelma Anderson, a nurse who had spent most of her youth in Coconut Grove, moved to Richmond Heights. She remembered having to leave home at 5:30 a.m. and take three buses just to get to her downtown job. Anderson recalled, nevertheless, "how thrilled I was that we were finally moving from a rented house . . . into our own home." With some fifteen miles of dirt road between Richmond Heights and Miami's downtown, the community, to many urban blacks, seemed distant enough to be "behind God's back." Still, even as it served to sequester black people, the neighborhood, like other bedroom communities, also outfitted them with certain suburban privileges.[24]

Leisure could, in some cases, be one of those privileges, despite concerns over white-owned drinking establishments. If investors opening a business remained committed to creating an actual destination (in the spirit of black tourism) and not simply turning a quick buck (as had long been the case in Colored Town), black residents could be quite welcoming to white-owned businesses in the suburbs. Brownsville residents, for example, had the distinction of close proximity to the Hampton House Motel and Villas. In 1957, Florence and Harry Markowitz, longtime clients and political allies of Luther Brooks, built the Hampton House as South Florida's suburban and more exclusive answer to hotels "over town." The Hampton House featured terrazzo floors, wrought-iron railings, Mediterranean-style architectural accents, and an upscale dining service replete with linen tablecloths, maître d' service, and valet parking. As a motel, it was also meant for the new black motorist who might desire air-conditioned rooms or prefer an in-ground swimming pool to the crowds at Virginia Key Beach.[25]

The Hampton House drew patrons as disparate in views and experience as Malcolm X, Milton Berle, Martin Luther King Jr., and Cassius Clay. No strangers to integrating predominantly Negro spaces, Luther Brooks and a few of his white business associates maintained a consistent presence in the Hampton House as well, as did Mayor Robert King High. Black businessmen and businesswomen from across the South also found their way to the Markowitzes' establishment as part of the larger tourist traffic of consumers and investors coming to South Florida and the Caribbean during the 1950s and 1960s. Such diversity put the Hampton House on a par with the Mary Elizabeth as one of the few locations in Miami that could effectively blend black and white patrons into a singular nightlife while helping the motel surpass other locations in accessibility and upscale atmosphere.

Just as the Markowitzes attempted to set the Hampton House apart from Overtown's hotels and night establishments, so, too, did the presence of that destination help Brownsville, as a neighborhood, stand apart from what lay "over town." "You had to be *dressed*," remembered David Miller, a onetime patron. "You couldn't walk into the Hampton House looking any kind of way." "When they opened that place," Miller added, "it was like a gold mine to us."[26] So exceptional had the Hampton House become that, in 1962, the Nationwide Hotel Association anointed Harry Markowitz the "Motel Man of the Year" at its annual convocation. Luther Brooks, a man "nationally known for his contributions to the betterment of Negro housing," served as a guest speaker at the event.[27] Markowitz, around this same time, opened a new black suburb near Richmond Heights, in Goulds. He also celebrated black consumption, in general, as a rich and, in 1962, still largely unex-

Figure 8.2. Hampton House advertisement, 1962. (Courtesy of the Black Archives History and Research Foundation of South Florida Inc.)

plored source of capital. "The Negro tourist and convention delegate spends a billion dollars a year in the United States," Markowitz explained. "That's a tremendous business which we've barely tapped."[28]

Growth, Not Progress

Seeming successes of black suburbanization at Liberty City, Richmond Heights, and Brownsville—to say nothing of the enduring ghetto downtown—encouraged a steady flow of nonwhites into the suburbs, and mirrored South Florida's wider growth trends. The year Richmond Heights opened, 1952, there were over ten thousand registered voters living in the Central Negro District. Four short years later, in 1956, that number dropped by nearly half. The *Brown* decision helped matters, as whites began fleeing their inner-ring suburbs for the promise of whiter school districts and job opportunities in Broward County. "For Sale," ran the real estate advertisements in the *Miami Times*: "Newly Opened to Colored—close to stores, churches, schools, buses and jitneys." White Miamians abandoned scores of three-bedroom concrete houses, some only eight years old. And black families were snapping them up, often with the help of newly available FHA or Veterans Administration loans, and many with mortgages offered by black insurance companies or individual developers.[29] In the northwest section of Dade County alone, there was an increase of over 300 percent in black residents during the 1950s.[30]

It helped that age-old "colored" institutions from the Central Negro District suddenly caught suburban fever. In 1957, Miami's flagship black newspaper, the *Miami Times*, closed its downtown offices and moved to the suburbs. This relocation accompanied, not coincidentally, the paper's endorsement of bulldozing the Central Negro District for highway building. Ministers, teachers, and physicians followed suit in their migrations, helping make South Florida's elite black electorate a decidedly more suburban one. Black theater troupes and musicians even began dramatizing life in the "old neighborhood" with plays and other cultural performances. One such play, *Goodbread Alley*, offered black suburbanites a scandalous rendering of prostitution and vice in Colored Town's most infamous quarter. With off-color language and dramatized violence, productions were deemed "adult entertainment only," and anyone under sixteen years old was barred.[31]

The pace of new housing construction and racial transitioning in Miami's suburban neighborhoods far exceeded the rate at which Dade County officials could effectively establish areas "fit" for black people.[32] Twenty-six different municipalities made up Dade County, each with its own city coun-

Figure 8.3. Richmond Heights, 1962. Suburban developers targeting black buyers made sure to tout the seemingly timeless benefits of property ownership. Here, sellers at Richmond Heights affirm widely accepted ideas about suburbs being the best place to raise children and make memories as a family. (Courtesy of the Black Archives History and Research Foundation of South Florida Inc.)

cil. Whenever county planners attempted to designate new areas for Negro expansion, developers would take advantage of their political connections, exploit bureaucratic lag times in city/county communications, and break ground on new "whites only" suburbs, thereby "eliminating . . . area[s] for minority group relocation purposes."[33] Also, white suburbanites who sat on the Dade County Commission and the county planning board were not above orchestrating government "inefficiencies" to protect their own property interests from possible black housing. One Dade County engineer deliberately misled federal and local housing officials about the likelihood of flooding on a particular tract of undeveloped land because planners had apparently earmarked the property, which was less than a mile from the engineer's Miami Springs home, for a Negro subdivision.[34] In search of agreeable Negro housing sites, officials also ran up against white builders who actively discouraged black buyers with pricing schemes—such as demanding balloon payments—or by simply drawing up restrictive covenants in direct violation of the law.[35]

By 1960, Miami's growth continued steadily, and two-thirds of *all* Dade County's nearly one million residents had been living at their current address for less than five years.[36] Under such mushrooming housing conditions, strategies of deliberate black containment, already hard to maintain, became even more difficult to plan centrally. In response to Dade County's perceived crisis in central planning, Greater Miami's voters, in 1957, established America's first metropolitan government. "Metro," as the initiative came to be called, suffered fierce opposition from landlord interests and white suburban communities, since both saw centralization as a threat to their autonomy. The measure passed, however, because Metro promised to help facilitate highway development, to lower taxes in the city of Miami, and to circumvent obstructionist politicking among "pork-choppers" in Florida's state legislature.

Under Metro, the actual practice of government "reform" for the first five years of the 1960s included the arrival of federal highway monies, more public housing, and better coordination of city and county services. And thanks to white homeowners, landlords, and black civic leaders, each new land regulation would improve practices of Negro containment. Landlords, in particular, became quite effective at using Metro's bigger bureaucracy to slow down the approval of public housing projects in the Central Negro District, their traditional stronghold, and redirect new projects to the city's black suburban districts.[37] Black reformers pushed for new black housing in those areas—"Negro areas"—where they knew they could get the quickest approval. And white homeowners, through sympathizers on the Metro commission, used the new county government to keep public housing largely away from their suburban communities, given that landlords had led most to believe that public housing all but assured racial integration and a decline in property values.[38] For good measure, some suburban developers in South Florida used restrictive covenants right up until President Lyndon Johnson signed the Fair Housing Act of 1968, just to give their communities a "traditional" appeal.

Still Selling History

Strategies of suburban development and racial restriction in the 1950s and 1960s conjured an earlier era in South Florida's real estate history. Miami, in fact, was still being called "the New Tropical Frontier" into the 1950s, and one geographer wondered in print "whether the white man will be successful in his latest invasion of the tropics."[39] In northwest Dade County, planning officials did their part to guide development along the lines of the old 1936 Negro Resettlement Plan. Through zoning variances and the conferral of permits, county bureaucrats continued driving black population growth away from Greater Miami's downtown business district and coastal areas. Ideal locations for black people seemed to be in the unincorporated black suburbs of Brownsville, or westward and northward from there. Yet, this plan, quite ironically, ran into the descendants of Progressive Era real estate developers Lon Worth Crow and Ernest Graham—families that intermarried and began developing new suburbs on a potential collision course with perceived black population growth.

Tales of Florida's frontier past still made money. By the start of the 1960s, multiple generations of Seminoles had grown up on their Broward County reservation, wrestling alligators and selling wooden tomahawks when they were not engaged in the more common practice of agricultural and dock work.[40] Lon Worth Crow Jr., son of the man so ceremoniously crowned in Indian feathers at the "Forward to the Soil" event in 1927, similarly hearkened to Florida's Native American roots. He celebrated his father's accomplishment and the longevity of the family mortgage company by plastering photos of Tony Tommie's surrender on the real estate pages of the *Miami Herald*. The accompanying caption read, "The Seminoles give up the sovereignty to the Everglades lands."[41]

Lon Crow Jr. wed Mary Graham, daughter of Ernest Graham, a Florida state senator, farmer, and onetime head of the Miami Chamber of Commerce's real estate committee. It was the elder Graham who arranged the partitioning of Seminole land after the "Forward to the Soil" event, and it was Graham who, as a fringe benefit of his work with a floundering sugar corporation, gained seven thousand acres of the Seminoles' "rich muck lands" on which to build his own dairy farm and family fortune in 1932. As children, Graham's three sons—Philip, William, and Bob—attended the very school for which Tony Tommie traded those many thousands of Seminole acres. And when the Graham brothers became adults, they opted to turn twenty-five hundred acres, or roughly a third of their estate, into a new suburb called Miami Lakes.[42]

Miami Lakes promised buyers a "Bit o' Scotland," with tiny lakeside neighborhoods and tree-lined streets spiraling like a conch shell out from a walkable, commercial town center. The development also had an "authentic" Scottish pub where patrons could buy such specialties as "cock-a-leekie," a soup made from leeks and chicken stock. What began as a quaint, remote subdivision grew quickly. The state of Florida recently finished a new Palmetto Expressway running right alongside the Grahams' property. When linked up with I-95, the Palmetto allowed Miami Lakes' residents to get to Miami Beach in less than twenty minutes. The family built and sold its first five model homes in 1962, and William, president of the Grahams' development corporation, began selling, hand over fist, an entirely novel housing type for South Florida—the town house. Shortly thereafter, William's brother, Phil, editor of the *Washington Post*, succumbed to manic depression and committed suicide. Lon and Mary eventually divorced. Bob, the youngest brother, finished his Harvard Law degree on his way to becoming Florida's thirty-eighth governor and, years later, a United States senator. Throughout Miami Lakes' early development and all the Graham family's personal life changes during the 1960s, their "Bit o' Scotland" remained under the protection of racially restrictive covenants.[43]

As during Miami's frontier years, black exclusion remained integral to the determination of property values. In 1967, William Graham explained to members of Dade County's Community Relations Board, "It is our policy not to sell to Negroes."[44] The community, in less than a decade, had grown to more than one thousand single-family homes, two golf courses, two hundred town houses and "villas," four churches, and an elementary school—all competitively priced, all white.[45] Yet, Miami Lakes was also the kind of community that, in its ties to a powerful Florida family, helped box in black people's housing options. The Grahams made sure to reject, flatly, any public housing projects. But even more than that, those potential black buyers whom realtors turned away dared not even pursue litigation out of a sense of futility. Challengers to the racial restrictions at Miami Lakes could expect, in the words of the county's chief civil rights officer, "wheels within wheels within wheels." Miami Lakes, in both aesthetic and legal terms, enjoyed, as a result, the reputation of being a "city of refuge" for those whites looking to flee safely the possibility of racial integration. As in most matters concerning real estate, word of mouth went a long way toward keeping blacks from even trying to lower the color barrier there in 1967.[46] The assassination of Martin Luther King Jr., a year later, provided President Lyndon Johnson with the political capital to win passage of the Fair Housing Act. This outlawed housing discrimination on the basis of race, color, religion, sex, and national origin. But well before then, the kinds of restrictive covenants employed at Miami Lakes were already becoming outdated, if bluntly effective, segregationist technology.

White Property Power

Since at least the landlord opposition to public housing in the 1930s and arguments against fair employment policies in the mid-1940s, whites had been improving the discursive power of property rights as a weapon against racial liberalism.[47] By the mid-1950s, white homeowners had become quite practiced at deploying the language of "private property," "freedom of choice," "self-help," "law and order," and "personal responsibility" to protect their racial entitlements and plausibly deny charges of individual racism. When segregationist US senators filibustered the 1964 Civil Rights Act, as just one example, they could safely claim to be acting in the interest of "free enterprise," without ever having to explain how government policies fused access to better education, employment opportunities, public services, and criminal and environmental justice to the housing in white communities.[48] Similar arguments appear throughout the records of the Metro–Dade County Commission and in the records of other local bodies nationwide.[49] In most cases, one did not need to even espouse bigoted ideas per se. The structures of inequality, such as weak government enforcement in the case of federal fair housing law, did much of the work.

Across the United States, white suburban homeowners, in their defense of segregation, could pass themselves off as ostensible defenders of the "free market." This became that much easier as many white communities responded to perceived threats of Negro "invasion" by privatizing city services and schools, defanging inclusive zoning measures, and creatively preempting open-housing and public housing measures. Rarely having to resort to racial terrorism by the 1960s, white suburbanites protected and hardened their racial power through antiregulation arguments in the courts, through the everyday proceedings of city and county governments, and at the ballot box through at-large voting, gerrymandering, and other creative approaches to black disenfranchisement.[50] The racism at America's political center became strikingly evident in California, a state rarely associated with the white supremacy of Dixie.[51] There, 60 percent of voters cast a ballot for Lyndon Johnson in 1964, and 65 percent voted to repeal California's fair housing law.[52]

What made the late 1950s and 1960s particularly important years in the modernization of racial segregation was the way in which homeowners and white landlords improved their ability to make common cause against racial liberalism, though not, as is commonly assumed, against the liberal state, as such. So-called backlash politics coming from the white grass roots found a ready-made ally in landlords who, dating back to the 1930s, had already developed the institutional and rhetorical means for profiting from segregation, both through the mechanisms of the local government and under constitutional protections of property rights. It was no accident, for example, that the chief Tallahassee lobbyist of Miami's Property Owners' Development Association (PODA), a landlord advocacy group, also served as the Dade County School Board's chief legal defender of racially segregated schools.[53] Through the 1950s and into the 1960s, PODA, Harry Markowitz's Free Enterprise Association, and the Miami Chamber's Committee against Socialized Housing continued to run full-page ads in local papers touting the benefits of "free enterprise" and stoking white homeowners' fears about falling property values and the "free association" public housing might encourage.[54]

Black pursuits of private property ran directly into these arguments. When Frank Legree, a black musician, attempted to move deep into the white section of Liberty City in January 1957, his white neighbors picketed his house by day ("WE WANT THIS NIGGER MOVED") and left threatening postcards by night ("Nigger, Don't move into this neighborhood"). The white residents of Liberty City had far fewer resources and none of the connections enjoyed by the Graham family and the eventual white residents of Miami Lakes. Instead, white Liberty City homeowners lobbied city officials unsuccessfully to condemn Legree's house and vandalized it, throwing bricks through the windows. Yet, even here, seemingly color-blind justifications for segregation were already emerging.

When rallying some two hundred of his neighbors (and a few whites from out of town), the spokesman for Liberty City's resistive white residents, David Hawthorne, told the crowd and reporters, "I don't hate Negroes and I'm sure most of you don't."[55] Hawthorne had been a chief organizer during the Carver Village incident in 1951. There, whites made no bones about

Figure 8.4. New neighbors, 1957. Whites in Liberty City picket the home of Frank Legree. (Courtesy of the Library of Congress.)

using the word *nigger* in signed correspondence to the governor and overtly threatening violence. Here, Hawthorne urged his neighbors against using more incendiary racial epithets, and encouraged them instead to put up "Not for Sale" signs. "They'll know what you mean." In an interview more than thirty years later, Legree recalled that, in response to the picketing, "I got my sprinklers, put in on my lawn, [and] turned the water up as high as I could." Protestors scattered and called the police. "When the police came," to Legree's surprise, "instead of getting *them*, the police carried *me* to jail."[56]

Through their calls for police and city commission protection, Edison homeowners asked only for their "liberties . . . to be restored" and their property to be protected.[57] Black buyers, by their estimation, endangered both, for reasons they could never actually articulate. By the mid-1960s, landlords and suburban developers continued to beat the drum of free enterprise and property rights in order to elicit the desired response from government officials and possible sympathizers. Landlords became especially fond of lambasting public housing as the den of "welfare cheats" and ongoing government waste, letting white suburban voters simply connect the racial dots.[58]

In the mid-1960s, the coming of urban renewal and highway construction provided white real estate speculators with new entrées to assume state power, new avenues to make money, and further means for many, in their search for profit, to undermine black property rights. Housing code enforcement served as an especially lively site of racist statecraft, as well-connected white rental speculators learned how to snatch property from the black elderly and economically fragile. One Miami man, described in the *US Congressional Record* as "Mr. Jones," had been in his home since before the "Big Blow" of 1926. As described by Morris Abrams, a local antipoverty activist, Jones fell victim to predacious real estate developers who, with an army of inspectors at their disposal, "rehabilitated . . . [him] to the poorhouse." After repeated visits from building inspectors and trips to the bank, first to withdraw his savings, and then to take out home improvement loans, "It becomes clear that Mr. Jones can't eat, let alone pay taxes and a loan. . . . Down comes his house, down come the limes, mangoes, hibiscus and croton . . . up comes the concrete monster—thirty families strong!" These were the deathbed whispers of Dr. William Sawyer echoing forward twenty years. "Our building code," Abrams pointed out, "was enforced to be confiscatory."[59]

Black-owned real estate, especially after years of permit denials and rejections of home improvement loans, did, at times, need to be torn down. But it was also true that black landlords and homeowners understood code enforcement as part of the suite of strategies whites used to take black people's real estate. Black tenants, not infrequently, got ground up in the resulting conflict.

A black Bahamian and second-generation client of Bonded Collection Agency, Ebenezer Stirrup Jr., owned over fifty rental properties in Coconut Grove given to him by his father, the senior Ebenezer, a man of infamous shrewdness.[60] In 1958, the son charged thirty-five dollars to forty-five dollars a month for four houses that, three years earlier, had been ordered demolished by the director of Miami's slum clearance office. When threatened with forcible condemnation, Stirrup threatened in turn, "I'm going to let those houses stay and rot down unless they give me a permit to repair them." When *Herald* reporters pressed Luther Brooks about the defiant stance of his client, Bonded's owner responded, "Stirrup does his own repairs on his houses. We just collect rent for him." Conditions in Stirrup's properties worsened over the 1960s. In September of 1967, the *Miami Herald* displayed headlines about four young boys who died in the black section of Coconut Grove. A house owned by Ebenezer Stirrup and managed by Bonded Rental Agency burned and collapsed on four children, ages 6, 5, 4, and 2½ years. No charges were ever filed or arrests made.[61]

For those black Miamians who could not afford, like Frank Legree, to move to the suburbs, tenement fires remained a particularly grave problem.[62] Few apartments were properly outfitted for Florida's winter cold snaps. A 1966 inspection of some nine hundred Dade County apartments showed that 90 percent lacked any kind of heating facilities whatsoever. Many renters still used wick-type heaters that carried an open flame, or they ran several space heaters that, being second- and thirdhand in many cases, routinely caused electrical fires. In one particularly active two-week period during the height of tourist season in 1966, three fires killed twelve people "over town," children among them. Two months later, two more children lay dead in one of the three-story concrete units that, just a decade earlier, were supposed to solve Miami's slum problem. In the second fire, Bessie Davis told her children, Willie and Ulysses, to leave the oven on and its door open as a way to heat their apartment. The two boys died from smoke inhalation when the gas from the stove ignited from a second, makeshift heating device, turning their apartment into an inferno. Such tragedies made it difficult even for white suburbanites to be agnostic about black people's housing conditions. And in the midst of chronic bureaucratic delays in urban renewal, the tenement fires in black Miami, according to the *Herald*, "[made] it clear that the city cannot wait for Urban Renewal to clean up miserable conditions in Miami's biggest slum."[63]

Cashing In, Cashing Out

Swelling tenant activism, increased repair costs, and continued negative publicity associated with black loss of life in the slums compromised much of the social fabric that propped up Jim Crow's ghetto. By August 1967, the *Miami Herald* reported that "Luther Brooks[,] . . . who was among the original opponents of public housing, said he and . . . his landlords have given up the fight."[64] "We are tired," Brooks explained, "of being accused of trying to keep poor people out of decent housing. . . . Private enterprise has received no real encouragement to do the job itself."[65] Just a month prior to Brooks's stated exasperation, urban unrest swept the streets of Detroit and Newark. Riots in those two cities were but the largest of twenty-three different street revolts that summer. Across the country, white profiteering in tenements and at the corner store stood alongside police brutality and underfunded schools on the list of black grievances.[66]

In Greater Miami, newspaper accounts of burned children and black militancy, steady reproach from more radical black leaders, and televised exposés moved the day-to-day human costs of slum dwelling into the public light.[67] One municipal judge, Meyer Brilliant, initiated what local papers were describing as a "crackdown on housing in the downtown Negro areas." Working with Mayor High and local investigators, the judge built over two dozen cases charging both landlords and their property managers for unpaid taxes and the terrible conditions of properties.[68]

Landlords, however, had the federal government on their side. The owners of Negro-occupied property provided the only relocation housing available for Miami's urban renewal projects. Imposing housing code too strictly would have, in fact, threatened the success of urban renewal, which, by 1967, it seemed no one wanted. "We are sympathetic to the needs of families," HUD officials in Atlanta wrote to Miami's housing office in February 1967. "We also recognize that city officials may receive strong pressure to enforce codes on properties in the area which do not meet code standards." "We are, however, unable," the letter continued, "to understand the necessity for the vigorous enforcement methods being used by the city in urban renewal projects during the execution stage." In the stated interest of saving urban renewal, HUD's Atlanta office threatened to defund local attempts at housing code enforcement. "We question the justification of expenditures . . . to bring the acquired properties up to the code requirements."[69]

Yet again, litigation against landlords tended to go nowhere.[70] Still, the negative press the 1967 cases generated further stained the reputation of all those affiliated with Miami's Negro housing industry. Luther Brooks saw how his public reputation, particularly among Miami's black residents, was continuing to deteriorate, and he complained of the "non-cooperation and abuse . . . owners have received at the hands of the general community."[71] Harry Markowitz, the same businessman who encouraged the building of new Negro hotels and touted black buying power in the 1950s, remarked by 1967, "I don't think you could find any savings and loan association that would make a loan on Negro property today." The profits bankers promised with the blessing of the Federal Housing Administration just a decade before no longer seemed likely. On black-occupied properties, banks now asked higher interest rates and as much as 60 percent down.[72] Finances were only part of the story, though. From Brooks's complaints of feeling unappreciated to the resignation of landlords, like Markowitz, who had fought and lobbied for black dollars for decades, there is every indication that white landlords would have continued fighting for their investment had black people not begun broadly rejecting the politics of paternalism.

As had happened to Luther Brooks thirty years earlier in Florida's economically depressed Black Belt, black migrations, in this case from downtown slums to suburbs, greatly impacted the relationship between white capital and black life. One could follow this in televised images of black militancy, in newspaper accounts about Miami's changing housing politics, or even in the leisure spaces of black Miami. At the Hampton House, Harry and Florence Markowitz noticed a change in the Negro musicians they hired for gigs. The Hampton House brought its patrons only the most "respectable" black entertainers, but Richard Strachan, a black pianist, recalled how one of his band members got "very aggressive" with the Markowitzes about the shabbiness of their venue. "It was the black power period by then," Strachan pointed out, and white ownership of anything associated with black life became a target of sharp criticism. Florence and Harry took exception to unsolicited recommendations about their decor, menu, and stage. The musician, in response, "told them if they didn't want to support the black community they could get the hell out. The Markowitzes didn't like that," and, not long after, they closed the Hampton House, citing lack of interest.[73]

Whether in housing or places of leisure, white real estate investors seemed fed up with a generation of Negroes who were increasingly untethered from the bonds of white philanthropy, or who seemed flippant and potentially hostile. Many black people, due perhaps to their constant movement and failure to escape poor housing, had little patience with the political world Jim Crow had built. And many white businesspeople, no longer content with their custodial role in the Jim Crow order, elected to opt out. Poor Negroes, Brooks maintained, would now be the government's responsibility. "We [private investors]," he explained, "are taking the cream."[74]

Such statements might lead one to believe that white capital was fleeing Miami's ghettos completely, or that landlords were not making money. Neither was true. Highway building and other urban redevelopment schemes, while sold as vehicles of black ownership through relocation grants, had folded scores of black landlords and homeowners under their demolition plans. Many black property owners simply could not recover. As Dorothy Graham, wife of Rev. Edward Graham, remembered of her displacement from Overtown, "I was too old to start over again, trying to get comparable living accommodations."[75] The liquidation of black property cleared the way for more speculative investment on the part of whites. White landlords owned 70 percent of the Central Negro District in 1950, and 80 percent ten years later. Black flight to the suburbs helped increase proportions of white ownership, certainly.[76] Still, by 1968, Liberty City—imagined at its inception as a possible black utopia in the Caribbean—had 92 percent of *its* homes and businesses owned by white people, too. Whites actually owned a greater percentage of Liberty City's housing in 1968 than whites had owned in Colored Town in 1928.[77] Most of Liberty City's absentee owners lived in

Philadelphia, New York, or a world away in any number of South Florida's white neighborhoods.[78] One five-block stretch in Liberty City housed some two thousand people and generated, in just one year, roughly $631,000 in rent for white landlords.[79] This money paid for family vacations, health care, and other benefits generally denied black tenants. And, while not the 27 to 30 percent returns from the 1950s, profits in the 1960s remained considerable, hovering at margins just over 20 percent.[80] Even an upper-level public housing official in Miami, Martin Fine, saw fit to include Negro housing in slum condition in his personal nest egg. He later defended his investment, saying his properties served as part of a "private urban renewal program."[81]

Urban renewal, like code enforcement, public housing, and Jim Crow itself, began as a reformist idea and rapidly turned to serving the interests of capital. And from investors' standpoint, urban renewal and public housing, in particular, provided the means to either solidify or liquidate, as needed, one's stake in rental real estate. If your tenants were too militant, perhaps even destructive, or your profit margins too small, the state could pay you for your property in the name of "progress." And if you could find black property owners whose homes might fail housing code inspection, the state, if you were properly connected, could supply you with the means to "buy in," condemning black "slums" and selling them to you for "redevelopment." Before the end of the 1960s, those who opted to cash out of Colored Town had their properties replaced with vacant lots.[82] Those who bought in replaced black single-family homes with "concrete monsters." The Central Negro District, in a matter of a few short years, became a rough combination of vacant lots and concrete buildings, with only a few shotgun shacks remaining as remnants of the old neighborhood. Black Miami suburbanites, in the meantime, bore witness to the continued hardening of their own neighborhoods under brick and stucco apartments.[83]

As a general feature of urban renewal, demolition tended to come swiftly, but the building of affordable housing units, because of landlord resistance, took much longer. Around the United States, roughly four hundred thousand residential units were demolished under urban renewal by 1 July 1967. Landlords ensured that fewer than eleven thousand low-rent public housing units were built on those sites.[84] In Miami, demolition began in the Central Negro District in 1965, first for the highway and then through a series of urban renewal zones. But construction of new housing in the urban renewal areas did not begin until 1969, which was when landlords who had existing interests in the community finally secured the desired terms on new building contracts. The largest builder in "renewed" Overtown was Apgar and Markham Construction Company. The owner of Apgar and Markham was Harry Markowitz, the same wealthy apartment owner and head of the Free Enterprise Association who developed black suburbs and owned the Hampton House—the same guy miffed by a musician wielding the rhetoric of Black Power, in fact. Markowitz would maintain his investment in black people, but it would come by means of urban renewal. His personal stake in black people, through the state, now happened from a distance.[85]

Redevelopment highlighted the fact that, for black and white property owners, all landlording was not equal. Indeed, once actual demolition began, the lived experience of land expropriation offered a study in racial contrasts. "When we really understood what was happening," remembered Marian Shannon, a black homeowner in the Central Negro District, "people . . . almost gave their homes away because there was nobody to advise them on how to deal with these people who were buying it up." Rachel Williams recounted, "They sent us [a] notice and a check for $7,000 for two double lots . . . and most of us got these checks from the city and we thought we just had to move." Learning later that she had sold her house and adjoining family residences at a significant loss, Williams lamented, "At the time, we were not educated to the point to know that we didn't have to take that."[86]

Property owners who held deeds to large rental projects profited at rates significantly higher than those homeowners caught in the path of redevelopment. State appraisers took both the current value of a structure and its *projected* revenue potential into account when considering condemnation payouts. A corporation of eight white investors packed ninety-two separate units on a lot equal in size to that owned by Rachel Williams. By the time the State Road Department's bulldozers arrived, they had received a government payout of over $340,000—nearly fifty times the $7,000 awarded Williams. Some enterprising developers even began buying up land and erecting apartments directly in the path of the expressway so they could then sell their property to the government at an inflated price.[87] The fantastic sums gained by landlords prompted one *Herald* editorial to remark, "Landlords who own property in Miami's Central Negro District slum area in the path of the North–South expressway are discovering 'gold' in their land."[88]

Landlords also learned how to profit from the relocation housing that was ostensibly to be provided by government agencies. Continued landlord intransigence, even after the 1953 public housing project at Para Villa, ensured that fewer than eight hundred of a promised fifteen hundred public housing units had been built in Miami by the early 1960s. By the time highway construction brought on the most frenzied years of demolition—roughly between 1965 and 1967—as many as three hundred families at a time, in several instances, were threatened with immediate homelessness.[89] Haley Sofge, the director of Dade County's Department of Housing and Urban Development (HUD), believed that, in order to circumvent "a highly-organized but small group of vocal slum landlords," he and his office needed "to fight program dogma, to experiment, and to innovate" in concert with rental property owners.[90] Under Sofge, Dade HUD positioned itself to make public housing the primary form of relocation housing. For those black residents displaced from downtown, HUD would lease existing properties from landlords rather than having to build every apartment from the ground up.[91] Local government, through this approach, saved tremendously on condemnation, demolition, and housing construction costs. It also gave tenants and the owners of apartment buildings a new property manager to take the place of an increasingly disengaged Bonded Rental Agency. Public housing in northwest Dade would now occupy the same "concrete monsters" that developers had brought to black suburbs over the previous decade. Sofge's office, in 1967, leased some five hundred privately owned properties for low-income, "turnkey" use.[92]

When Liberty Square opened thirty years earlier, it represented a welcome departure from the conditions of Colored Town. Black public housing in Liberty City, by the late 1960s, would serve as a continuation of horrible conditions, just under a different rent collector. Public housing remained without air-conditioning. Rooms were small. Apartments were short on electrical outlets. The grounds around apartments stayed unkempt and unsuitable for children. At least rent collectors no longer showed up at five and six in the morning. As the historian Arnold Hirsch explains, even in state actions, private investors had a hand in determining "whether a project got off the ground [and] its ultimate form." Liberty City's public housing, like highway building "over town," enabled scores of white landlords simply to walk away from what had been a half century's worth of safe investments in Negro poverty. Public housing, in Hirsch's words, won "its greatest support as relocation housing." And while that may have been true for many of the city's white landlords, there were many others who loathed public housing for precisely its effectiveness in relocating black slum dwellers.[93]

A Suburban Crisis

In June 1966, city officials unveiled still another comprehensive plan to renovate the face of metropolitan Miami; it showed, yet again, just how little had changed about the principles of racial segregation and urban growth. With an eighty-seven-acre highway interchange going up over the Central Negro District, the Miami City Commission approved a $7.2 million spending package to "arrest the decline of four of Miami's older and potentially pleasant neighborhoods." Edison Park, Buena Vista, Wynwood, and Santa Clara had been home to some of Miami's worst "white slums." Wynwood contained a Puerto Rican "barrio" that overlapped with Colored Town, and the redevelopment effort represented the first of several unsuccessful attempts to gentrify the area. Each of the four neighborhoods under consideration had suffered the loss of main-street, commercial corridors caught, like much of Overtown, in the path of the expressway.[94] Home values in these communities had declined by as much as 20 percent, and, in 1966, 75 percent of buildings in the neighborhood "[did] not meet minimum code standards."[95]

Redevelopment, in this instance, was supposed to preserve hopes for a white Miami that seemed, in spite of airline advertisements, increasingly remote. Some thirteen thousand white people had fled Miami between 1960 and 1965.[96] Most moved into Miramar, Hollywood, and other incorporated suburbs in Broward County. Others moved to Miami Lakes and Miami Shores. Then there were the thousands of migrating northerners who relocated to Florida, looking for freedom from state income tax and warm weather, but who avoided Dade County altogether.[97] The projected "revitalization zones" of the 1966 plan targeted those Miami communities that were hemorrhaging white residents the fastest and whose appeal to new arrivals, in the eyes of city officials, might be salvaged by pricing out working-class Puerto Ricans and other people of color. Each of the four target areas fell completely on the *east* side of Interstate 95, arguably the largest "race wall" yet built. The freeway, planners believed, would insulate and help "cure" these so-called sick neighborhoods from further blight and allow property values to recover. Federal monies went toward spot renewal, repair grants, sewer installation, and better code enforcement. Unlike "over town," there would be no blanket block clearings here.[98]

For decidedly white communities, Miami city and Dade County officials pursued, instead, a line of development being replicated by Broward's suburban governments. They gained grants and low-interest loans from the Department of Housing and Urban Development to provide the water-processing plants, parkland, libraries, and other amenities that, by virtue of black absence, would feel that much more appealing. Resource-rich communities would inspire white in-migration. For instance, the "whites only" library that officials built in Coral Gables with $40,000 from the Works Progress Administration in 1937 would be rebuilt, *this time* with $850,000 in federal funds. In place of Jim Crow, the geographic distance between Coral Gables and most of black Miami ensured that the library's patrons would remain almost exclusively white.[99]

At the very same time, Metro-Dade officials, in conjunction with the Miami Housing Authority, elected to concentrate and increase the density of existing black suburbs with new public housing projects. With the exception of housing for senior citizens, all new low-income housing development occurred in the city's northwest section, on the *west* side of I-95. Allapattah, Brownsville, Liberty City, and Opa-locka would become part of what urban historians will recognize as the "second ghetto." Like the ghetto of the Jim Crow era, the subtle class and residential distinctions in these neighborhoods would hardly be discernible from the bird's-eye view of downtown white planners.[100]

It perhaps did not help that the Metro-Dade Commission designated its public housing zone—or what it called the "Northwest Transition Area"—with, in the words of one judge, "the full concurrence of the representatives and spokesmen of the Negro community." Similar to the process that helped determine the scale of displacement caused by public housing at Para Villa in 1953, the Miami Housing Authority and Metro, in 1962, attained the endorsement of Theodore Gibson and other black civic leaders "whose interest in preventing discrimination," white officials reminded, "is a matter of common knowledge."[101] With the right kind of black people buying their way into single-family homes, formerly all-white suburbs, Gibson and others believed, would continue to open up. Moreover, the older black suburbs, the logic went, would not mind public housing if builders kept projects architecturally consistent with, or at least minimally invasive to, the surrounding community. Thus, as part of their agreement with black leaders and county officials, Miami's public housing administrators guaranteed that South Florida would not see the kinds of high-rise Negro developments going up in northern and midwestern cities. The drab, mammoth towers of Saint Louis's Pruitt-Igoe or Chicago's Cabrini-Green would have no counterpart in South Florida, housing officials assured. Public housing would instead consist strictly of scattered-site, low-rise developments. "I urge," Gibson said, "that the project be one of excellence, even if it requires a longer length of time to come into existence."[102] If residential desegregation, by Gibson's estimation, required sifting out the Negro "riffraff"—or skimming off what Luther Brooks called "the cream"—then the colored poor should at least not be confined to projects that carried the visible stigma of poverty.

Most new public housing, in the spirit of compromise, would be scattered in what was known as "unincorporated" Dade County, or those sections of the county in which people lived outside of the boundaries of any municipal government. On the Home Owners Loan Corporation maps of the 1930s, unincorporated Dade County fell under the great red swaths of

"D" areas that eventually surrounded Liberty Square and Edison Park. By the 1960s, these areas remained widely neglected because Dade's county government gave residents little say in how commissioners levied taxes or determined the placement of roads, schools, and other infrastructure. It was here, "out in the county," that poorer whites made their homes, and where white developers built black suburbia.

Brownsville, the black suburb Wesley Garrison fought to open to Negroes in 1946, was here in the unincorporated county. It boasted, after twenty years, homes valued at as much as thirty thousand dollars or forty thousand dollars, the same price as residences in Miami Lakes, despite the fact that black homes at that price tended to be less spacious. Even in the suburbs, to be black still meant paying more to get less. Brownsville also suffered from chronic stoppages in the flow of clean water, a lack of public parks, and constant flooding during rainstorms. The neighborhood did not get sidewalks until 1992.[103] In the view of some planners, Brownsville seemed an especially fitting site for public housing because there was still more open space there than in neighboring Liberty City.

In 1966, Donald Wheeler Jones, Theodore Gibson's successor at the Miami NAACP, read the development plans of the Miami Housing Authority as "deliberately perpetuated segregation," and demanded a federal investigation.[104] The case against the MHA fell apart quickly on the grounds that (1) there was no evidence of deliberate acts of individual or collective racism and (2) the MHA had consulted Gibson, Edward Graham, and other black leaders during site selection. To preserve the reputation of the MHA, Martin Fine—the public housing official who was also a slum owner—pointed out that residents had "free choice" to live anywhere that was available. Applicants could, of course, only choose from existing MHA locations, and, naturally, white people with options would hardly pick a "Negro" housing project, if they could help it. MHA officials rejected the idea, moreover, that their office should legislate desegregation. "I, personally, would never vote to force a man to move into a certain area," Fine remarked. "We are not obliged . . . to force integration." Don Jones retorted that, historically, the MHA "had no compunction about forcing a Negro to live in a Negro project."[105]

Hackles rose even more among black Miamians when Brownsville residents learned, in January 1967, that the Miami Housing Authority had slated their community for forty of what would eventually be nearly nine hundred low-income public housing units, accommodating some five thousand residents.[106] All of the initial units required demolitions and homeowner displacements. Brownsville residents pointed out that the 1967 project would be their neighborhood's second public housing allocation in three years. During the previous project, the MHA spent eight million dollars erecting some eighty-eight units of public housing. Despite that considerable government investment, Brownsville's public infrastructure remained largely outdated during the building of the project. More than forty families lost their homes to eminent domain. "While I am a staunch proponent of low rent public housing . . . and am certainly overjoyed to see hundreds of shacks and concrete monstrosities being torn down in the crime and vice infested Central Negro District," wrote one editorialist from the *Miami Times*, "my joy quickly turns to gloom when we take a good look at what is happening to the once proud Brownsville community."[107]

At the time of the earlier, 1964 development, "More than 100 Negroes," the *Times* reported, "filed objections to the . . . project."[108] And Harry Markowitz, to no avail, put the weight of his Free Enterprise Association behind black homeowners. Both Markowitz and the black press pointed out the negative impact public housing projects had on black suburban property values. Markowitz also charged that the Miami Housing Authority enjoyed zoning variances from the county commission that no private landlord could ever get. He knew because he had tried attaining such variances himself. Public housing was clearly gaining traction as the preferred form of low-cost black housing.

Compromising Brownsville

Brownsville's repeated run-ins with public housing represented housing policy as usual. For when the MHA, the Dade County Commission, and black leaders like Theodore Gibson agreed upon suburban site selection in northwest Dade County, they participated in what had become, by that time, standard government practice. In a technique pioneered by Chicago's Robert Taylor in the early 1940s, housing officials routinely viewed black suburbs as optimal places to put new government housing projects. Black suburban homeowners had resisted consistently. Still, as the argument went during the Jim Crow era, imposing Negro housing projects onto black homeowner communities allowed government officials to meet black people's obvious housing needs without giving the wider, white electorate or white city councils the impression that the government was trying to encourage racial integration. Black property values, in the wake of "public good" arguments for eminent domain, remained of minimal concern. When the promise of new suburbs seemed at hand after *Shelley v. Kraemer* (1948), older black suburbs became even more expendable. Housing planners around the country continued to put public housing in existing Negro neighborhoods, maintaining all the while that it represented a centrist—or, in the language of the day, "pragmatic"—approach to urban growth. Black property values, many assumed, could never get lower than they already were, relatively speaking. Officials also pointed to the new black suburbs opening up in remote corners of metropolitan areas, celebrating them as the best places to receive those who might possibly be displaced. The approach itself, conceived of by Taylor, a black liberal, had the added benefit of winning housing officials the support of an emergent generation of black liberals—the Ira Davises, Theodore Gibsons, and Frank Hornes of the country. These were reformers who were often forced to celebrate new public housing construction, not as instruments of segregation, but as instruments of slum clearance, Negro uplift, and much-needed market competition with profiteering white landlords.[109]

In other words, displacements of black people, like earlier forms of violence, were a show of racial solidarity, at least within the black liberal calculus. However, arguments for public housing as a public good were unpersuasive to Para Villa residents in 1953, and the same was true of Brownsville in 1967. For one thing, Brownsville, a community of eighteen thousand people, was hardly a "slum," at least not in the absolute terms that had become vogue in the age of wholesale block clearance and urban renewal.[110] Residents preferred to target individual properties, to pressure owners into meeting housing code, and preserve a community made predominantly of homeowners. The neighborhood, in the emergent context of Black Power, represented, for many, a kind of colored self-determination from times past and increasingly popular, contemporary notions of black community control. Brownsville was where black and white property rights advocates successfully killed racial zoning. It also bordered, and many of its residents came from, what used to be Railroad Shop, itself a symbol of the costs of landed white supremacy. Most residents also belonged to the Brownsville Improvement Association, arguably South Florida's strongest black homeowners group. Through it, residents, for almost a quarter century, successfully fought off the arrival of drinking establishments while going after black landlords who perpetuated slum housing in the neighborhood.[111] The association's founder, Neal Adams, a local grocery store owner, had become something of a household name for black Miamians over the course of Brownsville's development. Like Ira Davis or Lawson Thomas, Adams had been a longtime advocate of law-and-order approaches to the poor. As Dade's county government continued to open up new avenues for black property owners under the conference approach, Adams wound up serving on several zoning and anticrime committees.[112]

Less than a week after proposals for the 1967 public housing project came to light, the Brownsville Improvement Association demanded an audience with the Miami Housing Authority. Residents claimed they had been "clearly and definitely promised on several occasions that no additional public housing units would be built."[113] Athalie Range, who had by this point become Miami's first black city commissioner in an emergency appointment made by Robert King High, attended the meeting, and confessed, "I can't understand why everyone [from the Central Negro District] must come to the general area of Brownsville–Liberty City." She pointed to the vastness of Dade County—Florida's largest county—and said that, in keeping Brownsville free from relocated residents from "over town," "we have a prime opportunity to sit down and plan a moral community like Dade County Negroes have never had before."[114] "Moral communities" were widely understood as synonymous with suburban communities, partly for reasons having to do with popular culture, but also because of the power black homeowners had wielded with some success in suburban communities. South Floridians had also been told that the interstate highway and urban renewal efforts would serve as a decisive moral stroke against the stain of Jim Crow and lawlessness of the Central Negro District. Now, those poor residents, severed from their neighborhood by the blade of progress, would be planted right into the backyard of Miami's frustrated and fragile black middle class.

Regardless of one's color, the suburban ideal included a discernible distance from poor black people. For black suburbanites, in particular, suburbanization offered the added freedom of decoupling the seemingly natural association between "the Negro" and poverty. Much more was at stake than just the look of public housing, in other words. Animosity toward public housing, in general, was about Negroes, and, in Brownsville's case, it was about *the kind* of Negroes being housed. The nearly three thousand former Overtown residents being forced onto Brownsville, according to one correspondent at the *Miami Times*, "have been hard-core slum dwellers for most of their lives, and will bring with them their slum habits." Transplants from "over town" carried with them "social and economic problems which may include unemployment[;] . . . alcoholism; drug addiction; marital problems; incohesive family resulting from divorce, separation, or illegitimacy; poor housekeeping; criminal records; [and] psychological, psychiatric, or other health problems."[115] Within such characterizations of black Miami's poor residents, discussions of landlord practices, federal housing policies, collusion between city commissioners and developers, and other, more structural, factors tended to fade from view.[116]

An aversion to this population on the part Brownsville's black home-owners was, by the estimation of planning officials, "complicating" an otherwise straightforward plan. As one housing official told US lawmakers, "Opposition of the Negro middle class" is "compounding the problems in the Liberty City–Brownsville area."[117] The MHA tried to ease black discomfort with public housing by offering to build eleven four-bedroom single-family houses that, as public housing, would have been indistinguishable from the other suburban houses in the community. But the BIA's resistance was unflinching, befuddling Miami's housing officials. Said Vann Rhodes of the county's housing department, "I don't know what they want."[118] Norman Watson, head of Metro's Housing and Urban Development Agency, told reporters, "Few people, particularly the middle-class Negro, want public housing next to them; it's not a question of race, it's a question of status."[119]

It was, in fact, a question of property and history. At the January 1967 meeting Brownsville residents called to oppose public housing, two dozen black youth walked two laps around the meeting hall in silent protest with white housing officials looking on. Among the signs they carried were placards reading "Go to Hell Miami Housing Authority" and "Welcome new KKK." Invoking the Klan hardly seemed like a reach in the late 1960s when one understood what propertied Negroes had long held as one of Jim Crow's great evils—the elision of class distinctions among black people. A second great evil was black immobility, and that, too, seemed manifest in black suburbanites' inability to escape public housing. Athalie Range, who claimed the silent picketing by black youth gave her "cold chills," pointed out that Negro areas "are surrounded by walls without concrete."[120] Range knew full well all the *actual* concrete walls bounding and bisecting practically every neighborhood into which black people ever migrated.[121] Folk wisdom among black Miamians appreciated, moreover, the deep social costs Caribbean and American blacks bore under segregation and white land expropriation. Even with no knowledge of Robert Taylor, Frank Horne, or any number of black liberals who signed off, however begrudgingly, on black displacements, a simple recap of the previous twenty years testified to white people's habit of thrusting density and displacements onto black communities. With concrete monsters, private, mostly white capital, since the 1950s, had made Liberty City home to over-crowding almost as bad as that found "over town." A perceived "white" state had done something similar to the residents of Para Villa. The displacements public housing wrought in Brownsville in 1964, similarly, evoked memories of Railroad Shop. Displacements in the Central Negro District were ongoing.

Brownsville residents made the connections between past and present divestments in the stories they told public housing officials. Georgia Lee

Jones had been president of the Brownsville Junior High School PTA and was related, if only in shared predicament, to the apocryphal "Mr. Jones" whose story had been recounted to federal housing officials in hearings elsewhere. A former Railroad Shop resident, Georgia, as a younger woman, had been away at college when she got the hysterical phone call from her aunt, mideviction, on 1 August 1947. Twenty years later, she recounted for white Miami bureaucrats the grim details of family members "evicted from the old railroad shop addition." Jones also pointed out how the MHA, only three years earlier, condemned and demolished her own Brownsville house to build its 1964 project. Some Brownsville residents from the Central Negro District recounted their stories as well.[122]

Black animus against public housing was also historical in a different sense, for black Miamians were not just an increasingly suburban people; they had been—far longer, in fact—a landlording people. Similarly, the Brownsville Improvement Association was more than a simple collection of frustrated homeowners; it was also a corporation that owned rental real estate. At the time the MHA attempted to impose public housing on Brownsville, the BIA owned over a hundred apartments under the FHA's Section 236 program. This was the same federal housing product that Para Villa residents tried to use, unsuccessfully, to keep out the James E. Scott project.[123] The tactic of using the FHA to subvert public housing—one government program to oppose another—had transformed Liberty City from suburb to something else entirely. It was a tactic Neal Adams might have learned from Luther Brooks and E. F. P. Brigham in their failed effort to save Railroad Shop. It may have come from a chance conversation with Harry Markowitz at the Hampton House, from tuning in to Luther Brooks's radio show, or it may have been a strategy that black property owners simply discovered for themselves in their various battles against successive waves of leisure profiteers trying to buy a piece of black Miami. Whatever the strategy's source, Brownsville's residents estimated that, if they had to accommodate the downwardly mobile exiles of Overtown, they wanted to preserve their right, as landlords, to discriminate. Public housing had been anathema to landlords of any color, and what made it even more loathsome, in this instance, was that the MHA had no intention of screening out the "riffraff." As landlords, the BIA could choose its neighbors carefully and assume, through power of eviction, control over its tenants' conduct. Landlord paternalism turned into suburban protectionism.

The contradictions of self-interest and black solidarity would be as evident among Brownsville activists as they were with the black liberals who supported public housing. Investigative reporters would uncover that, only a few years after his stand against the MHA, Neal Adams—like Athalie Range and Ebenezer Stirrup Jr.—owned rental houses exhibiting a range of structural deficiencies: no closets, holes in roofs and walls, broken windows, and dozens upon dozens of other violations. Adams, by the time of the report, had been appointed by Governor Reuben Askew as a Dade County commissioner. The appointment came on the recommendation of Athalie Range, herself a member of Askew's cabinet. When interrogated about the condition of his property, Adams reverted to landlord talking points that were generations old. "I don't think [the housing] is bad, except maybe it's filthy. The tenants may not have done their job in keeping it clean."[124] Yet again, the politics of ownership made cultural explanations of black poverty seem like common sense.

The BIA's efforts to keep government housing out in 1967 proved to be of no avail. The proposed public housing would stay, and with it came diminished expectations for the future of Brownsville. To soothe black unrest, Miami's public housing officials allowed residents to name the project after the late Annie M. Coleman, a legendary community builder and property owner in her own right.[125] County officials also approved seventy-four thousand dollars in recreation facilities for Brownsville in order to meet longtime resident demands for a playground and community pool.[126] Still, in spite of these token investments, every week and a half in the summer of 1967, according to one report, one more suburban block in northwest Miami tipped from white to black.[127] The long, hot summer that brought the Detroit and Newark riots saw the emergence of a five-mile-long strip between NW Fifth Street, Overtown's southern border, and NW Eighty-Seventh Street. This ossifying black corridor served as the new center of black Miami, and, like the old Central Negro District, it was 90 percent Negro.[128]

Conclusion

When the debate over the Brownville housing projects raged hottest, Bill McBride of the *Miami Times* warned, "The conference table has been used in good faith by the Brownsville residents in an effort to make their grievances known to the power structure of Dade County. . . . Unless some immediate action will result from the use of this means, no Dade County Negro will ever respect the conference table again, and will resort to other means."[129] "Other means" came in August of the following year, when Liberty City and Brownsville erupted with South Florida's first racial upheaval. It may have coincided with the Republican National Convention, but there was little sense on the floor of the Miami Beach Convention Center that anything in sunny South Florida was out of the ordinary. Two years later, a second riot began at a Brownville grocery when conflicts over a white vendor's old stock and high prices precipitated a melee in which thirteen people were shot and fourteen policemen injured.[130] During this second conflict, Athalie Range's home became the rallying point for nearly three dozen "black peacemakers" who fanned out from her front steps in an effort to calm Brownsville residents and help enforce curfew.[131] Riots would again strike the Liberty City, Brownsville, and Overtown communities in 1980, and three more times in the 1990s.

As was often the case, "causes" seemed hard to pin down. Much of the postmortem coverage of the 1968 riot revolved around the police brutality and inflammatory, "get-tough" statements attributed to Miami's city police chief Walter Headley, a known advocate for "stop and frisk" and excessive use of shotguns and dogs. Even before the riot, Headley articulated his frustration with how "hoodlums," upon arrest, "throw civil rights in our faces." He believed that "community relations and all that sort of thing has failed. . . . Sending speakers out and meeting with Negro leaders . . . has amounted to nothing." "Felons will learn that they can't be bonded out of the morgue." Such statements rang in tones not just familiar to the likes of national law-and-order advocates such as United States senator Barry Goldwater, Chicago mayor Richard J. Daley, or then presidential candidate Richard Nixon; they echoed an earlier generation of black "law-and-order" property politics that inspired the push for Negro patrolmen some thirty years earlier. "We must get tough," Athalie Range explained, "if we are going to survive."[132]

There was also an enduring black employment problem. At the start of the 1960s, 42 percent of Miami's nonwhite families lived below the poverty line of three thousand dollars a year, and some 83 percent of black Miamians worked as either domestics or unskilled laborers, the second highest rate in the nation.[133] Federal antipoverty programs created to alleviate this condition in 1966 were deemed totally insufficient by 1967. Miami's local officials gutted most of these programs by February of 1968, and by the summer of that year, black Miamians were in the streets.[134] Most moderate observers, even when they granted the problems with law enforcement and jobs, seemed to miss the point. "By almost any standard," federal investigators determined, "the Miami disturbances were minor except to those involved."[135]

Few, it seemed, appreciated the deep infrastructural inequalities, the subversion of black property rights over several decades, and an aborted hope in suburbanization that finally caused Miami's "conference approach" to break down. Though Miami in 1968 served as a flashpoint in an apparent urban crisis sweeping the country, one could conceivably call the violence that beset Liberty City and Brownsville *suburban* riots, given what those communities once were and the ways in which black Miamians continued to understand and imagine them. Riots in onetime black suburbs would become a common feature of America's racial landscape from the late 1960s into the 1990s, in fact. Unable to stop the intentional devaluing of their communities, residents of communities beset by public housing, police brutality, and the denial of basic public services struck back against the very infrastructure of white supremacy. As in Miami, seemingly "minor" explosions racked black bedroom communities in Tampa Bay (1967), Louisville (1968), Youngstown (1969), and many other neighborhoods that, just a generation earlier, had been sold on a promise of black self-determination. All that made these riots "urban" was the specter of angry black people taking to the streets.

After the Brownsville housing projects went up and the fires of 1968 died down, Theodore Gibson found himself repeatedly trying to persuade black property owners to remain committed to the progressive potential of interracial negotiation and land liberalism, politics he had helped advance as a young priest in Coconut Grove twenty years before. At a 1968 meeting, he quarreled publicly with Ebenezer Stirrup Jr. and several members of the Coconut Grove Homeowners Protective Association about a twenty-eight million–dollar urban renewal plan proposed for their area. Stirrup told a crowd of over one hundred people, "Most proponents of urban renewal don't tell you of the unpleasant consequences that have happened in most other places." He highlighted how the state repeatedly defrocked black people of their estates, often at the behest of so-called reformers like Gibson, and he charged that the goal of urban renewal was "to gobble up the Negro section of Coconut Grove." In a turn of events with, by this point, near countless precedents, Gibson's hopes for urban renewal in Coconut Grove were thwarted through the combined efforts of black and white property owners. "We fought long and hard against apartments," one black Grove resident intimated. "We don't want apartments any more than the whites do." When government officials accused white Grove residents of racism, one Elizabeth Bettner threw Gibson's and Elizabeth Virrick's own visionary, interracial organizing on the table as evidence. "We've never had a race problem here. In fact, the white people in the Grove are the ones who have fought the most for civil rights." White homeowners, it seemed, had their stories, too.[136]

Many black people came to believe in land liberalism at the exact moment when more and more whites opted to retreat behind property rights

Figure 8.5. Confined to a "concrete monster," 1968. During the riot of 1968, the National Guard enforced a police curfew confining the residents of Liberty City to apartment buildings like this one. Guardsmen enforced that curfew by establishing a perimeter around the neighborhood that traced commonly understood color lines. (Courtesy of Corbis.)

arguments and their professed racial progressivism. These were not separate processes, but constituted, rather, a single social transformation. Property rights, the greatest form of protection allowed blacks in the late nineteenth and early twentieth centuries, ensured, by the 1960s, the elusiveness of racial integration and justice. Black people pursued, and would continue to pursue, property rights, nonetheless. Black suburbanization would grow almost exponentially in the 1970s and beyond. Still, what is offered by the fate of Brownsville, Liberty City, or for that matter Compton, California, and Prince Georges, Maryland, is, in many respects, a Jim Crow lesson. It is a testament to what happens when black people act in the interest of capital, and do so without the benefits of capital's greatest privilege—namely, whiteness.[137]

The Tragic City

Some people have begun to call Miami not the Magic City but the Tragic City.[1]

—Bernard Dyer, tenant organizer, 1971

Miami, like every American city, has more than a few tragic stories. Nearly sixty years from losing her family house at Railroad Shop and more than forty years after the Miami Housing Authority condemned her home in Browns-ville, Georgia Jones Ayers told reporters in 2006, "My grandchildren want to know where Granny was born. She wasn't born in Little Haiti. She was born in Railroad Shop's Colored Addition."[2] Now, with the neighborhood of her childhood having been renamed more than once, and with the physical evidence of Miami's black past getting bulldozed or annexed for urban rede-velopment all around her, Ayers tells anyone who will listen (and many who won't) the story of her family's evictions. For added historical effect, Ayers often tells these stories while drawing from her purse the original deed, dated 1897, that her forbearers from the Bahamas gained when they first made that now-faint footprint on South Florida's landscape.[3] Dade County School Board members, city and county commissioners, historic preservationists, re-porters, and, yes, even a few historians, have all been introduced to Miami's past through the stories that Ayers and others old enough to remember tell about the value of life and the cost of progress for those long ago deemed "colored."

Architecturally and among its people, much about South Florida con-sists of memories made from fragments of elsewhere.[4] In senior centers and churches, living rooms and college campuses, accounts of the Holocaust, *La Revolución*, and Tonton Macoutes mix with memories of when the Dodgers left Brooklyn, longings for classical British education in Jamaica, and more homegrown tales about "them damn Crackers." "In the new Florida," write historians Raymond Arsenault and Gary Mormino, "nearly everyone is a displaced person of one kind or another [and] lack of tradition has become a tradition."[5] Georgia Ayers might argue that some are more displaced than others. And in a place where the very earth under your feet seems to shift value and ownership from one generation to the next, the telling of stories may well be the only tradition, the only history, indeed the only politics, many Miamians of Ayers's generation have left.

In its recounting of the Jim Crow past, *A World More Concrete* has offered a Miami story of race, capital, and land that, at present, remains told in bits and pieces within archives, 'hoods, and high-rises. As with any self-respecting Miami story, few will agree completely with my choice of characters, communities, or even events. Yet, unlike most stories about South Florida, this account was not about an exceptional people enduring exceptional hardships in an exceptional place. Rather, this book has offered a regrettably commonplace and *un*exceptional story about how people sought and used power over the land to make and unmake wealth, neighborhoods, and individual and collective identities.

People everywhere endeavored to turn property into power, and vice versa. And in Greater Miami, political actors as diverse as Tony Tommie, Luther Brooks, and Athalie Range articulated their citizenship through their property rights. They also attempted to protect and expand those rights in the context of segregationist city building, at times contributing much to how Jim Crow actually worked. Jim Crow practices, conversely, drove transformations of both land and liberalism. They enriched and often confounded people who could never fully view the range of factors shaping their fates or decisions.

As demonstrated by South Florida's residents, ideas about property rights, especially in regard to the lived experience of race, were not simply the purview of white segregationists or of business interests warring against the New Deal state. Such ideas were the engine of real estate development, landlording, homeownership, demands for educational justice, law-and-order politics, and rental property management, broadly accepted and broadly practiced. And, as I have argued across the preceding chapters, the belief that a commitment to property rights could somehow bring about racial reform facilitated the hardening of several deeply troubling suppositions. Chief among these were racial assumptions about the deficiencies of black people, the apparent fitness of violence as an instrument of urban growth, the irrefutable goodness of suburbanization, the state's just commitment to protecting white property values, and approaches to governance that shifted the burden of "progress" in accord with perceived racial norms.[6] It was, indeed, widely held racial assumptions about real estate and state power that enabled property owners, again and again, to reach consensus through what were, at times, bitter conflicts. White landlords offered colored tenants and Jim Crow's broader black ghetto progress by way of paternalism, and paternalism, as we have seen, had a twin in practices of black racial uplift. What urban liberals and racial moderates offered the poor, by way of their earnest housing reformers, was demolition. And *this* process, in effect, differed little in its racial logic from white suburban protectionism.[7] In both instances, black people were the problem, suburbs the solution.

Even as the technology of urban development improved, white supremacy provided continuity and a certain set of shared values across the twentieth century. Lynching, forced labor conscription, or residential white terrorism represented expressions of white supremacy, to be sure. Yet, there was also a white supremacy to Progressive Era housing development, New Deal housing reform, and postwar land liberalism, in that black containment and displacement remained the easier of several hard choices. White supremacy, likewise, set the guidelines of suburban homeowner politics, in that poorer people of color, and black people especially, were principally considered a danger to property values. At the very same time, white supremacy made black people, as tenants, generators of fantastic profits.

Over Greater Miami's long history—the history of the United States, for that matter—it proved politically impossible to empower poor black tenants with civic authority and consistent means for self-determination. Jim Crow America had not been built for that. Its arbiters of landed power—planners, politicians, and property owners—advanced, instead, beliefs in blanket black inferiority while encouraging the formation of a political culture in which businesspeople determined what made for acceptable forms of economic growth and agreeable kinds of reform.[8] Since the days of the Colored Board of Trade, it was indeed a Jim Crow idea to argue for economic growth, conferences between property owners, and slow, qualified inclusion as the preferred path to racial progress.

Such remain the preferences today, with predictable results. Home prices, as in the 1930s, are still set on the basis of class exclusion and largely in relation to the location of black ghettos. Yet somehow, in the absence of strong fair housing enforcement, Americans expect the real estate market to help the United States finally realize racial integration.[9] Development schemes requiring massive displacements, carried out purportedly for the sake of economic growth, tend to target the black and brown poor through dramatic applications of eminent domain or the slow squeeze of gentrification.[10] The result of such redevelopment programs, in spite of new and ongoing promises of progress, has been the continued disassociation of majority-black communities with "good" schools, "safe" neighborhoods, and "moral" families. If there was one thing that remained true about the Jim Crow world, it was its uncanny ability both to make perfectly moral people do immoral things, and to make the absurd pass for common sense. That the rules of American capitalism continue to be set against the promises of American democracy suggests just how little has changed.

From Property to Power

Only people who were self-employed could advocate publicly. People who had bosses couldn't really advocate or step out front.[11]

—Frederica Wilson, Florida state representative, 2007

I don't know what [the tenants] were trying to prove, what they were trying to do to me. . . . I have a reputation in this community. They weren't anybody but poor people.[12]

—Garth Reeves, owner of the *Miami Times*, in response to tenant organizing at his Overtown apartment building, the Crispus Attucks Apartments, 1999

In recent years, scholars have produced brilliant work showing how notions of property rights determined "what happened" to the civil rights movement or left-leaning politics in the United States more generally.[13] Still, our general understanding of property rights and their ties to national political transformations remains largely one-sided, white-sided.[14] Political theorists have been slow to explore property ownership as a driving force in the evolution of black politics over the course of the twentieth century, even as scholars portray African Americans and other nonwhites as stalwart advocates of both suburbanization and gentrification.[15] Slower still have been political historians, whose recent attention to American conservatism has actually *narrowed* definitions of politics to the point where the most significant political acts are those that purportedly explain Republican electoral victories or Democratic capitulation.[16] Quite expectedly, preoccupations with "the rise of the Right" have breathed new life into the tendency to ignore nonwhites as agents of "mainstream" political change, except, of course, when addressing tightly framed "black" or "brown" concerns in the "multicultural" 1970s and beyond.[17] We have fundamentally misunderstood the integral place of property rights in the black political imagination, and, as a result, underplayed the role of black property politics in both the workings of white supremacy and the development of American liberalism.

In Jim Crow America, the right to speak for others, or simply to speak for oneself, remained bound to property. Owning land or buildings gave the otherwise disempowered or disenfranchised certain political entitlements. It assisted certain black people who, during years of mass voter intimidation and fraud, aspired to vote nonetheless. It granted colored people the opportunity to pay property taxes and thus to make claims on the state for better access to public amenities and services. And, in the eyes of other black people, property ownership gave one the status to be a spokesman for those otherwise marginalized by white statecraft. It made one a symbol of what "the Negro" was worth in an otherwise white world. The affirmative power of property created important political space for black people to shape the state.

Simultaneously, the underside of black property politics greatly diminished the positive possibilities colored people could access within American democracy and capitalism. In the preceding chapters, one finds civil rights and civic leaders who, as landlords, strong-armed their poor black tenants or willfully allowed their properties to collapse on top of black children. One finds middle-class black suburbanites who sought to isolate an emerging underclass. One finds multiple generations of black housing reformers who advocated for displacing black families, sometimes by the hundreds, for the purposes of improving the broader condition and reputation of "the Race." These, too, ought to be included among what the historian William Chafe called the "achievements of American liberalism," if only because they, too, originated from a political and governing culture that preserved certain white entitlements and certain black hardships.[18]

Remembering Overtown

We thought we were really Overtown . . . wherever we lived. We thought we were there forever.[19]

—Roberta Thompson, black Miamian

Maybe we should have fought for Overtown.[20]

—Enid Pinkney, black Miamian, historic preservationist

As of this writing, the destruction of Overtown serves as an especially compelling parable on racial injustice. It is akin to "Watts" or, more recently, "Katrina." It provides a metonym for neighborhoods lost and white supremacy in action. When Interstate 95 opened its southernmost leg in 1968, the highway had caused the direct expulsion of eighty-five hundred households from Miami's Central Negro District, and encouraged the flight of thousands more. "You couldn't fight it," recalled Maude Newbold, a former Overtown resident, in a 1997 interview. The highway "destroyed the cultural, the spiritual, the educational concept of the entire community. We lost our neighbors. We lost our friends. We lost our relatives. It was like death. . . . It destroyed us."[21] Variations on Newbold's account echo in documentaries, scholarly monographs, oral history archives, and records of city and county commission proceedings. For those who are old enough to remember, or who, at least, heard the stories, white people in city planning offices and riding atop bulldozers erased Colored Town's rich history and reduced a community that had admirably weathered decades of underdevelopment to something of a blank slate. The story remains a narrative of good defeated by evil. And it offers an account wherein an uncaring establishment repossessed black-owned businesses, black identity, and black economic futures; pared them down; packaged them for sale; and, in the words of one former resident, "sold them to white folks."[22] Compelling though that narrative may be, this book offers another.

First and foremost, I posit that narratives about Overtown's demise have little at all to do with the Central Negro District. They are about Brownsville, which in 2011 was called by one local paper "Miami's Most Blighted Neighborhood."[23] Jeremiads about Overtown are actually about unfailing poverty in Liberty City and Richmond Heights, or how the "war on drugs" decimated Bunche Park and Opa-locka.[24] They are not about the collapse of the city, but the failure of the suburbs. They are also, in many respects, about the Cuban "success story" and, more recently, the achievement of Haitian political power, as evidenced by a dozen suburban streets bearing Haitian names and accentuated by the erection of a statue of Toussaint Louverture on Martin Luther King Jr. Boulevard. Miami's black suburbs, without exception, experienced a rapid decline in the 1970s, as Miami–Dade County suffered the continuance of white flight. And the failed promise of black suburbia has helped fuel not just nostalgia for Jim Crow, but a collective pining for the imagined folkways of Jim Crow's ghetto.

What's largely forgotten, however, are the deplorable housing conditions, or more pointedly, the conditions that made slum clearance, urban renewal, and land expropriation of one kind or another seem, for many, like acts of civil rights reform during the years of these programs' actual implementation. "Negro removal," first popularized by James Baldwin and other social critics in the mid-1960s, has today become the shorthand term

Figure 9.1. Landmarking Little Haiti. (Photo by the author.)

for rewriting the past and portraying black Americans as somehow espousing longtime and blanket opposition to urban renewal and other forms of land liberalism.[25] Yet, for most residents of Negro ghettos during the actual 1950s and 1960s, slum clearance and urban renewal programs promised to help the collective social predicament and the collective reputation of black people. Bearing witness to the postwar prosperity that seemed so readily available to white Americans, many African Americans around the country believed mass condemnations of run-down Jim Crowed housing would, at minimum, launch otherwise contained black folk into the suburbs—the same suburbs now largely considered ghettos. The Para Villa homeowners asked, by black leaders, to sacrifice their homes for the James E. Scott project in 1953, or the residents of Brownsville and Coconut Grove who, in the late 1960s, would be asked—again, by black leaders—to make room for redevelopment and public housing, suffered under the same will-to-progress that sparked those first fragile hopes in black suburbia, the same progress fetish that would, in fact, drop eighty-seven acres of highway interchange in the middle of Miami's Central Negro District.

To be clear, black people were no more responsible for drawing up the plans to demolish Overtown than it was Kelsey Pharr or the Colored Board of Trade who pushed Herbert Brooks out of that train window in 1920. Nevertheless, similar to the way American Negroes fished Herbert out of Colored Town's tenements and handed him over to white law enforcement, black civic leaders who endorsed highway building and urban renewal had a deep familiarity with context and consequences of landed white violence and displacement. They knew what was likely to happen, and abetted anyway.

Negroes, white Americans, and immigrants all recognized the dilapidated housing of Miami's black people as a symbol of "the Negro's" political weakness. Some lamented it. Others reveled in it. Regardless of one's stance on the race question, most viewed housing reform as tantamount to improving colored folk's authority and autonomy. Remarking on the activities of the Coconut Grove Committee for Slum Clearance in the early 1950s, and stressing the link between black housing and black rights, one white real estate broker said, begrudgingly, "The next move is they will get all the Negroes to vote."[26]

As the 1950s became the 1960s and South Florida's black suburbs continued to grow, the respectability of "the Race" remained bound to what became of black life "over town." Apart from the possible conceit that could accompany one's perceived escape from the ghetto, the arguments some black suburbanites made in favor of urban renewal often dripped with condescension toward black poor and working people. Black Miami even saw a return of Victorian tones about "the Race" needing to control its wayward women.[27] "This once beautiful and carefree dame of the 20s and 30s is haggard and bare," wrote Lawrence Cooper, a *Miami Times* journalist, about Overtown in 1965. "Despite her tawdry appearance," Cooper assured, "there is hope. Her rebuilding and beautification by expert technicians are in progress. We hope that she will be a more sedate lady and follow the pattern of her suburban sisters and become a beauty again, minus her once dilapidated exterior." By the reformative hand of the federal bulldozer, Miami's black downtown would be made fit for bearing her family once more. "She will be [so] stripped of her rags and redressed in more sedate fineries that even those who forsook her may one day return and reclaim her."[28]

Black Miamians usually promoted urban redevelopment in less sexually suggestive terms. Still, both urban renewal and the eminent domain power on which it rested promised much for black Miami well into the late 1960s. "Urban Renewal Project to Encourage Integration," read a 1967 headline in the *Miami Times*.[29] When tethered to desegregation or the promise of black suburbanization, eminent domain facilitated among blacks and whites a shared discourse of progress that was vague enough to generate contradictory expectations from the governor's mansion down to the streets of the Central Negro District. Eminent domain was also concrete enough to promise a broad-based expansion of black civil rights and economic growth by leveling its power against Jim Crow's slums. From Negroes' position of relative lack, eminent domain sat at the center of a Faustian bargain in which propertied black politicos believed—and led others to believe—that demolishing slums would bring about racial equality, economic justice, and black political power. "You little black boys and you little white boys," Athalie Range explained of urban renewal to an integrated audience, "remember that Miami is a city making preparations. . . . You go to bed safe in the thought that our businessmen and leaders are burning the midnight oil so you will have the opportunity [to do better in the community]."[30]

As in the tale of Faust, the deal for the Central Negro District and post–Jim Crow Miami was one made between drastically unequal parties. Any gains black Miamians might have made by devaluing Brownsville or walking away from Overtown were abruptly sapped by increased Caribbean immigration, the asymmetrical protection of white suburbs, and the continued flight of white capital from black community building. Those events—Greater Miami in the 1970s, 1980s, and 1990s—require a book all their own. Suffice it to say, however, that Miami's fate was shared by every city where black leaders made similar bargains. The only exception was that the city of Miami, unlike, say, Atlanta or New Orleans, never got a black mayor out of the deal. The rise of Hispanic political power in South Florida ensured as much.

Practically everywhere black Americans attempted to steer liberalism from the late 1960s onward, they wound up trying to replace older forms of white paternalism or political patronage with only a fraction of the public and private resources local governments once enjoyed.[31] In some municipalities and county governments, seemingly "ineffective" black governance was a result of impersonal commitments to corporate growth designs or of the tax breaks that white executives demanded of their African American mayors.[32] In other places, poverty and racial segregation were preserved by ideological myopia and bald self-interest among a handful of city officials.[33] In others still, weak commitment to antipoverty measures on the part of government agencies and white labor leadership assured the permanence of poverty in Afro-America.[34]

Given how badly black Miami fared in the aftermath of urban renewal, it remains a great irony that it was not greedy developers or scheming executives but self-professed housing reformers who initiated Greater Miami's entry into the urban renewal era and sustained it through the 1960s.[35]

Further research may uncover similar dynamics elsewhere. Miami's most powerful white capitalists, such as Ed Ball or Harry Markowitz, found ways to shepherd land liberalism to serve their interests, no doubt. Still, in telling the story of origins and metropolitan transformations, historians must bear in mind that eminent domain, particularly in fast-growing metropolitan regions such as South Florida, began and did its chief work as a corrective for a world that threatened, again and again, to buckle under its own racial tensions.[36]

Afterlife

The new bridges, causeways and urban expressways will be significant landmarks in the near future.[37]

—Metropolitan Dade County Planning Department, 1960

The stretches of Overtown orbiting the highway overpasses had become, by 1967, what one report called "a bare, dangerous prairie. . . . The place is a jungle at night."[38] As a point of fact, however, life "over town," even after the building of I-95, was far from dead. New arrivals, almost exclusively poor, moved into what remained of the neighborhood. Most had come from slum communities elsewhere and knew what to expect. Older folk, not displaced and not interested in selling, also remained. Institutionally, little was left of the street life that had sustained Colored Town for so many decades. Gone were holiday *Junkanoo* processions—the shepherds, the costumes. Few felt comfortable being on the streets after midnight. A walk down the old "Little Broadway," NW Second Avenue, seemed like a parade of empty storefronts and abandoned buildings. In less than ten years, demolition crews had cut the number of dwelling units in half, leading to greater overcrowding in an increasingly desolate community.[39] Members of Overtown's NAACP chapter no longer felt safe enough to convene their evening meetings.[40] Luther Brooks no longer felt comfortable sending his rent collectors to make predawn runs to harvest rents from tenants, either. His men were being robbed constantly, and he decided to start collecting rent by mail. Brooks claimed to be "amazed" at how much his tenants preferred the new, less personal touch.[41]

The man who once claimed to "know what the Negro is thinking" noted how almost none of the ties that once bound tenants to landlords remained by the late 1960s. "None of the big property owners who got paid by Urban Renewal or the State Road Department . . . have reinvested in Negro housing."[42] The combination of white divestment and increased civil rights legislation finally led, in 1968, to tenants' gaining the right to sue landlords.[43] The increase in tenant organizing and litigation, however, created only a spike in evictions. In 1970, landlords were booting out tenants "over town" at the rate of two hundred to three hundred a month.[44] Between 1969 and 1974, developers did not erect a single building of new private housing in Dade's old black ghettos.[45] In aggregate, these changes made Overtown's black population less politically potent, even as it remained poor.

Wilhelmina Jennings and her family lived across the street from five rooming houses they owned on NW Ninth Street near NW Third Avenue in the Central Negro District. Jennings's grandfather, Shaddie Ward, first built the family real estate holdings in the 1910s. He was the same man who, alongside his children and neighbors, had famously made a stand against National Guardsmen who attempted to conscript a truckload of Negroes into gang labor after the terrible hurricane of 1926. Given their long history in Miami, the Jennings family bemoaned having to sell their property because of what they saw as a change in the quality of the community's residents. "The roughnecks began to come over, and all the people that would come to rent rooms . . . didn't use their culture like they should've. . . . That's why we bought out here [in Liberty City]."[46] Jennings used Bonded Rental Agency to collect the rent once the family moved out of the neighborhood. But, "We were having so much problems renting and collecting the rent . . . we just said, well, we'll close the whole thing down." With little hope the neighborhood would make a comeback, "We just decided to clean the lots . . . and houses off."[47]

By 1969, black people's apparent assumption of state power and the continued growth imperative among white businesspeople and politicians helped make the interstate highway a physical representation of interracial compromise and progrowth politics, even after Miami's suburban riots. Athalie Range's underexpressway park, in spite of its grand opening, became one of three parks in the Central Negro District that were never completed. Florida Power and Light Company, one of the principal donors, promised "all types of things," as one antipoverty advocate, Arthur King, remarked in 1971. FPL never installed lighting, and the city of Miami never even provided staff for basic upkeep of the park. A few years after the park's opening, city officials held a few public events under the expressway, hoping to maintain the goodwill that accompanied the park's inauguration. As Raymond Plumer, an employee in the Miami Parks and Recreation Department, put it: when the city shows up at the park, "We're there with our tokenism. I'm ashamed of it."[48]

Figure 9.2. Miami under the expressway, July 1969. With "concrete monster" apartments in the background, Mayor Stephen Clark addresses the media and residents of Miami's Central Negro District gathered under Interstate 95. Seated to Clark's left are City Commissioners David Kennedy and M. Athalie Range. To Clark's right sits Irwin Christie, a white politician who defeated Range four years prior through a blatant race-baiting campaign. Next to and behind Range are Edward T. Graham and Theodore Gibson, respectively. Both men served at various points as heads of the local NAACP chapter as well as city commissioners following Range's departure for a state position. (Courtesy of the Black Archives History and Research Foundation of South Florida Inc.)

The once illustrious Mary Elizabeth Hotel became a run-down tenement of over fifty apartments. By one telling in 1975, it contained "the elements of potential tragedy," including standing water, open electrical work, and padlocked fire doors.[49] During the 1980 Mariel boatlift, Immigration and Naturalization Services again reached out to Bill Sawyer, asking him, in effect, to resurrect his World War II–era job of helping blacks from the Caribbean settle into Miami's segregated cityscape. "When Castro started kicking the black Cubans out of Cuba, they called me to find housing for them because they wouldn't let them live anywhere else but Overtown."[50] As it had been during the 1950s, the Mary Elizabeth, quite ironically, became a waypoint for Cubans in transit.

Approaching old age by the mid-1970s, Bill Sawyer tried repeatedly, with other prominent family members, to get loans to repair the building. But once it became clear that urban renewal was not going to save Overtown, practices of redlining walled in the business, even at banks that, during the years of CORE's sit-ins, had helped tear down Jim Crow—banks where the Sawyers had held accounts for years. As explained by Bill's sister, Gwendolyn, "There are particular areas that are depressed like this, that bankers agree and draw a red line around, in which no monies flow through there from any of the financial institutions." "My mother," who owned the building, Gwendolyn added, "happens to be a woman, so she faces discrimination based on sex, age, *and* race."[51] Gwendolyn had trained in biology and chemistry, hoping to do what her older brother never could, and follow their father into the medical profession. Upon graduating from college, she pursued, instead, a career in law and politics, and became the first black woman to be elected to the Florida state legislature. Yet even she, an obvious "somebody" in Florida politics, "cannot get a loan from the First National Bank on [my mother's] behalf, nor can I even get to see the chairman of the board."[52] Less than a decade later, the city of Miami tore down the then sixty-year-old Mary Elizabeth Hotel under the auspices of its latest urban renewal program.[53]

Luther Brooks, through the late 1960s, remained committed to developing his multimillion-dollar archipelago city, Islandia. However, a lack of funding for infrastructure, coupled with a belligerent conservationist movement headed by longtime *Miami Herald* real estate reporter Juanita Greene, killed the effort.[54] Always the adroit businessman, Brooks found a way to make good. In a deal authorized under President Johnson and then carried out by the Nixon administration, the federal government purchased Islandia for $25 million to create Biscayne National Park. Brooks made $840,000 on land for which he had paid $187,000.[55] Brooks also got romance out of the deal, winning the affections of Juanita Greene during the Islandia affair. Given the back-and-forth between Brooks and the press over the years, the fact that Bonded's owner would divorce his wife, Gladys, and enter a relationship with Miami's chief muckraking journalist might seem surprising. (Or perhaps not, given Brooks's reputation as a charming and acute operator.) Greene, one of Brooks's harshest critics and political adversaries, would serve as his life partner till the end of his days.

It is Brooks's longest relationship that remains most pertinent here. For over thirty years, if Negroes rented their housing in Dade County, they almost assuredly rented a property built and/or managed by Luther Brooks. Part segregationist, part integrationist, and all capitalist, Brooks bedeviled Miami's self-styled progressives with realpolitik built from a masterful manipulation of the discourses of property rights, racial identity, and free enterprise.[56] Before selling off his company in the mid-1970s and dying painfully of bone cancer in the late 1980s, Brooks maintained a tight circle of black and white friends and business associates.[57] Among many he remained, for better or worse, a powerbroker of almost mythic proportions.

Luther Brooks, like everyone else in Jim Crow America (and, indeed, from our own time), does not fit into the good-versus-evil bedtime stories that typify popular historical treatments of American apartheid. But that's not from lack of trying. As one of Brooks's black clients, Jolien Taylor, proclaimed in 1959, "All the people in Miami—and Florida—are better off for Luther Brooks having lived among them. His name will never die."[58] A Dade County official who preferred to remain anonymous claimed that "Luther Brooks is the greatest salesman who ever lived. . . . But he's directly responsible for many of the bad housing conditions [in Miami], and don't let him tell you otherwise."[59] In 2007, a *Miami Herald* article on Florida's most infamous "civil rights villains" counted Brooks alongside openly brutal police chiefs, segregationist southern politicians, and others who, in the spirit of Sunbelt self-congratulation, "faded away quietly."[60] In response came the characterization provided by Juanita Greene, who pointed out that Brooks was an upright businessman, he owned not a single slum, and he remained popular among the black masses. "He was an easy target for do-gooders who didn't do their homework," she explained, and, besides, "Brooks died 19 years ago. The slums are still there."[61]

Indeed, they are. As much as people matter—and they matter a great deal—there is little to be gained by exalting or tearing down imperfect men and women. Therefore, in the account offered here, I elected, instead, to attend to the world people built, the world we, in large part, recognize today. In outlining the foundations, construction, and renovation of apartheid in Greater Miami, *A World More Concrete* has captured a sliver of our longtime investment in and dependence on racial segregation. If readers discern flecks of irreverence in the preceding pages, I make no apologies. Jim Crow has historically inspired transgressive behavior and curious demonstrations of solidarity. My hope was only to assign human complexity in the telling of a human story. Folly, perhaps, but it seemed like a good idea at the time.

ABBREVIATIONS

ARCHIVES

AALCC	African American Library and Cultural Center, Fort Lauderdale, FL
BA	Black Archives History and Research Foundation of South Florida, Miami, FL
FAMU	Florida A&M University, Black Archives, Tallahassee, FL
FLHS	Fort Lauderdale Historical Society, Fort Lauderdale, FL
FSU	Florida State University, Mildred and Claude Pepper Library, Tallahassee, FL
HASF	Historical Association of Southern Florida, Charles Tebeau Library, Miami, FL
HU	Howard University, Moorland-Spingarn Library, Washington, DC
LOC	Library of Congress, Washington, DC
MDPL	Miami Dade Public Library, Florida Room, Miami, FL
NA	National Archives and Records Administration, Washington, DC (Archives I)
NARA	National Archives and Records Administration, College Park, MD (Archives II)
SAF	State Archives of Florida, Tallahassee, FL
UF	University of Florida, George Smathers Library, Gainesville, FL
UM	University of Miami, Otto Richter Library, Coral Gables, FL
UNC	University of North Carolina, Louis Round Wilson Special Collections Library, Chapel Hill, NC

PERIODICALS

ADW	*Atlanta Daily World*
BAA	*Baltimore Afro-American*
BS	*Baltimore Sun*
CD	*Chicago Defender*
CDE	*Columbus Daily Enquirer* (Georgia)
CSM	*Christian Science Monitor*
CT	*Chicago Tribune*
EI	*Evening Independent*
FLN	*Fort Lauderdale News*
MG	*Montreal Gazette*
MGD	*Manchester Guardian*
MH	*Miami Herald*
MM	*Miami Metropolis*
MN	*Miami News*
MNT	*Miami New Times*
MT	*Miami Times*
NAN	*New York Amsterdam News*
NYT	*New York Times*
PBP	*Palm Beach Post*
PC	*Pittsburgh Courier*
PT	*Philadelphia Tribune*
OS	*Orlando Sentinel*
OSB	*Ocala Star-Banner*
SPT	*St. Petersburg Times*
SS	*Sun-Sentinel*
ST	*Seminole Tribune*
WAA	*Washington Afro-American*
WP	*Washington Post*

NOTES

INTRODUCTION: AMERICA'S PLAYGROUND

1. "Tot Lot Gets $20,000 from City Leaders," *MN*, 21 June 1969.
2. "Park Spells Happiness," *CSM*, 3 October 1969; "New Park Concept, Ms. Range's Idea," *WAA*, 12 August 1969; and "'Lost Land' Serves Kids," *CD*, 11 August 1969.
3. "'Lost Land' Serves Kids."
4. "Mini-park's a Great Idea," *MT*, 8 August 1969.
5. My use of the term *world* is meant to capture the physical, personal, and social aspects of segregationist regimes. For the interplay of these fields, see Henri Lefebvre, *The Production of Space* (Cambridge, MA: Basil Blackwell, 1991), 9–10.
6. Ta-Nehisi Coates, "Fear of a Black President," *Atlantic*, 22 August 2012, accessed 30 May 2013, http://www.theatlantic.com/magazine/archive/2012/09/fear-of-a-black-president/309064/4/?single_page=true; Marissa Chappell, *The War on Welfare* (Philadelphia: University of Pennsylvania Press, 2010); Jonathan Kozol, *Savage Inequalities: Children and America's Schools* (New York: HarperCollins, 1992); and Michelle Alexander, *The New Jim Crow: Mass Incarceration in the Age of Colorblindness* (New York: New Press, 2010).
7. J. Douglas Smith, *Managing White Supremacy: Race, Politics, and Citizenship in Jim Crow Virginia* (Chapel Hill: University of North Carolina Press, 2002); see also Eduardo Bonilla-Silva, *Racism without Racists: Color-Blind Racism and the Persistence of Racial Inequality in the United States* (Lanham, MD: Rowman and Littlefield, 2006). My thanks to James Dator for helping me appreciate *white privilege* as a historically specific euphemism for *white power*.
8. Joseph Crespino, *In Search of Another Country: Mississippi and the Conservative Counterrevolution* (Princeton, NJ: Princeton University Press, 2009), 4, 9. My point here is not to suggest that white people did not continue to practice racial terrorism after Jim Crow, only that the acceptability of white terrorism had, by the 1960s, greatly diminished. See, for instance, Timothy B. Tyson, *Blood Done Signed My Name: A True Story* (New York: Three Rivers Press, 2004).
9. In describing land as an expression of segregationist politics, I draw on William Novak's notion of infrastructural power; William J. Novak, "The Myth of a 'Weak' American State," *American Historical Review* 113, no. 3 (June 2008): 752–72.
10. "Florida Is Full of People, Sunshine—and Superlatives," *NYT*, 8 December 1946.
11. See Bryant Simon, *Boardwalk of Dreams: Atlantic City and the Fate of Urban America* (New York: Oxford University Press, 2004).

12. "Miami Beach, the All-Too-American City," *NYT*, 4 August 1968.
13. On the evolution of white supremacy from interpersonal violence to its less violent, more landed forms, see John W. Cell, *The Highest Stage of White Supremacy* (Cambridge: Cambridge University Press, 1982), esp. 18.
14. Bruce J. Schulman, *From Cotton Belt to Sunbelt: Federal Policy, Economic Development, and the Transformation of the South, 1938–1980* (Durham, NC, and London: Duke University Press, 1994).
15. Arnold R. Hirsch, *Making the Second Ghetto: Race and Housing in Chicago, 1940–1960* (Chicago: University of Chicago Press, 1998); Beryl Satter, *Family Properties: Race, Real Estate, and the Exploitation of Black Urban America* (New York: Metropolitan Books, 2009), esp. chap. 3; and Kevin Boyle, *Arc of Justice: A Saga of Race, Civil Rights, and Murder in the Jazz Age* (New York: Henry Holt, 2004), 9, 108–9, 202.
16. Commitments to American exceptionalism have contributed to a great deal of imprecision or outright denial about colonial practices in twentieth-century North America. The literature on this issue remains vast, nevertheless, thanks, in part, to a long list of scholars who have viewed US racism in an international frame. See Richard Wright's introduction and subsequent chapters in St. Clair Drake and Horace Cayton, *Black Metropolis: A Study of Negro Life in a Northern City* (1945; repr., Chicago: University of Chicago Press, 1993), xxiv–xv, 766–67. Many thanks to Davarian Baldwin on this score; Baldwin, *Land of Darkness: Chicago and the Making of Race in Modern America* (Oxford University Press, forthcoming); Stokely Carmichael and Charles V. Hamilton, *Black Power: The Politics of Liberation* (New York: Random House, 1967), 6–7; see also Cell, *Highest Stage of White Supremacy*, 15–16, 18; George M. Fredrickson, *White Supremacy: A Comparative Study in American and South African History* (Oxford: Oxford University Press, 1992); Nan Elizabeth Woodruff, *American Congo: The African American Freedom Struggle in the Delta* (Cambridge, MA: Harvard University Press, 2003); and, most recently, Carl H. Nightingale, *Segregation: A Global History of Divided Cities* (Chicago: University of Chicago Press, 2012), 74.
17. As a field, African history, when compared to its US counterpart, remains much further along in exploring the governing dynamics of colonial racial regimes. For particularly strong discussions of colonialism that inspired this book, see Pauline E. Peters, *Dividing the Commons: Politics, Policy, and Culture in Botswana* (Charlottesville: University Press of Virginia, 1994), 75; and Jocelyn Alexander, *The Unsettled Land: State-Making and the Politics of Land in Zimbabwe, 1893–2003* (Athens: Ohio University Press, 2006), 21. Eschewing discussions of comparative colonialism, students of US history tend to discuss interracial governance as part of the development of America's liberal democracy. Some of the most excellent studies in this vein include William H. Chafe, *Civilities and Civil Rights: Greensboro, North Carolina, and the Black Struggle for Freedom* (Oxford: Oxford University Press, 1981); Clarence Stone, *Regime Politics: Governing Atlanta, 1946–1988* (Lawrence: University Press of Kansas, 1989); and Robert Mickey, *Paths Out of Dixie: The Democratization of Authoritarian Enclaves in America's Deep South* (Princeton, NJ: Princeton University Press, 2013).
18. Earl Lewis, *In Their Own Interests: Race, Class, and Power in Twentieth-Century Norfolk, Virginia* (Berkeley: University of California Press, 1993); and Andrew Weise, *Places of Their Own: African American Suburbanization in the Twentieth Century* (Chicago: University of Chicago Press, 2004). For a great example of blacks appropriating the means of state violence to improve their situation under colonialism in Latin America, see Ben Vinson III, *Bearing Arms for His Majesty: The Free-Colored Militia in Colonial Mexico* (Palo Alto, CA: Stanford University Press, 2003).

19. During the 1970s, debates on the left over the nature of black neighborhoods as "internal colonies" hung on disagreements over the degree to which one ascribed to Marxian definitions of exploitation and the degree of state power whites could be shown to hold over black economic practice. This book, in its discussion of segregationist real estate policy and its ties to both economic growth and political culture, illustrates—though likely not once and for all—the reach of the Jim Crow state and its ability to create and sustain racialized and highly extractive housing markets. William K. Tabb, *The Political Economy of the Black Ghetto* (New York: Norton, 1970); Donald J. Harris, "The Black Ghetto as 'Internal Colony': A Theoretical Critique and Alternative Formulation," *Review of Black Political Economy* 2, no. 4 (Summer 1972): 3–33; and William K. Tabb, "Marxian Exploitation and Domestic Colonialism: A Reply to Donald J. Harris," *Review of Black Political Economy* 4, no. 4 (Summer 1974): 69–87.

20. See, for instance, Charles Denby, *Indignant Heart: A Black Worker's Journal* (Detroit: Wayne State University Press, 1989); and James D. Anderson, *The Education of Blacks in the South, 1860–1935* (Chapel Hill: University of North Carolina Press, 1988).

21. Dating back to at least the 1940s, housing reformers such as Charles Abrams and Robert Weaver, acting in the then emergent field of "race relations," detailed the role that housing played in acts of racial violence and in the preservation of beliefs in black inferiority. More recently, a new field described by historians Thomas J. Sugrue and Kevin M. Kruse as "the new suburban history" has detailed how suburban real estate, in particular, helped new forms of white supremacy emerge after the passage of the Civil Rights Act of 1964 and the Fair Housing Act of 1968. See Charles Abrams, "The Segregation Threat in Housing," *Commentary* 7, no. 2 (February 1949): 123–31; Wendell Pritchett, *Robert Clifton Weaver and the American City: The Life and Times of an Urban Reformer* (Chicago: University of Chicago Press, 2008), 121–29; and Kevin M. Kruse and Thomas J. Sugrue, eds., *The New Suburban History* (Chicago: University of Chicago Press, 2006).

22. See David M. P. Freund, "Marketing the Free Market: State Intervention and the Politics of Prosperity in Metropolitan America," in *The New Suburban History*, ed. Kevin M. Kruse and Thomas J. Sugrue, 11–32 (Chicago: University of Chicago Press, 2006); Kevin M. Kruse, *White Flight: Atlanta and the Making of Modern Conservatism* (Princeton, NJ: Princeton University Press, 2005); and Matthew D. Lassiter, *The Silent Majority: Suburban Politics in the Sunbelt South* (Princeton, NJ: Princeton University Press, 2006).

23. On assumptions about the inferiority of black culture within American social and political thought, see Khalil Gibran Muhammad, *The Condemnation of Blackness: Race, Crime, and the Making of Modern Urban America* (Cambridge, MA: Harvard University Press, 2010); and Daryl Michael Scott, *Contempt and Pity: Social Policy and the Image of the Damaged Black Psyche, 1880–1996* (Chapel Hill: University of North Carolina Press, 1997). For a particularly caustic critique of black urban culture and governance from the right, see Fred Seigel, *The Future Once Happened Here: New York, D.C., L.A., and the Fate of America's Big Cities* (New York: Encounter Books, 2000); and, from the center-left, see James T. Patterson, *Freedom Is Not Enough: The Moynihan Report and America's Struggle over Black Family Life from LBJ to Obama* (New York: Basic Books, 2010).

24. Becky M. Nicolaides, *My Blue Heaven: Life and Politics in the Working-Class Suburbs of Los Angeles, 1920–1965* (Chicago: University of Chicago Press, 2002); and Robert O. Self, *American Babylon: Race and the Struggle for Postwar Oakland* (Princeton, NJ: Princeton University Press, 2003).

25. Karen E. Fields and Barbara J. Fields, *Racecraft: The Soul of Inequality in America* (New York: Verso, 2012), 11, 16, 17; and David M. P. Freund, *Colored Property: State Policy and White Racial Politics in Suburban America* (Chicago: University of Chicago Press, 2007), 33–37.

26. See, for instance, Charlotte Brooks, *Alien Neighbors, Foreign Friends: Asian Americans, Housing, and the Transformation of Urban California* (Chicago: University of Chicago Press, 2009), 237–38; and Nicolaides, *My Blue Heaven.*

27. For two excellent looks at white supremacist land practices in the hands of non-whites, see Tiya Miles, *The House on Diamond Hill: A Cherokee Plantation Story* (Chapel Hill: University of North Carolina Press, 2010); and David A. Chang, *The Color of Land: Race, Nation, and the Politics of Landownership in Oklahoma, 1832–1929* (Chapel Hill: University of North Carolina Press, 2010).

28. Kevin Fox Gotham, *Race, Real Estate, and Uneven Development: The Kansas City Experience, 1900–2000* (Albany: State University of New York Press, 2002), 87.

29. Mindy Thompson Fullilove, *Root Shock: How Tearing Up City Neighborhoods Hurts America, and What We Can Do About It* (New York: Ballantine, 2004), 20. For an example of the argument that black displacement was simply the result of bureaucratic error, see, Milan Dluhy, Keith Revell, and Sidney Wong, "Creating a Positive Future for a Minority Community: Transportation and Urban Renewal Politics in Miami," *Journal of Urban Affairs* 24, no. 1 (2002): 75–95.

30. In recent years, scholars have been able to demonstrate vividly the extent of racial segregation (in the absence of formal apartheid) through creative combinations of census-based research and geographic information systems, or GIS. See, for instance, Emily Badger, "Watch These American Cities Segregate, Even as They Diversify," *Atlantic Cities,* 25 June 2012, accessed 23 September 2014, http://www.theatlanticcities.com/neighborhoods/2012/06/watch-these-us-cities-segregate-even-they-diversify/2346/; and Demographic Research Group, "The Racial Dot Map," accessed 23 September 2013, http://www.coopercenter.org/demographics/Racial-Dot-Map.

31. Two excellent exceptions to this trend, both centered on Chicago, are Laura Mc-Enaney, "Nightmares on Elm Street: Demobilizing in Chicago, 1945–1953," *Journal of American History* 92, no. 4 (March 2006): 1265–91; and Satter, *Family Properties.*

32. Charles E. Connerly, *"The Most Segregated City in America": City Planning and Civil Rights in Birmingham, 1920–1980* (Charlottesville: University of Virginia Press, 2005), 124; Christopher Silver, "The Changing Face of Neighborhoods in Memphis and Richmond, 1940–1985," in *Shades of the Sunbelt: Essays on Ethnicity, Race, and the Urban South,* ed. Randall M. Miller and George Pozzetta (Boca Raton: Florida Atlantic University Press, 1988), 114; and Irene V. Holliman, "Urban Renewal and Community Building in Atlanta, 1963–1966," *Journal of Urban History* 35, no. 3 (March 2009): 377.

33. This book, to paraphrase historian Adam Green, details both the will to struggle and the will to profit among black people; Green, *Selling the Race: Culture, Community, and Black Chicago, 1940–1955* (Chicago: University of Chicago Press, 2007), 12.

34. Since the 1970s, especially, black freedom organizations helped nurture an entire generation of politicos who (1) proved critical to gutting the old enforcement apparatus established under the Civil Rights Act, or (2) framed civil rights in the terms largely set by corporate America. Manning Marable, *How Capitalism Underdeveloped Black America: Problems in Race, Political Economy, and Society* (Boston: South End Press, 1983), 178–79; Stone, *Regime Politics,* esp. chap. 9; Heather Ann Thompson, *Whose Detroit? Politics, Labor, and Race in a Modern American City* (Ithaca, NY: Cornell University Press, 2001), esp. chap. 7; Guian McKee, *The Problem of Jobs: Liberalism,*

Race, and Deindustrialization in Philadelphia (Chicago: University of Chicago Press, 2008), 184; Thomas J. Sugrue, *Sweet Land of Liberty: The Forgotten Struggle for Civil Rights in the North* (New York: Random House, 2008), 433; Hasan Kwame Jeffries, *Bloody Lowndes: Civil Rights and Black Power in Alabama's Black Belt* (New York: New York University Press, 2009), 244; Matthew Countryman, *Up South: Civil Rights and Black Power in Philadelphia* (Philadelphia: University of Pennsylvania Press, 2006), 295; and Mary Frances Berry, *And Justice for All: The United States Commission on Civil Rights and the Continuing Struggle for Freedom in America* (New York: Knopf, 2009), 184, 217, 202. See also "NAACP Financial Freedom Center Celebrates One Year Anniversary," accessed 30 May 2013, http://www.naacp.org/blog/entry/naacp-financial -freedom-center-celebrates-one-year-anniversary; and "Financial Freedom Center," accessed 30 May 2013, http://www.naacp.org/pages/2347.

35. Robert Korstad and Nelson Lichtenstein, "Opportunities Found and Lost: Labor, Radicals, and the Early Civil Rights Movement," *Journal of American History* 75, no. 3 (December 1988): 786–811; Jacqueline Dowd Hall, "The Long Civil Rights Movement and the Political Uses of the Past," *Journal of American History* 91, no. 4 (March 2005): 1233–63; and Glenda Elizabeth Gilmore, *Defying Dixie: The Radical Roots of Civil Rights, 1919–1950* (New York: Norton, 2008).

36. The importance of established political and commercial networks was first outlined in Aldon D. Morris, *Origins of the Civil Rights Movement: Black Communities Organizing for Change* (New York: Free Press, 1984); see also Doug McAdam, *Political Process and the Development of Black Insurgency* (Chicago: University of Chicago Press, 1982).

37. In spite of all the attention granted to everyday forms of black resistance in recent decades, the political scientist Michael Hanchard points out that there is very little evidence that everyday forms of resistance culminate in formal political movements. Michael Hanchard, *Party/Politics: Horizons in Black Political Thought* (New York: Oxford University Press, 2006), 58. The most eminent works on everyday resistance in the Jim Crow South include Robin D. G. Kelley, "'We Are Not What We Seem': Rethinking Black Working-Class History in the Jim Crow South," *Journal of American History* 80, no. 1 (June 1993): 75–112, quote on 77. See also Elsa Barkley Brown, "Uncle Ned's Children: Negotiating Community and Freedom in Post-emancipation Richmond Virginia" (PhD diss., Kent State University, 1995); and Tera Hunter, *To 'Joy My Freedom: Southern Black Women's Lives and Labors after the Civil War* (Cambridge, MA: Harvard University Press, 1997).

38. Glenn T. Eskew, *But for Birmingham: The Local and National Movements in the Civil Rights Struggle* (Chapel Hill: University of North Carolina Press, 1997), 338; and Chafe, *Civilities and Civil Rights*.

39. Some of the best recent work exploring the contours of intraracial class conflict and the right of propertied Negroes to govern the perceived black collective include Michele Mitchell, *Righteous Propagation: African Americans and the Politics of Racial Destiny after Reconstruction* (Chapel Hill: University of North Carolina Press, 2004); Tomiko Brown-Nagin, *Courage to Dissent: Atlanta and the Long History of the Civil Rights Movement* (New York: Oxford University Press, 2011); Touré Reed, *Not Alms but Opportunity: The Urban League and the Politics of Racial Uplift, 1910–1950* (Chapel Hill: University of North Carolina Press, 2008); Carol Anderson, *Eyes off the Prize: The United Nations and the African American Struggle for Human Rights, 1944–1955* (Cambridge: Cambridge University Press, 2003); Millery Polyné, *From Douglass to Duvalier: U.S. African Americans, Haiti, and Pan-Americanism, 1870–1964* (Gainesville: University Press of Florida, 2011); and Green, *Selling the Race*.

40. Robin D. G. Kelley, *Freedom Dreams: The Black Radical Imagination* (Boston: Beacon Press, 2002), 9–10. See also Thomas F. Jackson, *From Civil Rights to Human Rights: Martin Luther King, Jr., and the Struggle for Economic Justice* (Philadelphia: University of Pennsylvania Press, 2007).

41. "Miami Condemned: Update '75" (station WCKT, Miami, 1975), University of Georgia Peabody Collection, accessed 28 May 2013, http://dlg.galileo.usg.edu/peabody/id:1975_75025_nwt_1.

42. "A Deserved Song of Praise," *MH*, 30 March 1996.

43. "Singing the Praises of 'Mama' Range," *MH*, 1 April 1996.

44. See, for instance, "Slum Areas Blight City, Range Says," *MN*, 13 June 1966.

45. Nicole Saunders, "We Can't Appreciate the Future Unless We Know the Past," *Essence* 35, no. 10 (February 2005): 32.

46. David T. Beito and Linda Royster Beito, *Black Maverick: T. R. M. Howard's Fight for Civil Rights and Economic Power* (Urbana and Chicago: University of Illinois Press, 2009); and Walter B. Weare, *Black Business in the New South: A Social History of the North Carolina Mutual Life Insurance Company* (Champaign: University of Illinois Press, 1973).

47. W. E. B. Du Bois, *The Autobiography of W. E. B. Du Bois: A Soliloquy on Viewing My Life from the Last Decade to Its First Century* (New York: International Publishers, 1968), 278–79; and David Levering Lewis, *W. E. B. Du Bois: The Fight for Equality and the American Century, 1919–1963* (New York: Owl Books, 2000), 188–89.

48. Roderick Waters, "Dr. William B. Sawyer of Colored Town," *Tequesta* 57 (1997): 67–80.

49. Andrew W. Kahrl, *The Land Was Ours: African American Beaches from Jim Crow to the Sunbelt South* (Cambridge, MA: Harvard University Press, 2012), 94–96.

50. Satter, *Family Properties*, 5.

51. George Lipsitz, articulating a widely held notion within critical race studies, writes of a "white spatial imaginary based on exclusivity and augmented exchange values" (28) and a "black spatial imaginary" defined by "radical solidarity" and generative— "continuously"—of "new democratic imaginations" (56–57). George Lipsitz, *How Racism Takes Place* (Philadelphia: Temple University Press, 2011). Lipsitz's ideas about white and black racial imaginary, which smack of uncharacteristic essentialism, are by no means confined to the academy. In their work on the Great Recession, antipoverty advocates no less eminent than Barbara Ehrenreich and Dedrick Muhammad accused self-interested blacks of having abandoned the legacy of Martin Luther King in favor of "embrac[ing] white culture"; "The Recession's Racial Divide," *NYT*, 12 September 2009. For a thoughtful critique of the black and white spatial imaginary, see Kahrl, *Land Was Ours*, 18.

52. For a fascinating study of one black family's managing of property ownership and racial identity over several generations, see Rebecca J. Scott and Jean M. Hébard, *Freedom Papers: An Atlantic Odyssey in the Age of Emancipation* (Cambridge, MA: Harvard University Press, 2012).

53. "Park Spells Happiness."

54. "Community Questions Police Relations," *MN*, 12 August 1968.

55. Thomas C. Holt, *The Problem of Race in the Twenty-First Century* (Cambridge, MA: Harvard University Press, 2000), 21.

CHAPTER ONE: THE MAGIC CITY

1. Population estimates for Seminoles based on the 1913 Indian Census Rolls, which listed 567 Seminoles in Florida. Ancestry.com, accessed 20 November 2011; original

source: RG 75 Records of the Bureau of Indian Affairs, *Indian Census Rolls, 1885–1940*; microfilm roll M595, NA, http://www.ancestry.com.

2. Harry A. Kersey Jr., "The Tony Tommie Letter, 1916: A Transitional Seminole Document," *Florida Historical Quarterly* 64, no. 3 (January 1986): 302.

3. The journalist and horticulturalist E. V. Blackman takes credit for coining the "Magic City" moniker in his book, *Miami and Dade County Florida: Its Settlement, Progress and Achievement* (Washington, DC: Victor Rainbolt, 1921), 86.

4. Arva Moore Parks and Gregory W. Bush, with Laura Pincus, *Miami, the American Crossroad: A Centennial Journey, 1896–1996* (Needham Heights, MA: Simon and Schuster, 1996), 28.

5. See, for instance, "Blacks Made a Major Contribution," *MN*, 10 February 1987.

6. John Sewell, *Memoirs and History of Miami, Florida* (Miami: Franklin Press, 1938), 134.

7. Hoyt Frazure, as told to Nixon Smiley, *Memories of Old Miami* (Miami: Miami Herald, 1964), 7–8, 15.

8. John Sewell, *Miami Memoirs* (Miami: Arva Moore Parks, 1987), 57, 59.

9. "Mayor and Other Candidates Addressed Civic Association," *MH*, 25 May 1915; US Congress, House, 62nd Cong., 2nd sess., H.R. Doc. 554 (1912), 23; and Daly Highleyman, *Pictures and Articles of the Early Days of Miami* (self-published, 1989), 24.

10. Frazure, *Memories of Old Miami*, 14.

11. Indian inspector Lorenzo D. Creel, quoted in Patsy West, *The Enduring Seminoles: From Alligator Wrestling to Ecotourism* (Gainesville: University Press of Florida, 1998), 8.

12. "Worries of the Seminoles through the European War," *MH*, 22 January 1916.

13. James Deering's massive Villa Vizcaya, started in 1912, employed over one thousand European artisans and thousands more colored people; Frazure, *Memories of Old Miami*, 18. See also "Where to Go, What There Is to Do and See," in *Guide Miami: A Guide to All Places of Interest in Metropolitan Dade County* (North Miami, FL: Interguide, 1966), 22.

14. "Miami Conservatory of Music," *MM*, 29 December 1908; and "Homes & Real Estate," *MN*, 5 September 1964.

15. "Wanted," *MH*, 14 January 1921; "Wanted," *MH*, 21 May 1917; "Wanted," *MH*, 26 March 1921; and "Opportunity for Colored Cooks," *MH*, 17 December 1920.

16. Elizabeth Clark-Lewis, "'This Work Had to End': African-American Domestic Workers in Washington, D.C., 1910–1940," in *Women and Power in American History: A Reader*, vol. 2, *From 1870*, ed. Kathryn Kish Sklar and Thomas Dublin (Upper Saddle River, NJ: Prentice Hall, 1991), 196.

17. Thomas A. Castillo, "Big City Days: Race and Labor in Early Miami, 1915–1925" (MA thesis, Florida International University, 2000), 59.

18. Carl Fisher to John La Gorce, 1920, cited in Thomas Albert Castillo, "Laboring in the Magic City: Workers in Miami, 1914–1941" (PhD diss., University of Maryland, 2011), 34.

19. Kenneth L. Roberts, *Sun Hunting* (Indianapolis: Bobs-Merrill, 1922), 18.

20. Ibid.

21. Ibid., 20.

22. Bryant Simon, *Boardwalk of Dreams: Atlantic City and the Fate of Urban America* (New York: Oxford University Press, 2004).

23. Castillo, "Laboring in the Magic City," 67.

24. Highleyman, *Pictures and Articles of the Early Days of Miami*, 22; "Homes & Real Estate"; and Adam G. Adams, "Some Pre-boom Developers of Dade County," *Tequesta* 17 (1957): 38.

25. Helen C. Freeland, "George Edgar Merrick," *Tequesta* 2 (1942): 1–7.
26. Frazure, *Memories of Old Miami*, 12–13.
27. Arthur E. Chapman, "The History of the Black Police Force and Court in the City of Miami" (PhD diss., University of Miami, 1986), 12, 15.
28. Ibid., 10, 12, 13, 15; Kip Vought, "Racial Stirrings in Colored Town: The UNIA [Universal Negro Improvement Association] in Miami during the 1920s," *Tequesta* 60 (2000): 57; and Paul S. George, "Colored Town: Miami's Black Community, 1896–1930," *Florida Historical Quarterly* 56, no. 4 (April 1978): 436.
29. Charles Johnson, interviewed by Alix Milfort, 22 August 1997, 46–47, Tell the Story Collection, BA.
30. As Jane Landers points out, Florida's importance within a migrating, black circum-Caribbean dates back to Africans living under Spanish colonialism in the sixteenth century; Landers, *Black Society in Spanish Florida* (Urbana: University of Illinois Press, 1999).
31. Claudrena N. Harold, "The Rise and Fall of the Garvey Movement in the Urban South, 1918–1942" (PhD diss., University of Notre Dame, 2004), 116.
32. Michael Craton, "Reshuffling the Pack: The Transition from Slavery to Other Forms of Labor in the British Caribbean, ca. 1790–1890," *New West Indian Guide / Nieuwe West-Indische Gids* 68, nos. 1–2 (1994): 23–75, esp. 55, 57.
33. Michael Craton and Gail Saunders, *Islanders in the Stream: A History of the Bahamian People*, vol. 2, *From the Ending of Slavery to the Twenty-First Century* (Athens: University of Georgia Press, 2000), 2.
34. David Shubow, "Sponge Fishing on Florida's East Coast," *Tequesta* 29 (1969): 4.
35. Howard Johnson, "Bahamian Labor Migration to Florida in the Late Nineteenth and Early Twentieth Centuries," *International Migration Review* 22, no. 1 (Spring 1988): 88–90, 93, 103.
36. Ira De Augustine Reid, *The Negro Immigrant: His Background, Characteristics and Social Adjustment, 1899–1937* (New York: Columbia University Press, 1939), 189.
37. "Overtown Is Waking Up," *MH*, 27 July 1986.
38. Warranty deed, 22 June 1900, the Papers of Dana A. Dorsey, Miami Metropolitan Archive, accessed 31 May 2013, http://digitool.fcla.edu/R/P9PB2D23CJ9MQ78KYKF2KUBJHIGIPSSE6HRI36DG1CU23XKNRC-00330?func=dbin-jump-full&object_id=73623&pds_handle=GUEST; and Ancestry.com, accessed 20 November 2011, original source: *1900 United States Federal Census, Coconut Grove, Dade, Florida*, microfilm roll T623_167, 35A, http://www.ancestry.com.
39. 1937 car insurance policy, the Papers of Dana A. Dorsey, Miami Metropolitan Archive; and correspondence from A. F. Given, public accountant, to Dana A. Dorsey, 24 June 1939, the Papers of Dana A. Dorsey, Miami Metropolitan Archive, accessed 31 May 2013, http://digitool.fcla.edu/R/P9PB2D23CJ9MQ78KYKF2KUBJHIGIPSSE6HRI36DG1CU23XKNRC-00330?func=dbin-jump-full&object_id=73623&pds_handle=GUEST. With the help of white investors and considerable Mexican labor, Dorsey secured over fifty thousand dollars in profits in 1939.
40. Dorothy Jenkins Fields, "Tracing Overtown's Vernacular Architecture," Florida theme issue, *Journal of Decorative and Propaganda Arts* 23 (1998): 326; "Below the Mason-Dixon Line," *PC*, 4 February 1933; Marvin Dunn, *Black Miami in the Twentieth Century* (Gainesville: University Press of Florida, 1997), 80, 81; and Roberta Thompson, interviewed by Electra Ford, 29 August 1997, 17, Tell the Story Collection, BA.
41. "No More Colored Picnics at the Ocean Beach," *MM*, 5 April 1912.
42. "Island Opposite Miami Sold for Colored Resort," *MM*, 1 May 1918.

43. "Blacks Recall Discrimination in Miami Beach," *MH*, 18 February 2001.

44. "Florence Gaskins," AT&T Miami Dade County African American History Calendar, 1994, BA, accessed 31 May 2013, http://www.theblackarchives.org/archon/index .php?p=digitallibrary/digitalcontent&id=84.

45. "Many Things Needed to Complete Plans for the Entertainment of Men," *MH*, 25 December 1918; "Big Parade of Colored People," *MH*, 4 July 1919; and "Julia Jenkins Baylor," AT&T Miami Dade County African American History Calendar, 1996, BA, accessed 31 May 2013, http://www.theblackarchives.org/archon/index.php?p =digitallibrary/digitalcontent&id=99.

46. "Green Is Held on Charge of Embezzlement," *MH*, 13 October 1917; "Epidemic Seems to Be Abating," *MH*, 16 October 1918; "The City Practically Broke Yet It Has Due and Collectable Sum of $4,800.10 from Citizens," *MH*, 5 January 1913; and "'Tag Day' for the Deep Water Fund Probable," *MH*, 21 January 1914.

47. Juliet E. K. Walker, *The History of Black Business in America: Capitalism, Race, Entrepreneurship* (New York: Macmillan Press, 1998), 182–224; see also Loren Schweninger, *Black Property Owners in the South, 1790–1915* (Urbana and Chicago: University of Illinois Press, 1990).

48. Andrew Zimmerman, *Alabama in Africa: Booker T. Washington, the German Empire, and the Globalization of the New South* (Princeton, NJ: Princeton University Press, 2010), 113.

49. Rebecca J. Scott, "Reclaiming Gregorio's Mule: The Meanings of Freedom in Arimao and Caunao Valleys, Cuba, 1880–1899," *Past and Present* 170 (2001): 181–216; Rebecca J. Scott and Jean M. Hébrard, *Freedom Papers: An Atlantic Odyssey in the Age of Emancipation* (Cambridge, MA: Harvard University Press, 2012), esp. chap. 4, "Crossing the Gulf"; and Thomas C. Holt, *The Problem of Freedom: Race, Labor, and Politics in Jamaica and Britain, 1832–1938* (Baltimore: Johns Hopkins University Press, 1991), 5.

50. Michael J. Klarman, *From Jim Crow to Civil Rights: The Supreme Court and the Struggle for Racial Equality* (Oxford: Oxford University Press, 2004), 10, 18, 95.

51. Dylan C. Penningroth, *The Claims of Kinfolk: African American Property and Community in the Nineteenth Century South* (Chapel Hill: University of North Carolina Press, 2002), 112, 129; see also Amy Dru Stanley, *From Bondage to Contract: Wage Labor, Marriage, and the Market in the Age of Slave Emancipation* (Cambridge: Cambridge University Press, 1998).

52. *Slaughterhouse Cases*, 83 U.S. 36 (1873).

53. *Civil Rights Cases*, 109 U.S. 3 (1883).

54. Wali R. Kharif, "Black Reaction to Segregation and Discrimination in Post-Reconstruction Florida," *Florida Historical Quarterly* 64, no. 2 (October 1985): 161–73.

55. "Negroes Ordered to Leave," *MM*, 31 July 1920; William F. Homes, "Whitecapping: Agrarian Violence in Mississippi, 1902–1906," *Journal of Southern History* 35 (May 1969): 165–85. Between 1890 and 1900, Negro landholdings in Quitman County, Georgia—Dana Dorsey's birthplace—had been more than halved, from forty-three hundred acres to less than two thousand acres; W. E. B. Du Bois, "The Negro Landholder of Georgia," *Bulletin of the United States Department of Labor* 35 (July 1901): 755.

56. Maurice Thompson, "The Court of Judge Lynch," *Lippincott's Monthly Magazine* 64, no. 380 (August 1899): 260. Many thanks to Ashraf Rushdy for introducing me to Thompson's work and for helping me think through the connection between racial violence and white popular sovereignty; see also W. E. B. Du Bois, "Georgia: Invisible Empire State (January 21, 1925)," in *The Age of Jim Crow*, ed. Jane Dailey (New York: Norton, 2008), 146.

57. Vought, "Racial Stirrings in Colored Town," 61.

58. Paul Ortiz, *Emancipation Betrayed: The Hidden History of Black Organizing and White Violence in Florida from Reconstruction to the Bloody Election of 1920* (Berkeley: University of California Press, 2005), xix.

59. Kidada E. Williams, *They Left Great Marks on Me: African American Testimonies of Racial Violence from Emancipation to World War I* (New York: New York University Press, 2012).

60. "S. Florida's Black Business Pioneers Paved Way for Others," *MH*, 31 January 2000.

61. "Miami and the Story of Its Remarkable Growth: An Interview with George E. Merrick published by the *New York Times*" (1925), 13, UM; and "Protest Mob Action," *MH*, 17 August 1915. Through white allies, the Colored Board of Trade remedied the fact that there was not a single park for all of Miami's five-thousand-plus Negroes; "Buy Two Public Parks for Negroes of Miami," *MM*, 21 August 1916.

62. Earl Lewis, *In Their Own Interests: Race, Class, and Power in Twentieth-Century Norfolk, Virginia* (Berkeley: University of California Press, 1993), 135.

63. "Miami and the Story of Its Remarkable Growth."

64. "Colored Board of Trade Open Letter to City Council," *MH*, 24 October 1915; and "Enthusiasm among Negroes," *MH*, 21 June 1918.

65. "Colored Board of Trade Wants Negro Hospital in Colored Town," *MH*, 14 October 1915; "Cannot Comply with Request for Colored Hospital," *MH*, 22 October 1915; and "Building for the Colored School Pupils," *MH*, 7 December 1917.

66. Thomas A. Castillo, "Chauffeuring in a White Man's Town: Black Service Work, Movement and Segregation in Early Miami," in *Florida's Labor and Working-Class Past: Three Centuries of Work in the Sunshine State*, ed. Robert Cassenello and Melanie Shell-Weiss, 143–67 (Gainesville: University of Florida Press, 2009); Dunn, *Black Miami in the Twentieth Century*, 94; and Paul George, "Policing Miami's Black Community, 1896–1930," *Florida Historical Quarterly* 57, no. 4 (April 1979): 440–41.

67. "Colored Board of Trade Wants Good Paving," *MH*, 27 August 1915; and Blackman, *Miami and Dade County Florida*, 24.

68. ". . . Disfigures the City," *MH*, 5 October 1911.

69. "Civic League of Miami Formally Organized at Rousing Meeting at the Fair Building Yesterday," *MH*, 21 October 1912.

70. "Colored Board of Trade Open Letter to City Council"; and "Officers Will Be Sustained," *MH*, 16 August 1912.

71. Tera Hunter, *To 'Joy My Freedom: Southern Black Women's Lives and Labors after the Civil War* (Cambridge, MA: Harvard University Press, 1997); and Micki McElya, *Clinging to Mammy: The Faithful Slave in Twentieth-Century America* (Cambridge, MA: Harvard University Press, 2007).

72. "Running a Frightful Risk," *MH*, 17 June 1915.

73. Nayan Shah, *Contagious Divides: Epidemics and Race in San Francisco's Chinatown* (Berkeley and Los Angeles: University of California Press, 2001), 121.

74. Samuel Kelton Roberts Jr., *Infectious Fear: Politics, Disease, and the Health Effects of Segregation* (Chapel Hill: University of North Carolina Press, 2009), 122.

75. "Progress Made against Leprosy," *MH*, 29 January 1914.

76. "Officers Will Be Sustained."

77. "Riversiders Favor Race Segregation and Want a Law," *MH*, 25 August 1915.

78. "K-Klux-Klan Methods Used to Make Negroes Move from Vicinity of Ave J and 4th," *MM*, 14 August 1915; "Police Asked to Protect Negroes in Colored Town," *MM*, 16 August 1915; and "Grave Duty of the Hour," *MM*, 16 August 1915.

79. "K-Klux-Klan Methods Used to Make Negroes Move."
80. "Committee to Push School Improvements," *MH*, 11 August 1915.
81. "The White Side," *MH*, 19 August 1915.
82. "Copy of Deed and Agreement between the Roland Park Montebello Company and Edward H. Bouton Containing Restrictions, Conditions, Etc. Relating to Northwood" (1930), Roland Park Company Records, box 318, Special Collections, Milton Eisenhower Library, Johns Hopkins University. Many thanks to Paige Glotzer for this source.
83. "Beautifying Our Suburbs, Parkways and Bungalows," *MH*, 13 August 1916.
84. "White Side."
85. "Getting at It by Vote," *MH*, 2 March 1916.
86. "Colored Board of Trade Open Letter to City Council."
87. "$150,000 to Be Probable Cost of Color Line," *MM*, 22 July 1920.
88. "Segregation of Races in Miami to Receive Careful Consideration," *MH*, 20 August 1915.
89. "Segregation Ordinance Up," *MH*, 7 January 1916.
90. "Colored Board of Trade Open Letter to City Council."
91. "Protest Mob Action."
92. Walter B. Weare, *Black Business in the New South: A Social History of the North Carolina Mutual Life Insurance Company* (Champaign: University of Illinois Press, 1973), 177.
93. Abram L. Harris, *The Negro as Capitalist: A Study of Banking and Business among American Negroes* (Philadelphia: American Academy of Political and Social Science, 1936), 182–83.
94. C. de Thierry, "Our Policy in the West Indies," in *Proceedings of the Royal Colonial Institute* 37, ed. Royal Commonwealth Society (London: Institute, 1906), 201; and Antonio Gaztambide-Géigel, "The Invention of the Caribbean," *Social and Economic Studies* 53, no. 3 (September 2004): 137. On segregation in the early twentieth-century Caribbean, see Michael L. Conniff, *Black Labor on a White Canal: Panama, 1904–1981* (Pittsburgh: University of Pittsburgh Press, 1985).
95. "Miami, Beautiful, Prosperous Has Many Colored Millionaires," *PT*, 20 March 1926.
96. Last will and testament of J. J. Hurd, 29 November 1916, and correspondence from C. J. Colsville to D. A. Dorsey, 11 February 1930, the Papers of Dana A. Dorsey, Miami Metropolitan Archive, accessed 31 May 2013, http://digitool.fcla.edu/R/P9PB 2D23CJ9MQ78KYKF2KUBJHIGIPSSE6HRI36DG1CU23XKNRC-00330?func=dbin -jump-full&object_id=73623&pds_handle=GUEST.
97. Lease to A. Goldstein & Son, 1 May 1925; lease to A. Athonyn and A. Bogianges, 20 August 1923; the Papers of Dana A. Dorsey, Miami Metropolitan Archive, accessed 31 May 2013, http://digitool.fcla.edu/R/P9PB2D23CJ9MQ78KYKF2KUBJHIGIPS SE6HRI36DG1CU23XKNRC-00330?func=dbin-jump-full&object_id=73623&pds _handle=GUEST.
98. Contract of sale between D. A. Dorsey and James Sanders, 16 November 1916; lease to Griff and Stein from D. A. Dorsey, 25 November 1929; the Papers of Dana A. Dorsey, Miami Metropolitan Archive, accessed 31 May 2013, http://digitool.fcla .edu/R/P9PB2D23CJ9MQ78KYKF2KUBJHIGIPSSE6HRI36DG1CU23XKNRC -00330?func=dbin-jump-full&object_id=73623&pds_handle=GUEST.
99. "White Side."
100. "Objects to Intrusion," *MH*, 16 December 1914.
101. "Vindicating Bahamians," *MH*, 7 August 1920.
102. W. E. B. Du Bois, quoted in David Levering Lewis, *W. E. B. Du Bois: Biography of a Race* (New York: Owl Books, 1993), 285.

103. "Colored Board of Trade Open Letter to City Council."

104. "Color Line Established to Satisfaction of All, City Will Buy or Condemn One and One-Half Blocks of Land in Disputed Territory; Avenue I, the Color Line Recommendations Made by Committees of Association, Accepted by City Council," *MM*, 19 October 1915.

105. "Riversiders Favor Race Segregation and Want a Law."

106. "K-Klux-Klan Methods Used to Make Negroes Move."

107. "Colored Board of Trade Open Letter to City Council."

108. "Segregation Law," *MH*, 29 November 1915.

109. "Segregation Law May Cost Money," *MH*, 20 November 1915.

110. "Drawing a Line between Sections Where Races Dwell," *MH*, 19 October 1915.

111. "At Miami, Fla . . . ," *Appeal* (St. Paul, MN), 29 April 1916.

112. Christopher Silver, "The Racial Origins of Zoning in American Cities," in *Urban Planning and the African American Community: In the Shadows*, ed. June Manning Thomas and Marsha Ritzdorf (Thousand Oaks, CA: Sage Publications, 1997), 25.

113. "Segregation Law a Misfit," *MH*, 29 October 1911; "Segregation in Baltimore," *MH*, 6 August 1913; and "Anti-Negro Law Invalid," *MH*, 28 April 1913.

114. *Buchanan v. Warley*, 245 U.S. 60 (1917); "Supreme Court to Pass on Segregation," *MH*, 6 July 1915; and "No Segregation," *MH*, 7 November 1917.

115. "Segregation Law."

116. "Appeal Taken in Segregation," *MH*, 8 May 1917.

117. "Segregation Law."

118. "Put Up or Shut Up," *MH*, 24 September 1915.

119. George, "Policing Miami's Black Community," 441.

120. "Encroachment of White Town Cause of Shooting, Colored Woman Has Close Call from Being Shot in Early Morning Raid by White Men," *MM*, 20 May 1920; see also "Council Probes Abuse of Negroes, Practice of Routing Colored Men out of Bed at Unearthly Hours Riles City Dads," *MM*, 2 August 1918.

121. Leon E. Howe, "Dynamiting Negro Houses in Miami," 2 July 1920, p. 1, RG 65 Federal Bureau of Investigation, Old German Files, Casefile OG 387852, Race Riots, Florida, Federal Bureau of Investigation, 1920, NA, Proquest Twentieth Century Black Freedom Struggles.

122. Correspondence to Claude Barnett, 10 May 1939, Claude A. Barnett Papers, Associated Negro Press, 1918–67, Part 3, Subject Files on Black Americans, Series C, Economic Conditions, "Funeral Directors, Especially Kelsey Pharr (Miami, Fla), 1934–1962" folder. Pharr lived at 911 Lemon Street (Fifth Street), less than a block from the "agreed-upon" racial border; Ancestry.com, accessed 9 December 2011, original source: *1920 United States Federal Census, Miami, Dade, Florida*, microfilm roll T625_216, 23A, http://www.ancestry.com.

123. Jerrell H. Shofner, "Florida and the Black Migration," *Florida Historical Quarterly* 57, no. 3 (January 1979): 285.

124. "$150,000 to Be Probable Cost of Color Line."

125. Estimates of what it would cost to buy out enough owners to create a buffer zone between Highland Park and Colored Town reached as high as $150,000 (ibid.), or the equivalent of $1.7 million in 2011.

126. Ibid.

127. "Final Anti-charter Meeting Staged in Park Monday Night," *MM*, 16 May 1921; and "Candidates Bar Negro Vote in City Elections," *MH*, 8 July 1921.

128. Miami City Charter, 1921, section 3 (ii), 6.

129. "Women Meet at Club to Hear Talk on Proposed City Charter," *MM*, 21 April 1921.

130. LeeAnn Bishop Lands, "A Reprehensible and Unfriendly Act: Homeowners, Renters, and the Bid for Residential Segregation in Atlanta, 1900–1917," *Journal of Planning History* 3, no. 2 (May 2004): 107; and Kristin Larsen, "Harmonious Inequality? Zoning Public Housing, and Orlando's Separate City, 1920–1945," *Journal of Planning History* 1, no. 2 (May 2002): 157. Atlanta's 1922 zoning power was overturned in *Bowen v. City of Atlanta*, 159 GA 145, 125 S.E. 199 (1924).

131. Charter of the City of Miami, approved 31 May 1913; Charter of the City of Miami, 1921, Section 3, "The City of Miami shall have the power . . . ," 6, point (ii). Charles E. Connerly, *"The Most Segregated City in America": City Planning and Civil Rights in Birmingham, 1920–1980* (Charlottesville: University of Virginia Press, 2005), 42.

132. "Joint Meeting Mapped District for Segregation," *MH*, 14 September 1915; and Howe, "Dynamiting Negro Houses in Miami."

133. Eric S. Yellin, *Racism in the Nation's Service: Government Workers and the Color Line in Woodrow Wilson's America* (Chapel Hill: University of North Carolina Press, 2013), 8; and Carl H. Nightingale, "The Transnational Contexts of Early Twentieth-Century American Urban Segregation," *Journal of Social History* 39, no. 3. (Spring 2006): 667–702. See also William E. Leuchtenburg, "The Progressive Movement and American Foreign Policy, 1898–1916," *Mississippi Valley Historical Review* 39, no. 3 (December 1952): 483–504; Robert Wiebe, *The Search for Order, 1877–1920* (New York: Westport, 1967), 166; C. Vann Woodward, *Origins of the New South, 1877–1913* (Baton Rouge: Louisiana State University Press, 1951), esp. chap. 14; Daniel Walden, "Race and Imperialism: The Achilles Heel of the Progressives," *Science and Society* 31, no. 2 (April 1967): 222–32.

CHAPTER TWO: BARGAINING AND HOPING

1. "Miami Points the Way to a Happier Life" (ca. 1920), Everest George Sewell Papers, manuscript box 8, HASF.

2. Albert Payson Terhune, *Black Caesar's Clan: A Florida Mystery Story* (New York: A. L. Burt, 1922); and David O. True, "Pirates and Treasure Trove of South Florida," *Tequesta* 6 (1946): 3–13.

3. "Miami Points the Way to a Happier Life."

4. "Wedge Your Way into the Ranks," *MH*, 13 December 1921.

5. Homer B. Vanderblue, "The Florida Land Boom," *Journal of Land and Public Utility Economics* 3, no. 3 (August 1927): 253.

6. "Miami, 1,681 in 1900, Now Third Florida City with 1920 Population 29,549," *MH*, 27 May 1920.

7. Arthur E. Chapman, "The History of the Black Police Force and Court in the City of Miami" (PhD diss., University of Miami, 1986), 10, 12, 13, 15.

8. Marvin Dunn, *Black Miami in the Twentieth Century* (Gainesville: University Press of Florida, 1997).

9. Thelma Peters, *Lemon City: Pioneering on Biscayne Bay, 1850–1925* (Miami: Banyan Books, 1976); Melanie Shell-Weiss, *Coming to Miami: A Social History* (Gainesville: University Press of Florida, 2009), 105–205; and Office of the County Manager, "Profile of the Black Population in Metropolitan Dade County" (January 1979), 63.

10. William C. Freeman, *Miami* (1921), accessed 3 September 2013, http://archive.org/stream/miami00mont#page/n0/mode/2up.

11. "Miami Realty Board Real Organization," *MH*, 13 March 1920; and "Realty Board for Men Only Is Verdict," *MH*, 26 March 1920.

12. Earl Royce Dumont, president of the Montray Corporation, a development firm, writing in Freeman, *Miami*, 1.

13. Works Projects Administration, *Miami and Dade County, Including Miami Beach and Coral Gables* (New York: Bacon, Percy, & Daggett, 1941), 173.

14. Helen C. Freeland, "George Edgar Merrick," *Tequesta* 2 (1942): 4.

15. George Merrick, *Coral Gables: Miami's Riviera* (ca. 1922), accessed 30 May 2013, http://archive.org/stream/coralgableshomes00merr#page/n1/mode/2up.

16. Ibid.

17. Hoyt Frazure, as told to Nixon Smiley, *Memories of Old Miami* (Miami: Miami Herald, 1964), 26; and Nixon Smiley, "The Story Behind the Miami Story," in *Guide Miami: A Guide to All Places of Interest in Metropolitan Dade County* (North Miami, FL: Interguide, 1966), 11.

18. "Miami and the Story of Its Remarkable Growth: An Interview with George E. Merrick published by the *New York Times*" (1925), 7, UM.

19. "Miami and the Story of Its Remarkable Growth," 12.

20. William A. Graham, "The Pennsuco Sugar Experiment," *Tequesta* 11 (1951): 42.

21. Frazure, *Memories of Old Miami*, 26.

22. Ibid., 28.

23. Ibid., 26, 28.

24. Sewell was president of the Miami Chamber of Commerce from 1915 to 1925, and mayor of Miami from 1927 to 1929 and 1933 to 1935. "E. G. Sewell for City Commissioner" (1935), Everest George Sewell Papers, manuscript box 8, HASF.

25. "Miami and the Story of Its Remarkable Growth," 14.

26. "Beat Storm to Get Film of Miami Ruin," *NYT*, 22 September 1926.

27. Frazure, *Memories of Old Miami*, 30–31.

28. "Miami Asks Nation for Help at Once," *EI*, 23 September 1926.

29. "Fruit Cake Must Ripen, Like Cheese to Be Good," *ADW*, 27 October 1934.

30. "The Forbidden City," *CD*, 2 October 1926; and "Is Miami a Sodom?," *MH*, 8 April 1922.

31. Wilhelmina Jennings, interviewed by N. D. B. Connolly, 3 February 2006, audio recording in author's possession; and Wilhelmina Jennings, interviewed by Stephanie Wanza, 8 August 1997, 2, Tell the Story Collection, BA.

32. Paul Farmer, *The Uses of Haiti* (Monroe, ME: Common Courage Press, 2005), 308. The records of the US Marines are too inconsistent to allow for anything other than a rough estimate of Haitians killed under American supervision during the occupation. The conservative figure is fifteen thousand, but it may have been as high as fifty thousand. Patrick Bellegarde-Smith, *Haiti: The Breached Citadel* (Toronto: Canadian Scholars Press, 2004). My thanks to Millery Polyné and Yveline Alexis for providing this lead.

33. "Miami Asks Nation for Help at Once."

34. Jennings, Connolly interview.

35. "Two Marines Shot in Gun Fight," *NYT*, 25 September 1926; the *Chicago Tribune* reported the shooting of Mabel as well, but left her unnamed: "Troops Patrol Miami Streets; Fear Race War," *CT*, 25 September 1926.

36. "Troops Patrol Miami Streets; Fear Race War"; and "Race Riot Offers Miami Diversion after Storm," *PT*, 2 October 1926.

37. Jennings, Connolly interview.

38. "Three Negroes Shot and Burned," *MGD*, 27 September 1926.

39. Ashraf H. A. Rushdy, *American Lynching* (New Haven, CT: Yale University Press, 2012), xi–xii, quote on xii.

40. Rushdy cites, for instance, the 1705 Virginia statue in which "any master who accidentally kills a slave in the course of correction 'shall be free of all punishment . . . as if such accident never happened.'" Ibid., 153.

41. Marian Moser Jones, "Tempest in the Forbidden City: Racism, Violence, and Vulnerability in the 1926 Miami Hurricane," *Journal of Policy History* (forthcoming).

42. "Flood Not God's Way to Punish Dixie Whites," *BAA*, 21 May 1927; see also "Walter White Finds Peonage Rife in Refugee Camps," *BAA*, 4 June 1927.

43. See, for instance, Kathleen Brown, *Good Wives, Nasty Wenches, and Anxious Patriarchs: Gender, Race, and Power in Colonial Virginia* (Chapel Hill: University of North Carolina Press, 1996), 5, 365, 366; and Jane Dailey, ed., *The Age of Jim Crow* (New York: Norton, 2008), esp. introduction.

44. Kevin Boyle, *Arc of Justice: A Saga of Race, Civil Rights, and Murder in the Jazz Age* (New York: Henry Holt, 2004), 141–43, 226, 249.

45. Shell-Weiss, *Coming to Miami*, 115.

46. Dunn, *Black Miami in the Twentieth Century*, 117–24, 133–39; see also Paul S. George, "Colored Town: Miami's Black Community, 1896–1930," *Florida Historical Quarterly* 56, no. 4 (April 1978): 432–47.

47. "White Musicians Were Cause of Miami Flogging," *CD*, 4 February 1922; and "Florida Mob's Atrocities Put 'Huns' to Shame," *CD*, 25 February 1922.

48. See, for instance, Matthew Frye Jacobson, "Annexing the Other: The World's Peoples as Auxiliary Consumers and Imported Workers, 1876–1917," in *Race, Nation, and Empire in American History*, ed. James T. Campbell, Matthew Pratt Guterl, and Robert G. Lee, 103–30 (Chapel Hill: University of North Carolina Press, 2007).

49. "Endeavoring to Trace a Negro Who Assaulted a White Woman," *MM*, 30 July 1920; and "Praiseworthy Action," *MM*, 31 July 1920. Kevin Boyle describes an alleged rape in Bartow, Florida, in 1901 wherein several trustees of the St. James AME Church proclaimed their solidarity with white lynch mobs based on little more than wild accusation. Black men actively participated in the manhunt and handed a sixteen-year-old black boy over to a white lynch mob. Boyle, *Arc of Justice*, 68. Black assistance was similarly integral to the 1955 Mississippi lynching of Chicago youth Emmett Till.

50. "Negro Suspect Leaps to Death from the Train," *MM*, 31 July 1920; "Negro Instantly Killed in Leap from Train," *MH*, 1 August 1920; Claudrena N. Harold, "The Rise and Fall of the Garvey Movement in the Urban South, 1918–1942" (PhD diss., University of Notre Dame, 2004), 122–23; and Shell-Weiss, *Coming to Miami*, 82–83.

51. "Guardsmen Patrol Miami," *NYT*, 3 August 1920.

52. "Militiamen Co-operate with Miami Authorities Following Demonstration of Negroes from Bahamas over Death of Herbert Brooks," *CDE*, 3 August 1920.

53. Leon E. Howe, "Dynamiting Negro Houses in Miami," 2 July 1920, 2, RG 65 Federal Bureau of Investigation, Old German Files, Casefile OG 387852, Race Riots, Florida, Federal Bureau of Investigation, 1920, NA, Proquest Twentieth Century Black Freedom Struggles.

54. "In Defense of Bahamians," *MH*, 3 August 1920.

55. Michael Hanchard and Michael Dawson, "Ideology and Political Culture in Black," in Michael Hanchard, *Party/Politics: Horizons in Black Political Thought* (New York: Oxford University Press, 2006), 88.

56. Dorothy Jenkins Fields, "Tracing Overtown's Vernacular Architecture," Florida theme issue, *Journal of Decorative and Propaganda Arts* 23 (1998): 332; and Grace Elizabeth Hale, *Making Whiteness: The Culture of Segregation in the South, 1890–1940* (New York: Vintage Books, 1999), 200.

57. Frantz Fanon, *Black Skins, White Masks* (New York: Grove Press, 1967), 110.

58. Loren Schweninger, *Black Property Owners in the South, 1790–1915* (Urbana and Chicago: University of Illinois Press, 1990), 231.

59. Michele Mitchell, *Righteous Propagation: African Americans and the Politics of Racial Destiny after Reconstruction* (Chapel Hill: University of North Carolina Press, 2004), 220–30.

60. The most withering critique of lynching as a defense of white womanhood remains Ida B. Wells, *Southern Horrors: Lynch Law and Its Phases* (New York: New York Age, 1892).

61. Melanie Shell-Weiss, "Coming North to the South: Migration, Labor, and City-Building in Twentieth Century Miami," *Florida Historical Quarterly* 84, no. 1 (Summer 2005): 91.

62. Bertha R. Comstock, "Life History: Kelsey L. Pharr, Negro Undertaker," 11 January 1939, Federal Writers Project, Miami, Florida, 5.

63. Ibid., 2–4; Ancestry.com, accessed 9 December 2011, original source: *1910 United States Federal Census, Salisbury West Ward, Rowan, North Carolina*, microfilm roll T624_1131, 7B, http://www.ancestry.com.

64. Comstock, "Life History," 4.

65. Kelsey Pharr, quoted in Dorothy Jenkins Fields, "Colored Town, Miami, Florida, 1915: An Examination of the Manner in Which the Residents Defined Their Community during This Era of Jim Crow" (PhD diss., Union Institute, 1996), 38–39.

66. Ibid., 36.

67. Shell-Weiss, *Coming to Miami*, 53–65.

68. "Patriotic League and Overseas Club Formed," *MH*, 29 August 1919.

69. "Communications," *MH*, 4 August 1920; Hugh Kingsmill, "A Modern Knight," *Bookman* (April 1934): 42–45, esp. 43; and John Fisher, "Keeping 'the Old Flag Flying': British Community in Morocco and the British Morocco Merchants Association, 1914–1924," *Historical Research* 83, no. 222 (November 2010): 721–46.

70. "Early Blacks Built Strong Foundation in Miami," *MT*, 5 February 2003.

71. Correspondence from J. Edgar Hoover to W. L. Hurley, 13 September 1920, RG 59 US Department of State, Entry 535–Office of the Counselor, Central File, 1917–28, Casefile 841-132: Over-Seas Club, Miami, Florida, British Organization, 1920, NA, Proquest Twentieth Century Black Freedom Struggles.

72. Howe, "Dynamiting Negro Houses in Miami."

73. Ancestry.com, accessed 20 November 2011, original source: *U.S. Passport Applications, 1795–1925*, NA; *Passport Applications, January 2, 1906–March 31, 1925*; microfilm roll 1458; Ancestry.com, accessed 20 November 2011, original source: *1920 United States Federal Census, Miami, Dade, Florida*, microfilm roll T625_216, 9B—both at http://www.ancestry.com. "Over Eight Thousand Pupils Are Enrolled in Dade County Schools," *MM*, 19 July 1920. J. Edgar Hoover's correspondence on the Overseas Club mistakenly says the school was run by "Bethel Lemasney." However, it was John Franklyn Bethel who was pastor of the church out of which Mary LeMasney, wife of John LeMasney, ran the LeMasney school; "British Subjects to Form Organization," *MH*, 28 August 1919.

74. Correspondence from J. Edgar Hoover to W. L. Hurley, 13 September 1920. Information on the LeMasneys' employment history comes from Ancestry.com, accessed 20 November 2011, original source: *1910 United States Federal Census, Paterson Ward 11, Passaic, New Jersey*, microfilm roll T624_906, 3A; Ancestry.com, accessed 20 November 2011, original source: *New York Passenger Lists, 1820–1957*, 1903, microfilm roll T715_333, 347—both at http://www.ancestry.com.

75. "Torch Given Queer Effigy of Guy Fawkes," *MH*, 6 November 1917. Meant to commemorate revolutionaries' failed attempt to blow up Parliament and assassinate King James in 1605, the none-too-subtle inversion of blacks play-lynching a white man did not go unnoticed, and city officials would eventually ban the holiday in the 1930s; Raymond A. Mohl, "Black Immigrants in Early Twentieth-Century Miami," *Florida Historical Quarterly* 65, no. 3 (January 1987): 296.

76. Correspondence from J. Edgar Hoover to W. L. Hurley, 13 September 1920.

77. Ibid.

78. Ancestry.com, accessed 20 November 2011, original source: *1920 United States Federal Census, Miami, Dade, Florida*, microfilm roll T625_216, 4A, http://www.ancestry.com.

79. Correspondence from J. Edgar Hoover to W. L. Hurley, 13 September 1920; and Leon E. Howe, "Dynamiting Negro Houses in Miami."

80. George Carter, quoted in Harold, "Rise and Fall of the Garvey Movement in the Urban South," 120. See also *Negro World*, 20 August 1921.

81. Mary G. Rolinson, *Grassroots Garveyism: The Universal Negro Improvement Association in the Rural South, 1920–1927* (Chapel Hill: University of North Carolina Press, 2007), 57.

82. "Disclaim Responsibility," *MH*, 6 July 1921; and "Interesting Revelations," *MH*, 15 July 1921.

83. "Tarred and Feathered," *Independent*, 17 September 1921.

84. "Will Try Negroes on Rioting Charge," *MH*, 5 July 1921.

85. Harold, "Rise and Fall of the Garvey Movement in the Urban South," 119.

86. "Opportunities Open for Enlistment in the Armey [sic] and Navy," *MH*, 17 April 1919.

87. Shell-Weiss, *Coming to Miami*, 86.

88. *Report by Bureau of Investigation Agent Leone E. Howe*, Miami, Florida, 7 July 1921, in *Marcus Garvey Papers and the Universal Negro Improvement Association Papers*, vol. 6, ed. Robert Hill (Berkeley: University of California Press, 1984), 340.

89. Kip Vought, "Racial Stirrings in Colored Town: The UNIA in Miami during the 1920s," *Tequesta* 60 (2000): 56–77, esp. 63.

90. "Higgs Takes Final Voyage from Miami," *MH*, 6 July 1921.

91. "Kidnap Negro Preacher; Cause Race Riot Alarm; Bridge Guard Shoots 2," *MH*, 2 July 1921; and "Kidnapping Bares Plot to Kill Whites in Key West," *MH*, 3 July 1921.

92. "Tar and Feather White Pastor of Negro Church," *MH*, 18 July 1921.

93. "Tarred and Feathered."

94. "Letter Writers Arouse Chief Dillon to Action," *MH*, 27 July 1921.

95. Robert A. Hill, ed. *The Marcus Garvey and Universal Negro Improvement Association Papers*, vol. 7, *November 1927–August 1940* (Berkeley: University of California Press, 1990), 168–70, quote on 168; Harold, "Rise and Fall of the Garvey Movement in the Urban South," 126; Vought, "Racial Stirrings in Colored Town," 57; "'Warrior Mother of Africa's Warriors of the Most High God': Laura Adorkor Koffey and the African Universal Church," in Richard Newman, *Black Power and Black Religion: Essays and Reviews* (West Cornwall, CT: Locust Hill Press, 1987), 133.

96. Vought, "Racial Stirrings in Colored Town," 71.

97. "Seminoles to Become Citizens on One Condition, Says Chief," *CSM*, 27 November 1926; and "Seminoles May Become Full-Fledged Citizens," *BS*, 19 December 1926.

98. "Seminole Indians Seek Citizenship in United States," *SPT*, 6 February 1927.

99. Ibid.

100. "Over Eight Thousand Pupils Are Enrolled in Dade County Schools."

101. "Tony Tommie Sends Letter," *MH*, 23 April 1916; and "The Seminoles in the 1920s," *ST*, 11 February 2000.

102. "Tony Tommie Runs Afoul of Law on Eve of Wedding," *MN*, 3 June 1926.

103. "Seminole Wedding to Gather Record Number of Indians Here," *MN*, 28 April 1928.

104. "Seminole Indians Seek Citizenship in United States."

105. Works Projects Administration, *Miami and Dade County*, 34.

106. Joseph T. Elvove, "The Florida Everglades: A Region of New Settlement," *Journal of Land and Public Utility Economics* 19, no. 4 (November 1943): 464–69, esp. 465; on the making of race in Manifest Destiny discourse, see Reginald Horsman, *Race and Manifest Destiny: The Origins of American Anglo-Saxonism* (Cambridge, MA: Harvard University Press, 1981).

107. Elvove, "Florida Everglades," 465–66.

108. Miami Chamber of Commerce, "First Seaboard Passenger Train Is Heralded by Capitalists as Proof of Miami's Greatness," *Miamian* 7, no. 9 (February 1927): 10, 33; and Miami Chamber of Commerce, "5,000 See Farming Begin on 'Glades; Seminoles Relinquish Sovereignty," *Miamian* 11, no. 10 (March 1927): 8–9.

109. Patsy West, *The Enduring Seminoles: From Alligator Wrestling to Ecotourism* (Gainesville: University Press of Florida, 1998), 70.

110. "Cameras Grind as Seminoles Turn Over Land," *MN*, 6 February 1927.

111. Miami Chamber of Commerce, "5,000 See Farming Begin on 'Glades," 8–9.

112. Ibid., 71; and West, *Enduring Seminoles*, 71.

113. HOLC Security Map Appendix, table 5, RG 195, Records of the Federal Home Loan Bank Board, Home Owners Loan Corporation, Records Relating to the City Survey File, 1935–40, entry 39, "Florida Miami" folder, box 81, NARA.

114. Works Projects Administration, *Miami and Dade County*, 63.

115. Ibid., 174.

116. Louis Fisher, "The Forward to the Soil Movement of Jews in Russia," *Menorah Journal* (1925), Papers of Joseph A. Rosen, Records of the Director of the American Jewish Joint Agricultural Corporation, 1922–44, subseries 2: American Relief Administration, American Jewish Joint Distribution Committee, American Society for Jewish Farm Settlements in the USSR (ASJFS), 1922–39, folder 19, 38 pp., YIVO Institute for Jewish Research, New York. Author saw finding aid only; accessed 1 June 2013, http://findingaids.cjh.org/?pID=109128.

117. "Tractors Invade the Everglades," *CSM*, 7 February 1927; and "Two Seminole Migrations," *CSM*, 14 March 1921.

118. West, *Enduring Seminoles*, 74.

119. "Seminoles Increase in the Everglades," *NYT*, 20 May 1930.

120. Kersey, "Tony Tommie Letter," 312.

121. West, *Enduring Seminoles*, 20.

122. "Lon Worth Crow, 80, Services Tomorrow," *MN*, 27 May 1958.

123. West, *Enduring Seminoles*, 71.

124. "Glades Truck Crops Ruined by Severe Cold," *MN*, 23 December 1927; "Blessings from an Ugly Piece of Land," *SPT*, 13 July 2003; and "Great Lakes," *SS*, 17 January 1994.

125. "Controversial 'Chief,'" *ST*, 14 April 2000.

126. Douglas Blackmon, *Slavery by Another Name: The Re-enslavement of Black Americans from the Civil War to World War II* (New York: Anchor Books, 2009), 5–9.

127. Nimmo, quoted in Harold, "Rise and Fall of the Garvey Movement in the Urban South," 117.

128. Native American history is particularly instructive when it comes to contextualizing violence between Indians as the product of imperialism and white supremacy. See, for instance, Ned Blackhawk, *Violence over the Land: Indians and Empires in the Early American West* (Cambridge, MA: Harvard University Press, 2008); Tiya Miles, *The House on Diamond Hill: A Cherokee Plantation Story* (Chapel Hill: University of North Carolina Press, 2010); and Philip J. Deloria, *Indians in Unexpected Places* (Lawrence: University Press of Kansas, 2004), esp. chap. 2, "Violence: The Killings at Lighting Creek."

CHAPTER THREE: JIM CROW LIBERALISM

1. "Luther Brooks: Behind the Scenes 'Mover,'" *MH*, 14 April 1963; and Hugh Douglas Price, "The Negro and Florida Politics, 1944–1954," *Journal of Politics* 17, no. 2 (May 1955): 203.
2. "Miracle Changes Face of Miami," *PC*, 30 November 1957; and "Luther Brooks, 80, Expowerbroker," *MH*, 31 December 1988.
3. "'General' Brooks Collects Rents," *MN*, 2 March 1962.
4. Gary R. Mormino, *Land of Sunshine, State of Dreams: A Social History of Modern Florida* (Gainesville: University Press of Florida, 2005), 45.
5. Roger Biles, *The South and the New Deal* (Lexington: University Press of Kentucky, 1994), 104.
6. "Miami's Slum District Is Worse Than Most," *MH*, 7 September 1934; and "Decent Homes for Decent Families: A Slum Clearance Program for Miami, Initiated by the City Planning Board," Ernest R. Graham Papers, box 20, "Urban Redevelopment Corporations, 1941" folder, UF.
7. Office of the County Manager, "Profile of the Black Population in Metropolitan Dade County" (January 1979), 65; Leome Culmer, interviewed by Stephanie Wanza, 13 August 1997, 9, Tell the Story Collection, BA; David C. Driskell, *Two Centuries of Black American Art* (Los Angeles: Los Angeles County Museum of Art; New York: Knopf, 1976); and Inter-county Regional Planning Commission, *Metropolitan Dade County Today: A Comparison with the Denver Inter-county Area* (Denver: Inter-county Regional Planning Commission, 1960), 2.
8. "Miami's Slum District Is Worse Than Most."
9. Amid mounting criticism that property managers drew exorbitant rents from Negro communities on behalf of white absentee landlords, Luther Brooks, in 1962, changed the name of his company from Bonded Collection Agency to Bonded Rental Agency.
10. *Miami City Directory*, 1935, pp. 167, 1005, UM; Ancestry.com, accessed 20 November 2011, original source: *Florida State Census, 1867–1945, Tenth Census of the State of Florida, 1935*, microfilm series S 5, 30 reels, http://www.ancestry.com.
11. "Miracle Changes Face of Miami." Bonded Collection Agency, "A Pictorial Review of Miami's 'Parade of Progress': What Is Being Done by Private Enterprise in Miami's Slum Clearance Program," 6; Bonded Collection Agency, "25 Years of Property Management and Community Service" (1959), 1; Bonded Rental Agency advertisement (ca. 1969), "Newspaper Clippings on Housing, 1966–1970"—all in Bonded Rental Agency Inc. Collection, BA.
12. Leonard Barfield, interviewed by N. D. B. Connolly, 23 February 2010, notes in author's possession.
13. "Who Is Responsible for This Condition?" *MH*, 16 August 1912.
14. US Census Bureau, *Housing: Supplement to the First Series Housing Bulletin for Florida: Miami: Block Statistics* (Washington, DC: Government Printing Office, 1942), 21–22.

15. Margie and George Harth, interviewed by N. D. B. Connolly, 9 March 2010.

16. John Hope Franklin and Alfred A. Moss Jr., *From Slavery to Freedom: A History of African Americans* (Boston: McGraw Hill, 2000), 421.

17. "Slum Area Rent Boosts in Miami Draw Ire, Favor," *WAA*, 16 August 1949.

18. US Census Bureau, *Housing*, 5.

19. Of the 434 dwellings without any toilet facilities whatsoever, 147—or 34 percent— of those were colored occupied; National Urban League, *A Review of Economic and Cultural Problems in Dade County, Florida as They Relate to Conditions in the Negro Population* (New York: National Urban League, 1943), 34–35.

20. Ibid., 35.

21. "Sanitation Conditions Fierce, Says Landlord," *MH*, 8 September 1934.

22. "Slum Area Survey Is Ordered by Miami," *MH*, 11 September 1934.

23. "Organized Crime Harmful to Miami," *EI*, 31 March 1933; and "Miami's New Deal: The People's Candidates . . . Gardner, Chartrand and Bridges," 19 March 1935, Everest George Sewell Papers, manuscript box 8, HASF.

24. "Rotary Hears Capone Scored by Dan Hardie," *MN*, 29 June 1928; "Dan Hardie Acts as His Own Witness at Sholtz Hearing," *PBP*, 9 November 1933; "Miami: The Way We Were," *MN*, 10 August 1985; Marvin Dunn, *Black Miami in the Twentieth Century* (Gainesville: University Press of Florida, 1997), 70; and N. D. B. Connolly, "Games of Chance: Jim Crow's Entrepreneurs Bet on 'Negro' Law and Order," in *What's Good for Business: Business and American Politics since World War II*, ed. Kim Phillips-Fein and Julian E. Zelizer, 140–56 (New York: Oxford University Press, 2012).

25. "Florida's Jobless Turn to Gambling," *NYT*, 14 August 1932.

26. Circuit Court of the Eleventh Judicial Circuit of Florida in and for the County of Dade, "The Situation in Miami," *Grand Jury Report*, 12 May 1947, 5; and Circuit Court of the Eleventh Judicial Circuit of Florida in and for the County of Dade, "Bolita," *Final Report of the Grand Jury*, 9 May 1967, 3.

27. "Stop Being a Sucker," *ADW*, 27 October 1951.

28. See Daniel Bell, "Crime as an American Way of Life," 50th anniversary issue, *Antioch Review* 50, nos. 1–2 (Winter–Spring 1992): 109–30.

29. "Crime: It Pays to Organize," *Time*, 12 March 1951; and Special Committee to Investigate Organized Crime in Interstate Commerce, *Kefauver Committee Interim Report #1, United States Senate*, 81st Cong., 2nd sess., report no. 2370, 18 August 1950, 2.

30. "Bolita Throwing Starts Again; Rent Collectors Are Hard Hit," *PBP*, 12 January 1932.

31. Russell Raymond Trilck, a South Florida landlord, worked through real estate and "several top police officials" to secure over six hundred thousand dollars in *bolita* revenue; "Hunt Key Man in Mich. Digit Probe," *CD*, 7 May 1959.

32. "High Says It's a Threat to Morals," *MH* (no date or page provided), WTVJ Collection, box 81, "Slum Clearance" folder 1, HASF.

33. "Land Owner Fights Bolita Ring Charge," *MN*, 26 February 1959.

34. "A Good Word for Miami," *MH*, 30 April 1922.

35. Roderick Waters, "Dr. William B. Sawyer of Colored Town," *Tequesta* 57 (1997): 67–80, esp. 67, 69, 70; Arthur E. Chapman, "The History of the Black Police Force and Court in the City of Miami" (PhD diss., University of Miami, 1986), 18.

36. Clarence Taylor, *Black Religious Intellectuals: The Fight for Equality from Jim Crow to the 21st Century* (New York: Routledge, 2002), 82.

37. Ibid., 83; Culmer interview, 5. On the politics of black respectability as they related to urban prostitution, see Victoria W. Wolcott, *Remaking Respectability: African American Women in Interwar Detroit* (Chapel Hill: University of North Carolina Press, 2001), 7.

38. Michele Mitchell, *Righteous Propagation: African Americans and the Politics of Racial Destiny after Reconstruction* (Chapel Hill: University of North Carolina Press, 2004), esp. chap. 5, "Making Home Life Measure Up."

39. Jack Kofoed, "Miami," *North American Review* (December 1929): 673, quoted in Arva Moore Parks and Gregory Bush, with Laura Pincus, *Miami, the American Crossroad: A Centennial Journey, 1896–1996* (Needham Heights, MA: Simon and Schuster, 1996), 90.

40. "Miami's Responsibility," *MH*, 20 September 1934.

41. "Sanitation Conditions Fierce, Says Landlord."

42. "Old Responsibility," *MH*, 10 September 1934.

43. "Sanitation Conditions Are Reported Better," *MH*, 16 September 1934.

44. "Sanitation Campaign Co-operation Sought," *MH*, 17 September 1934.

45. "Slum Area Survey Is Ordered by Miami."

46. "Expensive," *MH*, 16 September 1934.

47. "Sanitation Conditions Fierce, Says Landlord."

48. Ibid.

49. Shortly after this decision for vacant land development, a 1935 Kentucky Supreme Court decision would ensure that most public housing across the country went on vacant land rather than serving as an instrument of slum clearance. *U.S. v. Certain Lands in the City of Louisville* (1935); and "Housing Board Here to Conduct Survey," *MH*, 2 September 1934.

50. "Model Housing Project Is Dedicated Here," *MH*, 16 October 1936.

51. "5 Slum Clearance Projects Underway," *ADW*, 1 March 1937; and "Model Housing Project Is Dedicated Here."

52. "Memorandum Report on Miami, Florida, 36th Street Airport Section," 1 May 1944, 3, Records of the Committee on Fair Employment Practices, Part 1—Racial Tension File, 1943–45, Proquest Twentieth Century Black Freedom Struggles.

53. "Liberty Square Will Accommodate 10 Per Cent of Miami's Negro Population," *MH*, 29 July 1940.

54. Dorothy Jenkins Fields, "Tracing Overtown's Vernacular Architecture," Florida theme issue, *Journal of Decorative and Propaganda Arts* 23 (1998): 330; John A. Stuart, "Liberty Square: Florida's First Public Housing Project," in *The New Deal in South Florida: Design, Policy, and Community Building, 1933–1940*, ed. John A. Stuart and John F. Stack (Gainesville: University Press of Florida, 2008), 201; "Edison Court Opens Today," *MH*, 15 December 1939.

55. On white supremacy within congressional deal making over New Deal policy—or the so-called southern cage around US liberalism—see Ira Katznelson, *Fear Itself: The New Deal and the Origins of Our Time* (New York: Liveright Publishing, 2013), esp. 131–223. Katznelson's book, while fully acknowledging the role of southern politicians in drafting and revising New Deal legislation, attempts to draw a distinction between segregation, on the one hand, and "American values and visions," on the other (144). Contemporary scholars in the tradition of critical race theory, following the example of Ida B. Wells, W. E. B. Du Bois, Malcolm X, and others, make no such distinction, preferring to see white supremacy as constitutive of American values and statecraft. Evidence of practices of land development in South Florida affirms this latter view. See also Gary Peller, "Race Consciousness," in "Frontiers of Legal Thought III," *Duke Law Journal* 1990, no. 4 (September 1990): 758–847; Richard Delgado and Jean Stefancic, *Critical Race Theory: The Cultural Edge* (Philadelphia: Temple University Press, 2000); and Desmond King and Stephen Tuck, "De-centering the South:

314 / Notes to Pages 87–92

America's Nationwide White Supremacist Order after Reconstruction," *Past and Present* 194 (2007): 213–53.

56. Raymond A. Mohl, "The Origins of Miami's Liberty City," *Florida Environmental and Urban Issues* 12 (July 1985): 9–12, esp. 11.

57. "Making Miami White: Race, Housing, and Government Policy," *MT*, 12 June 2001; and "Model Housing Project Is Dedicated Here."

58. National Urban League, *Review of Economic and Cultural Problems in Dade County, Florida*, 26; and Dade County Planning Council, "Twenty-Year Plan for Dade County" (1936), quotation in National Urban League, *Review of Economic and Cultural Problems in Dade County, Florida*, 28–29.

59. Dade County Planning Council, "Twenty-Year Plan for Dade County," 27–28, 31. On the CCC in Dade County, see "Dade CCC Camp Observes Sixth Birthday Today," *MN*, 9 April 1939.

60. Stuart, "Liberty Square: Florida's First Public Housing Project," 192–93.

61. Liberty Square residents were required to make between $591 and $869 a year. Families in the white Edison Courts project were required to make between $722 and $963 a year. "Architects Perspective," *MH*, 28 July 1940; "Santa Claus Visits Slums When Edison Courts Open," *MH*, 16 December 1939; and Stuart, "Liberty Square: Florida's First Public Housing Project," 198, 211.

62. "Slum Area Survey Is Ordered by Miami."

63. "Clean-Up Activities Begin in Slum Areas," *MH*, 12 September 1934.

64. "Offer Big Bond for Bad Negro," *MH*, 22 November 1920.

65. "What Miami Colored People Are Doing for the Betterment of the Race in Every Way," *MH*, 27 November 1917.

66. "Condemned Houses Will Be Torn Down," *MH*, 14 September 1934.

67. Mary McLeod Bethune, "On the Home Soil," 17 March 1938, 2, Mary McLeod Bethune Papers, Bethune Foundation Collection, Part 3, Subject Files, 1939–55.

68. "Minutes of the Advisory Board," 2 April 1936, NARA, RG 196, box 299; and H. A. Gray to Clarence Coe, 24 October 1936, NARA, RG 196, box 299.

69. M. Athalie Range, interviewed by Stephanie Wanza, 28 August 1997, 28, Tell the Story Collection, BA; and Edward Braynon, interviewed by Stephanie Wanza, 6 August 1997, 26, Tell the Story Collection, BA.

70. James E. Scott, "Miami's Liberty Square Project," *Crisis* 49, no. 3 (March 1942): 87.

71. "The World Today," *PC*, 6 December 1941.

72. Glenda Elizabeth Gilmore, *Defying Dixie: The Radical Roots of Civil Rights, 1919–1950* (New York: Norton, 2008), 67–105; Robin D. G. Kelley, *Hammer and Hoe: Alabama Communists during the Great Depression* (Chapel Hill: University of North Carolina Press, 1990); and David Levering Lewis, *W. E. B. Du Bois: The Fight for Equality and the American Century, 1919–1963* (New York: Owl Books, 2000), 204, 256–65, 299, 306–11. See also W. E. B. Du Bois, "Negro Editors on Communism," *Crisis* (June 1932): 190–91, cited in Lewis, *W. E. B. Du Bois: Fight for Equality*, 627.

73. James B. Nimmo, quoted in Melanie Shell-Weiss, *Coming to Miami: A Social History* (Gainesville: University Press of Florida, 2009), 89.

74. "Miami Appoints Negro Policeman," *PC*, 16 January 1937; and "Miami Continues Reign of Terrorism," *PC*, 12 June 1937.

75. Correspondence to Mary McLeod Bethune from Edgar B. Young and correspondence from S. Bobo Dean to Walter Butler Co., 13 October 1936, "New Deal Agencies and Black America," Proquest Twentieth Century Black Freedom Struggles.

76. Shell-Weiss, *Coming to Miami*, 119.

77. Correspondence from Charles S. Thompson to the National Association for the Advancement of Colored People, 11 August 1931, "Miami, Florida White Primary" folder, Papers of the NAACP, Part 4, Voting Rights Campaign, 1916–50, Series C: Administrative File: Subject File—Discrimination, Proquest History Vault.

78. "The Horizon," *PC*, 13 May 1939.

79. "And Now, Negroes of Miami Not Only Register and Vote, but Are Showing the Way," *PC*, 22 June 1940.

80. Public Works Administration, "Allotted Projects," 29 March 1937, Series 450, box 13, 2, SAF.

81. "Gables Lays New Library Cornerstone," *MN*, 10 January 1937; and "Officials Dedicate Community House," *MH*, 10 January 1937.

82. "Miami's First Library for Negroes Formally Opened as Boys and Girls Hurry to Paint Small Home of Books," *MH*, 27 March 1938; and Fields, "Tracing Overtown's Vernacular Architecture," 325.

83. "Stadium Wins by Landslide Vote in Miami," *MH*, 5 December 1936; "Projects for Miami Involve Large Sums," *MH*, 3 January 1937; and "Orange Bowl Story Is Told in Detail," *MH*, 13 December 1937.

84. "Proposed Stadium Costing $225,000 to Be Constructed at Miami Field," *MH*, 3 May 1936; "Opening Roddey [*sic*] Burdine Stadium Is Set for Tonight," *MH*, 24 September 1937; "And Now, Negroes of Miami Not Only Register and Vote, but Are Showing the Way." On land development as integral to the success of the New Deal, see Jason Scott Smith, *Building New Deal Liberalism: The Political Economy of Public Works, 1933–1956* (Cambridge: Cambridge University Press, 2006).

85. Robert O. Self, *American Babylon: Race and the Struggle for Postwar Oakland* (Princeton, NJ: Princeton University Press, 2003), 117; and David M. P. Freund, "Marketing the Free Market: State Intervention and the Politics of Prosperity in Metropolitan America," in *The New Suburban History*, ed. Kevin M. Kruse and Thomas J. Sugrue, 11–32 (Chicago: University of Chicago Press, 2006), 15.

86. National Emergency Council for Florida, "Christmas," in *Biweekly Bulletin Concerning the Activities of Federal Agencies in Florida*, 15 December 1936, 2, Series 450, box 14, p. 2, SAF.

87. "FHA Insured Mortgages on 1,876 Residences in '39," *MH*, 17 December 1939.

88. Mid-Southside Better Housing Committee, "The Apparent Failure in One Respect of the Objectives of the Federal Housing Administration," 2 September 1935, Mary McLeod Bethune Papers, the Bethune Foundation Collection, Part 3, Subject Files, 1939–55, "Housing—Federal Programs, 1930s" folder; and St. Clair Drake and Horace Cayton, *Black Metropolis: A Study of Negro Life in a Northern City* (1945; repr., Chicago: University of Chicago Press, 1993), 212.

89. David M. P. Freund, *Colored Property: State Policy and White Racial Politics in Suburban America* (Chicago: University of Chicago Press, 2007), 285, 294, 327.

90. Kenneth Jackson, *Crabgrass Frontier: The Suburbanization of the United States* (Oxford: Oxford University Press, 1985), 198–99; and HOLC Security Map Summary, p. 1, RG 195, Records of the Federal Home Loan Bank Board, Home Owners Loan Corporation, Records Relating to the City Survey File, 1935–40, entry 39, "Florida Miami" folder, box 81, NARA.

91. Homer Hoyt, *The Structure and Growth of Residential Neighborhoods in American Cities* (Chicago: University of Chicago Press, 1939).

92. HOLC Security Map Area descriptions: "Downtown Northeast Section. Negro Area, Miami, Florida, Security Grade D," "Coconut Grove, Miami, Florida, Security Grade

D," RG 195, Records of the Federal Home Loan Bank Board, Home Owners Loan Corporation, Records Relating to the City Survey File, 1935–40, entry 39, "Florida Miami" folder, box 81, NARA.

93. Alec C. Morgan, *Report of Survey: Miami, Florida, for the Division of Research and Statistics, Home Owners Loan Corporation, Washington D.C.*, 19 September 1938, 25, RG 195, Records of the Federal Home Loan Bank Board, Home Owners Loan Corporation, Records Relating to the City Survey File, 1935–40, Entry 39, "Florida Miami" folder, box 81, NARA. See also Raymond A. Mohl, "Whitening Miami: Race, Housing, and Government Policy in Twentieth-Century Dade County," *Florida Historical Quarterly* 79, no. 3 (Winter 2001): 326.

94. HOLC Security Map Area descriptions: "Little River Section including Baywood and Morningside, Miami, Florida, Security Grade B," "Outlying western and Southern portion of Miami Shores, Florida, Security Grade B," "Western Section—Biscayne Park North Miami, Florida, Security Grade B," "Old Shenandoah, and major portions between S.W. 13th and 25th Avenue and 8th Street and the Florida East Coast RR, Miami Florida, Security Grade B," "South Central portion of Coral Gables, Coral Gables, Florida, Security Grade A"—all in RG 195, Records of the Federal Home Loan Bank Board, Home Owners Loan Corporation, Records Relating to the City Survey File, 1935–40, entry 39, "Florida Miami" folder, box 81, NARA.

95. Generally, the Cuban population in these decades before Castro's Communist revolution never surpassed 10 percent in any given neighborhood; HOLC Security Map Neighborhood descriptions: "South of 62nd Street from N.W. 17th Ave to N.E. 4 Ct., Miami, FL, Security Grade D," "Mush Isle and Allapattah Section, Miami, Florida, Security Grade C," "South of Flagler from River to S.W. 22nd Ave and South of Flagler to 15th Street, Security Grade C," "Shore Crest and Belle Meade, Miami, Florida, Security Grade A," "Newly developed portion of Old Shenandoah and immediately adjacent property, Miami, Florida, Security Grade A"—all in RG 195, Records of the Federal Home Loan Bank Board, Home Owners Loan Corporation, Records Relating to the City Survey File, 1935–40, entry 39, "Florida Miami" folder, box 81, NARA.

96. HOLC Security Map, "Southern Tip of Miami Beach, Security Grade C," RG 195, Records of the Federal Home Loan Bank Board, Home Owners Loan Corporation, Records Relating to the City Survey File, 1935–40, entry 39, "Florida Miami" folder, box 81, NARA.

97. The HOLC appraisers in Miami were Kenneth S. Keyes (Realtor), Thomas B. Hamilton (VP of South Atlantic Mortgage Company), Glenn Gold (VP of William H. Gold Company, mortgage brokers, builders, and developers), D. Earl Wilson (professional appraiser), Walter L. Harris (independent real estate broker), Roosevelt C. Houser (president, Florida Bond and Mortgage Company, mortgage brokers), Lon Worth Crow (president, Lon Worth Crow Company, Miami real estate broker and HOLC contract broker); HOLC Security Map Summary, 2; and Jeffery M. Hornstein, *A Nation of Realtors*: A Cultural History of the Twentieth Century American Middle Class* (Durham, NC: Duke University Press, 2005), 144.

98. Mohl, "Whitening Miami," 325–26.

99. Jackson, *Crabgrass Frontier*, esp. chap. 11; HOLC Security Map Appendix, table 18, RG 195, Records of the Federal Home Loan Bank Board, Home Owners Loan Corporation, Records Relating to the City Survey File, 1935–40, entry 39, "Florida Miami" folder, box 81, NARA; and Morgan, *Report of Survey*, 32.

100. US Census Bureau, *Housing*, 7–8, 21–22.

CHAPTER FOUR: PAN-AMERICA

1. In the Bahamas *Junkanoo* occurs on Boxing Day and New Year's Day. However, many black Miamians recall the *Junkanoo* procession happening at a number of key events throughout the year, including Christmas morning and during the Orange Blossom Classic parade, which commemorated the largest black college football game of the year; Rachel Williams, interviewed by Electra R. Ford, 19 August 1997, 13, Tell the Story Collection, BA; Joseph E. Dames II, interviewed by Electra R. Ford, 21 August 1997, 22, Tell the Story Collection, BA. On Jamaican *Jonkonnu,* see Kenneth M. Bilby, "Gumbay, Myal, and the Great House: New Evidence on the Religious Background of Jonkonnu in Jamaica," *African-Caribbean Institute of Jamaica Research Review* 4 (1999): 47–70.

2. Florida International University, Institution of Government, *The Historical Impacts of Transportation Projects on the Overtown Community* (Miami: Metropolitan Planning Organization of Miami-Dade County, 1998), 26; Williams interview, 13; Dames interview, 14–15; Mary Nairn Bloomfield, interviewed by Electra R. Ford, 21 August 1997, 9, Tell the Story Collection, BA; and Cleome Bloomfield, interviewed by Alix Milfort, 7 August 1997, 5, Tell the Story Collection, BA.

3. Office of the County Manager, "Profile of the Black Population in Metropolitan Dade County" (January 1979), 63.

4. On property as a bundle of rights, see Morton J. Horwitz, *The Transformation of American Law, 1870–1960: The Crisis of Legal Orthodoxy* (Oxford: Oxford University Press, 1992), 148–50; and Chris M. Hann, "Introduction: The Embeddedness of Property," in *Property Relations: Renewing the Anthropological Tradition,* ed. C. M. Hann (Cambridge: Cambridge University Press, 1998), 7.

5. "Property . . . presupposes a strong state only some of the time." Charles Geisler, "Ownership in Stateless Places," in *Changing Properties of Property,* ed. Franz von Benda-Beckmann, Keebet von Benda-Beckmann, and Melanie G. Wiber (New York and Oxford: Berghahn Books, 2006), 50.

6. James Weldon Johnson, "Self-Determining Haiti: The American Occupation," *Nation,* 28 August 1920, 236–38; James Weldon Johnson, "Self Determining Haiti: What the United States Has Accomplished," *Nation,* 4 September 1920, 265–67; James Weldon Johnson, "Self-Determining Haiti: Government of, by, and for the National City Bank of New York," *Nation,* 11 September 1920, 295–97; and James Weldon Johnson, "Self-Determining Haiti: The Haitian People," *Nation,* 25 September 1920, 345–47. See also Peter James Hudson, "The National City Bank of New York and Haiti, 1909–1922," *Radical History Review* 115 (Winter 2013): 91–114; and Brenda Gayle Plummer, "The Afro-American Response to the Occupation of Haiti, 1915–1934," *Phylon* 43, no. 2 (2nd quar. 1982): 125–43.

7. "What Is the League against Imperialism and for National Independence" (ca. 1929), Business Records, Membership—Save Haiti League, folder 89, Washington Conservatory of Music Collection, HU. On racism in American foreign policy during the Progressive Era, see also Daniel Walden, "Race and Imperialism: The Achilles Heel of the Progressives," *Science and Society* 31, no. 2 (April 1967): 222–32.

8. Joseph B. Lockey, "The Meaning of Pan Americanism," *American Journal of International Law* 19, no. 1 (January 1925): 105; James Brown Scott, "Good Neighbor Policy," *American Journal of International Law* 30, no. 2 (April 1936): 287–90; Ben F. Crowson, *Pan American Government: A General Survey of True Democracy and Politics in Latin America* (Washington, DC: Pan American Educational Center, 1942); and Mark T. Berger, "Civilising the South: The U.S. Rise to Hegemony in the Americas and

the Roots of 'Latin American Studies,' 1898–1945," *Bulletin of Latin American Research* 12, no. 1 (January 1993): 1–48.

9.   Hans Schmidt, *The United States Occupation of Haiti, 1915–1934* (New Brunswick, NJ: Rutgers University Press, 1995), 6; and Elizabeth Borgwardt, *A New Deal for the World: America's Vision for Human Rights* (Cambridge, MA: Belknap Press of Harvard University Press, 2005), 172–73.

10. A. Curtis Wilgus and Henry Gray, "Pan-American Histograph" (1940); Ben F. Crowson, *Pan American Government: A General Survey of True Democracy and Politics in Latin America* (Washington, DC: Pan American Educational Center, 1942); Federal Security Agency, "A Report on the Activities of the U.S. Office of Education in the Inter-American Field" (1943)—all from A. Curtis Wilgus Papers, box 64, folder 608, UM; and Berger, "Civilising the South."

11. William E. Brown Jr., "Pan Am: Miami's Wings to the World," Florida theme issue, *Journal of Decorative and Propaganda Arts* 23 (1998): 154–57; Thomas P. Caldwell, "The History of Air Transportation in Florida," *Tequesta* 1 (1941): 103–6; and Minister of Foreign Affairs, Dr. Saavedra Lamas of Argentina, quoted in Scott, "Good Neighbor Policy," 290.

12. Arva Moore Parks and Greg Bush, with Laura Pincus, *Miami, the American Crossroad: A Centennial Journey, 1896–1996* (Needham Heights, MA: Simon and Schuster, 1996), 100.

13. On race rumor during World War II, see Howard W. Odum, *Race and Rumors of Race: The American South in the Early Forties* (Baltimore: Johns Hopkins University Press, 1997). "WWII Veteran Recalls Sub Sinking," *MH*, 5 August 1985; Babatunde A. Onafuwa, "Praise the Lord! (And Pass the Ammunition): A Study of the Impact of World War II on a South Florida Community" (unpublished manuscript); Moe Katz, oral history, 28 January 1981; and Joe B. Oliver, oral history, 3 and 25 July 1980—all in Wars and Military Collection, FLHS.

14. August Burghard, oral history, 19 January 1981, Wars and Military Collection, FLHS.

15. Jack Kofoed, *Moon over Miami* (Whitefish, MT: Kessinger Publishing, 2007), 93, 111; correspondence from Chamber of Commerce secretary August Burghard to Roland Ritter, acting regional engineer of the Federal Works Agency, 2 July 1942, Wars and Military Collection, "WWII: Misc. Pamphlets" folder, Hoch Historical Society, FLHS; Philip J. Weidling and August Burghard, *Checkered Sunshine: The Story of Ft. Lauderdale, 1793–1955* (Gainesville: University of Florida Press, 1966), 238, 249, 251; Susan Gillis, *Fort Lauderdale: The Venice of America* (New York: Arcadia Press, 2004), 53, 108; "Boot Camp and Beaches," *SS*, 6 January 2002; August R. Sousa, "All This Is My Recollection of What Happened There . . ." (unpublished manuscript, April 1994), 1–5, Wars box, BA; see also Nathan Daniel Beau Connolly, "By Eminent Domain: Race and Capital in the Building of an American South Florida" (PhD diss., University of Michigan, 2008), 170–73.

16. "Summary of the Origins, Development, and Promotion of Overseas and International Air Transport by Pan American World Airways, Inc.," pp. 21, 47, box 200, folder 20, Pan American World Airways Inc. Records, UM.

17. Gary M. Mormino, "Midas Returns: Miami Goes to War, 1941–1945," *Tequesta* 57 (1997): 13, 22; and Brown, "Pan Am," 159.

18. Greater Miami Chamber of Commerce, Minutes of Committee on Pan American Relations, 18 September 1942, *Committee Meetings Minutes, vol. 2 (1941–1946)*, Greater Miami Chamber of Commerce Collection, HASF.

19. Marian D. Irish, "Foreign Policy and the South," *Journal of Politics* 10, no. 2 (May 1948): 306.

20. Johnson, "Self-Determining Haiti: What the United States Has Accomplished," 267.
21. Aline Helg, *Our Rightful Share: The Afro-Cuban Struggle for Equality, 1886–1912* (Chapel Hill: University of North Carolina Press, 1995); Barry Carr, "'Omnipotent and Omnipresent'? Labor Shortages, Worker Mobility and Employer Control in the Cuban Sugar Industry, 1910–1934," in *Identity and Struggle at the Margins of the Nation State: The Laboring People of Central America and the Hispanic Caribbean*, ed. Aviva Chomsky and Aldo Lauria-Santiago, 260–91 (Durham, NC: Duke University Press, 1998); George W. Westerman, "School Segregation on the Panama Canal Zone," *Phylon* 15, no. 3 (3rd quar. 1954): 276–87; and Harvey Neptune, *Caliban and the Yankees: Trinidad and the United States Occupation* (Chapel Hill: University of North Carolina Press, 2007), 9, 27.
22. Thomas Borstelmann, *The Cold War and the Color Line: American Race Relations in the Global Arena* (Cambridge, MA: Harvard University Press, 2001), 29; and Ira Katznelson, *Fear Itself: The New Deal and the Origins of Our Time* (New York: Liveright Publishing, 2013), esp. chap. 5, "Jim Crow Congress," 156–94.
23. Andrew B. Wertheimer, "Admitting Nebraska's Nisei: Japanese American Students at the University of Nebraska, 1942–1945," *Nebraska History* 83 (2002): 58–72.
24. City Planning Board of Miami, *Miami's Railway Terminal Problem* (6 January 1941), 9.
25. Ibid., 14, 15.
26. Correspondence from William W. Dohany, manager of the Better Business Division of the Miami Chamber of Commerce, to A. Curtis Wilgus, 7 April 1942, A. Curtis Wilgus Papers, box 65, folder 616, UM.
27. David Simpson Jr., executive secretary of the Miami Planning and Zoning Board, to members of the Miami Planning and Zoning Board, 26 February 1962. The Interama project was not fully abandoned until 1974.
28. *Time* magazine quotation in correspondence from Charles Sykes to A. B. Curry, 7 December 1944, Office of the Miami City Clerk, *Resolutions and Minutes of the City Commission, 1921–1986*, box 30, SAF.
29. Irish, "Foreign Policy and the South," 307.
30. United States Department of Commerce, *Foreign Commerce and Navigation in the United States*, vol. 2, *Shipments by Vessel*, 1947, cited in Irish, "Foreign Policy and the South," 316.
31. A. Curtis Wilgus, "Summary Report on Inter-American Center Activities in Florida" (1946), 6, A. Curtis Wilgus Papers, box 56, folder 510, UM.
32. Greater Miami Chamber of Commerce, Minutes of Committee on Pan American Relations, 18 September 1942.
33. Greater Miami Chamber of Commerce, Meeting Minutes of Conference on Tourist Promotion, 6 April 1945, 1, *Committee Meetings Minutes, vol. 2 (1941–1946)*, Greater Miami Chamber of Commerce Collection, HASF; and correspondence from Benton E. Jacobs, manager of the Miami News Bureau, to J. W. Power, director of the city of Miami's Publicity Department, 1 July 1946 and 7 July 1946, Office of the Miami City Clerk, *Resolutions and Minutes of the City Commission, 1921–1986*, box 33, SAF.
34. Saavedra Lamas, minister of foreign affairs of Argentina, quoted in Scott, "Good Neighbor Policy," 290; and agenda point 17, "Simon Bolivar Memorial," 17 January 1945, Office of the Miami City Clerk, *Resolutions and Minutes of the City Commission, 1921–1986*, box 31, SAF.
35. Wilgus, "Summary Report on Inter-American Center Activities in Florida," 7; and A. Curtis Wilgus, "Opinions of Leading Individuals in Florida" (1946), 2, 4, 5, A. Curtis Wilgus Papers, box 56, folder 510, UM; and "Miami," *CD*, 22 January 1949.

36. Millery Polyné, *From Douglass to Duvalier: U.S. African Americans, Haiti, and Pan Americanism, 1870–1964* (Gainesville: University Press of Florida, 2011), 8.

37. For impressive historical treatments of the role of black landowners, elites, or chiefs in the modernization of colonial economies—a variation of what occurred in Jim Crow America during the 1940s and 1950s—see Jocelyn Alexander, *The Unsettled Land: State-Making and the Politics of Land in Zimbabwe, 1893–2003* (Athens: Ohio University Press, 2006), 83–104; and Frantz Fanon, *The Wretched of the Earth* (New York: Grove Press, 1963), 148–205. See also Kevin K. Gaines, *American Africans in Ghana: Black Expatriates and the Civil Rights Era* (Chapel Hill: University of North Carolina Press, 2006).

38. Polyné, *From Douglass to Duvalier*, 90, 110, 128. See also Frank Andre Guridy, *Forging Diaspora: Afro-Cubans and African Americans in a World of Empire and Jim Crow* (Chapel Hill: University of North Carolina Press, 2010), 11.

39. Correspondence from Claude Barnett to Kelsey Pharr, 21 February 1950 and 5 April 1950, "Funeral Directors, especially Kelsey Pharr" folder, Associate Negro Press, Part 3, Subject Files on Black Americans, 1918–67, Series C—Economic Conditions, 1918–66, Claude Barnett Papers, Proquest Twentieth Century Black Freedom Struggles.

40. "Virgin Islands Governor to Address King of Club Forum," *ADW*, 21 January 1948.

41. Correspondence from Claude Barnett to Kelsey Pharr, 5 April 1950, 2 June 1952, 23 February 1957, 31 October 1957, and 7 March 1962; correspondence from Kelsey Pharr to Claude Barnett, 12 December 1961—all in "Funeral Directors, especially Kelsey Pharr" folder, Associate Negro Press, Part 3, Subject Files on Black Americans, 1918–67, Series C—Economic Conditions, 1918–66, Claude Barnett Papers, Proquest Twentieth Century Black Freedom Struggles.

42. Correspondence from Claude Barnett to Kelsey Pharr, 2 June 1952.

43. "Haitian Feted by High Southern Dignitaries," *NAN*, 2 November 1935.

44. "Florida Insults Stenio Vincent," *PC*, 16 December 1939; N. D. B. Connolly, "Timely Innovations: Planes, Trains, and the 'Whites Only' Economy of a Pan-American City," *Urban History* 36, no. 2 (2009): 257–58; and Plummer, "Afro-American Response to the Occupation of Haiti, 1915–1934," 142.

45. "Cuba Welcomes U.S. Tourists, Blames Air Line for Jim Crow," *BAA*, 13 July 1940; and "Pan American Lines Boasts of Race Equality," *CD*, 16 February 1946.

46. War Food Administration, *Consolidated Report of Jamaican Workers Assigned to Industrial Companies (War Manpower Commission)—Recruited: Division I, from 10-15 to 12-15-55*, 21 December 1944, RG 224, Records of the Office of Labor, General Correspondence, August 1943–December 1944, entry no. 6, box 13, "6-T27 War Manpower Commission Jamaicans" folder, NARA.

47. Ira De Augustine Reid, *The Negro Immigrant: His Background, Characteristics and Social Adjustment, 1899–1937* (New York: Columbia University Press, 1939), 529–31.

48. Thomas A. Guglielmo, "Fighting for Caucasian Rights: Mexicans, Mexican Americans, and the Transnational Struggle for Civil Rights in World War II Texas," *Journal of American History* 92, no. 4 (March 2006): 1212–37.

49. "An Agreement between the Governments of the United States of America and of Jamaica Modifying the Terms of an Agreement Dated the 2nd Day of April 1943 between the Aforesaid Governments," 4 March 1945, RG 224, Records of the Office of Labor, General Correspondence, 1945–47, entry no. 8, box 11, "Laborers 18 Jamaicans 1945" folder, NARA.

50. Mormino, "Midas Returns," 36.

51. United States Department of Agriculture, War Food Administration, "Work Agreement (Bahamian Dairy Workers)," 16 March 1943, RG 224, Records of the Office of Labor, General Correspondence, 1945–47, entry no. 8, box 11, "Laborers 18 Bahamians 1945" folder, NARA.

52. Herbert McDonald, *Welcome to the United States*, 1943, RG 107, Office of Assistant Secretary of War, Civil Aide to the Secretary Subject File, 1940–47, entry no. 188, box 212, "Jamaica Labor" folder, NARA.

53. Correspondence from W. A. Anglim, chief of operations, Berkeley, CA, to unnamed recipient, 24 May 1945, RG 224, Records of the Office of Labor, General Correspondence, 1945–47, entry no. 8, box 11, "Laborers 18 Jamaicans 1945" folder, NARA.

54. "Agreement between the Governments of the United States of America and of Jamaica Modifying the Terms of an Agreement Dated the 2nd Day of April 1943 between the Aforesaid Governments"; correspondence from L. A. Wheeler, Department of Agriculture, to Ruth B. Shipley, chief, Passport Division, State Department, 28 October 1943, RG 224, Records of the Office of Labor, General Correspondence, August 1943–December 1944, entry no. 6, box 10, "6-M26 Jamaican" folder, NARA; correspondence from George W. Hill, chief, Program Branch, War Food Administration, to American Miller, Chicago, IL, 25 July 1944, RG 224, Records of the Office of Labor, General Correspondence, August 1943–December 1944, entry no. 6, box 11, "6-R15 Jamaicans 1944" folder, NARA; and correspondence from K. A. Butler, assistant director of labor, War Food Administration, to Marvin Jones, administrator, War Food Administration, 9 June 1945, RG 224, Records of the Office of Labor, General Correspondence, 1945–47, entry no. 8, box 10, "Laborers 11 Recruitment—Requests" folder, NARA.

55. Correspondence from Mason Barr, chief, Interstate Foreign Labor Branch, to Belle City Malleable Iron Company, 14 October 1943, RG 224, Records of the Office of Labor, General Correspondence, August 1943–December 1944, entry no. 6, box 10, "6-M26 Jamaican" folder, NARA; correspondence from Lemuel L. Foster, race relations analyst, to Col. John L. Collins, re: "Bahama Farm Workers in New Jersey," 25 May 1943, RG 107, Office of the Assistant Secretary of War, Civil Aide to the Secretary Subject File, 1940–47, entry no. 188, box 212, "Jamaica Labor" folder, NARA; and correspondence from Guy Dowdy, state supervisor (Ohio), Emergency Farm Labor, to M. C. Wilson, deputy director of extension, in charge of farm labor, Department of Agriculture, 27 October 1944, RG 224, Records of the Office of Labor, General Correspondence, August 1943–December 1944, entry no. 6, box 10, "6-M26 Jamaican" folder, NARA.

56. Cindy Hahamovitch, *No Man's Land: Jamaican Guestworkers in America and the Global History of Deportable Labor* (Princeton, NJ: Princeton University Press, 2011), 100.

57. Correspondence from Guy Dowdy, state supervisor (Ohio), Emergency Farm Labor, to M. C. Wilson, deputy director of extension, in charge of farm labor, Department of Agriculture, 27 October 1944.

58. Memorandum from Truman K. Gibson Jr., acting civilian aide to the secretary of war, to John. J. McCloy, assistant secretary of war, 17 May 1943, RG 107, Office of the Assistant Secretary of War, Civil Aide to the Secretary Subject File, 1940–47, entry no. 188, box 212, "Jamaica Labor" folder, NARA; and correspondence from John J. McCloy, assistant secretary of war, to James F. Burns, director of economic stabilization, 18 May 1943, RG 107, Office of the Assistant Secretary of War, Civil Aide to the Secretary Subject File, 1940–47, entry no. 188, box 212, "Jamaica Labor" folder, NARA.

59. Gerald Horne, *Cold War in a Hot Zone: The United States Confronts Labor and Independence Struggles in the British West Indies* (Philadelphia: Temple University Press, 2007), 49.

60. Correspondence from George W. Hill, War Food Administration, to Lt. Col. Jay L. Taylor, deputy administrator, 17 May 1943, RG 224, Records of the Office of Labor, General Correspondence, March–July 1943, entry no. 1, box 15, "Farm Labor 3–4 Jamaican" folder, NARA.

61. War Problems Committee, "Estimated Labor Distribution by Counties, Florida 1943–44 Season: Oranges, Grapefruit, Tangerines, and Limes," 17 July 1943; quote in correspondence from L. L. Chandler, president, Goulds Growers Inc., and chairman of Farm Labor Committee for Florida Vegetable Committee, to US senator Claude Pepper and US representative Pat Cannon, 4 October 1943—both in Records of the Office of Labor, General Correspondence, August 1943–December 1944, entry no. 6, box 11, "6-R15 Florida July–December 1943" folder, NARA; "Agreement between the Governments of the United States of America and of Jamaica Modifying the Terms of an Agreement Dated the 2nd Day of April 1943 between the Aforesaid Governments"; and correspondence from G. W. Hill, Office of Labor, Department of Agriculture, to Experiment Station, FL, US Sugar Corporation, 29 September 1943, Records of the Office of Labor, General Correspondence, 1945–47, entry no. 8, box 11, "Laborers 18 Jamaicans 1945" folder, NARA. See also Jerrell H. Shofner, "The Legacy of Racial Slavery: Free Enterprise and Forced Labor in Florida in the 1940s," *Journal of Southern History* 47, no. 3 (August 1981): 414.

62. Correspondence from Albert Maverick Jr., acting chief, Operations Branch, to H. W. Rainey, chief of operations, Atlanta, GA, 14 August 1945, RG 224, Records of the Office of Labor, General Correspondence, 1945–47, entry no. 8, box 10, "Laborers 9 Personal Property" folder, NARA.

63. Hahamovitch, *No Man's Land*, 98.

64. Correspondence from Col. Philip G. Bruton, director, Army Corps of Engineers, to Pat Cannon, US House of Representatives, 13 October 1943; and correspondence from Col. Philip G. Bruton, director, Army Corps of Engineers, to Claude Pepper, US Senate, 13 October 1943—both in RG 224, Records of the Office of Labor, General Correspondence, August 1943–December 1944, entry no. 6, box no. 11, "6-R15 Florida July–December 1943" folder, NARA.

65. Raymond A. Mohl, "Black Immigrants in Early Twentieth-Century Miami," *Florida Historical Quarterly* 65, no. 3 (January 1987): 294.

66. Bill Sawyer, interviewed by Stephanie Wanza, 25 August 1997, 10–12, Tell the Story Collection, BA.

67. Ibid.

68. West Indian labor contracts were, like most else in Jim Crow, a site of negotiation. They tended to be more favorable than American Negro labor terms, but only marginally. Hahamovitch, *No Man's Land*, 99.

69. Greater Miami Chamber of Commerce, Minutes of the Industrial Management Council Executive Committee, 24 August 1943; Minutes of the Special Labor Study Committee, 22 November 1943, 2–5; 26 November 1943—all in *Committee Meetings Minutes, vol. 2 (1941–1946)*, Greater Miami Chamber of Commerce Collection, HASF.

70. Correspondence from H. Leslie Quigg to Miami City Managers Andrew Bloodworth and A. B. Curry, 23 January 1942 and 17 February 1942, respectively; 25 February 1945 meeting of the Miami City Commission, Office of the Miami City Clerk, *Resolutions and Minutes of the City Commission, 1921–1986*, box 28, SAF.

71. Correspondence from Lt. C. O. Huttoe to H. Leslie Quigg et al., 27 December 1941, Unnumbered and Undated Resolution, 30 December 1941, Office of the Miami City Clerk, *Resolutions and Minutes of the City Commission, 1921–1986*, box 28, SAF; and sworn testimony of H. Leslie Quigg, Suspension Hearing transcripts, 18 May 1944, Office of the Miami City Clerk, *Resolutions and Minutes of the City Commission, 1921–1986*, box 30, SAF.

72. James W. Loewen, *Sundown Towns: A Hidden Dimension of American Racism* (New York: New Press, 2005); Roberta Thompson, interviewed by Electra Ford, 29 August 1997, 22, Tell the Story Collection; Claude David, interviewed by Kitty Oliver, 8 September 1999 (audio recording), Crossing the Racial Divide Collection, AALCC; and Joe Wheeler, interviewed by Kitty Oliver, 24 September 1999 (audio recording), Crossing the Racial Divide / Kitty Oliver Collection, AALCC.

73. Peggy McKinney, interviewed by Alix Milfort, 14 August 1997, 10, Tell the Story Collection, BA.

74. On interracial leisure, see Bryant Simon, *Boardwalk of Dreams: Atlantic City and the Fate of Urban America* (New York: Oxford University Press, 2004); Lizabeth Cohen, *Making a New Deal: Industrial Workers in Chicago, 1919–1939* (Cambridge: Cambridge University Press, 1990); and Grace Elizabeth Hale, *Making Whiteness: The Culture of Segregation in the South, 1890–1940* (New York: Vintage Books, 1999).

75. "Merry-Go-Round," *SPT*, 17 March 1943.

76. M. Athalie Range, interviewed by Stephanie Wanza, 28 August 1997, 16, Tell the Story Collection, BA; Dames interview, 39; and Sam Dietz, interviewed by Kitty Oliver, 18 September 1999 (audio recording), Crossing the Racial Divide / Kitty Oliver Collection, AALCC.

77. L. R. Reynolds, "Florida Trip—Feb. 1–8, 1931," quoted in Eric Tscheschlok, "'So Goes the Negro': Race and Labor in Miami, 1940–1963, *Florida Historical Quarterly* 76, no. 1 (Summer 1997), 47.

78. "Miami," *CD*.

79. For a compelling discussion of African-American drowning deaths as a general feature of Jim Crow, see Andrew W. Kahrl, *The Land Was Ours: African American Beaches from Jim Crow to the Sunbelt South* (Cambridge, MA: Harvard University Press, 2012), esp. chap. 4, "Surviving the Summer."

80. For great social histories of numbers rackets in the urban North, for instance, see Victoria W. Wolcott, *Remaking Respectability: African American Women in Interwar Detroit* (Chapel Hill: University of North Carolina Press, 2001); and Davarian L. Baldwin, *Chicago's New Negroes: Modernity, the Great Migration, and Black Urban Life* (Chapel Hill: University of North Carolina Press, 2007).

81. "Murder Again!" *MT*, 20 October 1948; "Murder Again!" *MT*, 20 November 1948; and "Iceman Killed in Barroom Fight," *MT*, 18 December 1948.

82. "Bolita," *MN*, 14 April 1950.

83. Greater Miami Chamber of Commerce, Meeting Minutes of the Traffic Committee, 20 December 1940, 3, *Committee Meetings Minutes, vol. 2 (1941–1946)*, Greater Miami Chamber of Commerce Collection, HASF; Walter H. Headley Jr. interview, in Arthur E. Chapman, "The History of the Black Police Force and Court in the City of Miami" (PhD diss., University of Miami, 1986), 132; and "Trap White Cop in Extortion Plot," *PC*, 21 May 1949.

84. "Stabbed to Death by Common Law Husband," *MT*, 9 July 1949.

85. Doris J. Gramling interview, in Chapman, "History of the Black Police Force and Court in the City of Miami," 172.

86. Mercedes H. Brown, "Negro Youth Looks at Miami," *Crisis* 49, no. 3 (March 1942): 84.

87. "Swinging the News," *CD*, 21 January 1950; "Porter Found Selling Bolita at Beach Hotel," *MT*, 5 February 1949; Office of the Miami City Clerk, *Resolutions and Minutes of the City Commission, 1921–1986*, 28 January 1958, box 50, SAF; "Dade Grand Jury System Background" (2), 4 (1964), Don Shoemaker Papers, "Dade County Grand Jury" folder, box 6, UNC; T. J. English, *Havana Nocturne: How the Mob Owned Cuba . . . and Then Lost It to the Revolution* (New York: Harper, 2008), 56; and Circuit Court of the Eleventh Judicial Circuit of Florida in and for the County of Dade, "Bolita," *Final Report of the Grand Jury*, 10 May 1960, 7.

88. "Dixie's First Negro Judge Lauds His Own Appointment," *NAN*, 29 April 1950.

89. Chapman, "History of the Black Police Force and Court in the City of Miami," 122.

90. "Murder Again!" *MT*, 20 November 1948.

91. "'Life Too Cheap' Say Race Leaders," *ADW*, 24 November 1943.

92. Kelsey Pharr interview, in Chapman, "History of the Black Police Force and Court in the City of Miami," 134.

93. "Fla. Community Asks Stiff Penalty in Race Murders," *CD*, 13 November 1943.

94. Correspondence from Kelsey Pharr to Claude Barnett, 25 May 1939, "Funeral Directors, especially Kelsey Pharr" folder, Associate Negro Press, Part 3, Subject Files on Black Americans, 1918–67, Series C—Economic Conditions, 1918–66, Claude Barnett Papers, Proquest Twentieth Century Black Freedom Struggles.

95. Negotiating "minority status" in colonized nations routinely included providing black and brown people with gradual access to police positions in segregated enclaves, judgeships with authorities over minorities alone, and other highly monitored and mediated forms of state power. See Todd Shepard, *The Invention of Decolonization: The Algerian War and the Remaking of France* (Ithaca, NY: Cornell University Press, 2006), 155–59; Morton Sosna, *In Search of the Silent South: Southern Liberals and the Race Issue* (New York: Columbia University Press, 1977), 19; and Kimberly Johnson, *Reforming Jim Crow: Southern Politics and State in the Age before* Brown (Oxford: Oxford University Press, 2010). See also Karen Kruse Thomas, "The Hill-Burton Act and Civil Rights: Expanding Hospital Care for Black Southerners, 1939–1960," *Journal of Southern History* 72, no. 4 (November 2006): 823–70.

96. George Smathers, "St. Petersburg Speech," 6 April 1950, Saint Petersburg, FL, "Speeches and Statements by George Smathers" folder, box 1, Pepper-Smathers Collection, UF.

97. For cultural arguments explaining Caribbean radicalism, see W. A. Domingo, "Gift of the Black Tropics" in *The New Negro*, ed. Alain Locke (New York: Albert and Charles Boni, 1925), 345–46. See also Winston James, *Holding Aloft the Banner of Ethiopia: Caribbean Radicalism in Early Twentieth Century America* (London: Verso, 1998).

98. Charles W. Mills, *The Racial Contract* (Ithaca, NY: Cornell University Press, 1997).

99. Preston H. Smith II, *Racial Democracy and the Black Metropolis: Housing Policy in Postwar Chicago* (Minneapolis: University of Minnesota Press, 2012), 15, 19; Touré Reed, *Not Alms but Opportunity: The Urban League and the Politics of Racial Uplift, 1910–1950* (Chapel Hill: University of North Carolina Press, 2008), 191; and Wendy L. Wall, *Inventing the "American Way": The Politics of Consensus from the New Deal to the Civil Rights Movement* (Oxford: Oxford University Press, 2008), 167.

100. Office of the Miami City Clerk, *Resolutions and Minutes of the City Commission, 1921–1986*, 18 December 1946, box 33, SAF; and Howard N. Rabinowitz, "From Exclusion to Segregation: Southern Race Relations, 1865–1890," *Journal of American History* 63, no. 2 (September 1976): 325–50. See also Dan Carter, "Southern Political Style,"

in *The Age of Segregation: Race Relations in the South, 1890–1945*, ed. Robert Haws, 45–66 (Jackson: University Press of Mississippi, 1978), esp. 60–65; and David T. Beito and Linda Royster Beito, *Black Maverick: T. R. M. Howard's Fight for Civil Rights and Economic Power* (Urbana and Chicago: University of Illinois Press, 2009).

101. "The Adelphia Club . . . ," *Crisis* 49, no. 3 (March 1942): 97.

102. Correspondence from George Smathers to Ira Davis, 20 July 1954, "Political—1950 Campaign—misc." folder, box 319, George A. Smathers Papers, UF.

103. George A. Smathers, "Memorandum," 6 December 1949, "Political—1950 Campaign—misc." folder, box 319, George A. Smathers Papers, UF. On the stump in 1950, for instance, Smathers made sure to quote Lawson Thomas, an Adelphia Club member, who apparently believed that the Fair Employment Practices Commission, "if enacted, would set back one hundred years the progress the Negro has made in the U.S." "Speech Material FEPC," "General Information Concerning FEPC 1950, 52–53" folder, box 302, George A. Smathers Papers, UF.

104. Memorandum from George Weaver to Jack Kroll, 24 June 1949, folder 11, "Negro Organizations," box 37, Series 204A, RG 200, FSU.

105. Alex Lichtenstein, "The End of Southern Liberalism: Race, Class and the Defeat of Claude Pepper in the 1950 Florida Democratic Primary," unpublished paper presented at University of California, Santa Barbara, 26 September 2008, 8, used with written permission from Lichtenstein.

106. "And Now, Negroes of Miami Not Only Register and Vote, but Are Showing the Way," *PC*, 22 June 1940.

107. Miami Chamber of Commerce, Meeting Minutes of the Inter-racial Committee, 26 January 1945, *Committee Meetings Minutes, vol. 2 (1941–1946)*, Greater Miami Chamber of Commerce collection, HASF.

108. Parks and Bush, *Miami, the American Crossroad*, 84.

109. Eugenia Thomas, from screening of Virginia Key Beach Museum and State Park Oral History Project, 21 July 2005, Joseph Caleb Center, Miami.

110. See Victoria Wolcott, *Race, Riots, and Rollercoasters: The Struggle over Segregated Recreation in America* (Philadelphia: University of Pennsylvania Press, 2012); and Kahrl, *Land Was Ours*.

111. *Report of the Citizens' Committee Made Pursuant to Resolution 25779 of the City of Miami, October 28, 1953*, 7, Office of the Miami City Clerk, *Resolutions and Minutes of the City Commission, 1921–1986*, box 43, SAF.

112. Gwendolyn Sawyer Cherry, quoted in Roderick Waters, "Dr. William B. Sawyer of Colored Town," *Tequesta* 57 (1997): 74.

113. "Evidence Taken before the Citizens' Committee of the City of Miami, State of Florida on Tuesday, August 25, 1953, at 12:45 O'clock P.M., Room 221 of Shoreland Building, Miami, Florida," 172–73, Office of the Miami City Clerk, *Resolutions and Minutes of the City Commission, 1921–1986*, box 43, SAF.

114. "2,320 at Virginia Beach Sunday," *MT*, 5 February 1949; and "15,000 Worshippers Expected to Attend," *MT*, 16 April 1949.

115. "Evidence Taken before the Citizens' Committee of the City of Miami, State of Florida on Tuesday, August 25, 1953," 193.

116. Leah Sands, from screening of Virginia Key Beach Museum and State Park Oral History Project, 21 July 2005, Joseph Caleb Center, Miami; and Joyce Dent, interviewed by Kitty Oliver, 25 October 1999 (audio recording), Crossing the Racial Divide / Kitty Oliver Collection, AALCC.

117. "Miami Appoints Negro Policeman," *PC*, 16 January 1937.

118. Lawson Thomas interview, in Chapman, "History of the Black Police Force and Court in the City of Miami," 142.

119. Ralph V. White Sr. interview, in Chapman, "History of the Black Police Force and Court in the City of Miami," 233; and "Patrolman (Negro) City of Miami," MT, 6 November 1948.

120. "Foreword" and "What Leading Miamians Are Saying . . . ," in "A Welcome to Our Negro Policemen by the Citizens of Miami," 17 September 1944, Law Enforcement (Police) City of Miami Collection, BA.

121. Kahrl, Land Was Ours, 204–8.

122. "Two More Officers Describe Bolita Protection by Police," MN, 16 February 1960.

123. "Officer Beat Them, Two Say," MH, 10 October 1951.

124. Edward Kimble quotation in Jacob Bernstein, "Black in Blue," MNT, 13 November 1997.

125. African American Appointments by Year in Southern Cities, unpublished report (no date provided), "Law Enforcement (Police) City of Miami" Collection, BA.

126. Jennifer Fronc, "The Horns of the Dilemma: Race Mixing and the Enforcement of Jim Crow in New York City," Journal of Urban History 33, no. 1 (November 2006): 2–25; and Ronald H. Bayor, Race and the Shaping of Twentieth-Century Atlanta (Chapel Hill: University of North Carolina Press, 1996), esp. chap. 5.

127. William Wilbanks, Forgotten Heroes: Black Police Officers Killed in Dade County, 1944–1995 (Opa-locka, FL: Avanti Press, 1995), 4; "Police Bag 3,545 Law Violators in 6 Months of 1947," ADW, 26 February 1948; and "Florida Hails Record of Miami's Negro Policemen," CD, 23 October 1948.

128. "Bolita Ring Called Threat to Miami Negro Policemen," MH, 4 July 1946.

129. Thomas interview, in Chapman, "History of the Black Police Force and Court in the City of Miami," 141.

130. "Townsend Visits a Different Kind of Court in Miami," CD, 2 February 1952; and Chapman, "History of the Black Police Force and Court in the City of Miami," 125.

131. Ernesto Longa, "Lawson Edward Thomas and Miami's Negro Municipal Court," St. Thomas Law Review 18 (2005): 125–38, quote on 128.

132. Julio Capó Jr., "It's Not Queer to Be Gay: Miami and the Emergence of the Gay Rights Movement, 1945–1995" (PhD diss., Florida International University, 2011), 14; and Mormino, "Midas Returns."

133. Correspondence from Benton E. Jacobs, manager of the Miami News Bureau, to J. W. Power, director of the city of Miami's Publicity Department, 1 July and 7 July 1946.

134. Office of the Miami City Clerk, Resolutions and Minutes of the City Commission, 1921–1986, 15 October 1952, box 42, SAF; and Fred Fejes, "Murder, Perversion, and Moral Panic: The 1954 Media Campaign against Miami's Homosexuals and the Discourse of Sexual Betterment," Journal of the History of Sexuality 9, no. 3 (July 2000): 305–47.

135. "Outlaw KKK," MT, 5 February 1949; "Ku Klux Klan Almost a Joke in New South," WP, 17 April 1949; and "Florida Terrorism, Bombing Deaths Coincide with Ku Klux Recruiting Drive," WP, 6 January 1952. The banning of hoods and cross burnings occurred at an August convening of the Florida legislature in 1951.

136. Longa, "Lawson Edward Thomas and Miami's Negro Municipal Court," 132.

137. Bill Sawyer, interviewed by Stephanie Wanza, 7–8.

138. "William B. Sawyer, 89," MH, 30 April 2008.

139. "Dr. Sawyer to Build $40,000 Hotel at Miami," CD, 27 August 1921; "Mary Elizabeth Hotel," PC, 25 October 1930; "In Miami's Mary Elizabeth," NAN, 12 February 1949;

and Metropolitan Dade County Government, *Dade County Historic Survey Final Report: Summary of Survey Findings*, 55, "Buildings and Sites" Collection, BA.

140. John A. Stuart and Paul Silverthorne, "Pragmatism Meets Exoticism: An Interview with Paul Silverthorne," Florida theme issue, *Journal of Decorative and Propaganda Arts* 23 (1998): 379.

141. Marie M. White, "Society in Miami," *Crisis* (March 1942): 90; Fredericka Wanza, interviewed by Stephanie Wanza, 10 August 1997, 8, Tell the Story Collection, BA; Bill Sawyer, interviewed by Stephanie Wanza, 13; Bernice Sawyer, interviewed by Stephanie Wanza, 25 August 1997, 11, Tell the Story Collection, BA; Leome Culmer, interviewed by Stephanie Wanza, 13 August 1997, 15, Tell the Story Collection, BA; "Social Swirl," *ADW*, 23 September 1953; "Council Women Hear Reports at Recent Meeting," *ADW*, 1 September 1949; "Town Topics," *NAN*, 11 August 1951; "Fidel Castro's Sister Juanita Was a CIA Agent," *Guardian*, 26 October 2009, accessed 1 June 2013, http://www.guardian.co.uk/world/2009/oct/26/fidel-castro-sister-cia-agent; "Champion Louis Retires," *MT*, 5 March 1949; and "'Miss Puerto Rico' Crowned 'Miss Latin America,'" *MT*, 29 July 1950.

142. Bill Sawyer, interviewed by Stephanie Wanza, 20; and Stuart and Silverthorne, "Pragmatism Meets Exoticism," 379. For similar dynamics elsewhere, see Kamala Kempadoo, ed., *Sun, Sex, and Gold: Tourism and Sex Work in the Caribbean* (Lanham, MD: Rowman & Littlefield, 1999); and Simon, *Boardwalk of Dreams*, chap. 4.

143. Correspondence from Ramona Lowe to Claude Barnett, 12 August 1948, "NY. NY." folder, Associated Negro Press, Part 2, Associated Negro Press Organization Files, 1920–66, Claude Barnett Papers, Proquest database, Twentieth Century Black Freedom Struggles.

144. Enid Pinkney, interviewed by Stephanie Wanza, 5 August 1997, 16, Tell the Story Collection, BA.

145. "Financial Records—Orange Blossom Classic, Miami," box 3, folder 2, Jack Gaither Collection, FAMU.

146. "Hotel Patrons Fined, Jailed," *CD*, 18 June 1949.

147. Neptune, *Caliban and the Yankees*, 90–92; and Judith R. Walkowitz, *Nights Out: Life in Cosmopolitan London* (New Haven, CT: Yale University Press, 2012), 247–52.

148. Dorothy Graham, from screening of Virginia Key Beach Museum and State Park Oral History Project, 21 July 2005, Joseph Caleb Center, Miami.

CHAPTER FIVE: KNOCKING ON THE DOOR

1. "Attempt to Restrict Homes," *PC*, 16 February 1946.

2. Raymond A. Mohl, "Making the Second Ghetto in Metropolitan Miami, 1940–1960," *Journal of Urban History* 21, no. 3 (March 1995): 405–6.

3. "Attempt to Restrict Homes"; Charles G. Gomillion, "The Negro and Civil Rights," in *Negro Year Book: 1947*, ed. Jessie Parkhurst Guzman (Tuskegee, AL: Tuskegee Institute, 1947), 293.

4. Dade County Commission, County Planning Board Meeting Minutes, 14 August 1945, microfilm, MDPL.

5. Jason Scott Smith, *Building New Deal Liberalism: The Political Economy of Public Works, 1933–1956* (Cambridge: Cambridge University Press, 2006); and Elizabeth Borgwardt, *A New Deal for the World: America's Vision for Human Rights* (Cambridge, MA: Belknap Press of Harvard University Press, 2005).

6. "Burn Fiery Cross in Miami Section," *PC*, 11 August 1945. As Thomas J. Sugrue notes, concrete walls were artifacts of compromise between white developers who wanted

to build black housing and FHA appraisers and area residents concerned with black people's apparently negative impact on property values; Sugrue, *The Origins of the Urban Crisis: Race and Inequality in Postwar Detroit* (Princeton, NJ: Princeton University Press, 1996), 64.

7. National Urban League, *A Review of Economic and Cultural Problems in Dade County, Florida as They Relate to Conditions in the Negro Population* (New York: National Urban League, 1943), 7.

8. Mohl, "Making the Second Ghetto in Metropolitan Miami," 412–13.

9. "Florida Contestants . . . ," *MT*, 28 February 1959; "Special Warranty Deed between Garrison Investment Corporation and Dana A. Dorsey," 28 April 1931, box 2, file 2620; and "Special Warranty Deed between Wesley E. Garrison, Inc. and Dana Holding Company," 10 August 1933, box 2, file 2590—both in Papers of Dana A. Dorsey, Miami Metropolitan Archive.

10. "Florida Negro Demos Set to 'Bore from Within' with Newly Won Vote," *CD*, 9 February 1946.

11. Earl Lewis, "To Turn as on a Pivot: Writing African Americans into a History of Overlapping Diasporas," *American Historical Review* 100, no. 3 (June 1995): 782.

12. "Burn Fiery Cross in Miami Section."

13. "For Lease[:] Miami Beach Homes," *MN*, 2 November 1935.

14. "Zoning Law Argued in Miami Court," *PC*, 2 March 1946.

15. "State Republicans Plan Campaign," *EI*, 26 August 1940. Wesley Garrison actually loaned Solomon twenty-five hundred dollars to start the *Miami Whip*, a militant, if short-lived, black newspaper; "*Miami Whip* Sold to GOP Leader," *BAA*, 26 July 1947.

16. Title 42, US Code, section 1982.

17. Beryl Satter, *Family Properties: Race, Real Estate, and the Exploitation of Black Urban America* (New York: Metropolitan Books, 2009), 276–77.

18. "Florida Racial Zoning Law Declared Invalid," *PC*, 1 December 1945; and *State of Florida v. Wilson*, Supreme Court of Florida, 157 Fla. 342; 25 So. 2d 860; 1946 Fla. LEXIS 743, 30 April 1946.

19. "Attempt to Restrict Homes."

20. National Urban League, *Review of Economic and Cultural Problems in Dade County, Florida*, 7.

21. "Attempt to Restrict Homes."

22. "Zoning Law Argued in Miami Court"; *Dade County v. Palgar Home Builders*, 158 Fla. 50 (1946), 22 October 1946; and *State of Florida v. Wilson*.

23. Dade County Commission, Meeting Minutes, 3 April 1945, microfilm, Florida Room, MDPL; National Urban League, *Review of Economic and Cultural Problems in Dade County, Florida*, 38; "An Abstract of Title for Realty Securities Corp. to Lots 8, 9, 10, 11, 40, 41, 42, & 43 of Block 10 of Railroad Chops [*sic*] Colored Addition. From Security Abstract Company, Incorporator, Abstracts Prepared, Money Loaned and Invested, 33 N.E. First Avenue, Miami, Dade County, Florida, No 25056," "Neighborhoods and Communities" collection, box 3, BA.

24. Ashraf H. A. Rushdy, *American Lynching* (New Haven, CT: Yale University Press, 2012), 1–2, 4, 7.

25. This notion of white popular sovereignty survives in state legislation like the "Castle Doctrine," which allows gun owners to use lethal force and act with state-like impunity if they feel physically threatened. In Florida, as elsewhere, the racial implications of the "Castle Doctrine," also known as the "Stand Your Ground" law, became apparent in the 2012 Sanford, Florida, incident in which a seventeen-year-old

Miami youth, Trayvon Martin, was gunned down by a neighborhood watch member, George Zimmerman; "Race, Tragedy, and Outrage Collide after a Shot in Florida," *NYT*, 2 April 2012.

26. There's no shortage of literature on white residential terrorism in the post–World War II period. One of the best and most succinct accounts of white violence in defense of "homeowner rights" continues to be Arnold R. Hirsch, "Massive Resistance in the Urban North: Trumbull Park, Chicago, 1953–1966," *Journal of American History* 82, no. 2 (September 1995): 522–50.

27. Coined by the legal historian William Novak, "infrastructural power" functions as a sprawling, almost gossamer kind of authority that, unlike the more fragile forms of "despotic power," remains harder to pin down and root out. William J. Novak, "The Myth of a 'Weak' American State," *American Historical Review* 113, no. 3 (June 2008): 752–72.

28. Thomas J. Sugrue, *Origins of the Urban Crisis: Race and Inequality in Postwar Detroit* (Princeton, NJ: Princeton University Press, 1996), 81; and Arnold R. Hirsch, *Making the Second Ghetto: Race and Housing in Chicago, 1940–1960* (Chicago: University of Chicago Press, 1998), 40–67.

29. Scott Eyman, "World War II in Florida: The Two Invasions," *Sunshine*, 5 May 1985, 22; and Gary M. Mormino, "Midas Returns: Miami Goes to War, 1941–1945," *Tequesta* 57 (1997): 13.

30. Meg Jacobs, "'How About Some Meat?' The Office of Price Administration, Consumption Politics, and State Building from the Bottom Up, 1941–1946," *Journal of American History* 84, no. 3 (December 1997): 912, 914; and Meg Jacobs, *Pocketbook Politics: Economic Citizenship in Twentieth-Century America* (Princeton, NJ: Princeton University Press, 2007), 206.

31. Jacobs, "'How About Some Meat?,'" 936, 939–41.

32. "Rent Control Registration Starts Today," *MH*, 4 October 1943; and Wendy Plotkin, "Rent Control in Chicago after World War II: Politics, People, and Controversy," *Prologue* 20, no. 2 (1998): 113.

33. "Rent-Control End Is Urged by Realtors," *BS*, 21 November 1948.

34. *Report of the Secretary for the February Meeting of the Board*, "Board of Directors, Secretary's Report, 1947" folder, Papers of the NAACP, Part 16, Board of Directors, Correspondence and Committee Materials, Series B: 1940–55, Proquest History Vault; and Laura McEnaney, "Nightmares on Elm Street: Demobilizing in Chicago, 1945–1953," *Journal of American History* 92, no. 4 (March 2006): 1274.

35. Correspondence from Charles Wilson, chairman, Civil Rights Committee, to unnamed party living at 977 SW Fifth Street, Miami, 29 January 1947, President Truman's Committee on Civil Rights, 1947, Proquest Twentieth Century Black Freedom Struggles.

36. Franklin Delano Roosevelt, "Message to Congress on the State of the Union," 11 January 1944, in *Public Papers and Addresses of Franklin D. Roosevelt*, vol. 13 (New York: Harper, 1950), 41; see also Thomas J. Sugrue, *Sweet Land of Liberty: The Forgotten Struggle for Civil Rights in the North* (New York: Random House, 2008), xvii.

37. McEnaney, "Nightmares on Elm Street," 1282.

38. *Report of the Secretary for the February Meeting of the Board*, "Board of Directors, Secretary's Report, 1948" folder; *Report of the Secretary for the April 1949 Board Meeting*, "Board of Directors, Secretary's Report, 1949" folder; *Report of the Acting Secretary for the March 1950 Meeting of the Board*, "Board of Directors, Secretary's Report, 1950–1952" folder—all three in Papers of the NAACP, Part 16, Board of Directors, Cor-

respondence and Committee Materials, Series B: 1940–55, Proquest History Vault; and Plotkin, "Rent Control in Chicago after World War II," 120.

39. Plotkin, "Rent Control in Chicago after World War II," 113.

40. "Landlord and Tenant after OPA," *University of Chicago Law Review* 14, no. 2 (February 1947): 255.

41. Ewell E. Branscome, director and legislative chairman of the Greater Miami Apartment House Association, in Joint Committee on Housing, *Study and Investigation of Housing: Hearings before the Joint Committee on Housing*, 80th Cong., 1st sess., 27 October 1947, 1038; see also "Our Position on Rents," *MH*, 3 July 1946.

42. "Decontrol Drives Away Residents, Hurts Beach Business, Roth Says," *MN*, 29 May 1949.

43. Richard Wright, *12 Million Black Voices* (New York: Thunder's Mouth Press, 1988), 105; see also Hirsch, *Making the Second Ghetto*, 18–27.

44. Max Goodman, president, Miami–Miami Beach Tenant League Inc., in Joint Committee on Housing, *Study and Investigation of Housing: Hearings before the Joint Committee on Housing*, 80th Cong., 1st sess., 27 October 1947, 1043.

45. Harland Bartholomew and Associates, *A Preliminary Report upon Population, Land Uses and Zoning, Miami Beach, Florida* (September 1940), 8.

46. Perrine Palmer, mayor of Miami, in Joint Committee on Housing, *Study and Investigation of Housing: Hearings before the Joint Committee on Housing*, 80th Cong., 1st sess., 27 October 1947, 936.

47. For an especially insightful discussion of the lived experience of rental price and rent decontrol, see Laura McEnaney's "Nightmares on Elm Street."

48. Marjory Stoneman Douglas, "Coconut Grove, Florida, Faces Its Slums," 1950, Marjory Stoneman Douglas Papers, Series 3, articles and manuscripts, box 32, folder 17, UM; "Article 'Coconut Grove . . . ,'" *Ladies Home Journal* 10 (1950), 29, UM; and *Directorio de Miami, Miami Beach* (1951), 15, 27, 28, UM.

49. Edward T. Graham, Negro Service Council, in Joint Committee on Housing, *Study and Investigation of Housing: Hearings before the Joint Committee on Housing*, 80th Cong., 1st sess., 27 October 1947, 1020.

50. Palmer, in Joint Committee on Housing, *Study and Investigation of Housing*, 938.

51. Ibid., 935.

52. Ibid., 937.

53. Corienne K. Robinson, "Relationship between Condition of Dwellings and Rentals, by Race," *Journal of Land and Public Utility Economics* 22, no. 3 (August 1946): 296–302, esp. 298–99; William G. Grigsby, "Housing Markets and Public Policy," in *Urban Renewal*, ed. John Q. Wilson (Cambridge, MA, and London: Massachusetts Institute of Technology Press, 1966), 29; National Urban League, *Review of Economic and Cultural Problems in Dade County, Florida*, 40.

54. The Works Projects Administration reported in 1942, "In the Miami area there are no large blighted sections occupied by white families under substandard conditions"; *Report of Low Rent Housing Needs, Miami Florida and Vicinity* (Tallahassee: Florida State Planning Board and the Housing Authority of the City of Miami, 1942), 2, cited in National Urban League, *Review of Economic and Cultural Problems in Dade County, Florida*, 35. "The non-white tenant receives a distinctly higher proportion of substandard housing than does the non-white owner in the same rental ranges"; Robinson, "Relationship between Condition of Dwellings and Rentals, by Race," 300.

55. "'Rent Refugees' Are Leaving Miami Beach," *SPT*, 21 April 1949; and "Decontrol Drives Away Residents, Hurts Beach Business, Roth Says."

56. Raymond A. Mohl, "The Settlement of Blacks in South Florida," in *South Florida: The Winds of Change*, ed. Thomas D. Boswell, 112–17 (Miami: Association of American Geographers, 1991).

57. James J. Carney, "Population Growth in Miami and Dade County, Florida" *Tequesta* 6 (1946): 51; Philip J. Weidling and August Burghard, *Checkered Sunshine: The Story of Ft. Lauderdale, 1793–1955* (Gainesville: University of Florida Press, 1966), 252; and Susan Gillis, *Ft. Lauderdale: The Venice of America* (New York: Arcadia Press, 2004), 105–7.

58. Greater Miami Chamber of Commerce, Meeting Minutes of the Inter-racial Committee, 26 January 1945, *Committee Meetings Minutes, vol. 2 (1941–1946)*, Greater Miami Chamber of Commerce Collection, HASF; Gillis, *Fort Lauderdale: Venice of America*, 63; and Robe B. Carson, "The Florida Tropics," *Economic Geography* 27, no. 4 (October 1951): 322.

59. Alan Brinkley, *The End of Reform: New Deal Liberalism in Recession and War* (New York: Knopf, 1995), 269.

60. National Urban League, *Review of Economic and Cultural Problems in Dade County, Florida*, 38.

61. "Decent Homes for Decent Families: A Slum Clearance Program for Miami, Initiated by the City Planning Board," Ernest R. Graham Papers, box 20, "Urban Redevelopment Corporations, 1941" folder, UF; and Edward Braynon, interviewed by Stephanie Wanza, 6 August 1997, 29–31, quotations on 29, 30, Tell the Story Collection, BA.

62. Black Archives History and Research Foundation of South Florida, Narratives, "Railroad Shop," box 3, Neighborhoods and Communities Collection, BA.

63. "Railroad Shop: The Day a Community Died," *MH*, 23 September 2007.

64. "Decent Homes for Decent Families."

65. HOLC Security Map Area descriptions: "Musa Isles and Allapattah Section, Miami Florida, Security Grade C," and "South of 62nd Street from N.W. 17th Ave. to N.E. 4th Ct., Miami, FL, Security Grade D"—both in RG 195, Records of the Federal Home Loan Bank Board, Home Owners Loan Corporation, Records Relating to the City Survey File, 1935–40, entry 39, "Florida Miami" folder, box 81, NARA; Resolution 19821, 19 February 1947, Office of the Miami City Clerk, *Resolutions and Minutes of the City Commission, 1921–1986*, box 28, SAF; Resolution 18747, 7 March 1945, Office of the Miami City Clerk, *Resolutions and Minutes of the City Commission, 1921–1986*, box 31, SAF; and Resolution 17802, 29 April 1942, Office of the Miami City Clerk, *Resolutions and Minutes of the City Commission, 1921–1986*, box 28, SAF.

66. Carson, "Florida Tropics," 323; "Florida Is Full of People, Sunshine—and Superlatives," *NYT*, 8 December 1946; Eric S. Blake, Jerry D. Jarrell, and Edward N. Rappaport, "The Deadliest, Costliest, and Most Intense United States Tropical Cyclones from 1851 to 2004 (and Other Frequently Requested Hurricane Facts)," NOAA Technical Memorandum NWS TPC-4, National Weather Service, National Hurricane Center, accessed 1 June 2013, http://www.aoml.noaa.gov/hrd/Landsea/dcmifinal2 .pdf; and National Urban League, *Review of Economic and Cultural Problems in Dade County, Florida*, 39.

67. "The Situation at 'Railroad Shop,'" *MT*, 8 March 1947.

68. "City Atty. Promises People of 'Railroad Shop' a Square Deal," *ADW*, 22 October 1947.

69. "Force Church, Land Owners Off Property," *PC*, 26 July 1947.

70. "Evicted Residents 'Going Home,'" *MH*, 26 August 1977.

71. Ibid.

72. Ibid.

73. Andrea Robinson, "Railroad Shop," Neighborhoods and Communities Collection, box 3, BA; "35 Miami Families Evicted," PC, 9 August 1947; and Braynon interview, 29. Ronald H. Bayor discusses how, in 1947, Fulton County, GA, officials used whites-only public works projects—under the ruse of "slum clearance"—to facilitate their Negro-displacement strategy in the Bagley Park section of Atlanta; Bayor, *Race and the Shaping of Twentieth-Century Atlanta* (Chapel Hill: University of North Carolina Press, 1996), 58.

74. "35 Miami Families Evicted."

75. "Race Being Squeezed Out of Miami Area," PC, 30 August 1947.

76. Katherine Lumpkin Strachan, interviewed by Cynthia Strachan, 23 September 2005, in Cynthia Strachan, *Promises from the Palmetto Bush: The Genesis of Carver Ranches, FL, 1940–1949* (West Park, FL: Jusset Publishing, 2006), 20.

77. Loren Miller Address, 25 June 1947, NAACP National Convention, Papers of the NAACP, Part 1—Meetings of the Board of Directors, Records of Annual Conferences, Major Speeches, and Special Reports, Proquest History Vault.

78. Hirsch, *Making the Second Ghetto*, 30.

79. David M. P. Freund, *Colored Property: State Policy and White Racial Politics in Suburban America* (Chicago: University of Chicago Press, 2007), 42.

80. St. Clair Drake and Horace Cayton, *Black Metropolis: A Study of Negro Life in a Northern City* (1945; repr., Chicago: University of Chicago Press, 1993), 185.

81. "Slum Clearance a Must," MN, 6 February 1955.

82. Greater Miami Chamber of Commerce, Meeting Minutes of the Inter-racial Committee.

83. Robert C. Weaver, *Hemmed In* (1945), 3, RG 207, box 748, "Publications—Other Than HHFA Personnel" folder, NARA.

84. Carita Swanson Vonk, *Theodore R. Gibson: Priest, Prophet, and Politician* (Miami: Little River Press, 1997), 5.

85. "Apartments Will Rise on Former Slum Area," MN, 22 June 1947.

86. "OK Given $120,000 Project in Miami," PC, 17 July 1948.

87. "A Tidy Bit of 'Developing,'" MN, 3 February 1950.

88. *Guide to Greater Miami and Dade County, Including Miami Beach and Coral Gables*, American Guide Series, compiled and written by the Florida Writers' Project, Work Projects Administration, Sponsored by the Miami City Commission (1940), 231–32.

89. Planning Board of the City of Miami, Slum Clearance Committee, and Dade County Health Department, *Dwelling Conditions in the Two Principal Blighted Areas* (1950), 41; and Melanie Shell Weiss, *Coming to Miami: A Social History* (Gainesville: University Press of Florida, 2009), 135.

90. Vonk, *Theodore R. Gibson*, 39; "Still Unsettled," MT, 22 January 1949; correspondence from Elizabeth Virrick to Malcolm Wiseheart, 7 March 1949, Elizabeth Virrick Papers, "Correspondence, Memos, etc., 1949–1967" folder, box 1, HASF; and Raymond A. Mohl, "Elizabeth Virrick and the 'Concrete Monsters': Housing Reform in Postwar Miami," *Tequesta* 51 (2001): 11.

91. As an example of this folk census figure, Mount Zion AME's Edward Graham testified before Congress in 1947 that "the Negro is 'stored in' 7½ deep"; Graham, in Joint Committee on Housing, *Study and Investigation of Housing: Hearings before the Joint Committee on Housing*, 80th Cong., 1st sess., 27 October 1947, 1019; and Mohl, "Elizabeth Virrick and the 'Concrete Monsters,'" 7.

92. Helen Muir, *Miami: USA* (Coconut Grove, FL: Hurricane House, 1953), 265–66; and Mohl, "Elizabeth Virrick and the 'Concrete Monsters,'" 12.

93. Greater Miami Chamber of Commerce, Minutes of Public Health Committee, June 26 (no year provided), *Committee Meetings Minutes, vol. 2 (1941–1946)*, Greater Miami Chamber of Commerce Collection, HASF; and Muir, *Miami: USA*, 265–66.

94. "Still Unsettled," *MT*, 22 January 1949; and "South Florida Mourns Elizabeth Virrick—Hon. Dante B. Fascell," 9 May 1990, as reflected in the *Congressional Record* of the Library of Congress, Thomas Collection, accessed 1 June 2013, http://thomas.loc .gov/cgi-bin/query/z?r101:E09MY0-457.

95. Mohl, "Elizabeth Virrick and the 'Concrete Monsters,'" 14.

96. Correspondence from Elizabeth Virrick to Malcolm Wiseheart, 7 March 1949; and Mohl, "Elizabeth Virrick and the 'Concrete Monsters,'" 8–9.

97. "Coconut Grove Zoning Still Kicked Around," *MT*, 8 January 1949.

98. Office of the County Manager, "Profile of the Black Population in Metropolitan Dade County" (January 1979), 67; "Coconut Grove Zoning Still Kicked Around"; and Abe Aronovitz, untitled statement, 18 February 1949, Elizabeth Virrick Papers, "Correspondence, Memos, etc., 1949–1967" folder, box 1, HASF.

99. "Slum Clearance," 15 September 1948, Office of the Miami City Clerk, *Resolutions and Minutes of the City Commission, 1921–1986*, box 36, SAF.

100. "Slum Clearance and Public Housing in Greater Miami," *MH*, 17 April 1950; "The Big Difference," *MT*, 9 July 1949; "Crossing His Path," *MT*, 23 July 1949; and "Housing Experts Say Slum Clearance May Be Segregated Ruse," *MT*, 3 September 1949.

101. "Miami Landlords Say City's Housing Action against Group," *ADW*, 14 October 1948.

102. "More Floridians to Be Made Homeless by Eviction," *PC*, 20 September 1947.

103. "Move to Halt Mass Eviction," *PC*, 23 August 1947; and "Park Property Worth $67,550, Jury Rules," *MN*, 11 February 1949. In addition to the value of the land, the city of Miami paid five thousand dollars in attorney's fees to E. F. P. Brigham.

104. "Both Sides Give Their Arguments on Proposed Low-Cost Housing Project for Miami," *MN*, 25 June 1950.

105. "Voice of America to Tell Grove's Slum Clearance Work," *MH*, 14 December 1950; and letter from Elizabeth Virrick of the Coconut Grove Citizens Committee to Carroll Seghers II of the Black Star media company, 20 December 1950, Elizabeth Virrick Collection, box 14, HASF.

106. Sugrue, *Sweet Land of Liberty*, xxv.

107. National Urban League, *Review of Economic and Cultural Problems in Dade County, Florida*, 38, 98.

108. "Race Being Squeezed Out of Miami Area."

109. "35 Miami Families Evicted."

110. "Evicted Residents 'Going Home.'"

111. Resolutions 19135 and 19137, 2 January 1946, Office of the Miami City Clerk, *Resolutions and Minutes of the City Commission, 1921–1986*, box 37, SAF; and "Rail Road Shop Keeping in Touch: August 28th, 1977 30 Year Reunion," Railroad Shop binder, Neighborhoods and Communities Collection, box 3, BA.

112. I first heard of Thomas's possible involvement discussed, matter-of-factly, at a black historic preservationists meeting in 2005 in the black Miami suburb of Brownsville. As with most questions of community memory and land, whether neighborhood accounts of Thomas's involvement are actually true matters less, perhaps, than whether older black Miamians believe it to be true. See Sara Berry, "Tomatoes, Land and Hearsay: Property and History in Asante in Time of Structural Adjustment," *World Development* 25, no. 8 (1997): 1236.

113. Coconut Grove Citizens Committee for Slum Clearance, *They Said It Could Not Be Done: 14th Anniversary Report to Members* (ca. 1962), Elizabeth Virrick Collection, box 14, "Scrap Book," HASF; and Mohl, "Elizabeth Virrick and the 'Concrete Monsters,'" 17, 19.

114. Arnold R. Hirsch, "Choosing Segregation: Federal Housing Policy between *Shelley* and *Brown*," in *From Tenements to the Taylor Homes: In Search of an Urban Housing Policy in Twentieth-Century America*, ed. John F. Bauman and Kristin M. Szylvian (University Park: Pennsylvania State University Press, 2000), 216.

CHAPTER SIX: A LITTLE INSURANCE

1. "*Times* Select Sawyer, Ward, Nickerson as Outstanding Citizens," *MT*, 28 January 1950.

2. "Miss Puerto Rico Crowned 'Miss Latin America,'" *MT*, 29 July 1950.

3. "Wealthy M.D. Succumbs in Miami, Fla.," *PC*, 5 August 1950.

4. Bill Sawyer, interviewed by Stephanie Wanza, 25 August 1997, 3, 59, Tell the Story Collection, BA.

5. "Neighbors NE," *MH*, 19 October 1989.

6. "Condemned Plus 65" (station WCKT, Miami, 1961), University of Georgia Peabody Collection, accessed 28 May 2013, http://dbs.galib.uga.edu/cgi-bin/parc.cgi?userid=galileo&query=id%3A1961_61013_pst_1&_cc=1.

7. "'General' Brooks Collects Rents," *MN*, 2 March 1962.

8. "Depreciated Shacks Bringing Top Profits," *MH*, 6 November 1959. Beyond the 8 to 9 percent for Brooks, the landlord was responsible for paying all fees and expenses, including labor and materials used by Bonded Rental's twenty-four-man maintenance department; "Slumlords' Agent: A Matter of Profit," *MN*, 15 October 1974.

9. Harvey argues that if landlord returns dropped below 10 percent, owners would most often abandon their investment. See David Harvey, *The Urbanization of Capital: Studies in the History and Theory of Capitalist Urbanization* (Baltimore: Johns Hopkins University Press, 1985), esp. chap. 3.

10. Margie and George Harth, interviewed by N. D. B. Connolly, 9 March 2010. In 1962, Elizabeth Virrick corroborated this astounding figure, telling a reporter from the *Miami News*, "Most of the owners of Negro housing get their investment back in three years." Perhaps as further evidence of its veracity, Brooks for years evaded the question of his landlords' profit margins, until 1974, when a host of political and demographic factors lowered it to 10 percent; "'General' Brooks Collects Rents"; and "Slumlords' Agent."

11. Leonard Barfield, interviewed by N. D. B. Connolly, 23 February 2010, notes in author's possession.

12. "Luther Brooks, 80, Expowerbroker," *MH*, 31 December 1988. Limited financial records and client information for Bonded Collection Agency are also available at the Black Archives History and Research Foundation of South Florida Inc., Miami.

13. "Biggest Property Owners? Here's List of the Top 15," *MH*, 6 November 1959; "Slumlords' Agent"; "Luther Brooks, 80"; and Bonded Rental Agency advertisement (ca. 1969), "Newspaper Clippings on Housing, 1966–1970," Bonded Rental Agency Inc. Collection, BA.

14. "Miami Condemned: Update '75" (station WCKT, Miami, 1975), University of Georgia Peabody Collection, accessed 28 May 2013, http://dlg.galileo.usg.edu/peabody/id:1975_75025_nwt_1.

15. Charles E. Connerly, *"The Most Segregated City in America": City Planning and Civil Rights in Birmingham, 1920–1980* (Charlottesville: University of Virginia Press, 2005),

2–3; and David M. P. Freund, *Colored Property: State Policy and White Racial Politics in Suburban America* (Chicago: University of Chicago Press, 2007).

16. Robert C. Weaver, *Dilemmas of Urban America* (Cambridge, MA: Harvard University Press, 1967), 19; Raymond Vernon, "The Changing Economic Function of the Central City," in *Urban Renewal*, ed. John Q. Wilson (Cambridge, MA, and London: Massachusetts Institute of Technology Press, 1966), 16; and M. Athalie Range, interviewed by Stephanie Wanza, 28 August 1997, 9–10, Tell the Story Collection, BA.

17. Edward Graham in Joint Committee on Housing, *Study and Investigation of Housing: Hearings before the Joint Committee on Housing*, 80th Cong., 1st sess., 27 October 1947, 1019–20.

18. Thomas W. Hanchett, *Sorting Out the New South City: Race, Class, and Urban Development in Charlotte, 1875–1975* (Chapel Hill: University of North Carolina Press, 1998), esp. chap. 5, "Creating Black Neighborhoods"; and LaDale Winling, "Building the Ivory Tower: Campus Planning, University Development, and the Politics of Urban Space" (PhD diss., University of Michigan, 2010), 93–95.

19. City Planning Board of Miami, "Railway Terminal 14th Street Plan" (26 December 1941), 1; City Planning Board of Miami, *Miami's Railway Terminal Problem* (6 January 1941), 8; and City Planning Board of Miami, *Report of City Planning Board of Miami Relative to New Railway Terminal* (1940), 55.

20. US Census Bureau, *Housing: Supplement to the First Series Housing Bulletin for Florida: Miami: Block Statistics* (Washington, DC: Government Printing Office, 1942), 21–22; Metropolitan Dade County Planning Department Comprehensive Plan Division, *Urban Growth in Dade County Florida: Planning Staff Report No. 2* (Metropolitan Dade County, March 1960), 5, WTVJ Collection, "Metro Land Use Plan" folder, box 50, HASF; Charles D. Thompson, "The Growth of Colored Miami," *Crisis* 49, no. 3 (March 1942): 83; and Planning Board of the City of Miami, Slum Clearance Committee, and Dade County Health Department, *Dwelling Conditions in the Two Principal Blighted Areas* (1950), 41.

21. "Miracle Changes Face of Miami," *PC*, 30 November 1957; and Bonded Collection Agency, "A Pictorial Review of Miami's 'Parade of Progress': What Is Being Done by Private Enterprise in Miami's Slum Clearance Program," 6, 14, 21, Bonded Rental Agency Inc. Collection, BA.

22. "Voice of the People: Slum Conditions Not One-Man Blot," *MH*, 29 April 1958.

23. "Miracle Changes Face of Miami."

24. Bonded Collection Agency, "Pictorial Review of Miami's 'Parade of Progress,'" 11–12, 21.

25. "Merry Christmas," a notice from Abe Schonfeld Properties and Bonded Collection Agency to Schonfeld's tenants, December 1956, Bonded Rental Agency Inc. Collection, "Newspaper Clippings on Housing, 1960 and Back to 1952," BA.

26. Office of the County Manager, "Profile of the Black Population in Metropolitan Dade County" (January 1979), 56; "Solomon Faced Death; Earned Undying Fame," *PC*, 22 June 1940; and "Over 500 Negro Arrests in Albany," *PC*, 23 December 1961.

27. "Miracle Changes Face of Miami"; and Langston Hughes, "Ballad of Sam Solomon," published in "Poet's Corner," *New York Amsterdam Star-News*, 12 July 1941.

28. "Solomon Pioneered Miami Vote Surge," *PC*, 30 November 1957.

29. "Here's How No's Beat Merger," Bonded Rental Agency Inc. Collection, "Newspaper Clippings on Housing, 1960 and Back to 1952," BA.

30. "Rent Collector Pounding Pavements," *MH*, 22 November 1957.

31. *Negro Housing in Greater Miami and Dade County: A Pictorial Presentation* (ca. 1951), UM, 45.

32. Enid Curtis Pinkney, interviewed by N. D. B. Connolly, 26 September 2006, notes and recording in author's possession.

33. C. Vann Woodward, *The Strange Career of Jim Crow* (New York: Oxford University Press, 1955), 51.

34. For intimacy and its connections to political power, see Nell Irvin Painter, "Three Southern Women and Freud: A Non-exceptionalist Approach to Race, Class, and Gender in the Slave South," in Painter, *Southern History across the Color Line*, 93–111 (Chapel Hill: University of North Carolina Press, 2002); and Ann Laura Stoler, "Tense and Tender Ties: The Politics of Comparison in North American History and (Post) Colonial Studies," in *Haunted by Empire: Geographies of Intimacy in North American History*, ed. Ann Laura Stoler, 23–70 (Durham, NC: Duke University Press, 2006).

35. *Zora Neale Hurston: A Life in Letters*, ed. Carla Kaplan (New York: Random House, 2003), 631.

36. William Alexander Percy, "Fode (1941)," in *The Age of Jim Crow*, ed. Jane Dailey, 150–60 (New York: Norton, 2008); and Micki McElya, *Clinging to Mammy: The Faithful Slave in Twentieth-Century America* (Cambridge, MA: Harvard University Press, 2007).

37. Zora Neale Hurston, "A Negro's Point of View about NAACP and Political Activity," *OS*, 17 July 1952.

38. "Vote-Buying Charge Called Lie in Miami," *PC*, 4 November 1950.

39. David T. Beito and Linda Royster Beito, *Black Maverick: T. R. M. Howard's Fight for Civil Rights and Economic Power* (Urbana and Chicago: University of Illinois Press, 2009); and Douglas Flamming, *Bound for Freedom: Black Los Angeles in Jim Crow America* (Berkeley and Los Angeles: University of California Press, 2004), 239–42.

40. Zora Neale Hurston, *Their Eyes Were Watching God* (1937; repr., New York: Harper-Collins, 1998), 36–50; see also Zora Neale Hurston, "Mrs. Ruby McCollum!," *PC*, 28 March 1953.

41. Hurston, *Their Eyes Were Watching God*, 46.

42. Glen Feldman, prologue to *Before* Brown: *Civil Rights and White Backlash in the Modern South*, ed. Glen Feldman (Tuscaloosa: University of Alabama Press, 2004), 7. The wild swings in membership numbers and political visibility among civil rights organizations in the Deep South also points to the propensity of black Americans to see political agency by means other than overt protest; see, for instance, Jeanne Theoharis, *The Rebellious Life of Mrs. Rosa Parks* (Boston: Beacon Press, 2013), 17, 29. Long after her death, Hurston's fieldwork on intimacy and black political power would prove instrumental for scholars recreating "a hidden history of unorganized, everyday conflict waged by African-American working people"; Robin D. G. Kelley, "'We Are Not What We Seem': Rethinking Black Working-Class History in the Jim Crow South," *Journal of American History* 80, no. 1 (June 1993): 76.

43. For examples of labor organizing in black Miami, see Thomas A. Castillo, "Miami's Hidden Labor History," *Florida Historical Quarterly* 82, no. 4 (Spring 2004): 438–76; Alex Lichtenstein, "Putting Labor's House in Order: Anticommunism and Miami's Transport Workers' Union, 1945–1949," *Labor History* 39 (Winter 1998): 7–23; and Melanie Shell-Weiss, *Coming to Miami: A Social History* (Gainesville: University Press of Florida, 2009).

44. Correspondence from Dr. Thomas Lowrie to William T. Andrews, 14 July 1931; "Attached letter sent to this list . . . ," 17 July 1931; and "List of Prominent Race Members in Miami, Fla."—all in Papers of the NAACP, Part 4, Voting Rights Campaign, 1916–50, Series C: Administrative File: Subject File—Discrimination, "Miami, Florida White Primary" folder, Proquest History Vault.

45. Paul S. George, "Colored Town: Miami's Black Community, 1896–1930," *Florida Historical Quarterly* 56, no. 4 (April 1978): 440.

46. Chanelle Nyree Rose, "Neither Southern nor Northern: Miami, Florida and the Black Freedom Struggle in America's Tourist Paradise, 1896–1968" (PhD diss., University of Miami, 2008), 16.

47. In the 1930s, colonial officials in the Congo, looking to negotiate food resources, labor unrest, and workforce productivity in Belgian mines, relied on what they called a "responsible" African commercial elite to facilitate white authoritarian rule; David M. Gordon, *Nachituchi's Gift: Economy, Society, and Environment in Central Africa* (Madison: University of Wisconsin Press, 2006), 91, see also 65, 72.

48. Harvard Sitkoff, *A New Deal for Blacks: The Emergence of Civil Rights as a National Issue: The Depression Decade* (Oxford: Oxford University Press, 1978), 152–53. For rent strikes in postwar Harlem, see Martha Biondi, *To Stand and Fight: The Struggle for Civil Rights in Postwar New York City* (Cambridge, MA: Harvard University Press, 2003), 114.

49. Glenda Elizabeth Gilmore, *Defying Dixie: The Radical Roots of Civil Rights, 1919–1950* (New York: Norton, 2008), 51–66.

50. E. Franklin Frazier, *Black Bourgeoisie* (New York: Collier Books, 1957), 129–91.

51. Ibid., 129.

52. Abram L. Harris, *The Negro as Capitalist: A Study of Banking and Business among American Negroes* (Philadelphia: American Academy of Political and Social Science, 1936), 183.

53. In their condemnations of materialism among black people, Frazier and Harris echoed earlier thinkers, most notably Alexander Crummel, Ana Julia Cooper, and, a mentor of theirs, W. E. B. Du Bois; Jonathan Scott Holloway, *Confronting the Veil: Abram Harris, Jr., E. Franklin Frazier, and Ralph Bunche, 1919–1941* (Chapel Hill: University of North Carolina Press, 2002), 23–30.

54. The seminal article on black resistance in the Jim Crow South is still Robin D. G. Kelley's "'We Are Not What We Seem.'" On forms of political engagement different from those outlined by Kelley, see David T. Beito and Linda Royster Beito, "T. R. M. Howard: Pragmatism over Strict Integrationist Ideology in the Mississippi Delta, 1942–1954," in *Before Brown: Civil Rights and White Backlash in the Modern South*, ed. Glen Feldman, 68–95 (Tuscaloosa: University of Alabama Press, 2004).

55. Frazier, *Black Bourgeoisie*, 107.

56. Leslie Brown, *Upbuilding Black Durham: Gender, Class, and Black Community Development in the Jim Crow South* (Chapel Hill: University of North Carolina Press, 2008); Tomiko Brown-Nagin, *Courage to Dissent: Atlanta and the Long History of the Civil Rights Movement* (New York: Oxford University Press, 2011), 62–68; and Christopher Silver and John V. Moeser, *The Separate City: Black Communities in the Urban South, 1940–1968* (Lexington: University Press of Kentucky, 1995), 48–61.

57. J. Douglas Smith, *Managing White Supremacy: Race, Politics, and Citizenship in Jim Crow Virginia* (Chapel Hill: University of North Carolina Press, 2002).

58. "Decontrol of Rents Voted by Hialeah," *MN*, 3 May 1949.

59. Raymond A. Mohl, *South of the South: Jewish Activists and the Civil Rights Movement in Miami, 1945–1960* (Gainesville: University Press of Florida, 2004), 20, 65–66.

60. Burnett Roth, in Joint Committee on Housing, *Study and Investigation of Housing: Hearings before the Joint Committee on Housing*, 80th Cong., 1st sess., 27 October 1947, 988, 992.

61. Edward Graham, interviewed in Arthur E. Chapman, "The History of the Black Police Force and Court in the City of Miami" (PhD diss., University of Miami, 1986), 127.

62. "Daily News Index," *MN*, 27 December 1949.

63. Matilda Graff, "The Historic Continuity of the Civil Rights Movement," printed in Raymond A. Mohl, *South of the South: Jewish Activists and the Civil Rights Movement in Miami, 1945–1960* (Gainesville: University Press of Florida, 2004), 89. Robin Kelley describes how communist organizers from the North expected to find downtrodden blacks in Alabama during the 1930s. But much to their surprise, white communists found blacks well steeped in a radical, grassroots organizing tradition. Robin D. G. Kelley, *Hammer and Hoe: Alabama Communists during the Great Depression* (Chapel Hill: University of North Carolina Press, 1990).

64. St. Clair Drake and Horace Cayton, *Black Metropolis: A Study of Negro Life in a Northern City* (1945; repr., Chicago: University of Chicago Press, 1993), 212.

65. Charlotte Brooks, *Alien Neighbors, Foreign Friends: Asian Americans, Housing, and the Transformation of Urban California* (Chicago: University of Chicago Press, 2009), 117–18.

66. "Slum Area Rent Boosts in Miami Draw Ire, Favor," *WAA*, 16 August 1949. For the most influential discussion of FHA discrimination among historians, see Kenneth Jackson, *Crabgrass Frontier: The Suburbanization of the United States* (Oxford: Oxford University Press, 1985); Arnold R. Hirsch, *Making the Second Ghetto: Race and Housing in Chicago, 1940–1960* (Chicago: University of Chicago Press, 1998); and Freund, *Colored Property*.

67. George Merrick, "Real Estate Development Past and Future," transcript of address to the Southeastern Convention of Realty Boards, 29 November 1937, RG 196, box 298, NARA, cited in John A. Stuart, "Liberty Square: Florida's First Public Housing Project," in *The New Deal in South Florida: Design, Policy, and Community Building, 1933–1940*, ed. John A. Stuart and John F. Stack (Gainesville: University Press of Florida, 2008), 212.

68. D. Bradford Hunt, *Blueprint for Disaster: The Unraveling of Chicago Public Housing* (Chicago: University of Chicago Press, 2009), 25.

69. House Select Committee on Lobbying Activities, *Housing Lobby: Part 2 of Hearings before the Joint Committee on Lobbying Activities*, 81st Cong., 2nd sess., 19, 20, 21, 25, 26, 27, 28 April 1950; 3, 5, and 17 May 1950, 365–68.

70. Don Parson, "The Decline of Public Housing and the Politics of the Red Scare: The Significance of the Los Angeles Public Housing War," *Journal of Urban History* 33, no. 3 (March 2007): 400–417, esp. 406; and Alexander von Hoffman, "A Study in Contradictions: The Origins and Legacy of the Housing Act of 1949," *Housing Policy Debate* 11, no. 2 (2000): 299–326, esp. 311.

71. "Property Owners Protest New Zoning," *MT*, 21 May 1949.

72. Miami Chamber of Commerce, Meeting Minutes of the Inter-racial Committee, 26 January 1945, *Committee Meetings Minutes, vol. 2 (1941–1946)*, Greater Miami Chamber of Commerce collection, HASF.

73. "Property Owners Protest New Zoning."

74. "Miami Plans Negro Jury Panel, More Race Police and End of Slums," *CD*, 10 July 1948.

75. "Race Being Squeezed Out of Miami Area," *PC*, 30 August 1947.

76. "Estimates of Mortgage Insurance Commitments on Negro Housing," 1946, 1948, 1949, RG 207, Race Relations Program 1946–48 Collection, "Housing Programs—FHA" folder, box 747, NARA.

77. Interoffice memo from Herbert C. Redman, zone commissioner, Federal Housing Administration, to A. L. Thompson, racial relations advisor, Housing and Home Fi-

nance Agency, 1 November 1949, 4, RG 207, Housing and Home Finance Agency Racial Relations Collection, "Miami, Florida Race Relations" folder, box 750, NARA.

78. HOLC Security Map Appendix, table 11, Records of the Federal Home Loan Bank Board, Home Owners Loan Corporation, Records Relating to the City Survey File, 1935–40, entry 39, "Florida Miami" folder, box 81, NARA; and intraoffice memo from Frank S. Horne, 3 April 1953, RG 207, Housing and Home Finance Agency Racial Relations Collection, "Miami, Florida Racial Relations" folder, box 750, NARA.

79. Leo Grebler, David M. Blank, and Louis Winnick, *Capital Formation in Residential Real Estate: Trends and Prospects* (Princeton, NJ: Princeton University Press, 1956), 146.

80. Ibid., 147.

81. Raymond A. Mohl, "Elizabeth Virrick and the 'Concrete Monsters': Housing Reform in Postwar Miami," *Tequesta* 51 (2001): 16.

82. "'Concrete Slums' Beat Zoning Deadline," *MT*, 18 May 1957.

83. "Miracle Changes Face of Miami."

84. "Is Your Rent Too High?," *MT*, 28 May 1955.

85. Barfield interview.

86. Between 1940 and 1950, the number of Negro-occupied dwellings in Dade County almost doubled, from nearly 11,300 to about 22,300; "Dade Negro Housing Has Nearly Doubled in Past Ten Years," *MH*, 6 May 1951.

87. "Rev. Gibson's First Inspiration," *MN*, 11 April 1965.

88. Elizabeth Virrick, "New Housing for Negroes in Dade County, Florida," in *Studies in Housing and Minority Groups*, ed. Nathan Glazer and Davis McEntire (Berkeley: University of California Press, 1960), 140.

89. Ira P. Davis, quoted in "FHA Charged with Blocking Negro Housing Improvement—Exhibit III," 2 July 1948, RG 207, Housing and Home Finance Agency Racial Relations Collection, "Miami, Florida Race Relations" folder, box 750, NARA.

90. "F.H.A. Housing," *MT*, 30 April 1949.

91. *Negro Housing in Greater Miami and Dade County*, 31.

92. Clarence Taylor, *Black Religious Intellectuals: The Fight for Equality from Jim Crow to the 21st Century* (New York: Routledge, 2002), 91.

93. "Florida Physician Builds 80-Unit Housing Project," *ADW*, 12 January 1950; and "Project in Florida May Solve Problem of Minority Housing," *PC*, 21 January 1950.

94. *Negro Housing in Greater Miami and Dade County*, 12.

95. David M. P. Freund, "Marketing the Free Market: State Intervention and the Politics of Prosperity in Metropolitan America," in *The New Suburban History*, ed. Kevin M. Kruse and Thomas J. Sugrue, 11–32 (Chicago: University of Chicago Press, 2006).

96. "Public Housing in Dade County: Statement of Non-federal Contribution," RG 207, General Records of the Department of Housing and Urban Development; Model Cities Reports, 1966–73, "Florida; FL 4 (part)—FL 5; Vol. 2, Part 1" folder, box 49, NARA.

97. Mohl, "Elizabeth Virrick and the 'Concrete Monsters,'" 19; and "Slum Clearance vs. Rehousing," *MN*, 8 April 1950.

98. *Miami Herald*, quoted in "Tale of Two Cities," *SPT*, 1 July 1950.

99. "Both Sides Give Their Arguments on Proposed Low-Cost Housing Project for Miami," *MN*, 25 June 1950.

100. Harth and Harth interview.

101. Barfield interview.

102. "When DuBreuil Took Trip Paid by Brooks," *MN*, 24 July 1961.

103. "How Harth Got Job," *MH*, 7 April 1958.

104. "Slum Group Would Testify before House Lobby Probers," *MN*, 21 April 1950; and "Tale of Two Cities."
105. "In the Bag," *MN*, 14 April 1950.
106. "Government Housing Is Not Slum Clearance," *MN*, 15 April 1950.
107. "Wiseheart, Bouvier Seek Negro Area," *MN*, 9 August 1951.
108. "Edison Center Meeting Called," *MN*, 12 August 1951; Stetson Kennedy, "Miami: Anteroom to Fascism," *Nation*, 22 December 1951, 546–47; telegram to Governor Fuller Warren from Mr. and Mrs. M. L. Hammack of 1017 NW 114th Street, Miami, 16 August 1951, Papers of Governor Fuller Warren, Series 235, folder 9, box 21, SAF. See also telegram to Governor Fuller Warren from Mr. and Mrs. Fred Coleman of 1052 NW 65th Street, 17 August 1951, Papers of Governor Fuller Warren, Series 235, folder 9, box 21, SAF.
109. "Tenants Ignore Threats in Miami," *PC*, 18 August 1951; and "Group to Seek Evacuation of Carver Village Negroes," *MH*, 24 September 1951.
110. Charles Abrams, *Forbidden Neighbors: A Study of Prejudice in Housing* (New York: Harper & Brothers, 1955), 125.
111. "Blast Rocks Apartment," *NYT*, 23 September 1951; Abrams, *Forbidden Neighbors*, 125; "Condemnation of Property—Carver Village," 19 September 1951, Office of the Miami City Clerk, *Resolutions and Minutes of the City Commission, 1921–1986*, box 40, SAF; Louie Bandel, interview in Arthur E. Chapman, "The History of the Black Police Force and Court in the City of Miami" (PhD diss., University of Miami, 1986), 118; and Kennedy, "Miami: Anteroom to Fascism."
112. Teresa Lenox, "The Carver Village Controversy," *Tequesta* 50 (1990): 39–51, 42; and "City Turns Down Demand to Evict Bombing 'Cause,'" *MH*, 25 September 1951.
113. "Project Bombing Fails to Rout Negro Tenants," *NAN*, 6 October 1951.
114. Hirsch, *Making the Second Ghetto*, 89–92.
115. Timothy B. Tyson, *Blood Done Signed My Name: A True Story* (New York: Three Rivers Press, 2004), 54.
116. Connerly, *"Most Segregated City in America,"* 3.
117. John Egerton, *Speak Now Against the Day: The Generation before the Civil Rights Movement in the South* (New York: Knopf, 1995); and Kevin M. Kruse, *White Flight: Atlanta and the Making of Modern Conservatism* (Princeton, NJ: Princeton University Press, 2005), 53.
118. *Prohibiting Certain Acts Involving the Use of Explosives*, Hearing before the Subcommittee on Housing of the Committee on the Judiciary, House of Representatives, 85th Cong, 2nd sess., Washington, DC, 18 June 1958 (Washington, DC, 1958), 23.
119. On the pervasiveness of homegrown anticommunism in Miami, see Gregory W. Bush, "'We Must Picture an Octopus': Anticommunism, Desegregation, and Local News in Miami, 1945–1960," *Tequesta* 65 (2005): 48–63; Kennedy, "Miami: Anteroom to Fascism"; and Abrams, *Forbidden Neighbors*, 126.
120. "4 Inquiries Comb Florida Bombing," *NYT*, 28 December 1951; "Negro Leader's Wife Also Dies in Bombing," *NYT*, 4 January 1952; and Ben Green, *Before His Time: The Untold Story of Harry T. Moore, America's First Civil Rights Martyr* (New York: Free Press, 1999).
121. Letter to Governor Fuller Warren, 3 February 1952; and correspondence from Lillian B. Gilkes to Governor Fuller Warren, 23 January 1952—both in Papers of Governor Fuller Warren, Series 235, folder 6, box 64, SAF; correspondence from Charlie Clark, executive assistant to Governor Fuller Warren, to E. W. Burch, 23 January 1952, sent in response to an expressed outrage on the part of Mrs. Burch over the presence

of Negro guests dining in the Governor's Mansion, Papers of Governor Fuller Warren, Series 235, folder 8, box 64, SAF.

122. Correspondence from Loyal Compton, press secretary to Governor Fuller Warren, to Cullen E. McCoy, editor of the *Tallahassee Record Dispatch*, 28 December 1951, Papers of Governor Fuller Warren, Series 235, folder 6, box 64, SAF; "4 Give Up to U.S. Marshal in Miami on Perjury Charges in Terrorism," *NYT*, 11 December 1952; and "First Fruits," *Time* magazine, 22 December 1952.

123. "Urban League Backs Vocational School Fight," *MT*, 26 July 1952.

124. Interoffice memo from Warren R. Cochrane, director of the Racial Relations Branch of the Public Housing Administration, to Frank S. Horne, assistant to the administrator of the Housing and Home Finance Agency, 11 July 1952, RG 207, Housing and Home Finance Agency Racial Relations Collection, "Miami, Florida Racial Relations" folder, box 750, NARA; "Amending Cooperation Agreement—Miami Housing Authority," 17 December 1958, Office of the Miami City Clerk, *Resolutions and Minutes of the City Commission, 1921–1986*, "Resolutions 30487–30518, December 17, 1958" folder, box 51, SAF; intraoffice memo from A. R. Hanson, director of Housing and Home Finance Agency Atlanta Field Office, to Hubert M. Jackson, race relations staffer, 15 August 1952, 3, RG 207, box 750, "Miami, Florida Racial Relations" folder, NARA; Lenox, "Carver Village Controversy," 50; and "5-Man Committee Will Seek Solution on Negro Housing," *MN*, 25 October 1951.

125. "Hialeah Crowd Boos Negro Housing Plan," *MH*, 16 January 1951; "Dade Backing Promised in Housing Plan," *MH*, 2 March 1951; and intraoffice memo from Hanson to Jackson, 15 August 1952, 3.

126. *Bonded Rental Agency, Inc., v. City of Miami*, 192 So. 2d 305 (1966); *City of Miami v. Schonfeld*, 197 So. 2d 559 (1967); *Dukes v. Pinder*, 211 So. 2d 575 (1968); and letter from J. T. Knight, Miami Housing Authority, to John P. Broome, Public Housing Administration, 15 April 1953, 3, RG 207, Housing and Home Finance Agency Racial Relations Collection, "Miami, Florida Racial Relations" folder, box 750, NARA.

127. "Negroes Plan $10 Million Slum Clearance Project," *Jet*, 11 June 1953, 37.

128. Intraoffice memo from Hanson to Jackson, 15 August 1952, 3–5; and letter from Knight to Broome, 15 April 1953, 3.

129. "Statement of Robert Weaver," ca. 1948, 6, "Restrictive Covenant, May 1948–May 1953, Jan. 1960" folder, National Urban League Papers, Part III, box 76, LOC.

CHAPTER SEVEN: BULLDOZING JIM CROW

1. "Evidence Taken before the Citizens' Committee of the City of Miami, State of Florida on Tuesday, August 25, 1953, at 12:45 O'clock P.M., Room 221 of Shoreland Building, Miami, Florida," 200–201, Office of the Miami City Clerk, *Resolutions and Minutes of the City Commission, 1921–1986*, box 43, SAF.

2. "Evidence Taken before the Citizens' Committee of the City of Miami, State of Florida on Tuesday September 8, 1953, at 8 O'clock P.M., at the Bayfront Auditorium, Miami, Florida," 284, Office of the Miami City Clerk, *Resolutions and Minutes of the City Commission, 1921–1986*, box 43, SAF.

3. "Resolutions 26318–26345, March 17, 1954," Office of the Miami City Clerk, *Resolutions and Minutes of the City Commission, 1921–1986*, box 44, SAF.

4. Charles M. Grigg and Lewis M. Killian, "The Bi-racial Committee as a Response to Racial Tensions in Southern Cities," *Phylon* 23, no. 4 (4th quar. 1962): 379–82; and Lewis G. Watts, "Social Integration and the Use of Minority Leadership in Seattle, Washington," *Phylon* 21, no. 2 (2nd quar. 1960): 136–43. What I call the "confer-

ence approach" could be understood as a variation of what William H. Chafe, in 1980, called the "progressive mystique." For Chafe, "the 'progressive mystique' . . . [advanced] that conflict is inherently bad, that disagreement means personal dislike, and that consensus offers the only way to preserve a genteel and civilized way of life." I modify Chafe's contention by exploring how discourses about and practices preserving landlords' property rights stood at the foundation of reaching political consensus and governing apartheid. Chafe, *Civilities and Civil Rights: Greensboro, North Carolina, and the Black Struggle for Freedom* (Oxford: Oxford University Press, 1981), 7.

5. The National Urban League's 1943 report on the black experience in Dade County takes nearly one hundred pages to make the case for equalization, not desegregation, in Greater Miami; *A Review of Economic and Cultural Problems in Dade County, Florida as They Relate to Conditions in the Negro Population* (New York: National Urban League, 1943).

6. Elaine R. Samet, "Quiet Revolution in Miami," *Progressive* 29, no. 4 (April 1965): 34.

7. Ibid.

8. Dade County Council on Human Relations, *Report of the Committee on Public Accommodations* (ca. fall 1958), reprinted in Raymond A. Mohl, *South of the South: Jewish Activists and the Civil Rights Movement in Miami, 1945–1960* (Gainesville: University Press of Florida, 2004), 140.

9. "Evidence Taken before the Citizens' Committee of the City of Miami, State of Florida on Tuesday, August 25, 1953," 193.

10. Allan Keiler, *Marian Anderson: A Singer's Journey* (Urbana and Champaign: University of Illinois Press, 2002), 259; and "Mixed Miami Throng Hears Miss Anderson," *NYT*, 27 January 1952. Black and white audience members sat in alternate rows at this event.

11. "Rev. Edward T. Graham Used Cunning to Help Integrate Beach Hotels," *MT*, 6 October 2004.

12. See, for instance, "Program for the 1954 General Convention of Alpha Phi Alpha Fraternity, Inc., December 27–30, Miami, Florida," *Sphinx* 39, no. 4 (December 1954): 1.

13. Frank Andre Guridy, *Forging Diaspora: Afro-Cubans and African Americans in a World of Empire and Jim Crow* (Chapel Hill: University of North Carolina Press, 2010), 192.

14. "State's TB Workers Invited to Health Education Institute," *ADW*, 22 August 1952; "Miami Beach Hotels Welcome NEA Negro Delegates," *PC*, 11 July 1953; "Behind the Headlines," *PC*, 10 October 1953; "NNIA Holds Thirty-Third Session in Miami, Fla.," *PC*, 26 September 1953; "Florist to Form National Group," *ADW*, 2 April 1953; "Insurance Men Head for Miami," *PC*, 19 September 1953; and "Rogers Says," *PC*, 21 February 1953.

15. "Miami Mayor Apologizes for Lincoln Day Bias," *PC*, 19 February 1955.

16. Gerald Posner, *Miami Babylon: Crime, Wealth, and Power—A Dispatch from the Beach* (New York: Simon and Schuster, 2009), 58–59; see also "Patterson Won't Fight in Miami If Jim Crow Holds," *PC*, 7 January 1961.

17. "Two Negro Units Clash on Bus Drive Pressure," *MH*, 14 June 1956; and "Ye Editor's Notebook," *MT*, 17 June 1956.

18. For nearly a year, Miami city bus drivers and their managers successfully held off desegregation in public transportation on the grounds that the Miami Transit Company functioned as a private subcontractor, not a government agency. It had, in other words, the right to regulate itself. "Segregated Bus Seating Dead in Miami," *MT*, 5 January 1957; and "City Seeks to Delay Bus Integration," *MT*, 17 August 1957.

19. Chanelle Rose, "The 'Jewel' of the South? Miami, Florida and the NAACP's Struggle for Civil Rights in America's Vacation Paradise," *Florida Historical Quarterly* 86, no. 1 (Summer 2007): 58.

20. "Citation: Father Theodore Gibson" (June 1961), "1961 Church" folder, Papers of the NAACP, Part 1, Supplement, 1961–65, Series A: Administrative File, Annual Convention, 52nd Annual Convention, 10–16 July 1961, Philadelphia, Proquest History Vault.

21. "Negroes Integrate Crandon Park," *MT*, 28 November 1959.

22. Garth Reeves, interviewed by Julian Pleasants, 19 August 1999, 16, accessed 1 June 2013, http://ufdc.ufl.edu/UF00005526/00001/16j?search=garth+%3dreeves.

23. Ibid., 17–18.

24. "Racial Rift in Miami," *NYT*, 31 May 1961; see also Andrew W. Kahrl, *The Land Was Ours: African American Beaches from Jim Crow to the Sunbelt South* (Cambridge, MA: Harvard University Press, 2012), 154.

25. "Request for Publicity—Negro Tourist Facilities," 4 November 1953, Office of the Miami City Clerk, *Resolutions and Minutes of the City Commission, 1921–1986*, box 43, SAF.

26. See, for instance, "Ft. Lauderdale Sells Golf Course," *MT*, 13 July 1957. On privatization as a vehicle for continued racial segregation, see Kevin M. Kruse, *White Flight: Atlanta and the Making of Modern Conservatism* (Princeton, NJ: Princeton University Press, 2005), esp. chap. 9.

27. Richard J. Strachan, *Dade County Schools, Students, Communities: A True Story* (New York: Carlton Press, 1993); and "Integration to Close 4 Negro High Schools," *MT*, 3 October 1964.

28. "379 Assigned to Orchard Villa School," *MT*, 10 October 1959; and Marvin Dunn, *Black Miami in the Twentieth Century* (Gainesville: University Press of Florida, 1997), 230.

29. See, for instance, *Rice v. Arnold*, 54 So. 2d 114 (1951); *Garmon v. Miami Transit Company*, 151 F. Supp. 953 (1957); and *Ward v. City of Miami, Florida*, 151 F. Supp. 593 (1957).

30. LeRoy Collins, "Talk to the People of Florida on Race Relations," radio and television address, 20 March 1960, Jacksonville, FL, accessed 2 June 2013, http://digitalcommons.unf.edu/eartha_materials/31/.

31. "The Governor's Inaugural Address," *MT*, 12 January 1957.

32. James C. Cobb, *The Selling of the South: The Southern Crusade for Industrial Development, 1936–1980* (Baton Rouge and London: Louisiana State University Press, 1982), 123; and Tom Wagy, *Governor LeRoy Collins of Florida: Spokesman of the New South* (Tuscaloosa: University of Alabama Press, 1985).

33. "Starting Points for Discussion" (ca. 1960), 1, 4, RG 100, Series 226, Records of Florida's Advisory Commission on Race Relations, 1957–61, "Florida Communities—Miami" folder, box 8, SAF.

34. Southern Regional Council, "Roots of Racial Tension: Blighted Housing and Bomb Violence," *New South* 7, nos. 6, 7 (June–July 1952): 2.

35. See, for instance, Christopher Klemek, *The Transnational Collapse of Urban Renewal: Postwar Urbanism from New York to Berlin* (Chicago: University of Chicago Press, 2011); and Samuel Zipp, *Manhattan Projects: The Rise and Fall of Urban Renewal in Cold War New York* (Oxford: Oxford University Press, 2010).

36. Robert E. Lang and Rebecca R. Sohmer, "Legacy of the Housing Act of 1949: The Past, Present, and Future of Federal Housing and Urban Policy," *Housing Policy Debate* 11, no. 2 (2000): 291–98. On urban renewal as a cultural force, see Leandro Benmergui, "The Alliance for Progress and Housing Policy in Rio de Janeiro," *Urban History* 36, no. 2 (August 2009): 303–26; Zipp, *Manhattan Projects*; and Klemek, *Transatlantic Collapse of Urban Renewal*.

37. "City Lacks Curbs on Slum Projects," *MN*, 5 April 1957.

38. Reapportionment finally came in 1962 with *Baker v. Carr*, 369 US 186 (1962); LeRoy Collins, interview by Joe B. Frantz, 15 November 1972, 19, Civil Rights during the Johnson Administration, 1963–69, Part 3—Oral Histories, Proquest Twentieth Century Black Freedom Struggles; and Loren P. Beth and William C. Havard, "Committee Stacking and Political Power in Florida," *Journal of Politics* 23, no. 1 (February 1961): 57–83, esp. 60, 61.

39. "Miami Condemned: 1961" (station WCKT, Miami, 1961), University of Georgia Peabody Collection, accessed 28 May 2013, http://dbs.galib.uga.edu/cgi-bin/parc.cgi ?userid=galileo&query=id%3A1961_61012_pst_1-2&_cc=1.

40. Ibid.

41. Robert B. Fairbanks, "The Failure of Urban Renewal in the Southwest: From City Needs to Individual Rights," *Western Historical Quarterly* 37, no. 3 (Autumn 2006): 303–25; and Elizabeth Tandy Shermer, "Counter-organizing the Sunbelt: Right-to-Work Campaigns and Anti-union Conservatism," *Pacific Historical Review* 78, no. 1 (2009): 81–118.

42. "Governor Asks Slum Rule Study," *MH*, 20 November 1959.

43. "Build Miami a New Heart," *MH*, 11 March 1957.

44. Raymond A. Mohl, "Stop the Road: Freeway Revolts in American Cities," *Journal of Urban History* 30, no. 5 (July 2004): 686–87.

45. City Commissioner George DuBreuil used this $193 million figure in his rebuttal against freeway revolters in 1957; "Protest to Proposed Expressway," 20 February 1957, Office of the Miami City Clerk, *Resolutions and Minutes of the City Commission, 1921–1986*, box 49, SAF.

46. "Unruly Throng Disrupts Road Hearing," *MN*, 7 February 1957; and "Demolish Slums and Start Anew," *MH*, 19 March 1957.

47. Mohl, "Stop the Road," 684.

48. Ibid., 685.

49. "Miami's Expressway," *MT*, 2 March 1957.

50. Harold M. Rose, "Metropolitan Miami's Changing Negro Population, 1950–1960," *Economic Geography* 40, no. 3 (July 1964): 225.

51. "How Will Expressways Affect You?" *MN*, 3 February 1957.

52. "The Proposed Expressway," *MT*, 19 March 1957.

53. "Your Money's Ending Slums—but Not Here," *MH*, 15 December 1957.

54. *Grubstein v. Urban Renewal Agency of the City of Tampa*, 115 So. 2d 745 (Fla. 1959); Nancy Raquel Mirabal, "Telling Silences and Making Community: Afro Cubans and African Americans in Ybor City and Tampa, 1899–1915," in *Between Race and Empire: African Americans and Cubans before the Cuban Revolution*, ed. Lisa Brock and Digna Castañeda Fuertes, 49–69 (Philadelphia: Temple University Press, 1998). Precedent for the *Grubstein* ruling had been set in *Adams v. Housing Authority of Daytona Beach*, 60 So. 2d 663 (Fla. 1952).

55. "Governor Asks Slum Rule Study."

56. "Draft: Commission Members and Their Background," 8 September 1960, RG 100, Series 226, Records of Florida's Advisory Commission on Race Relations, 1957–61, "Florida Communities—Master File" folder, box 7, SAF.

57. "Governor's Advisory Commission on Race Relations," RG 100, Series 226, Records of Florida's Advisory Commission on Race Relations, 1957–61, "Commission Minutes" folder, box 1; "Starting Points for Discussion," 3; and memorandum from J. E. Gibbs, Florida A&M University College of Law, to J. R. E. Lee Jr., Florida A&M University and a member of the Governor's Advisory Committee on Racial Relations, 1957, RG 100,

Series 226, Records of Florida's Advisory Commission on Race Relations, 1957–61, "Housing" folder, box 3—all at SAF.

58. Maude Newbold, interviewed by Stephanie Wanza, 29 August 1997, 23, Tell the Story Collection, BA; and Dorothy McIntyre, interviewed by Kitty Oliver, 15 September 1999 (audio recording), Crossing the Racial Divide / Kitty Oliver Collection, AALCC.

59. Chanelle Nyree Rose, "Neither Southern nor Northern: Miami, Florida and the Black Freedom Struggle in America's Tourist Paradise, 1896–1968" (PhD diss., University of Miami, 2008), 333.

60. Mohl, *South of the South*, 53.

61. Ibid.

62. Shirley M. Zoloth, "Civil Rights Correspondence and Miami CORE Reports and Minutes, 1957–1960," in Mohl, *South of the South*, 192–93.

63. Matilda Graff, "The Historic Continuity of the Civil Rights Movement," printed in Mohl, *South of the South*, 89, 98.

64. Jim Carrier, *A Traveler's Guide to the Civil Rights Movement* (Orlando, FL: Harcourt Books, 2004), 196.

65. Zoloth, in Mohl, *South of the South*, 194.

66. Correspondence from Edward T. Graham to Theodore Gibson, 8 August 1960, RG 100, Series 226, Records of Florida's Advisory Commission on Race Relations, 1957–61, "Florida Communities—Miami" folder, box 8, SAF.

67. Ibid.

68. Correspondence from John B. Turner to Edward T. Graham, 9 August 1960, RG 100, Series 226, Records of Florida's Advisory Commission on Race Relations, 1957–61, "Florida Communities—Miami" folder, box 8, SAF.

69. *Community Report of the Fowler Commission on Race Relations*, 2 December 1960, RG 100, Series 226, Records of Florida's Advisory Commission on Race Relations, 1957–61, "Florida Communities—Master File" folder, box 7, SAF.

70. "Memorandum for Leaders in Dade County," 17 October 1960, RG 100, Series 226, Records of Florida's Advisory Commission on Race Relations, 1957–61, "Florida Communities—Miami" folder, box 8, SAF.

71. Ibid.

72. Juanita Greene, in Committee on the Judiciary, *Cuban Refugee Problems: Hearings before the Subcommittee to Investigate Problems Connected with Refugees and Escapees of the Committee on the Judiciary, United States Senate*, 87th Cong., 1st sess., part 1, 6 December 1961, 75.

73. Correspondence to Governor LeRoy Collins from Bill Killian, "Re: Cuban Situation in Dade County," 21 April 1958; "Re: Attack on Cuban Representative Rodolfo Masferrer," 22 April 1958; "Re: Cuban Situation in Miami," 24 April 1958; correspondence from Alonso Hidalgo Barrios, consul general of Cuba, to Miami mayor Robert King High and Miami police chief Walter Headley, 6 July 1959; correspondence from Frank Kappel, supervisor of criminal intelligence, to Thomas J. Kelly, metropolitan sheriff, "Subject: Incident on July 4th, 1959 Involving Alonso Hidalgo, Consul of Cuba in Miami," 31 July 1959—all in RG 102, Series 776B, Governor LeRoy Collins Papers, Administrative Correspondence, 1957–61, "Dade County 1959" folder, box 62, SAF. Correspondence from Miami mayor Robert King High to Cody Fowler, chairman of Governor's Commission on Race Relations, 31 March 1960; "Memorandum for Leaders in Dade County"; and "An Ordinance Creating a Community Relations Board . . ." (1960), 1—all in RG 100, Series 226, Records of Florida's Ad-

visory Commission on Race Relations, 1957–61, "Florida Communities—Miami" folder, box 8, SAF.

74. Dade County Council on Human Relations, "Suggested Presentation for Discussion Leaders," 29 January 1959, reprinted in Mohl, *South of the South*, 146.

75. Miami Planning and Zoning Board, *Generalized Land Use Plan for the City of Miami* (Comprehensive Planning Staff, 1959), x.

76. *Congressional Record*, House, vol. 113, 90th Cong., 1st sess., 14 December 1967, 36651.

77. "Miami's Civil Rights Activism Was Sparked Long before Advent of MLK," *MT*, 31 December 1992; and "Community Relations Board to Deal with Racial Tensions Here," *MT*, 15 June 1963. Letter from Frank C. Hart Jr., mayor of Bal Harbor, to Cody Fowler, chairman of Governor's Commission on Race Relations, 4 April 1960; see also letter from G. H. Colnot, mayor and town manager of Lauderdale-by-the-Sea, to Cody Fowler, 31 March 1960—both in RG 100, Series 226, Records of Florida's Advisory Commission on Race Relations, 1957–61, "Florida Communities—Miami" folder, box 8, SAF.

78. "Jobless Citizens Resent Cuban Hiring but Officials Claim No Competition," *MH*, 2 December 1960.

79. Allan Morrison, "Miami's Cuban Refugee Crisis," *Ebony* (June 1963): 100.

80. Art Hallgren, interviewed by Jack Bass, 20 May 1974, Southern Historical Collection Program, University of North Carolina, 4, accessed 4 September 2013, http://dc.lib .unc.edu/cdm/compoundobject/collection/sohp/id/8897/rec/1.

81. Melanie Shell-Weiss, *Coming to Miami: A Social History* (Gainesville: University Press of Florida, 2009), 179.

82. "Cheap Cuban Labor Creating Dangerous Situation in Miami," *St. Joseph Gazette*, 15 March 1963.

83. Alejandro Portes and Alex Stepick, *City on the Edge: The Transformation of Miami* (Berkeley: University of California Press, 1993), 41.

84. "Refugees Taking Over Cuba Numbers Game?" *MT*, 15 June 1963.

85. "Unwelcome Guests," *Wall Street Journal*, 6 May 1963; and Farris Bryant, interview by Joe B. Frantz, 5 March 1971, 11, Civil Rights during the Johnson Administration, 1963–69, Part 3—Oral Histories, Proquest Twentieth Century Black Freedom Struggles.

86. "Low Price Latins Undermine," *Jet*, 9 November 1961, 16.

87. "Cuban Refugees Take Jobs from Fla. Negroes," *Jet*, 21 March 1963, 19.

88. Luther Brooks, in Committee on the Judiciary, *Cuban Refugee Problems: Hearings before the Subcommittee to Investigate Problems Connected with Refugees and Escapees of the Committee on the Judiciary, United States Senate*, 87th Cong., 1st sess., part 1, 13 December 1961, 281–82.

89. Black women, under what was then called Aid to Dependent Children (ADC), were entitled to eighty-one dollars a month. Widespread concern about ADC discouraging marriage led lawmakers, in 1962, to add *Families with* to the acronym, making it *AFDC*.

90. Brooks, in Committee on the Judiciary, *Cuban Refugee Problems*, 281–82.

91. "Sweeting Town All Jammed Up," *MN*, 1 March 1962.

92. National Urban League, "Housing Statistics, June 1960–June 1964, n.d." folder, part III, National Urban League Papers, box 73, NA.

93. Brooks, in Committee on the Judiciary, *Cuban Refugee Problems*, 276.

94. "Pastors Battle Slum Landlord L. Brooks," *PC*, 7 December 1957.

95. "'Puppet' Cry Rocks Mayor Race," *MH*, 23 November 1957.

96. "Backers of Reese Blast at Dumond," *MN*, 22 July 1961.

97. "Mayor Asks Probe in Slum Clearance," *MN*, 17 March 1958; "Influence Got Job for Frank Kelly," *MH*, 21 March 1958; Morty Freedman, "'Dear Frank' Note to Kelly Saves Slum Owner $15,000," *MH* (n.d. and no page no. provided); and Morty Freedman, "Slum Agent Has Right Friends," *MH* (ca. 1958, no page no. provided)—both in Bonded Rental Agency Inc. Collection, "Newspaper Clippings on Housing, 1960 and Back to 1952," BA.

98. "How Harth Got Job," *MH*, 7 April 1958.

99. "Probe Asked of Tenement Fee Lapse," *MH*, 19 January 1960; and *Bonded Rental Agency, Inc., v. City of Miami*, 192 So. 2d 305 (1966).

100. "Pastors Battle Slum Landlord L. Brooks."

101. "Slum Laws Effective—If Used," *MH*, 29 March 1958.

102. Thomas J. Wood, "Dade County: Unbossed, Erratically Led," *Annals of the American Academy of Political and Social Science* (1964): 67; and "Obsequies for the Late Charles Albert Lockhart," Bonded Rental Agency Inc. Collection, BA.

103. Wood, "Dade County," 67.

104. Litigation wasn't brought against Luther Brooks's company until 1965–66; *Washington v. Bonded Rental Agency, Inc.*, 181 So. 2d 752 (1966). The company escaped liability.

105. "'General' Brooks Collects Rents," *MN*, 2 March 1962.

106. "I'll Block Play Area for Whites, He Says," *MN*, 15 June 1960.

107. "To Tell the Truth," *MT*, 25 May 1963.

108. "*Herald*'s Slum Clearance Series Gets Reporter's Comments," *MT*, 29 March 1958.

109. "Voice of the People: Slum Conditions Not One-Man Blot," *MH*, 29 April 1958.

110. Bonded Collection Agency, "25 Years of Property Management and Community Service" (1959), 9, Bonded Rental Agency Inc. Collection, BA.

111. Wood, "Dade County," 69; and Morty Freedman, "Mayor Says 'Nix' to Ol'-Pal Pix," *MH* (n.d. and no page no. provided), Bonded Rental Agency Inc. Collection, "Newspaper Clippings on Housing, 1960 and Back to 1952," BA.

112. Correspondence from Art Green to Luther Brooks, "Re: Governor Elect Haydon Burns–Charles Lockhart," 9 November 1964, Bonded Rental Agency Inc. Collection, BA; "Did Poverty Aide Sabotage Project?" *MH*, 30 November 1966; and Governor Haydon Burns—Robert King High Debate 1964, no. 1, video 379, v-34 and v-35 EA009, S. 828, SAF.

113. "Anti-poverty Aide Also Serves Landlords," *MH*, 5 November 1966.

114. Mary Givens, "Why We Had to Organize," *The Goulds Club News* (unpublished leaflet), 27 April 1966, 2, Bonded Rental Agency Inc. Collection, "Newspaper Clippings on Housing, 1966–1970," BA.

115. "Poverty Pays in Dade," *SPT*, 3 November 1966.

116. "Anti-poverty Aide Also Serves Landlords"; and "Did Poverty Aide Sabotage Project?"

117. "Approving Wilbur Smith's Expressway Plan," 19 December 1956, Office of the Miami City Clerk, *Resolutions and Minutes of the City Commission, 1921–1986*, box 48; "Objection to Proposed Change in Ramp of Proposed Downtown Interchange of Expressway," 2 February 1958, box 50—both in SAF; Keith Revell, "Chronology of Important Transportation Decisions in the Area, 1950–1990," in *The Historical Impacts of Transportation Projects on the Overtown Community*, ed. Institution of Government, Florida International University (Miami: Metropolitan Planning Organization of Miami–Dade County, 1998), 46; Wilbur S. Smith and Associates, *Alternatives for*

Expressways: Downtown Miami, Dade County, Florida (New Haven, CT: Wilbur S. Smith and Associates, 1962), cited in Mohl, "Stop the Road," 684; and "How Expressways Affect You—Crosstown Links in the Future," *MN*, 8 February 1957.

118. Leome Culmer, interviewed by Stephanie Wanza, 13 August 1997, 16, Tell the Story Collection, BA.

119. *Eyes on the Prize II: Back to the Movement, 1979–1983* (Boston: Blackside; Alexandria, VA: PBS Video, 1990).

120. "Luther Brooks for Urban Renewal," *MN*, 22 January 1964.

121. "Luther Brooks, 80, Expowerbroker," *MH*, 31 December 1988.

122. "Miami Rent Collector Keeps Pot Boiling for Islandia Future," *MN*, 28 October 1962; and "A Florida City That Never Was," *NYT*, 8 February 2012.

123. "Miami Condemned: 1961."

124. "Soaring Negro Rents Arouse Commission," *FLN*, 9 December 1959; "Negro Rent Fracas Probed," *FLN*, 13 December 1959; "Relief for Tenants Is Still Far Off," *MH*, 14 December 1959; and "League Queries Hopefuls," *MH*, 29 December 1959.

125. "Soaring Negro Rents Arouse Commission"; "Negro Rent Fracas Probed"; "Relief for Tenants Is Still Far Off"; "League Queries Hopefuls"; "Negro Is Candidate for City Commission in Fort Lauderdale, *OSB*, 5 March 1957; and "They Can't Keep Us Down," *Sphinx* 45, no. 1 (February 1960): 18.

126. "World Premiere!," *Broadcasting: The Businessweekly of Television and Radio* 61, no. 10, 4 September 1961, 6.

127. "Pun Phun," *MT*, 20 May 1961.

128. "Where Do We Go from Here?," *Ink* 14, no. 1 (September 1961): 1.

129. "Calypso for City Commissioners," *Ink* 14, no. 2 (October 1961): 2.

130. "Where Poverty Is Paradise," *NAN*, 21 August 1965.

131. "Negroes Plan March over Exiles in Jobs," *MN*, 1 March 1963.

132. "Save Urban Renewal," *Ink* 16, no. 5 (January 1964): 2; see also Irene V. Holliman, "Urban Renewal and Community Building in Atlanta, 1963–1966," *Journal of Urban History* 35, no. 3 (March 2009): 369–86.

133. Miami-Metro News Bureau, "Press Release," 8 June 1961, 2, WTVJ Collection, "Negroes-Miami" folder, box 62, HASF; "Dade County Negro Still at Crossroads," *MT*, 26 August 1966; and Sonny Wright, interviewed by Electra Ford, 30 August 1997, 22, Tell the Story Collection, BA.

134. Correspondence from Donald Wheeler to Robert King High, cited in John D. Skrentny, *The Minority Rights Revolution* (Cambridge, MA: Harvard University Press, 2002), 413.

135. "Stop Frisk Law Passed by Miami," *MH*, 15 September 1965.

136. "The Editor's Notebook," *MT*, 29 June 1963; "Join Motorcade and Public Meeting . . . ," 10 December 1966, "56:4 Jan. 1967" folder, Papers of the SCLC, Proquest Twentieth Century Black Freedom Struggles; "X-Way Force-Outs May Live in Pre-fabs," *MH*, 29 August 1967; and "Metro Told Districts Only Means of Representation," *MT*, 22 September 1967.

137. "Some Negro Groups Hurting Cause," *MN*, 9 August 1963.

138. "Negroes Ignore Call to March on City Hall," *MN*, 29 August 1966.

139. "Slumlords' Agent: A Matter of Profit," *MN*, 15 October 1974.

140. *Congressional Record*, House, vol. 113, 90th Cong., 1st sess., 14 December 1967, 36652.

141. Stokely Carmichael and Charles V. Hamilton, *Black Power: The Politics of Liberation* (New York: Random House, 1967), 5.

142. Largely deriving from the work of Frantz Fanon and arguments made by Kenneth Clark over the course of the *Brown* case, proponents of militant Black Power advanced that black Americans had suffered psychic afflictions under white supremacy. As articulated by Elizabeth Southerland, an activist with the Student Nonviolent Coordinating Committee, at a rally in New York in 1967, "Black Power is not racism. It is nationalism with a purpose. To undo the psychic damage of white racism. To build our communities." "Black Power—An Ideology of Blackness," *MG*, 19 July 1967.

143. Bernard Dyer, *Oversight of Federal Housing and Community Development Plans in the State of Florida*, Hearing before the Subcommittee on Housing of the Committee on Banking and Currency, House of Representatives, 92nd Cong., 1st sess., Miami, FL, 8 October 1971 (Washington, DC, 1971), 218.

144. "Don't Blame Landlords for Slums," *MH*, 26 March 1966.

145. "Middle Ground in the Slums," *MN*, 18 May 1967.

146. "Range Outlines Plan to Fight Housing Bias," *MN*, 4 February 1969.

147. "Housing Change Approved," *MH*, 24 January 1967; and "Housing Court: Way to Better Living," *MH*, 8 May 1967. For Miamians' advocacy of the "Baltimore model" of tenant court, which is more landlord focused, see "Task Force Says Model City Tenants Need 'Housing Court,'" *MN*, 4 February 1969.

148. *Congressional Record*, House, vol. 113, 90th Cong., 1st sess., 14 December 1967, 36652.

149. "Tenant Court Urged to Upgrade Housing," *MH*, 10 May 1967; and *Baltimore Plan* (1953), Encyclopedia Britannica Film, accessed 2 June 2013, http://www.archive.org/details/baltimore_plan.

150. "Athalie Range Backs Plan for Tenants School—'No Pressure,'" *MH*, 4 May 1967.

151. "Middle Ground in the Slums."

152. The first house was at 1178 NW Sixty-Second Street. Range moved her tenant to 1184 NW Sixty-Second Street, a few doors down. "Slum War Finally Showing Results," *MH*, 26 February 1967.

153. "Athalie Range Backs Plan for Tenants School."

154. "Landlords 'Ignore' Ordinance," *MH*, 1 March 1967.

155. "Miami Condemned: Update '75" (station WCKT, Miami, 1975), University of Georgia Peabody Collection, accessed 28 May 2013, http://dlg.galileo.usg.edu/peabody/id:1975_75025_nwt_1.

156. See Daryl Michael Scott, *Contempt and Pity: Social Policy and the Image of the Damaged Black Psyche, 1880–1996* (Chapel Hill: University of North Carolina Press, 1997); and Khalil Gibran Muhammad, *The Condemnation of Blackness: Race, Crime, and the Making of Modern Urban America* (Cambridge, MA: Harvard University Press, 2010).

157. "Housing Court: Way to Better Living."

158. "'Homemaking' School," *MH*, 3 May 1967.

159. "Athalie Range Backs Plan for Tenants School"; "Middle Ground in the Slums."

160. Rev. Clay Evans, quoted in Beryl Satter, *Family Properties: Race, Real Estate, and the Exploitation of Black Urban America* (New York: Metropolitan Books, 2009), 176.

161. Ibid., 186.

162. Tomiko Brown-Nagin, *Courage to Dissent: Atlanta and the Long History of the Civil Rights Movement* (Oxford: Oxford University Press, 2011), 270.

163. "Tenants Organizing to Fight Substandard Housing Units," *MT*, 30 September 1966.

164. Shell-Weiss, *Coming to Miami*, 198.

165. "Negro Leadership Is Deplored," *Spokesman-Review*, 5 June 1966.

166. Letter from Jimmie L. Chatmon to Martin Luther King Jr., 21 December 1966, "56:4 Jan. 1967" folder, Papers of the SCLC, Proquest Twentieth Century Black Freedom Struggles.

167. "The Staff of Employees of the Bonded Collection Agency, Inc.," *MT*, 26 December 1959; and "People, Places, Things," *MT*, 12 March 1960.
168. "Around Miami," *MT*, 26 August 1966.
169. Kelsey Pharr, quoted in Dorothy Jenkins Fields, "Colored Town, Miami Florida, 1915: An Examination of the Manner in Which the Residents Defined Their Community during This Era of Jim Crow" (PhD diss., Union Institute, 1996), 38–39.
170. "City Golf Course Ordered Integrated," *MT*, 4 May 1957.
171. In the *Ward* case, the city had previously allowed blacks to use the municipal course on Mondays only, as a means of saving the city the expense of having to build a separate golf course for blacks. With there no longer being a state segregation policy or a racist subcontractor to blame for the continued exclusion of blacks, the city had no choice but to open the course to every Miamian; *Ward v. City of Miami, Florida*.
172. Graff, quoted in Mohl, *South of the South*, 98.
173. "Miami Condemned: 1961."

CHAPTER EIGHT: SUBURBAN RENEWAL

1. "Dade NAACP Puts Shoe on Other Foot," *MN*, 4 March 1962.
2. As the historian Kent B. Germany explains of postwar liberalism generally, "The majority antipoverty strategy [of the War on Poverty] was to make individuals more adaptable to the demands of the marketplace, to turn the poor and segregated into better capitalists and capitalism into a better system for the poor and segregated." Kent B. Germany, "The Politics of Poverty and History: Racial Inequality and the Long Prelude to Katrina," *Journal of American History* 94 (December 2007): 745.
3. Miami-Metro News Bureau, "Press Release," 8 June 1961, 2, WTVJ Collection, "Negroes-Miami" folder, box 62, HASF; and "Dade NAACP Puts Shoe on Other Foot."
4. "Dade NAACP Puts Shoe on Other Foot."
5. For a more contemporary exploration of this theme, see Ellis Cose, *Rage of a Privileged Class: Why Are Middle-Class Blacks Angry? Why Should America Care?* (New York: Harper Perennial, 1992).
6. Wendy L. Wall, *Inventing the "American Way": The Politics of Consensus from the New Deal to the Civil Rights Movement* (Oxford: Oxford University Press, 2008), 286.
7. Elaine R. Samet, "Quiet Revolution in Miami," *Progressive* 29, no. 4 (April 1965): 34.
8. Robin D. G. Kelley, "'We Are Not What We Seem': Rethinking Black Working-Class History in the Jim Crow South," *Journal of American History* 80, no. 1, (June 1993): 75–112, quote on 77. Quite independent of Kelley, resistance remains the default intellectual preoccupation of those taking on the study of Jim Crow segregation and American racism more generally. The literature privileging black resistance over other historical processes in Jim Crow America is far too large to outline here. A few of the more finely executed and recent examples include Glenda Elizabeth Gilmore, *Defying Dixie: The Radical Roots of Civil Rights, 1919–1950* (New York: Norton, 2008); Leslie Brown, *Upbuilding Black Durham: Gender, Class, and Black Community Development in the Jim Crow South* (Chapel Hill: University of North Carolina Press, 2008); and Isabel Wilkerson, *The Warmth of Other Suns: The Epic Story of America's Great Migration* (New York: Random House, 2010).
9. Robin Kelley puts forth the idea of a "radical imagination" in his book *Freedom Dreams: The Black Radical Imagination* (Boston: Beacon Press, 2002), 9–10; Michael P. Johnson and James L. Roark, *Black Masters: A Free Family of Color in the Old South* (New York: Norton, 1984); Edward P. Jones, *The Known World* (New York: Harper-Collins, 2009); and Steven Hahn, *A Nation under Our Feet: Black Political Struggles in*

the Rural South from Slavery to Emancipation (London and Cambridge, MA: Belknap and Harvard University Press, 2003), esp. chap. 4.

10. See Millery Polyné, *From Douglass to Duvalier: U.S. African Americans, Haiti, and Pan-Americanism, 1870–1964* (Gainesville: University Press of Florida, 2011); Victoria W. Wolcott, *Remaking Respectability: African American Women in Interwar Detroit* (Chapel Hill: University of North Carolina Press, 2001); and Samuel Kelton Roberts Jr., *Infectious Fear: Politics, Disease, and the Health Effects of Segregation* (Chapel Hill: University of North Carolina Press, 2009).

11. Christopher Silver, "The Racial Origins of Zoning in American Cities," in *Urban Planning and the African American Community: In the Shadows*, ed. June Manning Thomas and Marsha Ritzdorf, 23–42 (Thousand Oaks, CA: Sage Publications, 1997). For an example of black seaside property owners who hired a white police officer to stand guard outside their community, keeping it free from Negro "undesirables," see Andrew W. Kahrl, *The Land Was Ours: African American Beaches from Jim Crow to the Sunbelt South* (Cambridge, MA: Harvard University Press, 2012), 100–101. One can find the litany of "technologies" that whites have used to maintain suburban exclusion over the last century in Gerald Frug, "The Legal Technology of Exclusion in Metropolitan America," in *The New Suburban History*, ed. Kevin M. Kruse and Thomas J. Sugrue, 205–20 (Chicago: University of Chicago Press, 2006). See also Mary Patillo, *Black on the Block: The Politics of Race and Class in the City* (Chicago: University of Chicago Press, 2007).

12. *Crisis* 49, no. 3 (March 1942).

13. Correspondence from Claude Barnett to H. E. S. Reeves, 5 April 1950, "MT" folder, Associated Negro Press, Part 2, Associated Negro Press Organization Files, 1920–66, Claude Barnett Papers, Proquest Twentieth Century Black Freedom Struggles.

14. Rowan noted that the only place with slums possibly worse than Miami was Galveston, Texas, also a coastal community; Carl Thomas Rowan, *South of Freedom* (New York: Knopf, 1952), 120.

15. Mary Nairn Bloomfield, interviewed by Electra R. Ford, 21 August 1997, 15, Tell the Story Collection, BA; and "Exodus from the Inner City," *MH*, 5 September 1993.

16. Urban League of Greater New York, "An Untapped Housing Market," 1948, 8, "Market Analysis, Apr. 1948" folder, National Urban League Papers, Part III, box 74, LOC.

17. Special thanks to Andrew Kahrl for reminding me of the containment aspects of early black suburbanization. Andrew Weise, *Places of Their Own: African American Suburbanization in the Twentieth Century* (Chicago: University of Chicago Press, 2004); Thomas J. Sugrue, *Sweet Land of Liberty: The Forgotten Struggle for Civil Rights in the North* (New York: Random House, 2008), 424; and Gwendolyn Thompkins, "Return to New Orleans: Pontchartrain Park," accessed 2 June 2013, http://www.npr.org/templates/story/story.php?storyId=5036200.

18. On the hopes black slum dwellers placed in slums, see J. W. Follin, director, Division of Slum Clearance and Urban Redevelopment, Housing and Home Finance Agency, "Urban Renewal Program; Relocation Responsibilities or Local Agencies, Community and Federal Government," 7 September 1954, address before the Annual Conference, National Urban League Inc., Fort Pitt Hotel, Pittsburgh, PA, "Urban Renewal, Sept. 1954–July 1956" folder, National Urban League Papers, Part III, box 318, LOC.

19. "A Resolution of the Miami City Commission Urging Miami–Dade County to Codesignate Northwest 17th Avenue from Northwest 36th Street to Northwest 71st Street, Miami, Florida, as 'M. Athalie Range Avenue,'" City of Miami Legislation, file

no. 07-00302a, 9 March 2007, accessed 28 July 2012, http://egov.ci.miami.fl.us/Legistarweb/Attachments/33775.pdf.

20. M. Athalie Range, interviewed by Teresa Alexander, 22 March 2002, Turner Tech Oral History Archive, accessed 30 May 2013, http://digitool.fcla.edu/R/7KVHPVMFA1S 8RGG6EEYSYR7GEL6SUYUHV66BRD5IYYPJQLVPHN-02531?func=results-jump -full&set_entry=000002&set_number=000596&base=GEN01-FCL01.

21. "School Fracas Settled—No School," *MT*, 23 July 1965.

22. "Richmond Heights Development Will Be Resumed Soon," *MN*, 25 January 1953.

23. "Petition," Neighborhoods and Communities Collection, "Richmond Heights" folder, box 2, BA.

24. "Richmond Heights Challenge to Negro Community Builders," *MN*, 20 May 1951. Thanks to Donnalyn Anthony for her understanding of Miami residents' sense of Richmond Heights' distance from "the rest" of black Miami. Thelma Vernell Anderson Gibson, with Helen Lawrence McGuire and Howard Carter Sr., *Forbearance: The Life Story of a Cocoanut Grove Native* (Homestead, FL: Helena Enterprises, 2000), 94–95, 140.

25. "Past Glory Fades into History," *SS*, 18 February 2001.

26. Ibid.

27. "Hotel Body Ends Convention in Miami," *NAN*, 10 November 1962; and "Hotel Men Re-elect Ted Hagans as President," *CD*, 17 November 1962.

28. "Dade NAACP Puts Shoe on Other Foot," *MN*, 4 March 1962.

29. "For Sale," *MT*, 10 May 1958; and "Court Opens All FHA Housing to Negroes," *MT*, 25 July 1959.

30. Harold M. Rose, "Metropolitan Miami's Changing Negro Population, 1950–1960," *Economic Geography* 40, no. 3 (July 1964): 225.

31. "*Goodbread Alley* Slated for Bunche Theater," *MT*, 9 February 1957.

32. "Negro Zone Proposal Is Rejected," *MH*, 7 July 1946.

33. Federal Housing Administration interoffice correspondence from A. L. Thompson, racial relations advisor, to Herbert C. Redman, zone commissioner, 12 July 1948, 5, RG 207, Housing and Home Finance Agency Race Relations Program 1946–58 collection, "Miami, Florida" folder, box 750, NARA.

34. Letter from Ernest I. Katz, Law Offices of Katz and Fuller, to Warren Lockwood, assistant commissioner in charge of field operations, Federal Housing Administration, 29 October 1948, 3, RG 207, Housing and Home Finance Agency Race Relations Program 1946–58 Collection, "Miami, Florida" folder, box 750, NARA; and "Too-Long Delayed Negro Housing Problem Demands Solution Now," *MH*, 24 September 1951.

35. Stuart B. McIver, *The Greatest Sale on Earth: The Story of the Miami Board of Realtors, 1920–1980* (Miami: E. A. Seeman Publishing, 1981), 145.

36. *Congressional District Data Book*, 88th Cong., House Document 132 (Washington DC: Government Printing Office, 1964), 95.

37. "Apartment Owners' Group Delays Miami-Metro Merger Attempt," *MN*, 18 July 1966.

38. "Proposed Amendment to Cooperation Agreement—Miami Housing Authority," 10 December 1958, Office of the Miami City Clerk, *Resolutions and Minutes of the City Commission, 1921–1986*, box 51, SAF.

39. Robe B. Carson, "The Florida Tropics," *Economic Geography* 27, no. 4 (October 1951): 337.

40. Patsy West, *The Enduring Seminoles: From Alligator Wrestling to Ecotourism* (Gainesville: University Press of Florida, 1998), 110.

41. Patsy West, "Miami's Muck-Lands Promotion Threatened Seminole Sovereignty," *South Florida Magazine* 19, no. 1 (Winter 1992): 16.

42. Senator Bob Graham, "Hialeah Memories," cited in Arva Moore Parks and Greg W. Bush, with Laura Pincus, *Miami, the American Crossroad: A Centennial Journey, 1896–1996* (Needham Heights, MA: Simon and Schuster, 1996), 123.

43. "Miami Sights That Are Seldom Seen," *BS*, 24 August 1969; "Blessings from an Ugly Piece of Land," *SPT*, 13 July 2003; "Graham's Rising Clout Mirrors Florida's Growth," *SS*, 6 May 2003; "Great Lakes," *SS*, 17 January 1994; and "Miami Lakes Comes of Age," *MH*, 8 March 1987.

44. "Housing Segregation Is Noted in 3 More Cities," *CD*, 4 February 1967.

45. "New Town Where Cattle Grazed," *CT*, 30 January 1971.

46. "College Prof Denied Home," *MT*, 13 January 1967.

47. Anthony S. Chen, *The Fifth Freedom: Jobs, Politics, and Civil Rights in the United States, 1941–1972* (Princeton, NJ: Princeton University Press, 2009), 88–89.

48. "Senate Extends Rights Sessions," *NYT*, 13 March 1964.

49. Kevin M. Kruse, *White Flight: Atlanta and the Making of Modern Conservatism* (Princeton, NJ: Princeton University Press, 2005); and Matthew D. Lassiter, *The Silent Majority: Suburban Politics in the Sunbelt South* (Princeton, NJ: Princeton University Press, 2006).

50. US Supreme Court cases critical to the preservation of racial inequality in the 1970s include *San Antonio Independent School District v. Rodriguez*, 411 U.S. 1 (1973); *Millikan v. Bradley*, 418 U.S. 717 (1974); *Village of Arlington Heights v. Metropolitan Housing Corporation*, 429 U.S. 252 (1977); and *Regents of the University of California v. Bakke*, 438 U.S. 265 (1978). See also Eduardo Bonilla Silva, *Racism without Racists: Color-Blind Racism and the Persistence of Racial Inequality in the United States* (Lanham, MD: Rowman and Littlefield, 2006).

51. Ties between the South and California have been exhaustively explored by historians in recent years. There remains, nevertheless, a common assumption that in California and the wider West resides a more progressive racial politics than in southern states. Among work exploring the South/West link, and what it meant for American politics, see Darren Dochuk, *From Bible Belt to Sunbelt: Plain-Folk Religion, Grassroots Politics, and the Rise of Evangelical Conservatism* (New York: Norton, 2011); Charles M. Payne, "'The Whole United States Is Southern!' *Brown v. Board* and the Mystification of Race," *Journal of American History* 91, no. 1 (June 2004): 83–91; Donna Jean Murch, *Migration, Education, and the Rise of the Black Panther Party in Oakland, California* (Chapel Hill: University of North Carolina Press, 2010), esp. pt. 1, "City of Migrants, 1940–1960"; and Scott Kurashige, "The Many Facets of *Brown*: Integration in a Multiracial Society," *Journal of American History* 91, no. 1 (June 2004): 56–68.

52. Daniel HoSang, *Racial Propositions: Ballot Initiatives and the Making of Postwar California* (Berkeley: University of California Press, 2010), 70; and Robert O. Self, *American Babylon: Race and the Struggle for Postwar Oakland* (Princeton, NJ: Princeton University Press, 2003), esp. chap. 4, "Redistribution."

53. "School Lawyers Ask Judge to Throw Out Case," *OSB*, 15 November 1957; and "Slum Property Owners Block Blight Removal," *MH*, 18 December 1957.

54. Correspondence from Don Shoemaker, editor of the *Miami Herald*, to James S. Knight, 30 July 1959, Don Shoemaker Papers, UNC; and "We're Stuck with Slums," *MH*, 1 May 1959.

55. "Angry Residents to Protest Negroes' Move into Area," *MN*, 16 January 1957.

56. *Eyes on the Prize II: Back to the Movement, 1979–1983* (Boston: Blackside; Alexandria, VA: PBS Video, 1990).

57. "Angry Residents to Protest Negroes' Move into Area."

58. "Landlords Still Fight Public Housing; Claim Cheats," *MT*, 28 May 1965.

59. Morris Adams, *Oversight of Federal Housing and Community Development Plans in the State of Florida*, Hearing before the Subcommittee on Housing of the Committee on Banking and Currency, House of Representatives, 92nd Cong., 1st sess., Miami, FL, 8 October 1971 (Washington, DC, 1971), 314.

60. "2 Facing Prosecution in Grove," *MH*, 10 June 1949; "Warrant Issued for Landlord," *CD*, 18 June 1949; and "Pioneer Miami Developer Dies at 84," *MT*, 23 November 1957.

61. Marvin Dunn, *Black Miami in the Twentieth Century* (Gainesville: University Press of Florida, 1997), 37, 41; Melanie Rebecca Shell-Weiss, "'They All Came from Someplace Else': Miami, Florida's Immigrant Communities, 1896–1970" (PhD diss., Michigan State University, 2002), 119; "Warrant Issued for Landlord"; "Rich Landlord Answers Court," *CD*, 15 April 1950; Morty Freedman, "He'll 'Let Houses Rot'— and Does," *MH* (n.d. and no page no. provided), Bonded Rental Agency Inc. Collection, "Newspaper Clippings on Housing, 1960 and Back to 1952," BA; Marjory Stoneman Douglas, "Coconut Grove, Florida, Faces Its Slums" (1950) and "Article 'Coconut Grove . . . ,'" *Ladies Home Journal* 10 (1950): 15—both in Marjory Stoneman Douglas Papers, folder 17, box 32, UM; and "4 Boys Killed in Grove Fire," *MN*, 20 September 1967.

62. "Fire Killing 10 Spurs Crackdown," *MN*, 7 February 1966.

63. "Enforce Housing Code, Slum-Dwellers Plead," *MH*, 11 October 1966; "2 Tots Die, Trapped in Flaming Apartment," *MH*, 20 December 1966; and "House Blaze Injuries Fatal to Father, Son," *MH*, 21 February 1966.

64. "Private Landlords Giving Up Fight," *MH*, 8 August 1967.

65. Ibid.

66. For an excellent discussion of black animus against white merchant creditors during the 1968 riots, see Louis Hyman, *Debtor Nation: The History of America in Red Ink* (Princeton, NJ: Princeton University Press, 2011), 174–90.

67. "We Can't Wait 10 Years to Clean Up Slums," *MN*, 22 February 1966; "The Slums Make Slum-Dwellers," *MH*, 30 March 1966; and "City Maps Tight Slum Laws," *MN*, 14 March 1966.

68. "City Prepares Warrants to Arrest Landlords," *MH*, 12 March 1966; "Crackdown on Slums Is Mapped in Miami," *MH*, 22 November 1966; "Rental Firm Charged with 9 Violations," *MN*, 8 March 1967; and "City Cases against 2 Landlords Delayed," *MN*, 10 March 1967.

69. "Vigorous Enforcement of Housing Code Hit," *MN*, 10 March 1967.

70. "Slum Owner Wins Another Fight in Court," *MN*, 23 April 1966; and "City Loses Round to Rent Firm," *MH*, 18 April 1966.

71. "Low Income Housing Not Popular with Investors," *MT*, 17 November 1967.

72. "Private Landlords Giving Up Fight."

73. "Past Glory Fades into History."

74. "Private Landlords Giving Up Fight."

75. Dorothy Graham, interviewed by Stephanie Wanza, 5 August 1997, 22, Tell the Story Collection, BA.

76. Planning Board of the City of Miami, Slum Clearance Committee, and Dade County Health Department, *Dwelling Conditions in the Two Principal Blighted Areas* (1950), 41; and "Miami Condemned: 1961" (station WCKT, Miami, 1961), University of Georgia Peabody Collection, accessed 28 May 2013, http://dbs.galib.uga.edu/cgi-bin/parc.cgi?userid=galileo&query=id%3A1961_61012_pst_1-2&_cc=1.

77. US Census Bureau, *Housing: Supplement to the First Series Housing Bulletin for Florida: Miami: Block Statistics* (Washington, DC: Government Printing Office, 1942), 21–22.

78. Eric Tscheschlok, "Long Time Coming: Miami's Liberty City Riot of 1968," *Florida Historical Quarterly* 74, no. 4 (Spring 1996): 448.

79. Bernard Dyer, *Oversight of Federal Housing and Community Development Plans in the State of Florida*, Hearing before the Subcommittee on Housing of the Committee on Banking and Currency, House of Representatives, 92nd Cong., 1st sess., Miami, FL, 8 October 1971 (Washington, DC, 1971), 218.

80. "Miami Condemned: 1961."

81. Steve Rogers, "Authority Chief Defends His Slum Property," *MH* (no date provided, ca. January 1967), Bonded Rental Agency Inc. Collection, "Newspaper Clippings on Housing, 1966–1970," BA; and "House Partly Owned by Housing Boss Cited," *MH*, 14 July 1967.

82. "Private Building in Slums Called Bad Risk for Owner," *MH*, 15 November 1967.

83. "Law Sought to Halt 'Concrete Slums,'" *MT*, 6 April 1957; and "'Concrete Slums' Beat Zoning Deadline," *MT*, 18 May 1957.

84. National Commission on Urban Problems, *Building the American City: Report of the National Commission on Urban Problems to the Congress and the President of the United States* (New York: Praeger, 1969), 163.

85. "More Removal Than Renewal to Urban Plan," *MN*, 3 September 1968; "And Now, Tearing Down Slum Walls," *MN*, 13 February 1967; "At Last! Urban Renewal Building to Start," *MT*, 14 February 1969; and Keith Revell, "Chronology of Important Transportation Decisions in the Area, 1950–1990," in *The Historical Impacts of Transportation Projects on the Overtown Community*, ed. Institution of Government, Florida International University (Miami: Metropolitan Planning Organization of Miami–Dade County, 1998), 47.

86. Marian Shannon, interviewed by Yvonne Daly, 15 August 1997, 14, Tell the Story Collection, BA; Rachel Williams, interviewed by Electra Ford, 30 August 1997, 21, Tell the Story Collection, BA; and Genevieve Lockhart, interviewed by Yvonne Daly, 13 August 1997, 10–20, Tell the Story Collection, BA.

87. "'Buildup' Clutters Expressway's Path," *MH*, 5 February 1958; and "The Gables That Is Best Forgotten," *MT*, 24 January 1957.

88. "Modern Gold Rush Hits Miami Slum Core," *MH*, 20 November 1966; and "There's 'Gold' in Miami Slums," *MN*, 20 November 1966.

89. Revell, "Chronology of Important Transportation Decisions in the Area," 58–59.

90. Haley Sofge, "Public Housing in Miami," *Florida Planning and Development* 19, no. 3 (March 1968): 1.

91. On the insufficiency of privately owned housing to meet minimum building requirements for relocation housing, see "Slum Owners Challenge on Units," *MN*, 3 January 1966; and "Slum Owners' List Falls Far Short," *MN*, 19 January 1966.

92. *Congressional Record*, House, vol. 113, 90th Cong., 1st sess., 14 December 1967, 36648.

93. Arnold R. Hirsch, *Making the Second Ghetto: Race and Housing in Chicago, 1940–1960* (Chicago: University of Chicago Press, 1998), 264.

94. Marcos Feldman, "The Role of Neighborhood Organizations in the Production of Gentrifiable Urban Space: The Case of Wynwood, Miami's Puerto Rican Barrio" (PhD diss., Florida International University, 2011), 46.

95. Feldman, "Role of Neighborhood Organizations in the Production of Gentrifiable Urban Space," 49; and "7.2 Million Jobs OKd to Rescue Northwest Area," *MN*, 13 June 1966.

96. *Congressional Record*, House, vol. 113, 90th Cong., 1st sess., 14 December 1967, 36647.

97. John R. Tunis, "If You're Thinking of Florida," *Progressive* 24 (February 1960): 37–39.

98. "7.2 Million Jobs OKd to Rescue Northwest Area"; and "City Has Medicine for Sick Neighborhoods," *MH*, 20 June 1966.

99. "HUD News," 27 September 1967, George A. Smathers Papers, "Dept. of HUD-Releases 1967" folder, box 262, UF. Throughout the late 1960s, press releases from the Department of Housing and Urban Development, available in the George Smathers Papers at the University of Florida special collections, detail the millions of dollars South Florida's suburban communities received for flood prevention, the building of libraries, water-processing plants, and other infrastructure. See also "Suburban Renewal in Pennsylvania," *University of Pennsylvania Law Review* 111, no. 1 (November 1962): 61–110.

100. Raymond A. Mohl, "Making the Second Ghetto in Metropolitan Miami, 1940–1960," *Journal of Urban History* 21, no. 3 (March 1995): 395–427.

101. *Thompson v. Miami Housing Authority*, 251 F. Supp. 121 (1966).

102. "Town Homes Included in Urban Renewal Plan," *MN*, 1 December 1966.

103. "A Dream Being Set in Concrete," *MH*, 23 May 1993. The average three-bedroom concrete ranch house in South Florida, by comparison, was going for fifteen thousand dollars.

104. "Housing Authority Accused of Bias," *MH*, 16 September 1966.

105. "'Free Choice' in Public Housing Called Sham," *MT*, 21 October 1966.

106. "Commissioner Range Urges, 'Rework Brownsville Plan,'" *MH*, 7 February 1967; "Betrayal Charges Leveled at Housing Authority by BIA," *MT*, 3 February 1967; and "Brownsville Housing Fight Nears Solution," *MT*, 23 June 1967.

107. "Shacks Left Standing While Good Houses Come Down," *MT*, 15 April 1966.

108. "$8,000,000 City Housing Project Gets Go Ahead," *MT*, 9 May 1964.

109. Preston Smith II, *Racial Democracy and the Black Metropolis: Housing Policy in Postwar Chicago* (Minneapolis: University of Minnesota Press, 2012), 55–63; and D. Bradford Hunt, *Blueprint for Disaster: The Unraveling of Chicago Public Housing* (Chicago: University of Chicago Press, 2009), 58–59.

110. "County Should Build Brownsville Pool Now," *MT*, 2 September 1966. In the 1961 documentary "Miami Condemned," Wayne Ferris described Brownsville as part of Miami's "2000 Dade County slum acres." Such a description, common to observers of black housing generally, failed to account for the diverse housing stock in the neighborhood, much of which was not "substandard"; "Miami Condemned: 1961."

111. "Northwest Slum Building Must Be Repaired or County Will Order Its Destruction," *MN*, 15 November 1957; "Attempt to Build Bar Fails Again," *MN*, 13 February 1964; and "Brownsville Residents Fight Bar in Area," *MT*, 27 April 1963.

112. "First Negro Elected to Crime Unit," *MN*, 7 May 1965.

113. "Betrayal Charges Leveled at Housing Authority by BIA."

114. "Commissioner Range Urges, 'Rework Brownsville Plan.'"

115. "County Should Build Brownsville Pool Now."

116. "Miami Condemned: 1961."

117. *Congressional Record*, House, vol. 113, 90th Cong., 1st sess., 14 December 1967, 36648.

118. Ibid.

119. "Low Income Housing Not Popular with Investors."

120. "Commissioner Range Urges, 'Rework Brownsville Plan.'"

121. Kirk Nielsen, "The Wall," *MNT*, 5 February 1998, accessed 8 June 2013, http://www.miaminewtimes.com/content/printVersion/238245/.

122. "Betrayal Charges Leveled at Housing Authority by BIA"; and Eugenia Thomas, interviewed by Yvonne Daily, 14 August 1997, 7–8, Tell the Story Collection, BA.

123. "Table 2: Other Federally Assisted Housing, Existing, Under Construction and in Development Stage, Dade County, 1969," *Oversight of Federal Housing and Community Development Plans in the State of Florida*, Hearing before the Subcommittee on Housing of the Committee on Banking and Currency, House of Representatives, 92nd Cong., 1st sess., 8 October 1971, 128.

124. "Miami Condemned: Update '75" (station WCKT, Miami, 1975), University of Georgia Peabody Collection, accessed 28 May 2013, http://dlg.galileo.usg.edu/peabody/id:1975_75025_nwt_1.

125. "Urban Renewal: Houses, Hopes to Rise," *MH*, 3 July 1966.

126. "Brownsville Sends SOS," *MN*, 14 April 1967.

127. *Congressional Record*, House, vol. 113, 90th Cong., 1st sess., 14 December 1967, 36647.

128. "Some Wouldn't Break Up the Ghettos—Yet," *MH*, 9 August 1967; and *U.S. Congressional Record*, House, vol. 113, 90th Cong., 1st sess., 14 December 1967, 36651.

129. "Betrayal Charges Leveled at Housing Authority by BIA."

130. "Little Gratitude for Riots Here, Mrs. Range," *MN*, 20 July 1970.

131. "Miami Racial Storm Calmed as Blacks List Grievances," *MT*, 20 June 1970.

132. George Lardner Jr., "Epidemic of 'Law and Order,'" *Nation*, 19 February 1968, 231–34.

133. In New Orleans, 84 percent of black people worked as domestics or unskilled laborers. National Urban League Papers, "Housing Statistics, June 1960–June 1964" folder, box 73, LOC.

134. "Poverty Program Criticized," *MT*, 27 October 1967; "Crippled EOPI Program's [Economic Opportunity Program Inc.] Life Will Be Short," *MT*, 9 February 1968; and "460 Poverty Workers to Be Cut," *MT*, 16 February 1968.

135. National Commission on the Causes and Prevention of Violence, *Miami Report: The Report of the Miami Study Team on Civil Disturbances in Miami, Florida during the Week of August 5, 1968* (Washington, DC: Government Printing Office, 1969), 28.

136. "Negroes in Grove Organize to Fight Renewal Project," *MN*, 3 April 1968; and "Urban Development Project Delayed by Citizen Concern," *BAA*, 17 January 1970.

137. Josh Sides, "Straight into Compton: American Dreams, Urban Nightmares, and the Metamorphosis of a Black Suburb," *American Quarterly* 56, no. 3 (2004): 583–605.

CONCLUSION: THE TRAGIC CITY

1. Bernard Dyer, *Oversight of Federal Housing and Community Development Plans in the State of Florida*, Hearing before the Subcommittee on Housing of the Committee on Banking and Currency, House of Representatives, 92nd Cong., 1st sess., Miami, FL, 8 October 1971 (Washington, DC, 1971), 216–17.

2. "'The True History,'" *MH*, 17 February 2006.

3. Eighteenth- and nineteenth-century African American history often travels on the person of present-day African Americans. In their landmark study of Mount Laurel, New Jersey, the authors of *Our Town* describe how families with deep roots in their neighborhood, sometimes going back over two hundred years, kept the manumission papers of a long-passed ancestor. These documents served to help blacks lay a kind of deep historical claim to their communities, especially in the face of new zoning regulations that threatened to erase the black residents of Mount Laurel; David L. Kirp, John P. Dwyer, and Larry A. Rosenthal, *Our Town: Race, Housing, and the Soul of Suburbia* (New Brunswick, NJ: Rutgers University Press, 1997), 2.

4. See, for instance, Marianne Lamonaca, "Whose History Is It Anyway? New Deal Post Office Murals in South Florida," in *The New Deal in South Florida: Design, Policy, and Community Building, 1933–1940*, ed. John A. Stuart and John F. Stack, 120–57 (Gainesville: University Press of Florida, 2008); and Melanie Rebecca Shell-Weiss, "'They All Came from Someplace Else': Miami, Florida's Immigrant Communities, 1896–1970" (PhD diss., Michigan State University, 2002).

5. Raymond Arsenault and Gary R. Mormino, "From Dixie to Dreamland: Demographic and Cultural Change in Florida, 1880–1980," in *Shades of the Sunbelt: Essays on Ethnicity, Race, and the Urban South*, ed. Randall M. Miler and George E. Pozzetta (Boca Raton: Florida Atlantic University Press, 1989), 181. See also Melanie Shell-Weiss, *Coming to Miami: A Social History* (Gainesville: University Press of Florida, 2009).

6. For an exploration of black commercial practice as intellectual history, see Davarian L. Baldwin, *Chicago's New Negroes: Modernity, the Great Migration, and Black Urban Life* (Chapel Hill: University of North Carolina Press, 2007).

7. On the link between demolition and widely accepted ideas about urban progress, see Andrew R. Highsmith, "Demolition Means Progress: Urban Renewal, Local Politics, and State-Sanctioned Ghetto Formation in Flint, Michigan," *Journal of Urban History* 35, no. 3 (March 2009): 348–68.

8. For ideas about black cultural deficiency widely accepted, even among African Americans and progressives, see Daryl Michael Scott, *Contempt and Pity: Social Policy and the Image of the Damaged Black Psyche, 1880–1996* (Chapel Hill: University of North Carolina Press, 1997); and Khalil Gibran Muhammad, *The Condemnation of Blackness: Race, Crime, and the Making of Modern Urban America* (Cambridge, MA: Harvard University Press, 2010).

9. "The zeal with which Federal officials carried out policies of discrimination in the early days of the Government's housing effort has not been matched by a similar enthusiasm in carrying out their current legal mandate of equal housing opportunity"; US Commission on Civil Rights (1972), quoted in US Commission on Civil Rights, *Understanding Fair Housing* (February 1973), 7, accessed 30 May 2013, https://www.law.umaryland.edu/marshall/usccr/documents/cr11042.pdf.

10. See Stephanie Farquhar, "Making a University City: Cycles of Divestment, Urban Renewal and Displacement in East Baltimore" (PhD diss., Johns Hopkins University, 2012); and Derek S. Hyra, *The New Urban Renewal: The Economic Transformation of Harlem and Bronzeville* (Chicago: University of Chicago Press, 2008).

11. "Losing a Generation," *MH*, 31 May 2007.

12. Kathy Glasgow, "The Apartment Building from Hell," *MNT*, 12 August 1999, accessed 6 June 2013, http://www.miaminewtimes.com/1999-08-12/news/the-apartment-building-from-hell/.

13. Nancy MacLean, "Neo-Confederacy versus the New Deal: The Regional Utopia of the Modern American Right," in *The Myth of Southern Exceptionalism*, ed. Matthew D. Lassiter and Joseph Crespino, 308–29 (New York: Oxford University Press, 2010); Anthony S. Chen, *The Fifth Freedom: Jobs, Politics, and Civil Rights in the United States, 1941–1972* (Princeton, NJ: Princeton University Press, 2009); Kim Phillips-Fein, *Invisible Hands: The Making of the Conservative Movement from the New Deal to Reagan* (New York: Norton, 2009); Kevin M. Kruse, *White Flight: Atlanta and the Making of Modern Conservatism* (Princeton, NJ: Princeton University Press, 2005); and Matthew D. Lassiter, *The Silent Majority: Suburban Politics in the Sunbelt South* (Princeton, NJ: Princeton University Press, 2006).

14. As evidence of the segregation problem within the American historical profession, precious few books considered to be African American, urban, or civil rights history have been granted consideration as fundamental reinterpretations America's more general political history. Among these stand Thomas J. Sugrue's oft-cited *Origins of the Urban Crisis*, which, through a reframing of the racial contradictions within New Deal–era governance, helped substantially revise narratives about the rise and fall of American liberalism; Sugrue, *The Origins of the Urban Crisis: Race and Inequality in Postwar Detroit* (Princeton, NJ: Princeton University Press, 1996).

15. Andrew Weise, *Places of Their Own: African American Suburbanization in the Twentieth Century* (Chicago: University of Chicago Press, 2004); Mary Patillo-McCoy, *Black Picket Fences: Privilege and Peril among the Black Middle Class* (Chicago: University of Chicago Press, 1999); and Mary Patillo, *Black on the Block: The Politics of Race and Class in the City* (Chicago: University of Chicago Press, 2007).

16. Matthew D. Lassiter, "Political History beyond the Red-Blue Divide," *Journal of American History* 98, no. 3 (December 2011): 760–64.

17. See, for instance, Kim Phillips-Fein, "Conservatism: A State of the Field," *Journal of American History* 98, no. 3 (December 2011): 723–43; and Daniel T. Rodgers, *Age of Fracture* (Cambridge, MA: Harvard University Press, 2011).

18. William H. Chafe, *The Achievement of American Liberalism: The New Deal and Its Legacies* (New York: Columbia University Press, 2003).

19. Roberta Thompson, interviewed by Electra R. Ford, 29 August 1997, 21, Tell the Story Collection, BA.

20. Enid Curtis Pinkney, interviewed by N. D. B. Connolly, 26 September 2006, notes and audio recording in author's possession.

21. Maude Newbold, interviewed by Stephanie Wanza, 29 August 1997, 25, 29, Tell the Story Collection, BA.

22. Rachel Williams, interviewed by Electra R. Ford, 19 August 1997, 25, Tell the Story Collection, BA.

23. "Brownsville Is Miami's Most Blighted Neighborhood," *MNT*, 10 February 2011, accessed 8 June 2013, http://www.miaminewtimes.com/2011-02-10/news/brownsville -is-miami-s-most-blighted-neighborhood/full/.

24. My thanks to Donna Murch for thinking through the war on drugs and black nostalgia. See also Michelle R. Boyd, *Jim Crow Nostalgia: Reconstructing Race in Bronzeville* (Minneapolis: University of Minnesota Press, 2008).

25. James Baldwin, interview with Kenneth Clark, WGBH-TV, 24 May 1963, in *Conversations with James Baldwin*, ed. Fred L. Standley and Louis H. Pratt (Oxford: University Press of Mississippi, 1989), 42; see also E. Michael Jones, *The Slaughter of Cities: Urban Renewal as Ethnic Cleansing* (South Bend, IN: St. Augustine Press, 2004).

26. Martin Millspaugh, Gurney Breckenfeld, and Miles L. Colean, eds., *The Human Side of Urban Renewal: A Study of the Attitude Changes Produced by Neighborhood Rehabilitation* (Baltimore: Fight Blight, 1958), 152.

27. Michele Mitchell, *Righteous Propagation: African Americans and the Politics of Racial Destiny after Reconstruction* (Chapel Hill: University of North Carolina Press, 2004). See also Ronald Walters, ed., *Primers for Prudery: Sexual Advice for Victorian America* (Baltimore: Johns Hopkins University Press, 2000).

28. "Miami—But It's My Town," *MT*, 28 May 1965.

29. "Urban Renewal Project to Encourage Integration," *MT*, 13 January 1967.

30. "Eliminate Miami's Slums, Then Beautify: Mrs. Range," 29 August 1967, WTVJ Collection, box 81, "Slum Clearance" folder 1, HASF.

31. Kent B. Germany, *New Orleans after the Promises: Poverty, Citizenship, and the Search for the Great Society* (Athens: University of Georgia Press, 2007).

32. Clarence N. Stone, *Regime Politics: Governing Atlanta, 1946–1988* (Lawrence: University Press of Kansas, 1989), esp. chap. 9.

33. Hasan Kwame Jeffries, *Bloody Lowndes: Civil Rights and Black Power in Alabama's Black Belt* (New York: New York University Press, 2009), 244; and Matthew Countryman, *Up South: Civil Rights and Black Power in Philadelphia* (Philadelphia: University of Pennsylvania Press, 2006), 295.

34. Heather Ann Thompson, *Whose Detroit? Politics, Labor, and Race in a Modern American City* (Ithaca, NY: Cornell University Press, 2001), esp. chap. 7; Guian McKee, *The Problem of Jobs: Liberalism, Race, and Deindustrialization in Philadelphia* (Chicago: University of Chicago Press, 2008), 184; and Thomas J. Sugrue, *Sweet Land of Liberty: The Forgotten Struggle for Civil Rights in the North* (New York: Random House, 2008), 433.

35. Marc Weiss and Arnold Hirsch, for instance, both tender similar characterizations of urban renewal's top-down origins. "Urban renewal," Weiss writes, "owes its origins to the downtown merchants, banks, large corporations, newspaper publishers, realtors, and other institutions with substantial business and property interests in the central part of the city." Arnold Hirsch makes the same argument a slightly different way in his oft-quoted *Making the Second Ghetto*. He writes the following of Chicago's urban renewal coalition: "After World War II . . . developers asked for, and got, expanded powers of eminent domain, relocation assistance, and subsidies. . . . In the 1930s private enterprise had been unleashed to provide low- and moderate-income housing with little effect. In the 1950s it talked the government not only into giving it new bootstraps, but also into hauling them up two-thirds of the way." Weiss, "The Origins and Legacy of Urban Renewal," in *Federal Housing Policy and Programs: Past and Present*, ed. J. Paul Mitchell (New Brunswick, NJ: Center for Urban Policy Research, 1985), 254; Hirsch, *Making the Second Ghetto: Race and Housing in Chicago, 1940–1960* (Chicago: University of Chicago Press, 1998), 263–64.

36. As James Q. Wilson explained, "Urban renewal is in part a method for intervening in [the market for land and housing] to change its operation or eliminate its frictions." Wilson, introduction to *Urban Renewal*, ed. James Q. Wilson (Cambridge, MA, and London: Massachusetts Institute of Technology Press, 1966), xvii.

37. Metropolitan Dade County Planning Department Comprehensive Plan Division, *Amenity: Planning Staff Report No. 6* (Metropolitan Dade County, September 1960), 39, WTVJ Collection, "Metro Land Use Plan" folder, box 50, HASF.

38. *Congressional Record*, House vol. 113, 90th Cong., 1st sess., 14 December 1967, 36648.

39. Edwin Shirley, *Oversight of Federal Housing and Community Development Plans in the State of Florida*, Hearing before the Subcommittee on Housing of the Committee on Banking and Currency, House of Representatives, 92nd Cong., 1st sess., 8 October 1971, 191.

40. Shell-Weiss, *Coming to Miami*, 199.

41. "Holdups Halt Slum Rental Collectors' Rounds," *MN*, 9 May 1969.

42. "Private Landlords Giving Up Fight," *MH*, 8 August 1967.

43. "Tenants Can Sue Landlords," *MT*, 30 August 1968.

44. "Housing Evictions at Crisis Point," *MN*, 6 March 1970.

45. "Slumlords' Agent: A Matter of Profit," *MN*, 15 October 1974.

46. Wilhelmina Jennings, interviewed by N. D. B. Connolly, 3 February 2006, audio recording in author's possession.

47. Wilhelmina Jennings, interviewed by Stephanie Wanza, 8 August 1997, 20, 23, Tell the Story Collection, BA.

48. "Central District Woes Are Ignored, Panel Told," *MN*, 10 September 1971.
49. "Miami Condemned: Update '75" (station WCKT, Miami, 1975), University of Georgia Peabody Collection, accessed 28 May 2013, http://dlg.galileo.usg.edu/peabody/id:1975_75025_nwt_1.
50. "Neighbors NE," *MH*, 19 October 1989.
51. "Miami Condemned: Update '75."
52. Ibid.
53. Bill Sawyer, interviewed by Stephanie Wanza, 25 August 1997, 44–45, Tell the Story Collection, BA.
54. Charles Lee, in "Letters to the Editor," *MN*, 2 September 1965; and *National Parks: America's Best Idea*, episode 6, "Morning of Creation (1946–1980)," prod. Ken Burns, 1 hour 54 min. (Alexandria, VA: PBS Video, 2009), DVD.
55. "Luther Brooks, 80, Expowerbroker," *MH*, 31 December 1988.
56. Art Green, "Landlord and Tenant Legislation in the Florida Legislature—1971," Bonded Rental Agency Inc. Collection, BA.
57. Among Bonded's last clients was Leonzie Jones, a black man who made his fortune through a trash-hauling company and rental properties. Margie and George Harth, interviewed by N. D. B. Connolly, 9 March 2010, notes in author's possession.
58. Bonded Collection Agency, "25 Years of Property Management and Community Service" (1959), 11, Bonded Rental Agency Inc. Collection, BA.
59. "'General' Brooks Collects Rents," *MN*, 2 March 1962.
60. "Civil Rights Villains Faded Away Quietly," *MH*, 5 June 2007.
61. "Brooks Was No 'Slumlord,'" *MH*, 12 June 2007.

INDEX

HISTORICAL STUDIES OF URBAN AMERICA
Edited by Timothy J. Gilfoyle, James R. Grossman, and Becky M. Nicolaides

Series titles, continued from front matter